Agency and Action

ROYAL INSTITUTE OF PHILOSOPHY SUPPLEMENT: 55

EDITED BY

John Hyman and Helen Steward

CAMBRIDGE
UNIVERSITY PRESS

CAMBRIDGE
UNIVERSITY PRESS

University Printing House, Cambridge CB2 8BS, United Kingdom

One Liberty Plaza, 20th Floor, New York, NY 10006, USA

477 Williamstown Road, Port Melbourne, VIC 3207, Australia

314-321, 3rd Floor, Plot 3, Splendor Forum, Jasola District Centre, New Delhi - 110025, India

79 Anson Road, #06-04/06, Singapore 079906

Cambridge University Press is part of the University of Cambridge.

It furthers the University's mission by disseminating knowledge in the pursuit of education, learning and research at the highest international levels of excellence.

www.cambridge.org
Information on this title: www.cambridge.org/9780521603560

A catalogue record for this publication is available from the British Library

ISBN 978-0-521-60356-0 Paperback

Contents

Preface   v

Notes on Contributors   vii

Agency and Actions   1
JENNIFER HORNSBY

Two Ways of Explaining Actions   25
JONATHAN DANCY

Anscombe on 'Practical Knowledge'   43
RICHARD MORAN

Action, the Act Requirement and Criminal Liability   69
ANTONY DUFF

Emotion, Cognition and Action   105
DAVID CHARLES

Kantian Autonomy   137
TERENCE IRWIN

The Structure of Orthonomy   165
MICHAEL SMITH

Normativity and the Will   195
R. JAY WALLACE

Can Libertarians Make Promises?   217
ALFRED MELE

Intention as Faith   243
RAE LANGTON

The Destruction of the World Trade Center and the
Law on Event-identity   259
MICHAEL S. MOORE

Preface

The philosophy of action is principally concerned with human action. Its main aims are to explain the distinction between activity and passivity in human life and to describe the circumstances in which an action by a human being is correctly described as voluntary, intentional, or culpable. These are obviously fundamental problems in ethics and jurisprudence. But a satisfactory philosophy of action will depend on a theory of belief and desire, of practical reasoning, and of causation. So the philosophy of action is also closely connected with the philosophy of mind, with logic and with metaphysics.

Although Aristotle, Aquinas and Bentham made permanent contributions to the philosophy of action, recent interest in the subject stems from work published between six and three decades ago. This work was initially focused on the definition of voluntary action, but it rapidly came to embrace the other topics mentioned. At stake was the classical positivist view, expounded with particular clarity by Mill, that the human sciences are comparable to the exact natural sciences in their infancy:

> The Science of Human Nature [Mill wrote] may be said to exist, in proportion as the approximate truths, which compose a practical knowledge of mankind, can be exhibited as corollaries from the universal laws of human nature on which they rest. (*A System of Logic*, Bk. 6, Ch. 3.)

The principal writers in the 1940s and 1950s opposed this positivist idea. They argued that the objects studied by the exact natural sciences undergo predictable changes under the impact of reproducible forces, whereas the behaviour of human beings exhibits a rational order, is imbued with meaning, and is responsive to norms and values—norms and values which are themselves modified by the conduct of human beings in their changing historical circumstances.

Since the 1960s, however, the predominant view has changed. The logic of sentences used to report actions, and the connections between the concepts of agent, action, event and cause have been examined more scrupulously than they had been previously. And the orthodoxy is now a combination of ideas drawn from the positivist and the anti-positivist traditions. Some philosophers regard this as a plausible synthesis; others regard it as an unstable compound.

Preface

This book includes papers about the nature of actions them-selves; about self-knowledge, emotion, autonomy and freedom in human life; and about the place of the concept of action in the crim-inal and civil law. They are all published here for the first time. Taken together, they cover the entire range of the philosophy of action; and they demonstrate that the concept of action, which was mangled and misunderstood for centuries, now occupies a central position in ethics, metaphysics and jurisprudence.

In our view, the resurgence in the philosophy of action is one of the most exciting developments in philosophy in the last fifty years. We were fortunate to gather together many of the most astute and influential philosophers working in this area today, for the 2002 Royal Institute of Philosophy Conference, where the papers collected in this book, or their ancestors, were read. We are very grateful to Tom Moore and Glenn Lake for the remarkable efficiency and good humour with which they took care of the administrative work associated with the conference; and also to John Gardner, John Tasioulas, David Mackie and Christopher Taylor, all of whom contributed substantially to the conference's success. We would also like to thank the Royal Institute of Philosophy itself, the Faculty of Philosophy in the University of Oxford, the Mind Association, Cambridge University Press and Oxford University Press for their generous support.

John Hyman
Helen Steward

Notes on Contributors

Jennifer Hornsby is Professor of Philosophy at Birkbeck College, London. She is the author of *Actions* (Routledge & Kegan Paul, 1980) and *Simple Mindedness: A Defence of Naïve Naturalism in the Philosophy of Mind* (Harvard University Press, 1996).

Jonathan Dancy is Professor of Philosophy at the University of Reading. He is the author of *An Introduction to Contemporary Epistemology* (Blackwell, 1985), *Moral Reasons* (Blackwell, 1996) and *Practical Reality* (OUP, 2000).

Richard Moran is Professor of Philosophy at Harvard University. He is the author of *Authority and Estrangement: An Essay on Self-Knowledge* (Princeton University Press, 2001).

Antony Duff is Professor of Philosophy at the University of Stirling. He is the author of *Intention, Agency and Criminal Liability* (Blackwell, 1990), *Criminal Attempts* (OUP, 1996) and *Punishment, Communication and Community* (OUP, 2000).

David Charles is a Fellow of Oriel College, Oxford. He is the author of *Aristotle's Philosophy of Action* (Duckworth, 1984) and *Aristotle on Meaning and Essence* (OUP, 2002).

Terence Irwin is Susan Linn Sage Professor of Philosophy at Cornell University. He is the author of *Aristotle's First Principles* (OUP, 1988), *Classical Thought* (OUP, 1989) and *Plato's Ethics* (OUP, 1995).

Michael Smith is Professor of Philosophy at the Research School of Social Sciences, Australiam National University. He is the author of *The Moral Problem* (Blackwell, 1994).

R. Jay Wallace is Professor of Philosophy at the University of California, Berkeley. He is the author of *Responsibility and the Moral Sentiments* (Harvard University Press, 1994).

Alfred Mele is Professor of Philosophy at Florida State University. He is the author of *Autonomous Agents* (OUP, 1995), *Self-Deception Unmasked* (Princeton University Press, 2001) and *Motivation and Agency* (OUP, 2003).

Notes on Contributors

Rae Langton is Professor of Moral Philosophy at the University of Edinburgh. She is the author of *Kantian Humility: Our Ignorance of Things in Themselves* (OUP, 1998).

Michael S. Moore is Charles R. Walgreen Jr. Professor of Law and Co-Director of the College of Law at the University of Illinois. He is the author of *Law and Psychiatry: Rethinking the Relationship* (CUP, 1984), *Act and Crime* (OUP, 1993) and *Placing Blame: a General Theory of the Criminal Law* (OUP, 1997).

Agency and Actions

JENNIFER HORNSBY

Among philosophical questions about human agency, one can distinguish in a rough and ready way between those that arise in philosophy of mind and those that arise in ethics. In philosophy of mind, one central aim has been to account for the place of agents in a world whose operations are supposedly 'physical'. In ethics, one central aim has been to account for the connexion between ethical species of normativity and the distinctive deliberative and practical capacities of human beings. Ethics then is involved with questions of moral psychology whose answers admit a kind of richness in the life of human beings from which the philosophy of mind may ordinarily prescind. Philosophy of mind, insofar as it treats the phenomenon of agency as one facet of the phenomenon of mentality, has been more concerned with how there can be 'mental causation' than with any details of a story of human motivation or of the place of evaluative commitments within such a story.

This little account of the different agenda of two philosophical approaches to human agency is intended only to speak to the state of play as we have it, and it is certainly somewhat artificial. I offer it here as a way to make sense of attitudes to what has come to be known as the *standard story of action*. The standard story is assumed to be the orthodoxy on which philosophers of mind, who deal with the broad metaphysical questions, have converged, but it is held to be deficient when it comes to specifically ethical questions. Michael Smith, for instance, asks: 'How do we turn the standard story of action into the story of 'orthonomous action?', where orthonomous action is action 'under the rule of the right as opposed to the wrong'.[1] Smith is not alone in thinking that the standard story is

[1] This is Smith's question in 'The Structure of Orthonomy', the paper he presented to the conference on which the present volume is based. The quotation from Smith below is taken from the handout he used at the conference.

At the conference Michael Smith responded to my own paper by saying that the standard story could be retold so as to avoid my objections to it. The present, much revised, version is aimed at showing that that which I find objectionable in the standard story cannot simply be evaded. I thank Michael for his contribution to discussion there, Tom Pink and Miranda Fricker for comments they gave me on a draft of the earlier version, and the editors for comments on a draft of the present version.

Jennifer Hornsby

correct as far as it goes but lacks resources needed to accommodate genuinely ethical beings. Michael Bratman is another philosopher who has this thought; and I shall pick on Bratman's treatment of human agency in due course.

The standard story is sometimes encapsulated in the slogan: 'Beliefs and desires cause actions'. In the version of Smith's that I shall consider here, it says:

> Actions are bodily movements that are caused and rationalized by an agent's desire for an end and a belief that moving her body in the relevant way will bring that end about.

Smith's unpacking of the slogan shows how reason is supposed to enter the story: the word 'rationalize' is used in conveying that that which causes an action constitutes the agent's reason for it.[2] For the purposes of the present paper, it need not matter very much exactly how the story is formulated. My objection to the standard story will be that—despite the fact that the word 'agent' appears in definitions like Smith's—*the story leaves agents out*. Human beings are inelimin- inable from any account of their agency, and, in any of its versions, the standard story is not a story of agency at all.

The claim I intend by saying that the story leaves agents out is not answered by adding states of mind of different sorts from beliefs and desires to the causes of bodily movements. For what concerns me is the fact, as I see it, that 'belief-desire psychology' as it is understood in the standard story can cover none of the ground where human agency is found, and cannot do so even when it is sup- plemented with further mental states.[3] The popularity of the stan- dard story then seems very unfortunate. It is not merely that that which supplements it inherits its crucial flaw. It is worse than that. For when the standard story is the base line for questions in moral

---

[2] This use of 'rationalize' is taken from Donald Davidson's 'Actions Reasons and Causes', *Journal of Philosophy*, **60**, (1967) 685–700, reprinted in his *Essays on Actions and Events* (Oxford University Press, 1980) 3–19, in which the seeds of the standard story were sown.

[3] In 'The Possibility of Philosophy of Action', *in Human Action, Deliberation and Causation*, ed. Jan Bransen and Stefaan Cuypers (Dordrecht: Kluwer Academic Publishers, 1998), 17–41, Michael Smith defends the standard story, which he there calls the basic Humean story, to the hilt. He aims to show just how widely the story has application (how- ever much one might need to embellish it in order to deal with all of the various cases). My present concern, one might say, is not with any of the particular claims in that paper, but with the general picture of agency that lies behind it.

psychology, a shape is imposed on those questions that they should never have been allowed to take on. Meanwhile the orthodoxy in philosophy of mind is silently reinforced.

Before I criticize Bratman's attempt to supplement the standard story (§3), I want to draw attention to what I shall call its *events-based character*, and to explain how and why that is a source of trouble (§1). Events-based accounts introduce a conception of the causal order in which agents have no place (§2). The causal role that agents actually occupy disappears in an account, which is events-based (§4).

1

There are some ideas in the background of the standard causal story which I should start by spelling out. The basic idea is that there is a category of particulars called 'events', and that some of the things in this category—spatiotemporal things that can happen only once—merit the title actions. Thus any of the following may on occasion apply to an event: 'a mosquito's biting me', 'the chocolate's melting', 'Don's falling from the cliff', 'Jones's stealing the jewels', 'Helen's waving her right arm'. And, very likely, the last two phrases here—but (*human* action being implicitly understood) only these two—apply to events that are actions. As we have seen, *bodily movements* (some of them) are said to be actions in the standard story. That is because such things as stealing the jewels are things that people do by moving their bodies; and if Jones stole the jewels by moving his body thus and so, then his stealing the jewels is (the same event as) his moving his body thus and so. 'His stealing the jewels' describes a bodily event by allusion to an effect that it had.[4]

Some of this is already controversial. And I need to set some controversies aside now in order to move on. There are philosophers who object to the whole idea that actions are events. I think that their objection will be easier to understand when some of its sources have emerged. (Without defending the idea that actions are events in the present paper, I would suggest that its innocence may be manifest when it is freed from everything with which it has so often and so readily been wrongly associated. Much of the opposition to the idea is explained [I believe] by the alacrity with which philosophers whose outlook is 'naturalistic' have moved from this idea to events-based accounts of agency: see §§4 and 5 *infra*.) Again, there

[4] For a defence of the idea that actions are described in terms of effects they have and the thesis about the individuation that underlies this claim, see Davidson's 'Agency', reprinted in *Essays on Actions and Events*, cit. n.2, 43–61.

are philosophers who allow that actions are events, but who draw upon a conception of events different from the standard story's own. I hope that it will come to be evident that errors I find in the standard story are not a product of its conception of events as such (see n.14 below). Then again, there are those who allow that an action can be an event of someone's moving their body but who don't believe that such an event is a movement. They refuse to equate (say) *a*'s moving her leg with *a*'s leg's movement. Here I agree, but leave expression of my own disbelief for much later because I want to avoid muddying the waters for the present. For the time being, then, let us simply follow the standard story in speaking as if bodily movements were the events which are redescribed in terms of effects or results they have—redescribed so as to reveal interesting things done by someone who moved their body in some way.

An account of action which is *events-based*, as I shall mean this, assumes more than that actions are such redescribable bodily movements. It also assumes that the phenomenon of human agency, and not just a category of events, is delimited when it is said which events are actions. And it takes it that the causal truths about agency can be formulated as claims about causation of, or by, an action—as claims about particulars. (See Smith's version quoted above in which both of these assumptions are implicit.) An events-based account thus accords a very central role to events, having recourse to them both in marking out the phenomenon of agency, and in a causal depiction of it.

The events-based character of the standard story is what I shall criticize to begin with. One way to see the error of its first assumption is to think about failures to act (in a certain sense). One way to see the error of its second assumption is to think about how action-explanation works. I take each of these in turn now.

1.1 The key notion in much theory of action has been that of doing something *intentionally*. This is evidently the notion that has informed the standard story, which takes 'believe' 'desire' and 'do intentionally' to form a sort of conceptual trio. Behind the use of 'intentionally' is the thought that one keeps track of what is significant in someone's life as an agent if one attends to what they *intentionally do*. That was one of Davidson's principal claims in his paper 'Agency'.[5]

---

[5] Cited in previous note. That paper beings with the question 'What events in the life of a person reveal agency?'. The question puts in place the assumption that the phenomenon of human agency will be delimited when it is said which events are actions.

But someone can do something intentionally without there being any *action* that is their doing the thing. Consider A who decides she shouldn't take a chocolate, and refrains from moving her arm towards the box; or B who doesn't want to be disturbed by answering calls, and lets the telephone carry on ringing; or C who, being irritated by someone, pays that person no attention. Imagining that each of these things is intentionally done ensures that we have examples of agency in a sense that Davidson's claim brought out. But since in these cases, A, B and C don't move their bodies, we have examples which the standard story doesn't speak to.

It might be thought that the standard story needs to take the emphasis off *bodily movements*. And certainly it seems that the story would encompass more than it does if actions weren't defined by reference to the body and its movements.[6] If D's temptation to take a chocolate was so powerful that she had to tense her muscles in order to hold herself back, then arguably 'her refraining from taking a chocolate' would apply to an event even though her body did not move: it would apply to D's tensing her muscles, perhaps. Still to adapt the standard story in order to let in an example such as this would not address the real point here, which is that in cases like the three imagined, there simply is no event— no particular—which is the person's intentionally doing the relevant thing. In the cases of A, B and C, that which ensures that something is done intentionally is not a matter of the occurrence of an event at all. Of course there will be plenty of events in the region of these agents at the time at which they do their things. But as the cases are imagined, none of these events is someone's doing something intentionally. One might put the point by saying that 'there is no positive performance' on the part of A or B or C, and that when actions are taken to be events, they are 'positive performances'.

Notice that one cannot put the point by saying that there are 'negative actions' on the parts of A, B and C. Of course not: where 'action' is taken in the standard story's sense, there could not be any

---

[6] The doubt about assimilating actions to bodily movements mentioned a few paragraphs back is different. The question there was this: Assuming that an agent moved her body on some occasion when there was an action, then is it her bodily *movement* with which the action is to be identified? Here the question is this: Should the class of actions be so circumscribed that it is required that an agent move her body for there to be an event which is an action?

such thing as a negative action.[7] It is true that philosophers who are interested in categories such as *omitting, refraining, letting happen* sometimes speak of these as categories of 'negative actions'. But then they don't use the word 'action' as having application to events. It may put a strain on those who raise questions about 'negative actions' to use the word as the standard story does—so that it is denied application as soon as there is no event which can be identified as an action. (This is why speaking of 'a positive performance' can help to make the point about the examples.) Still the strain is something that one has to put up with if one adopts the terminology of the standard story in order to evaluate it. The bodily movements of which the story speaks are spatiotemporal particulars. And in any of its versions, the standard story finds actions among such particulars—among events. To that extent, it fails to deal with examples where there is (in its own sense) no action. If such examples appeared to have been included in the story, perhaps that is because it is so easy to forget that 'action' is used there in a semi-technical, philosophers' sense.

1.2 If it were a matter of its preferring one conception of agency to another, then the standard story could not be faulted for leaving out cases where there is no 'positive performance'. And one can imagine someone thinking that there are reasons to hold on to a relatively narrow conception of agency, which treats the territory of agency as defined by the domain of the events which are actions. (It might, for instance, be thought that certain questions in metaphysics receive a particularly sharp formulation by reference to this domain.) Still the problem with the standard story's narrow conception is not that it serves only certain purposes: it doesn't even serve its own.

The reason why the standard story doesn't serve its own purposes is that it purports to work with a rather general conception of agency, deriving from a model of action-explanation. We saw that proponents of the standard story take the notion of being *intentionally* done to provide a hallmark of agency. This is thought to provide a hallmark because of its connexion with 'reason-explanation'—explanation which speaks about agents' beliefs and desires. A's, B's and C's cases count as agency on this reckoning, because one can construct tales of

---

[7] There are no such things as negative particulars: cp. D. H. Mellor, *The Facts of Causation* (London: Routledge, 1995), pp.131–4. Notice that the presence of the word 'not' in a verb-phrase that applies to some agent need not correspond to there being no action: it could correspond to the occurrence of an action that is negatively described. Equally a positive description can sometimes be given of cases where there is no action (in the standard story's sense): she spoiled the show by not turning up.

what each of them believed and desired which will appropriately explain their doing their things—not moving, letting the 'phone ring, not paying attention to X. So the standard story locates examples in a certain explanatory setting in order to characterize them as examples of agency, yet, by treating actions as events in accordance with the standard story, it ensures that there are cases that belong in that setting but don't have a place in the story.

Well, a proponent of the standard story might acknowledge that there are more explanations in the 'belief-desire' style than there are events (sc. 'positive performances') about which his story could be told, but respond by suggesting that action-explanation comes in two sorts. The suggestion would be that there are explanations in which the occurrence of an event—of a bodily movement—is explained and the standard story can straightforwardly be told; and there are, in addition, explanations in which the standard story cannot be told, although some other, related story, which also mentions 'beliefs and desires', no doubt can. But the suggestion is actually not at all plausible. For when we ask why someone did something, expecting to learn about what they thought or wanted, we don't always need to consider whether or not there was a positive performance on their part; explanation can carry on in the same vein, whether there was or not. One might discover that it was because she wanted to wreak revenge on the producer that she spoiled the show, and it not matter very much whether, for example, she put a sleeping tablet into the principal performer's drink (so that her spoiling the show was an event that was her putting ...) or she simply failed to turn up (so that there was no *event*, or at least no bodily movement of hers, that was her spoiling the show). Either way, we say that she spoiled the show because she wanted to wreak revenge; and it makes no odds here whether the case is of such a sort that we can construct a statement 'Her wanting to wreak revenge caused [an event which was whatever bodily movement was] her Φ-ing'.

In the version of Smith's that we looked at, the standard story contains such causal statements as: 'Her desiring ... and her believing ... caused and rationalized a bodily movement'. Simplifying a bit, we can say that the standard story's causal statements are on the following style and pattern:[8]

[8] The simplification assumes that w is a cause of that of which d and b are a cause. It is actually unclear how the 'and' of 'd and b caused m' (a desire and a belief caused a movement) is supposed to work: cp. nn.13 and 15 *infra*. But I take it that those who tell the standard story will assent to 'Desires cause actions', just as they assent to 'Desires and beliefs cause actions'.

(SS) Her desire ... caused [an event which was] her bodily movement.

What we have just seen is that it is sometimes impossible to find a statement in this style, and implausible that we should be looking for statements in two different styles. That surely suggests that our focus should be on the sort of causal claim which comes naturally and which applies in every case:

(*) She did such and such because she desired... .

Causal statements like this hardly need defence: they are statements of a kind that we commonly recognize to be true.[9]

One may wonder now why causal claims like (SS), which are part of the standard story, should ever have been made. For even where there is an event of the agent's doing something, its occurrence is surely not what gets explained. An action-explanation tells one about the agent: one learns something about her that makes it understandable that she should have done what she did. We don't want to know (for example) why there was an event of X's offering aspirins to Y, nor why there was the actual event of X's offering aspirins to Y that there was. What we want to know is why X did the thing she did—offer aspirins to Y, or whatever.[10] When we are told that she did it because she wanted to help in relieving Y's headache, we learn what we wanted to know.

[9] I cannot defend the idea that action-explanation is causal in the present paper. About it, I would say what I say, in n.5 *supra* about the idea that actions are events

[10] I don't think that I need to take issue with Davidson's claims in 'The Logical Form of Action Sentences' [reprinted in his *Essays on Actions and Events*, cit. n.2]: one can accept that some of the sentences that give the explanantia of some action-explanations implicitly contain an existential quantifier whose domain is events, without thinking that any of the explanations is focused on the occurrence of an event. The objection that may be raised here will be that someone who allows any sort of equivalence between 'a Φ-d' and 'there was an event of a's Φ-ing' is compelled to think that action- explanation is the explanation of events' occurrences. But I think the objection relies on a failure to appreciate the hypersensitivity of 'explains why ...' contexts. Consider that there may be circumstances in which we are interested to know why *Mary* stole the bicycle, and other circumstances in which we are interested to know why Mary *stole* the bicycle; and different answers to the questions will satisfy our interests in the different circumstances. (See Jonathan Bennett, §14 of *Events and Their Names* (Oxford University Press, 1988) 32–3 for a spelling out of this example.) My claim is that when someone seeks an action-explanation, typically what she is interested to know is why someone did something.

Now the standard story's proponents say that 'Actions are caused by a desire and a belief of the agent'. So they not only take the occurrence of a particular to be causally explained when an action-explanation is given, they also assume that items in a realm of particulars are what do the explaining. Hence their recurrent talk of 'belief-desire pairs' as causes, and of beliefs and desires as 'token' states. This is not the place to issue a challenge to the very idea of token states as they figure in the philosophical orthodoxy.[11] But we can notice that those who treat a state of mind a person was in—wanting to help, as it might be—as if it were a particular inside that person, appear to confuse two quite different uses of 'state'. And it is surely the events-based character of the standard story which gives rise to the idea that action-explanations record truths about causally-related particulars. Only when events are on the scene would there be any incentive to move from (*) to (SS). (*) gives the form of some action-explanations as normally understood; (SS) purports to see particulars standing in a relation of 'cause'.[12]

It will have to suffice here to have questioned the conception of action-explanation that an events-based account characteristically leads to. First, a causal explanation of why someone did something could not always be the explanation of an event's occurrence (for want sometimes of a 'positive performance'). Secondly, an action-explanation doesn't ever seem to be focused on saying why an event occurred. Once these points are appreciated, perhaps the habit of thinking that action-explanations mention items which combine with one another in the production of an event will start to be undermined.[13]

[11] Helen Steward's challenge, in Part II of *The Ontology of Mind: Events, Processes and States* (Oxford University Press, 1997), is devastating. There is no ontological category into which can be lumped both the things which those who tell the standard story call 'states' and the things which they call 'events'.

[12] 'Cause' is sometimes used in such a way that any 'because'-statement (or, perhaps, any 'because'-statement which is genuinely causal) licenses a statement of the form 'C causes E'. I needn't quarrel with this usage, insofar as 'Q because P' might be equivalent to 'C causes E *where 'C' and 'E' abbreviate 'the fact that P' and 'the fact that Q'*. My quarrel here is with the move from 'Q because P' to '*c* caused *e*', where '*c*' and '*e*' are taken to name something in the category of particulars.

[13] A different way to undermine this habit is to show that there are no intelligible causal statements which mix together things in a category of events with things in a category of conditions (where so-called 'token' states would need to be reckoned in the category of conditions). This is the

Jennifer Hornsby

2

The foregoing is meant to indicate that agency is misconceived in an events-based account of it. Examples where there is no 'positive performance' suggest that the account leaves things out, and they point towards the impossibility of accommodating agency to its view about the operation of causality. Perhaps that view—of causality operating through items linked in causal chains—is the correct view of causal truths in some areas. But the truths that make up the phenomenon of agency seem not to belong in a world in which causality operates only in such a manner.[14]

I come now to a more direct way of showing that agency cannot be captured if one takes this view of causality's operation. I suggest that if one attempts to locate agency within the confines of such a view, one fails.

Consider Hume on the subject of bodily movements' production:

> We learn from anatomy, that the immediate object of power in voluntary motion, is not the member itself which is moved, but certain muscles, and nerves, and animal spirits, and, perhaps, something still more minute and more unknown, through which the motion is successively propagated, ere it reach the member itself whose motion is the immediate object of volition. [T]he power, by which this whole operation is performed is, to the last degree, mysterious and unintelligible. ... [W]e have no power [to move our limbs]; but only that to move certain animal spirits, which, though they produce at last the motion of our limbs, yet operate in such a manner as is wholly beyond our comprehension.[15]

[14] I hope that it will be evident now that the view about the operation of causality that I put into question need not be founded in the standard story's conception of events. At the outset of §1, I noted that some philosophers draw on a different conception: an example would be Jaegwon Kim. The criticisms of the standard story in §1 have relied upon a specific conception of events (upon the only conception, I should say, which allows that they are genuinely particulars). But I believe that my claims against "events"–based accounts have application also when "events" is understood in different (but all of them philosophically familiar) ways.

[15] *An Enquiry Concerning Human Understanding* (1748), §7.I

conclusion of an argument of Davidson's 'Causal Relations' (reprinted in his *Essays on Actions and Events*, cit. n.2, 149–62). For a spelling out and endorsement of the relevant argument, see Helen Steward, 'On the notion of cause "philosophically speaking" ', in *Proceedings of the Aristotelian Society*, XCVII, 1997, 125–40. From the perspective of Steward's article, it must seem an irony that Davidson's writings about action should so much have influenced those who tell the standard story.

Hume's account of how limb movements come about provides one way of filling out one part of the standard story. But it is impossible to believe that Hume has succeeded in offering any part of any story of human agency. The lesson from anatomy, supposedly, is that the only effects we can produce are events in our brains, and thus, as Hume himself puts it, 'totally different from' the effects that we intend. But it is undeniable that among the effects we produce when we do something intentionally, there are some that we intend—whether bodily movements, or events in the region beyond our bodies. And if we do produce intended effects, then we can produce them. It is true, of course, that advances in neurophysiology have made the production of limb movements less incomprehensible than Hume took it to be. But the present point is not that Hume could not comprehend how our limbs come to move, but that, with an events-based account as his only resource, he finds himself saying that we *cannot* ('have no power to') move them.[16]

In Hume's story of agency, there is no place for beings who can move their bodies. Thomas Nagel has said that 'There seems no room for agency in a world of neural impulses, chemical reactions, and bone and muscle movements'. When he presented 'his problem of autonomy', Nagel adopted an external perspective from which 'the agent and everything about him seems to be swallowed up by the circumstances of action; nothing of him is left to intervene in those circumstances'. If you try to imagine your actions as part of the flux of events, then you won't succeed, Nagel said. 'The essential source of the problem is a view of ... the order of nature. That conception, if pressed, leads to the feeling that we are not agents at all.'[17]

Some commentators share Nagel's anxiety. Not everyone has gone along with it, however. Those who have got used to thinking that someone's doing something intentionally is constituted by states and events see no difficulty about discovering examples of human agency in the picture on show from Nagel's external perspective. But perhaps one can appreciate the source of some of

[16] Hume's denial of causal powers is well-known of course. But I think that its consequences for an account of human agency are insufficiently appreciated. (I take these consequences to be revealed in the particular passage, though no doubt there could be more argument about this. I don't suggest that Hume really thought that no one can move their limbs. His compatibilist arguments always take it quite for granted that human beings can take their place in the causal nexus.)

[17] See *The View from Nowhere*, Oxford University Press, 1986) pp. 110–11).

Jennifer Hornsby

Nagel's anxiety by thinking about where Hume was led by his assumption that instances of agency consist of items—volitions, and then movements of muscles, nerves, animal spirits and, eventually, limbs—linked on causal pathways. It is surely because there seems to be no place for a sort of being that can move itself in his account that Hume is led to the conclusion that we cannot move our limbs. Where Hume plumps for a manifestly false conclusion, Nagel tells us that we find problems.[18]

The problem now would seem to be that agency cannot be portrayed in a picture containing only psychological states and occurrences and no agent making any difference to anything. It is no wonder that some of those who share Nagel's worry take it to be a problem for the standard story of action.[19]

3

Michael Bratman, so far from sharing Nagel's worry, thinks that it is obvious that an account of our agency had best be 'embedded in the event causal order'. He recognizes that 'in some cases we suppose ... that the agent ... is not merely the locus of a series of happenings, of causal pushes and pulls'. And he is led to seek a fuller account of actions' aetiology than the standard story provides. In a series of recent articles, Bratman builds upon that story, adding

[18] In Ch. VII of op. cit. n.19, Nagel discusses a question which 'applies even to the activity of spiders' before he introduces two different problems relating specifically to human agency. I have not been careful to distinguish here between Nagel's various problems, thinking as I do that they should all be solved together. I have said more about the problem that Nagel calls the problem of autonomy in 'Agency and Causal Explanation', in *Mental Causation*, eds. J. Heil and A. Mele (Oxford University Press, 1993) 129–53 (reprinted in *Philosophy of Action*, ed. A. Mele, Oxford Readings in Philosophy 1997).

[19] David Velleman introduces his problem about agency by reference to Nagel's puzzle in 'What Happens When Someone Acts?', Mind 101, pp. 461–81 (reprinted at 123–43 in his *The Possibility of Practical Reason*, Oxford University Press, 2000); but he settles for the view that the standard story is adequate if someone's agency falls short of what is needed for a case of 'agency *par excellence*'. I think then that Velleman fails to address what Nagel had supposed to be a *quite general* puzzle. I discuss Velleman's treatment in this and subsequent of his papers in my 'Agency and Alienation', in *Naturalism in Question*, ed. Mario De Caro and David Macarthur (Harvard University Press, 2004).

further states to its beliefs and desires.[20] I look at his account now in order to illustrate the direction in which philosophers are led if they think that treating distinctively human forms of agency is a matter of bolstering the standard story.

Bratman is right, of course, to think that the standard story is conceptually inadequate insofar as it mentions only beliefs and desires. Everyone agrees that a life-like account of human agency will include states of mind of many more sorts than these. And Bratman himself has done more than anyone else to show that agents' intentions cannot be reduced to their beliefs and desires.[21] But to agree to this is not to accept the strictures of what Bratman calls a 'broadly naturalistic psychology', wherein phenomena are all to be seen as 'consisting in some, perhaps, complex, causal structure involving, events, states and processes'.[22] These strictures, rather than its simple shortage of mental states, are what lead Bratman to think that the way to treat agency is to add further pieces of psychological machinery to the standard story's states.

In Bratman's account a distinction falls between action determined or governed by an agent—confined to adult human beings, and '(merely) motivated behaviour'—found for instance among children who have beliefs and desires but do not yet have the conceptual resources for normative deliberation. The question what makes someone a *full-blown agent* of X is a question about the type of psychological functioning—beyond what is found where behaviour is motivated merely—from which X issues.[23] Bratman postulates that where agency is full-blown, actions are caused by higher-order reflexive policies. Any such policy has a content of this

---

[20] The paper by Bratman on which I mainly focus in the present section is 'Two Problems About Human Agency,' *Proceedings of the Aristotelian Society* (2000–2001) 309–26. (I have just quoted from p.311.) I also draw on his 'Reflection, Planning, and Temporally Extended Agency', The *Philosophical Review, 109* (2000) 35–61: the phrase 'embedded in the event causal order' occurs there. In this, Bratman not only endorses 'naturalistic psychology', but also maintains that an agent's identity over time should be treated as consisting 'primarily in overlapping strands of various kinds of psychological ties' between 'states and attitudes'. It is a good question whether such a reductionist conception of personal identity is enforced by 'naturalistic psychology', but certainly no accident that someone should subscribe to both.

[21] See his *Intention, Plans and Practical Reason* (Harvard University Press, Cambridge Mass., 1987).

[22] 'Two Problems ...', op. cit. n.20, p.312.

[23] Ibid. p.310.

sort: Treat desired end E as providing reasons in one's motivationally effective deliberation, and treat it so as a result of having this policy.[24] The proposal is that when action is the upshot of such a policy, there is a strong form of agency, so that 'the *agent* is the source of, determines, directs, governs the action, and is not merely the locus of ... causal pushes and pulls'.

Well, there doesn't seem to be any ordinary evidence that people regularly operate with second-order, reflexive policies of Bratman's kind. The fact that people show consistency in exhibiting one or another virtue certainly doesn't seem to provide evidence. When you call someone 'considerate', for example, it doesn't seem that you say that their actions are caused by the presence of a policy to treat respect for others' feelings as providing reasons in their motivationally effective deliberation and so to treat it as a result of having the policy. (If it really were as a result of a policy that someone showed consideration, then its content most probably would be 'Be considerate'.) It is not clear what could persuade us that anyone pursues policies of Bratman's kind. Certainly it seems very unlikely that many people would readily assent to possessing them. And it will be doubtful that many of us would be prepared to settle for a definite list of ends to encompass all of what we do as self-determined agents. At the very least, then, it is implausible that many adult human beings will be revealed as full-blown agents on Bratman's account of the matter. Yet presumably few adult human beings only ever go in for what Bratman calls '(merely) motivated behaviour'.

Suppose, however, for the sake of argument, that we go along with Bratman's policies. Suppose that we can define the ends we desire, and that we have the relevant policies in respect of each of them, and that such policies sometimes account for what we do. Even so, we surely should not want to say that someone is self-determined only insofar as the presence of such a policy actually explains what they do at some time. Consider a segment of someone's life history—a day's worth, say. Even allowing that, within this segment, policies with a second-order reflexive content sometimes cause actions, we shall not think that this shows that the person's self-determination is sometimes switched on. Much of what is done by a self-determined agent is not at all remarkable, so that most likely very many of the examples of agency found in such a segment will be quite mundane, and lack any distinctly rational or ethical deliberative history. The property of being a self-determined agent surely does not derive from particular occasions when

[24] Ibid. pp.321–4.

some distinctive sort of state of mind—a special kind of policy or whatever it might be—kicks in to produce an action.

There are two sorts of objection to Bratman in the foregoing. Firstly, he postulates states of mind which are not plausibly states of ordinary people. Secondly, he assumes that we have to consider what is for an *action* to be of an especially high-grade sort in order to come to understand particular forms of *agency*. (This assumption is also present in Smith, when he raises the question what it is for an action to be orthonomous.) The assumption flows from allegiance to the standard story. The story tells us how the events that are actions are caused. And Bratman (like Smith) thinks that we have to find a particularly high-grade sort of cause for the actions of a self-determined (or orthonomous) agent.

Life would be tough if pursuing second-order reflexive policies were the only option for a genuinely ethical agent. Pursuing them would be cognitively taxing and interfere with exercising more ordinary capacities—capacities to react appropriately to the particularities of the various situations in which one may find oneself. These other capacities can be taken for granted if one rejects the assumption that characterizing self-determined agency is a matter of marking out a special class of events. For then our claim to self-determination can be founded in a conception of human agents as the kind of beings who consciously act under the influence of a wide variety of considerations, including so-called normative reasons. And an account of agents and their motivation can then make allusion to quite disparate factors, including, for instance, traits of character and emotional reactions.[25] Provided that human beings themselves are acknowledged to be part of the subject matter in action-explanation, a story about what someone does on occasion need not be focused upon actions and their history among other events, states and processes; it can be focused upon the agent and the difference that she made.

4

The idea that human beings make a difference—that they cause things, or bring them about—is surely a very ordinary and familiar one. Bratman tells us that 'it is difficult to know what it means to

[25] I say this in order to point towards a different direction from Bratman's in which to go in order to answer questions like Bratman's. I don't mean to deny that there are plenty of good questions in the region of Bratman's own.

say that the agent, as distinct from relevant psychological events, processes and states, plays ... a basic role in the aetiology and explanation of action.'[26] But I think that Bratman's difficulty must be a consequence of his espousal of an events-based account of agency. When one reflects upon what is present in that account, it can seem as if the only alternative to thinking of actions as 'embedded in an event causal order' were to treat agents as 'fundamentally separate and distinct elements in the metaphysics'[27]—as if any agent would have to encroach upon the causal chains that lead up to actions.

There is another view, however; and I think that it is a part of common sense. If we want to know what it means to say that an agent (as distinct from events and so on) brings things about, then we need only to think about what is ordinarily meant when this is said. That is what I explore next (4.1). We shall discover that events-based accounts are ruled out when it is accepted that agents bring about the things that they actually do (4.2). When the actual causal role of agents is grasped, it becomes evident why the standard story is not a story of human agency (4.3).

4.1 An event of someone's doing something is usually an event of their bringing something about. A driver slams on the brakes and she brings it about that the car comes to a sudden stop; the event that is her slamming on the brakes brings it about that the car comes to a sudden stop. A tea drinker puts her cup on the table; the result of the event of her putting it there is that the cup is on the table. The thought here—that a person's doing something is typically that person's bringing something about—relies on the fact that typical action verbs are causatives of one or another sort. The causative character of action language reflects agents' abilities to affect things. When agents do things by moving their bodies, they draw on causal knowledge, some of which is knowledge of relations of event causation, including knowledge of what their bodies' movements cause. (A foot pressed against the appropriate pedal applies the brakes; braking causes stopping; and so on.) In taking up the language of events, then, one is able to recapitulate in an explicit way a kind of knowledge that agents exploit in affecting things beyond themselves.

The idea that actions are events that can be redescribed in terms of their effects or results was part of the background of events-based accounts. We see now that this idea fits in with a general way

---

[26] See 'Reflection, Planning', op. cit. n.20, p.39
[27] Ibid.

of spelling out the causative character of action language: something the driver did was to bring the car to a sudden stop, and the car's arriving at a sudden stop was an effect of the driver's action; something the tea drinker did was to put the cup on the table, and the cup's being on the table was a result of her putting it there. Although an event ontology is made explicit here, there is no call to import the two assumptions of an events-based account of agency. In the first place, to claim that there are events which merit the title 'actions' is not to adopt a conception of agency which confines examples of agency to the occurrence of events. For the upshot of agents' drawing on their causal knowledge can perfectly well be that they *don't* move their bodies. (So it was in the case of A, B and C, who, knowing that their moving would not have conduced to what they wanted, did things intentionally without there being any *action.*) Secondly, the claim that actions are events that are usually described in terms of their effects and results says nothing about the aetiology of actions. Taking a view about the language of action and its causative character can hardly settle the question of what kind of story to tell about the causation and explanation of action. Accepting that actions are events is one thing, endorsing an events-based account of agency quite another.

4.2 Advocates of events-based accounts are not alone in thinking that once events are on the scene, any causal question relating to human agency concerns the causation of the events that are actions. There are also the Agent Causationists who say that *agents* are causes of actions.[28] It is when this is said that it looks as though agents were intruders among events states and processes,

---

[28] I introduce the initial capitals in 'Agent Causation' in order to suggest a distinctive doctrine—that of e.g. Richard Taylor (see further, next n.). Robert Kane, in *The Oxford Handbook of Free Will* (2002) p. 23, talks about the common practice of introducing a hyphen in 'agent causation' in order to indicate that a special kind of relation is intended. Well, many philosophers have had particular theoretical intentions when they have defined notions of agent causation; save for that, I don't think that we'd be inclined to think that there's anything special about it.

Others who are called agent causationists include Timothy O'Connor and John Bishop. There is much agreement between the view I put forward here and theirs. But O'Connor and Bishop both define actions as *relations* (and perhaps, then, they do introduce a notion which is 'special' in the sense meant by Kane). Thus they abandon the idea in the background of events-based accounts, which, as it seems to me, can be perfectly acceptable.

17

encroaching there as 'fundamentally separate and distinct elements in the metaphysics'.

But in order to defend the causal role of agents, there is no need to say that they cause actions. Indeed there is every reason to say that agents do *not* cause actions. Consider again the examples of the driver and the tea drinker. What did they cause, or bring about? The driver caused (among other things) the car's coming to a halt; the tea drinker brought it about that (among other things) her cup was on the table. These things, which they caused or brought about, are the effects or results of their actions. What agents cause, then, are not the events that are their actions, but the effects or results in terms of which their actions may be described.[29] And when we think of agents causing things, we don't think of them imposing themselves in causal chains that lead up to their actions.[30]

[29] And that is why it is not an ordinary notion of agent causation which is used when Agents are said to Cause actions (see preceding n.). Bringing in an agent to do some of the causal work of the states and events of an events-based theory can be a consequence of confusing actions with their effects or results. One sees this confusion in the following passage from Richard Taylor's *Action and Purpose* (Prentice-Hall, Englewood Cliffs, 1966. The quotation is at p.111 of the 1973 edition reprinted by Humanities Press, New York; I have added the numbering):

> (1) In acting, I make something happen, I cause it.... (2) It seem[s] odd that philosophers should construe this as really meaning, not that I, but rather some event process or state not identical with myself should be the cause of that which is represented as my act. (3) It is plain that ... I am not identical with any such event process or state as is usually proposed as the 'real cause' of my act. (4) Hence, if ... I sometimes cause something to happen, ... it is false that an event process or state not identical with my self should be the real cause of it.

The philosophers, the oddness of whose construal Taylor points out at (2), claim that an event, state or process causes his action. But in order to arrive at their claim, one has to confuse 'acting' with the 'something' that he makes happen, or causes, in acting. In putting the cup on the table (say) that which he makes happen, or causes, is that the cup is on the table. His action, however, is his putting the cup on the table. Thus to represent that some event process or state caused the cup to be on the table is not to represent that some event state or process caused his putting it there. Nothing is said about the cause of his putting it there. Thus Taylor's assertion at (4) can be rejected. An event not identical with the agent (sc. an action) is a cause of that which an agent causes to happen. This does not conflict with Taylor's claims at (1) and (3), which are obviously true.

[30] In Ch.VII of *Actions* (Routledge, 1980), I suggested that the question of the irreducibility of agent causation comes down to the question

Those who speak as if an action were an event one candidate for whose cause is an agent make it seem as if an action might be identified independently of any agent. But an event that merits the title 'action' is *a person's* intentionally doing something. And such events do not belong in a causal order from which people themselves might be missing. Their effects and results are caused by people situated in the causal world in which they intervene, and knowledge of which they rely on for their doings to lead to outcomes they want. Evidently this world, which we know and inhabit, although it is not a world from which events are absent, is not 'the event causal order' of which Bratman spoke. But nor is it a world into which people intrude.

Bratman and Smith, when they raised questions about what it is for an agent of a certain sort to be at work, turned these into questions about what sort of psychological cause is in operation. Like others who tell the standard story, they suppose that citing states and events that cause a bodily movement carries the explanatory force that might have been carried by mentioning the agent. But unless there is an agent, who causes whatever it is that her action does, questions about action-explanation do not even arise. An agent's place in the story is apparent even before anyone enquires into the history of the occasion.

To see this, consider that when one has an action-explanation, one knows why someone did something, and that that is to know why they played a particular causal role—why *a* brought it about that *p*, say. The explanation does not tell one *what* causal role a played: one already knows this when one knows what a did. If one finds out *why* a did whatever it was, then one comes to know things about a which make it understandable that she should have brought it about that p. But it then becomes more fully intelligible why it came about that *p* only insofar as this had already be understood by reference to *a*'s part in bringing it about. It might be that the agent actively intervened—so that there was a "positive performance" on her part—, or it might be that the agent intentionally let matters take their course. Either way, one must have taken a view of what the agent did—what role she played—, before one can speak to the

---

whether 'is an action of' can be analysed in terms of event-causal notions. It now seems to me that the principal thesis of that book—namely that actions are events that we always describe in terms of their effects—leads rather directly to the answer *No*. We don't know which events are *a*'s actions unless we know what a—the agent—caused. And we couldn't know what it is for something to be *a*'s action without knowing that things like a can cause things.

question of why she did it. In cases where the agent can be said to have intervened, there will be an event that was her action. But that could not mean that one needs to switch one's attention to an event causal order in order to uncover the agent's motives and reasons in such cases.

The fact that our attention is never directed towards an event causal order when it comes to action-explanation makes it clear why the same sort of explanation should subsume cases where there is no event which is an action as well as cases where there is (§1.1). And it helps to show why (SS) of §1.2 ought never to command our assent, although (*) perfectly well can.

4.3 Before concluding, I should say something about *bodily movements*. (I indicated that I would postpone expression of my own disbelief in the standard story's accounting of these back at the start of §1). What it will be important now to realize is that the agent's role—as cause of what her actions cause—still has application in connection with moving the body. Recognizing this will help to pinpoint where the standard story goes wrong. And it will also enable us to understand better why Hume should have been led to say that we can only produce effects totally different from any that we intend.

We move our bodies in order to effect changes beyond them. The driver, for instance, produced a movement of her foot for a purpose. Thanks to her causal knowledge, her moving her foot on the brake pedal belonged in a causal sequence that culminated in the car's coming to a halt. Her action then is describable as her moving her foot, as her slamming on the brakes, and as her bringing the car to a halt. But there is no possible reason to say that it is a foot's movement. Would anyone be inclined to think of someone's moving her foot as a foot's movement unless they imagined that a person's activity could be dissolved into the goings-on of states and events? The movement of a foot is not an action: it is not an agent's doing anything.

It is not a mere quibble to insist that someone's moving a bit of their body is their doing something, and that the movement they produce is not. For when the label 'action' is attached to bodily movements—to events which aren't actions—the events which *are* actions (to which 'action' had always been supposed to apply) are left out of account. Proponents of the standard story identify actions with bodily movements. And the identification gives their game away. Given that agents cause what their actions cause, an agent's place in any causal story must be the place of her actions.

But then agents and the events that really are actions are obliterated with a single stroke when bodily movements are identified with actions. In the standard story no-one ever does anything.

When actions are removed from the scene, not only are agents removed, but also their capacities cannot be recorded. We saw that when one considers the teachings of anatomy as Hume relates these, human agents, with their usual powers of movement and abilities intentionally to do things, are not in sight. Hume denied us our normal capacities of movement. But if it is allowed, against Hume, that we can move our bodies, and can produce such effects as we know would be produced by moving them, then our actions will be thought of as exercises of our capacities. (When the driver, who is capable of moving her right foot [and knows how to put the brakes on etc.] exercises a capacity of movement, there is an event/action of her slamming on the brakes.) Agents then are seen as bodily beings who have a place in causal sequences which lead from influences upon them to the comprehensible effects that they have beyond them. It is only to be expected now that the facts about what we do are not recorded by speaking of items which operate 'in such a manner as is wholly beyond our comprehension'.

5

I hope to have elicited the force of my claim that human agents are ineliminable from any proper story of their agency. Nagel was right to think that the very idea of agency is threatened when we try to picture action from an objective or external standpoint. For in any picture of action, agents will be seen causing things. And since agents are not visible from the external standpoint, we must refuse the suggestion that we might account for agency from it. Some philosophers are inured to the external standpoint; others impose it as their own—for instance whey they are led from the idea that actions are events to events-based accounts of agency. But we have established now that this was never the standpoint of anyone who had anything to say about people and what they do; and that treating actions as events incurs no commitment to any events-based account.

It may yet be thought that I exaggerate when I say that the standard story is not a story of human agency at all. Many people suppose that it is only a kind of shorthand that leads philosophers to favour a slogan like the summary version of the standard causal story—'beliefs and desires cause actions'. What this means, so these people say, is that 'a person's believing something and a person's desiring something causes that person's doing something'. According to this line, agents' mental states and their actions are really mentioned, even if agents themselves are not highlighted, in the language of the shorthand and of the standard story. Well, I think that what is represented now as shorthand is actually a way of talking that changes the subject. And I want to say something about why the change of subject should so frequently go unobserved.

Notice that even when what is alleged to be shorthand is given in its unabbreviated version, still the agent's role in action could not be conveyed. For when an account of the causal transaction in a case of agency is given in the claim that a person's believing something and a person's desiring something causes that person's doing something, it is assumed that the whole of the causal story is told in an action-explanation. The fact that the person exercises a capacity to bring something about is then suppressed. It is forgotten that the agent's causal part is taken for granted as soon as she is said to have done something. The species of causality that belongs with the relevant idea of a person's exercising her capacities is concealed.

There are many reasons why this should remain concealed, and why so many philosophers should have settled for a picture of agency like the one presented in the standard story's events-based account. There is the ease with which it is forgotten that 'action' is used in a semi-technical, philosophers' sense when the causal underpinnings of agency are in question (see §1.1). There is the readiness with which the very different uses of the word 'state' are confused (see §1.2). And perhaps there is a tendency simply (unreflectively) to equate a person's moving her body with the movement that she makes. But none of these slides and confusions is as powerful as the outlook which encourages them and which they encourage. From this outlook, the only possible reality is one in which any causal fact fits into an account in which everything that does any causal work is an event or state. Thus the correct and ordinary idea that to explain what human beings do is to give a kind of causal explanation is thought to be amenable to reconstruction as the idea that some events have causes belonging in a category of psychological occurrences.

Many philosophers with this outlook nod in the direction of the standard story, and offer it a sort of shallow endorsement. They assume that what they have to say about human agency is compatible with the story, without troubling to investigate it. I examined Bratman's account of full-blown agency in order to see where the standard story leads when it is explicitly told and taken seriously. I hoped to show that, whatever our metaphysical outlook might be, we can appreciate that we need to be released from the straitjacket of the standard story to give a realistic account of human agency. (Bratman's second-order reflexive policies should strike us, I think, as states at best of superhumans—states introduced in order to compensate for a deficiency in what can be uncovered among what is 'embedded in the event causal order'.)

Bratman's work is instructive because he follows where the story leads. Those whose endorsement of the story is more shallow than Bratman's might be less willing than he is to accept what I take to be its consequences. But given the prevailing 'naturalistic' outlook, it is not surprising that so many philosophers should sometimes pay the standard story lip service. And the widespread acceptance of the story among philosophers of mind may make it seem as if the outlook itself had some support. Thus even those whose accounts of agency actually exclude the standard story may blithely suppose that they might always be recast to conform to it. After all, the standard story isn't *obviously* wrong. It is obvious only that its vocabulary is inadequate. This obvious thought leads to the idea that the story needs to be supplemented; the question whether the causal notions that belong in an account of human agency are contained in the story is then overlooked.

I suggest that a 'naturalistic' outlook engenders the story, and that the story sustains that outlook; we have an orthodoxy whose presuppositions aren't examined by most of those who perpetuate it. Peter Strawson once said that it takes a really great philosopher to make a really great mistake.[31] I can't help thinking that, these days, it takes a really great number of philosophers to contrive in the persistence of a really great mistake.

[31] 'Self, Mind and Body' in *Freedom and Resentment and Other Essays* (Methuen & Co. Ltd., London, 1974).

Two Ways of Explaining Actions

JONATHAN DANCY

I

In my *Practical Reality*[1] I argued that the reasons for which we act are not to be conceived of as psychological states of ourselves, but as real (or maybe only supposed) states of the world. The main reason for saying this was that only thus can we make sense of the idea that it is possible to act for a good reason. The good reasons we have for doing this action rather than that one consist mainly of features of the situations in which we find ourselves; they do not consist in our believing certain things about those situations. For instance, the reason for my helping that person is that she is in trouble and I am the only person around. It is not that I believe both that she is in trouble and that I am the only person around. Give that the (good) reason to help is that she is in trouble etc., it must be possible for my reason for helping to be just that, if it is indeed possible for one to act for a good reason. In fact, this sort of thing must be the normal arrangement. The reasons why we act, therefore, that is, our reasons for doing what we do, are not standardly to be conceived as states of ourselves, but as features of our situations.

I further argued that the explanations of action that we give when we specify the agent's reasons for acting—sometimes called rational or rationalizing explanations—are unusual in being non-factive. What this means is that for the explanation to be correct as an explanation, it is not required that what is offered as *explanans* in fact be the case. When we give the agent's reasons for doing what he did, the sort of light that is thereby cast on his actions does not seem in any way to require that things should actually have been as he took them to be. For the purposes of these explanations, then, there is no reason to insist that the explanans should be the case. If an agent's reason for what he does is that p, the fact that he is wrong about whether p should not persuade us that his reason was something else, something that he was not wrong about. This general philosophical point can be supported, or confirmed, by looking at some (carefully crafted) examples. A perfectly correct explanation of an act might be:

[1] Oxford: Clarendon Press, 2000.

His reason for doing it was that it would increase his pension.

But such an explanation cannot be factive, in the sense given above, since it can perfectly well be expanded thus:

His reason for doing it was that it would increase his pension, but he was sadly mistaken about that.

Now this claim, if true, seems to establish immediately that the sort of explanation at issue, which I call (for reasons which will be investigated in due course) a normative explanation, is not itself a causal explanation. For causal explanations are factive, whatever else they are, and need to be so for the purposes which they serve; but my 'normative' explanation is non-factive. Still, this in itself does little to tell us whether, in addition to the normative explanation, there might not *also* be available a causal explanation of some sort or other. Indeed, it might be the case that suitable causal explanations can just be read off the normative ones; if someone acts for the reason that p, he is caused to act by his belief that p. For each normative explanation, then, a shadow causal explanation seems to be just waiting in the wings. Why suppose otherwise? This is the issue which the present paper is about. In pursuing it, I will take it as granted for present purposes that I am right in the account I give of the reasons for which agents act. Normative explanations give the agent's reasons for doing what she did, and they are the only explanations that do this. Causal explanations, then, whatever their form, will not be attempting to do this as well. For if they do, we will most probably have two competing accounts of the agent's reasons, and this is exactly what we are *not* supposing when we entertain the possibility that the normative explanation be supplemented in some way by a causal explanation. The causal explanation we give will indeed be an explanation of the action, but it will not explain the action by laying out the agent's reasons for doing it. It will be doing something else.

Despite the fact that the causal explanation is not intended to be in direct competition with the normative one, in the sense just discussed, my suspicions are that any causal explanation we try to provide will eventually prove to be offering a competing account of the agent's reasons. I cannot show this to be the case in general. What I will be trying here to do is to show that it is true for one characteristic suggestion about the sort of causal explanation that is at issue in the present context. That suggestion comes in various forms, weaker and stronger. The weaker version is:

C: S acts for the reason that p only if S is caused to act by his believing that p.

The stronger version is:

C*: What it is for S to act for the reason that p is for S to be caused to act by his believing that p.

Now p here could be more or less simple. It might just be 'it is time to have lunch' or it might be 'having lunch would be good and now is the moment'. This is just a contrast between a more and a less complex belief. Now my own view is that if action is caused by any mental state, that state could be purely cognitive. But the position one would expect to find favoured by those who want to promote the sort of causal explanation that I am here discussing would claim that we need both belief and desire if an action is to ensue. To make explicit room for this, both C and C* could be complicated in the same way, by introducing considerations to do with desires. Let us take p now to be the more complicated 'having lunch would be good and now is the moment'. We then get something like:

Cd: S acts for the reason that p only if S is caused to act by his believing that p and by 'relevant' desires of his.
C*d: What it is for S to act for the reason that p is for S to be caused to act by his believing that p and by 'relevant' desires of his.

It is worth trying to lay out the considerations which might lead someone to suppose that something on the lines of Cd or even C*d must be true, even if we admit that my normative explanations are the ones—indeed, the only ones—that specify the agent's reasons. The vaguest of these would be the thought that there must be some psychological story to be told in addition to the normative one. There must be such a psychological story because only such a thing could render it intelligible how it could be the case that S acted for the reason that he did. This thought would only take us as far as Cd, I think, not all the way to C*d; all we would have would be a necessary condition.

So what we have so far is that there must be some psychological story to be told in addition to the normative one, but that this story should not be in the business of specifying the agent's reasons. Instead, as I have now said several times, the causal explanation and the normative explanation will be explanations of the same thing, but they will not be the same explanation of that thing. I said above that this was because one explanation is factive and the other is not.

27

But this claim needs to be taken cautiously. There are factive explanations of action in terms of the agent's reasons. For instance, we have the non-factive:

His reason for doing it was that it would increase his pension.

But we have factive ways of saying the very same thing, for instance:

He did it because it would increase his pension.

I take it that unlike the former, the latter cannot coherently be continued 'but he was sadly mistaken about that', which is the mark of its factivity. Should we say, then, that we have here two explanations of the same thing, two 'rational' or rationalizing explanations, one of which is factive and one of which is not? In general, such a situation is no cause for complaint. But I think that the explanation itself is not a factive one; there are just factive ways of wording it. The word 'because' renders the explanation factive, but only in the sense that it commits the explainer to the truth of the explanans; the explanation itself, which might have been given in other terms, remains stubbornly non-factive. That is, the fact that the explanation can be given in non-factive form shows that it is a non-factive explanation, even though that very explanation can be given in ways that (for trivial reasons to do with the use of certain words) are themselves factive. In the latter cases, it is not the explanation itself that is factive, but the form of words that we use to express it.

There is a further reason for saying that the causal explanation is not the very same explanation as the normative one. This is just that the causal explanation does not explain the action in terms of the agent's reason for doing it. Since that is exactly the way in which the normative explanation works, the two explanations cannot really be just two ways of saying the same thing.

Another possible reason why they cannot be the same explanation is that one is causal and the other is normative. This suggestion, however, needs careful handling. If we had said that one explanation is causal and the other is not, we would have had a clear contrast, but we would have begged a crucial question - the question whether a normative explanation might not *also* be causal (or vice-versa). There is a natural inclination, of course, to say that causal things are quite different from normative things. We have all read about the differences between the realm of reasons and the realm of causes, or between the space of law and the space of reasons. But the notion of normativity is notoriously slippery, and it is especially slippery in the present context, where we have not yet asked what is meant by calling the 'rational' explanation normative. To answer this question, we need to run through some possibilities. Here they are:

1. The explanation is normative because it is a good explanation. (Reply: so is the causal one.)
2. The explanation is normative because it specifies the agent's reason, and reasons are normative. (Reply: an explanation is not normative just because something that it appeals to is normative; an explanation of one physical change in terms of another is not for that reason among the physical things.)
3. The explanation is normative because it specifies a good reason. (Reply: plenty of these normative explanations appeal to something that is not a good reason; they appeal to something that the agent mistakenly acted on as a reason when in fact it was no reason at all.)
4. The explanation is normative because it specifies something that the agent took to be a reason—that is, because it appeals to a normative belief of the agent's. (Reply: same as 2 above.)
5. The explanation is normative because someone who wields it is displaying a capacity to distinguish between those things that are comprehensibly taken to be goods and those that are not, or because it appeals to normative laws.

This last one, which we have reached by a process of gradual elimination, seems to me to be defensible, indeed to be correct. Its relevance is that an explanation of action is only effective to the extent that it reveals a comprehensible good (that is, something that can be comprehensibly taken to be a good, even if it is not actually a good). If an action-explanation of the style that we are considering failed even to do this, we would, I think, deem it no explanation at all. So such explanations are worth calling normative.

The point now should be, of course, that causal explanations are not like this. The ability to wield them in no way depends on or evinces a capacity to distinguish between those things that are comprehensibly taken to be goods and those that are not. Nor, so far as one can tell, does it involve any appeal to normative laws. One might take it to be a distinctive feature of causal explanations that one does not need this sort of evaluative knowledge in order to wield them (except in special cases, of course). In this they would differ from my normative explanations. If all this is right, it would establish that we are dealing here with two explanations, not one; for no causal explanations can also be normative.

What is more, the contrast which has here emerged would be *some* reason, at least, to say that the causal explanation cannot *constitute* the success of the normative one, as C* would have us believe. It cannot be that what it is for one explanation to be sound is for the other to be sound, if to wield one we need this sort of evaluative knowledge and to wield the other we do not.

But this point depends on accepting that causal explanations do not require this sort of evaluative backing. And not everyone agrees with this. First, John McDowell (to give one prominent example) maintains that intentional explanations are both rational and causal. This, however, is irrelevant to our present topic. In McDowell's supposedly causal intentional explanations beliefs of the agent function as *explanantia*, in a way intended to chime with their being the agent's reasons for doing what he did. But this shows that McDowell's explanations are rival accounts of the reasons for which the action was done, and the causal explanations I am officially dealing with in this paper are exactly not of this type. To repeat, the latter allow that my normative explanations are the only ones that explain by appeal to the agent's reasons, but suppose that some (merely) causal explanation is also somehow appropriate. And here a doubt enters my mind, for there is a suspicion that what we have been calling so far the causal explanation—that is, the right-hand side of C and of C*, is not itself *purely* causal. It clearly has a causal element, at least as we are presently expressing things, but there is some reason to suppose that there is an evaluative element lurking hidden within it. The next section tries to say what that evaluative element is and where it is hiding. What will emerge, I think, is that evaluative knowledge is indeed required for us to wield the supposedly causal explanation offered by the right-hand side of C. This removes the worry that our causal explanation cannot be what it is for a normative explanation to be sound, but only at the risk of diminishing the difference between the two explanations, in a way that threatens to collapse that difference altogether.

II

The clue to this issue, as I see it, lies in a revealing epithet which often appears unremarked in statements of Humean conceptions of motivation (which are themselves supposedly causal in style). An intentional action, we are told, cannot occur in the absence of a pair of distinct states in the agent, one belief and another desire, which states are to function as causes. But not just this: there is the further requirement that the belief and the desire be somehow 'appropriate' to each other; we must have an 'appropriate' pairing if we are to have the sort of explanation of action that the Humeans conceive themselves to be talking about. What this means is that an explanation of someone's taking the bus that appeals to his wanting to get to the market and believing that the bus is a convenient way of getting there is a good explanation of the Humean sort. A bad explanation of the Humean sort would be one that explained an action of putting on one's hat because one believes that it is raining and wants to wear a hat if it is not raining. The latter, we are told, is *no* explanation, because the belief and the desire are not appropriately related.

Let us then consider the difference between two supposedly causal explanations:

A: S Φ's because S believes that p and S desires to Φ if p
B: S Φ's because S believes that p and S desires to Φ if not-p[2]

One of these explanations seems to have some kind of advantage over the other. We can see how it might be that the 'process' specified by A should occur. We cannot see how it might be that the 'process' specified by B should occur. But what is the ground for this difference in attitude? Is it that we have learnt by experience that things work the A-way and not the B-way, by and large? I doubt it. We cannot suppose that our preference for A-type explanations rests on empirical knowledge of how the mind works. Indeed, it seems that there is something non-empirical here, and if it is non-empirical it must be a priori. But what could tell us a priori that A-type explanations do somehow explain when B-type explanations don't? It looks on the face of things as though, if they really are both causal explanations of S's Φ-ing, they should both be equally comprehensible, both equally capable of capturing the way things happened. But we know in advance that this is not so.[3] One of them seems to make sense of the agent, or to make the agent make sense, in a way that the other does not.

It seems to me that the obvious suggestion here is that our a priori preference for A-type explanations is grounded in exactly that fact, the fact that in 'making sense' of the agent they portray him as

[2] I have expressed these in belief/desire terms, but it would have been equally possible to have written them purely cognitively. A could have been: S Φ's because S believes that p and S believes that it would be good to Φ if p.

[3] For the contrast I am working with here to be effective, it is important that one should not seek to supplement B with some further clauses that would turn it back into the sort of causal explanation that 'makes sense'.

Jonathan Dancy

rational, as responding to rational norms, in a way that B-style explanations do not. In what follows I consider how that might work, and try to argue that no answer emerges that is really compatible with the supposedly causal nature of A-type explanations. I don't, however, think that this can be established just on the basis of the fact that our preference for one form of supposedly causal explanation over another is normatively grounded. It seems to me that the normativity of the grounding does not show that A-style explanations are offering a conception of the agent's reasons that is in direct competition with my own. The problem will rather turn out to be that the normative and the 'causal' explanations are too close for the latter to be what is claimed for them.

The obvious way to understand the suggestion that our a priori preference for A-type explanations is grounded in rational norms would be to suppose that these explanations make an implicit appeal to principles of rationality.[4] Allowing this, what sort of principle or principles might be involved? Given the way in which I have formulated A-type and B-type explanations, two candidates suggest themselves:

PR1: R ($\exists p$ [S believes that p and desires to Φ if p] $\rightarrow$ S Φ's).
PR2: R (S Φ's $\rightarrow$ $\exists p$ (S believes that p and desires to Φ if p)).

I don't mean to suggest that these are the only possible candidates, nor even that it is clear that these ones make sense, let alone that they are true. I think there are the gravest difficulties in understanding them and the potential relation between them. (For instance, PR2 is clearly a rational requirement to the effect that every action should be done for a reason. But PR1 is not a requirement at all, since it clearly remains possible that, though S believes that p and desires to Φ if p, rationally speaking he should not Φ, since he has (what one might call) stronger reasons to do something else. It is an open question, then, what sort of claim is made by principles like PR1.[5]) But for my purposes, I need something reasonably specific as a stalking horse, and I am going to use these.

The crucial feature of PR1 and PR2, for my purposes, is that they are rational requirements on a relation between beliefs and desires

---

[4] As a card-carrying particularist, I would not myself accept this idea that norms necessarily rest on principles, but I go along with it here for the sake of argument.

[5] A possible answer to this question is suggested in John Broome's 'Normative Requirements', in J. Dancy ed. *Normativity* (Oxford: Blackwell, 2000), 78–99.

of the agent's, on the one side, and action on the other. One might for this reason call them subjective principles, in contrast to 'objective' principles such as:

PR3: R [(p & it is good for S to Φ if p) -> S Φ's].

Objective principles of this sort are principles of reason. By this I mean that they tell us what S has reason to do, in my sense of 'reason'; they specify good reasons for S to Φ. Given that in the present paper we are officially accepting my account of reasons, at least in broad terms, we must also be accepting that principles of this sort are in place, available. And what I want now to argue is that, if so, it is hard to see what role to ascribe to the subjective principles which one might suppose to emerge from these objective ones in some way. The general idea might be that where PR3 is in place, then a subjectivised version of it (something like PR1) must also be in place. The question will then be what is the relation between the objective and the subjective principle. I suggested above that in offering A-type explanations we portray our agent as responding to a norm of rationality. The first question should then be: if so, to which sort of norm is the agent to be thought of as responding, the objective sort or the subjective sort? But to this question, the answer seems clear. Agents who deliberate and act in the light of their deliberations do not say to themselves 'Well, I believe that p and desire to Φ if p; so even if I am wrong in believing that p and wrong to desire to Φ if p, still I should Φ (or at least will breach no rational constraint if I do)'. That is, agents do not deliberate on their own states of mind as input; they deliberate on and act in the light of how (as they see it) things are. So if the agent is responding to any principle or norm of rationality, it will be to an objective norm which tells him what he has reason to do in which situations, not to a subjective one at all. Agents neither do nor should respond to subjective norms.

But this raises in a stark form the question what role the subjective norm is playing, if it is not supposed to be that in responding to which the agent displays his rationality. We are allowing now that in order to make sense of the agent, we need to display the objective norm to which he is responding—even if the norm to which he is responding does not in fact apply to the case in hand. An agent is shown to be acting rationally if, as we might put it, he is shown to be trying to do what there is good reason to do, even if as a matter of fact he is quite mistaken on that front. If he is mistaken, then though he is trying to follow where the reasons lead he is failing in that attempt, and has ended up doing what he has no good reason to do.

There is a certain temptation to say at this point that instead of accusing the agent of failing to act according to objective norms, we should congratulate him for succeeding in acting in accordance with subjective ones. He is getting something right, at least. But to fail in the attempt to follow objective norms of rationality is not the same as to succeed in the attempt to follow subjective norms; there is a success condition involved in the former that is not in the latter. And that success condition is what tells us, not only what the agent is trying to do, but also what he is not trying to do.

My first point, then, is that even if A-style explanations portray the agent as acting according to rational norms, those norms are not subjective ones of the style of PR1 and PR2, but objective ones. In which case it is worth asking what is the difference between my normative explanations of action and the supposedly causal explanations which we are imagining adding to them. Both of them portray the agent as attempting to live up to norms of objective reason. Both of them, one might add, fail if the agent cannot be shown to be responding to an intelligible good. (More on this point below.) At this point it is beginning to look as if A-type explanations are so close to normative ones that they must either be identical with them or in competition with them. But this is exactly not the picture we were working towards.

III

In response to this worry, we might suggest that, despite the admitted similarities, there remains a crucial difference between the A-type explanation and my normative explanation, in that the former is causal where the latter is not. I will pursue that response in the next section. Before doing that I want to ask what other role might be played by subjective norms like PR1 and PR2 than the one we have just considered and rejected. There seem to be two further possibilities. The first is that such principles specify further reasons, reasons of a subjective sort, in addition to the objective ones specified by objective norms. These further reasons are not considerations that the agent should be attending to, but they are genuine reasons for him to act nonetheless. The second possibility is that what these principles do is to show that when the agent acts or even only tries to act in the light of objective norms, he acts rationally.

On either of these two accounts the operation of subjective principles is subordinate to that of objective ones. If they play the second role, subjective principles establish the rationality of an agent who is responding (so far as he can tell) to the corresponding objective principles of good reasons. But if they play the first role, that of specifying further sets of reasons, subjective principles are parasitic on objective ones in a different way. What we do, in working from an objective to a subjective principle, is to turn a requirement or reason which would obtain if things were as the agent supposes into one that in fact obtains for an agent who merely takes things to be so, whether they are so or not. Another way of putting this is to say that we start from a statement about a requirement or reason that would be in place if the agent were right in what he believes, and then say that a different requirement or reason is *already* in place because that other one would be, were circumstances different from the way they actually are. Now the objective principle, we may say, does indeed specify the (good) reasons for the agent to act. But if the subjective principle is derived from the objective one in the way that I have just suggested, we should take it that it itself specifies *different* reasons for the agent—reasons that can apply here even when the first reasons don't. So the subjective principle we have been working with (something like PR1) does look as if it is in the business of specifying what we might call real but subjective reasons. But now we are in danger of saying that if one were to act in the light of a subjective principle, one should be acting in the light of the reasons it specifies, namely that one believes that p and that if p it would be good to Φ. But that is just to say that the features that we originally offered as causes—S's believing that p and so on—are in fact now being offered as reasons. They are being offered as *good* reasons, and *also* as considerations in the light of which the agent is to act, that is, as features that are to be the agent's reasons. But if that is right, the supposedly causal explanation of action surreptitiously offers its own specification of the agent's reasons. The only advance that has been made is that those reasons are additional to the objective ones rather than replacements for them. But I view this as no advance at all. There are too many reasons around.[6]

So on the first of the two roles that subjective principles might be playing, they will really be offering a competing conception of reasons (though they will not be offering to replace objective reasons with subjective ones). But I think that we should anyway abandon this first role. The features specified by the subjective principles are not offered as further good reasons, reasons that are additional to those specified in objective principles. There are in fact, according to all the relevant objective principles, no reasons for

[6] I argue this last point in more detail in Ch. 3 of my *Practical Reality*.

our agent to act, as things in fact stand. For we are supposing that none of the things specified as reasons in the relevant objective principles are in fact the case. It would be better to think of subjective principles as specifying conditions for a sort of subjective rationality, in addition to the objective sort of rationality involved in acting for a good reason. Objective principles, then, link what we might call objective rationality to acting in response to the reasons actually present in the case. Subjective principles say that where the agent is acting in ways that would be objectively rational if things were as he supposes, he is *already* subjectively rational even though he is doing something that he has no reason to do. So it is misleading to think of the two principles as being concerned with rationality in the same sense. Instead, the objective ones are concerned with what there is reason to do, and subjective ones are concerned with an independent question whether the agent is acting rationally. The hope is that we will be able to say that someone can be acting rationally even when doing something that there is no reason to do.

Subjective principles could play this role even if one is not required, or even permitted, to act 'in the light of' them at all. Indeed, it has become rather obscure what demands such a principle does lay on one—how it affects one's normative score, as it were. It has begun to look as if subjective principles are not ones than can even be obeyed, which is a bit disconcerting. The idea we are working with is that they determine—at least in part—someone's normative status with respect to a subjective form of rationality, but we should pay no attention to them in deciding how to act.

But how does someone acquire this sort of normative status? As I suggested above, one does it by seeking to act in accordance with an *objective* principle. If one seeks so to act, one acquires that normative status even if one fails in the endeavour. But to fail in one's attempt to act in accordance with an objective principle is not the same as to succeed in acting in accordance with a subjective one. In the former, as I have already suggested, there is a success condition involved which there is not in the latter. So it seems to me that we don't need subjective principles of rationality in addition to objective ones, and so that if our preference for A-type explanations is normatively based, it must be based on objective ones which themselves make no reference to belief and desire at all.

IV

I now return to the suggestion raised at the start of the previous section, that there is a difference between my normative explanations and the supposedly causal A-type explanations, which is exactly that though both portray the agent as attempting to respond to objective norms, still one of these explanations is causal and the other is not.

This idea, however, is not well supported by the suggestion that our preference for A-type explanations is grounded in normative principles like PR1 and PR2. For the purposes of such principles, it is not required merely that while you are Φ-ing there should be some p such that you believe that p and desire to Φ if p. Your Φ-ing only becomes rationally intelligible if there is some suitable relation between your action and the specified belief-desire pair. What relation could that be? Could it be causal?

Think of the matter in terms of PR2; rationality requires that, if one acts, one has appropriately interrelated beliefs and desires. But it is not just that one should have them. It would be no good at all if, though one had them all right, the action was done, as one might put it, for quite other reasons. (We can't in fact put it this way because we granted at the outset that the agent's beliefs and desires are not the reasons for which she acts. Perhaps we should rather say that it would be no good if the action came about in quite another way.) It is also necessary that the action be appropriately related to the beliefs and desires. Again, the question is what relation is at issue here.

One thing we know already, however, is that that relation cannot be causal. We know this because there cannot be a rational norm that requires one to be *caused* to act by A-type pairings of beliefs and desires. Rationality might demand that one acts *in the light of* such beliefs and desires (whatever that is to turn out to mean). But this has to be something that one is capable of doing or not doing. Being caused to act by these beliefs and desires is not something one is capable of doing or not doing. One cannot even *try* to do it. It is not, in the relevant sense, up to us what causes our actions, and so it cannot be rationally required of us that our actions be caused in one way rather than another. So we cannot understand PR2 as requiring of us a causal relation between our beliefs and desires and our actions. And by the same token the relation at issue in PR1 cannot be causal.

Some might seek to evade this conclusion by adjusting our conception of what is to count as the cause at issue. The previous paragraph was expressed in terms of states of agents causing actions. Perhaps it is obviously senseless to require of us that certain of our states cause us to act in one way rather than another. But it is not so obviously senseless to require of us that we act because we believe this and desire that, intending this 'because' still to be a causal one.[7] The difference between this way of running the causal explanation and the one we have been largely considering is that for the latter, the causes are states that we have got into, while for the new suggestion the cause is thought of as including, or even just as being, the person who is in that state; it is I who believe this, not a state that I am in, that functions as cause. There is, I think, a lot to be said for this new suggestion. But even when we conceive things in this more human way, I would still say that there cannot be a rational norm that requires one to act *because* one believes that *p*—and the reason for this is still that it is not up to us what causes our actions, though it is up to us what are the reasons for which we are acting.

If our preference for A-type explanations is grounded in normative principles that do not demand any causal relation between explanandum and explanans, how are we to hold on to the thought that such explanations are causal? We reject B-type explanations on normative grounds; causally, one might say, they are in perfect order. So the sort of intelligibility that they are capable of providing must be different from the sort provided by A-type explanations. Crucially, desires only contribute to A-type explanations if they are desires for intelligible goods; these explanations fail if the desire appealed to is itself unintelligible. But no such complaint is in place where B-type explanations appeal to an unintelligible desire. It doesn't matter for them whether the desire is unintelligible or not. But there is no form of causation that is subject to the demand that a desire can only cause (in that sense) if it is intelligible.

This does not itself mean that A-type explanations are really disguised form of reasons-explanation. The 'because' in them need not be understood as 'for the reason that'. But it does mean that the causal status of A-type explanations is in doubt, for two reasons. First, it is not as if the relevant normative principles themselves *recommend* any causal relation between mental states and action, so that if they are satisfied, some form of causation must be going on. Second, the sort of intelligibility generated by an A-type explanation is quite different from that generated by B-type ones, which all allow to be causal. And if the causal status of A-type explanations is in doubt, we cannot explain our preference for them *as causal* by appeal to the normative principles. It is not that this is somehow the right sort of causing.

[7] I owe this thought, and the need to respond to it, to Helen Steward.

To prevent the supposedly causal explanation from collapsing back into my normative one, we have to say that A was caused to act by his seeing some point in so acting. But that sort of supposedly causal explanation can only be viewed as similar but preferable to B-style explanations if it is normatively preferable. (It cannot have a *causal* advantage.) And this shows that the light it casts is not causal. If Humeans are right in thinking that B-style explanations are not the sort of explanation they are in the business of giving, then A-style explanations are not causal at all.

Effectively, we have not seen how to understand these explanations as both causal and normative at once. The normative underpinning of A-type explanations is at odds with their supposedly causal nature.

V

We were looking for a relation between mental states and action that was neither causal nor normative. What relation could that be?

In this connection, it is worth pausing to consider how it is with moral norms. Sometimes people suppose that there is a certain self-reference in a moral norm. What they mean by this is that a principle 'pay your debts' really says something like 'you should pay your debts because of that, i.e. because they are your debts'. I don't want to endorse this suggestion here at all, but only to try to relate it to the principle of rationality we are discussing. Our rationality principle might say 'Where you believe that p and desire to Φ if p, you should Φ because of that'. The question I am raising is what sort of 'because of that' is at issue in this if it is not the normative one that means 'for that reason'.

My underlying suspicion, of course, is that our a priori preference for A-type explanations is in fact grounded in a prejudicial conception of the reasons for which the agent acts. A prejudicial conception, in the present context, is one that is at odds with the conception offered by the normative explanation; in particular, one that took the agent's reasons to be his own mental states (e.g., his believing that p) as opposed to supposed features of the situation (that p) would be prejudicial in the sense intended here. My suspicion is that PR1 itself gives us such an account. But it would be wrong to assume this too quickly. PR1 tells us, very roughly, that rationality thinks well of us if we Φ where we believe that p and desire to Φ if p, so long as we are Φ-ing 'in the light of' our believing and desiring these things. (I am here, as before, using the

phrase 'in the light of', as before, to denote the supposedly intermediate relation which is neither causal nor normative—contrary to
my usual practice.) Does this amount to demanding that our believing and desiring these things be our reason for Φ-ing when we Φ?
If so, we would have established that defenders of C are implicitly
committed to an account of agents' reasons that is in competition
with that of the normative explanation. But it may not be so. The
demand that we act in the light of our believing that p and desiring
to Φ if p may be compatible with the insistence that when we do so
act, our reasons for Φ-ing be that p and (something like) that it
would be good to Φ if p.[8] For this to be the case, each intentional
action stands in two distinct relations, one to the believings in the
light of which the agent acts, and one to the things believed which
are the reasons for which he acts. And there are distinct normative
principles requiring our actions to stand in both those relations at
once.

But how are we to put together these two sets of principles,
principles of reason, as we might put it, and principles of light? If
there really are two sets of principles operating at once, they must
be combinable somehow. They must be combinable either
internally, in the agent, or externally, in what one might call the
court of rational assessment. But I have already argued that neither
way will work. In both cases, it turns out that what is in operation
is in one way or another an objective principle, not a subjective one.
The conclusion that there is no relation in between the reasons-
relation and the causal one becomes very tempting indeed. There is
nothing for the 'in the light of' relation to be. That relation was to
be neither normative nor causal. It could not be normative, because
if it was PR1 and PR2 would be in competition with the normative
account of agents' reasons; and it could not be causal because
causality cannot be required. But now we have begun to wonder
what can be the sense in which PR1 requires of him (or, more
gently, recommends) that he act, as we put it, 'in the light of' his

---

[8] I have here converted the desire to Φ if p into a belief that it would be
good to Φ if p. I don't think that this conversion makes any difference to
the point at issue (the relation between causal and normative explanations),
even though it will seem to some to be an abandonment of Humeanism,
properly conceived. I have argued elsewhere that a purely cognitive form
of Humeanism in the theory of motivation is better than the familiar
mixed belief/desire theory (Dancy, 1993, chs. 1–2; 2000, ch. 4). For this to
be the case, we must think of Humeanism simply as the claim that intentional actions are caused by suitable combinations of believings in the
agent.

believing that p and desiring to Φ if p? There seems to be nothing left for this to mean.

VI

A crucial part of my argument has been the supposition that the most plausible way of explaining our a priori preference for A-type explanations is by appeal to certain rational norms, and thereby to principles of rationality that turn out inconveniently to be objective rather than subjective in style. However this may be, one might suggest that, though the explanation that I focused on is plausible, it is not the only plausible one.[9] A different explanation might be not so much normative as causal. It might claim that the concepts of belief and desire are so interrelated as to generate the a priori preference for A-type explanations over B-type ones. Suppose, for instance, that we conceive of a desire that p as a disposition to do whatever, given one's beliefs, will increase the probability of its becoming or remaining the case that p. And we conceive of a belief that p as a disposition to do whatever action is likely to promote one's ends, given that p. Now with this sort of interconnection between the two concepts, it seems natural that we will have a preference for explanations that, as one might put it, follow the flow of that interconnection. And that preference will be, in the relevant sense, a priori. (The point could also be put in functional terms.)

It is important for this alternative explanation that the possibility of B-type explanations be still allowed. For otherwise the A-type explanations will not be suitably causal. If they are causal, it should be an empirical, not a conceptual, question which states of the relevant types in fact did the causing this time. So B-type explanations should remain possible. And it is not clear to me how to retain their possibility within this new conceptually based approach. We have to tread a fine line here between saying that this is how the explanations *should* work and that this is how they usually work. We are supposed to be treading this line by saying that A-type explanations have a sort of conceptual *imprimatur*, though it is not one that renders B-type explanations literally incoherent. I don't see how to do this. I understand the idea of an empirical preference (because things normally go that way) and that of a normative preference (because they should go that way), but I don't understand the idea of a conceptual preference. If our concepts are,

[9] Not only might one suggest this; Michael Ridge did suggest it to me, at the conference.

as it were, designed for the case where things do go that way, how can those concepts be used to characterize a case in which thing don't go that way?

There is a further question about whether these dispositional explanations are really causal at all. The matter turns on two issues: whether the explanantia in these cases are sufficiently independent of the explanandum, and whether the dispositions which act as explanantia are required to be present in advance, as it were. This last depends on whether we conceive of dispositions of this sort as functioning as causes of the things which they are dispositions to do. Maybe for our larger purposes we do not need really to worry about that. My official target in this paper is the view that in addition to the normative explanation of action there could be a distinct causal explanation that appeals to the agent's beliefs as causes. If it turns out that the latter explanations are not properly conceived as causal, not everyone will be much upset about that. There is a yet further question whether these conceptually based explanations are entirely free of normative grounding; but I leave that for others to determine.[10]

[10] Many thanks to Wayne Davis for vigorous discussion of these issues, and to Michael Morris (of Sussex) and Helen Steward for helpful suggestions about a penultimate draft.

Anscombe on 'Practical Knowledge'

RICHARD MORAN

Among the legacies of Elizabeth Anscombe's 1957 monograph *Intention* are the introduction of the notion of 'practical knowledge' into contemporary philosophical discussion of action, and her claim, pursued throughout the book, that an agent's knowledge of what he is doing is characteristically *not* based on observation.[1] Each idea by itself has its own obscurities, of course, but my focus here will be on the *relation* between the two ideas, how it is that the discussion of action may lead us to speak of non-observational knowledge at all, and how this notion can be part of the understanding of a kind of ordinary knowledge that we have reason to consider practical rather than speculative. Anscombe mentions several quite different things under the heading of 'non-observational knowledge', and she first introduces the notion of the non-observational for purely dialectical purposes, associated with the task of setting out the field she wants to investigate, in a way that avoids begging the very questions she means to raise. She needs a way of distinguishing the class of movements to which a special sense of the question 'Why?' applies, but which doesn't itself employ the concepts of 'being intentional' or 'acting for a reason'. Section 8 begins: "What is required is to describe this class without using any notions like 'intended' or 'willed' or 'voluntary' and 'involuntary'. This can be done as follows: we first point out a particular class of things which are true of a man: namely the class of things which he *knows without observation*." (p. 13) She first illustrates this by the example of knowledge of the position of one's limbs, the immediate way one can normally tell, e.g., whether one's knee is bent or not. But examples of this sort are in fact ill suited to shed light on the idea of 'practical knowledge', which is the true focus of the idea of the non-observational in the study of action. When we see this we will be better able to see why Anscombe is concerned with the non-observational in the first place, and how this concern is tied to other characteristic Anscombian theses, for instance that an action will be intentional under some descriptions but not others, and that practical knowledge is distinguished from

[1] G. E. M. Anscombe, *Intention* (Cambridge, USA, Harvard, 2000; originally published by Basil Blackwell, 1957).

speculative knowledge in being "the cause of what it understands" (p. 87). And we will be able to understand how it is that an agent can be said to know without observation that he is doing something like painting the wall yellow, when this knowledge so patently involves claims about what is happening in the world, matters which it seems could *only* be known observationally.

What I hope to show is how the very idea of the non-observational comes to assume such an important role in Anscombe's understanding of action, something she herself says very little about. Her account of practical knowledge is part of the more general project of reconciling what I take to be two commonplaces. On the one hand the agent's own conception of what he is doing is not just another description, side by side with all the others, but has some claim to determine what the action itself is. There is a privileged relation, though not incorrigible, between what the agent is doing and what he takes himself to be doing. And on the other hand there is the commonplace that one can simply fail to do what one means to do, or do something quite other than what one takes oneself to be doing. I do not attempt to show that Anscombe's notion of practical knowledge is perfectly clear, nor that her appeal to the 'non-observational' character of this knowledge is without problem. (Indeed, one of my purposes here is to untangle the quite distinct strands of this appeal, and to claim that they cannot all be expected to do the same kind of work in her argument.) But I do want to argue that both her appeal to a distinct kind of knowledge in action, distinct from theoretical knowledge, and her characterization of it as in some sense 'non-observational', have motivations that are deeper, more interesting, and more defensible than is commonly assumed.

1. Some varieties of the non-observational

A—The first and in some ways still most oft-cited example Anscombe gives of what she means by 'non-observational knowledge' is the awareness a person normally has of his basic bodily position:

> "A man usually knows the position of his limbs without observation. It is without observation because nothing *shews* him the position of his limbs; it is not as if he were going by a tingle in his knee, which is the sign that it is bent and not straight." (p. 13)

Certain aspects of this idea have been contested, of course, but it seems undeniable that a person does have an awareness of his bodily position and bodily movements which is different from the knowledge he may have of another person's position and movements by *watching* what they do. Normally one doesn't need to look down at one's leg to tell if it is bent or not, and while there may be kinesthetic sensations which accompany such awareness, it is not plausible that it is on the basis of attending to *them* that one can tell one's bodily position. For one thing, there are just too many different such positions which one *can* report on immediately and accurately, and it's hard to believe either that there *are* distinct sensations correlated with all these different positions *or* that one's ability to distinguish such sensations could possibly be what underwrites such knowledge. Agreement on this point is not crucial, however, for what is more important is the fact that the idea of the 'non-observational' in this context cannot do the sort of work the notion must carry in the rest of Anscombe's argument, with respect to extended actions, both present and future. We can see this when we compare this case to the second class of cases.

B—In several places, Anscombe speaks of 'practical knowledge' of what one is currently doing, where this is contrasted with, e.g., visual aids to knowledge and action. Examples include the knowledge that I am painting the wall yellow (p. 50), opening the window (p. 51), pushing the boat out (p. 54), and the knowledge of what one is writing without looking (p. 53 and p. 82). What is striking is that in these examples of ordinary actions, essential reference is made to events taking place *outside* the boundaries of the person's body, and yet Anscombe insists that *this* sort of knowledge of 'what I am doing' is *also* not based on observation.

> I have argued that my knowledge of what I do is not by observation. A very clear and interesting case of this is that in which I shut my eyes and write something. I can say what I am writing. And what I say I am writing will almost always in fact appear on the paper. Now here it is clear that my capacity to say what is written is not derived from any observation. In practice of course what I write will very likely not go on being very legible if I don't use my eyes; but isn't the role of all our observation-knowledge in knowing what we are doing like the role of the eyes in producing successful writing? That is to say, once given that we have knowledge or opinion about that matter in which we perform intentional actions, our observation is merely an aid, as the eyes are an aid in writing. (p. 53)

How is it possible for the knowledge of what one is writing to be non-observational? It might be thought that non-observational knowledge of bodily position could still be the real basis for knowledge of extended actions, if we took a kind of two-factor approach to the knowledge of what one is doing, restricting its non-observational content to the confines of one's body and then adding to it the empirical knowledge of one's surroundings and the impact of one's body upon them. That is, it could be claimed that, to the extent that the idea of 'non-observational knowledge' is granted any plausibility at all, the *scope* of such knowledge is restricted to the boundaries of the agent's body, essentially the sort of awareness that a person has of the disposition and movements of his limbs (our category (**A**) here). The *appearance* of a similar awareness that extends *beyond* the body, as in the cases involving writing etc. that Anscombe is discussing above, could be explained away as the result of the agent's combining of his immediate bodily awareness with his fully empirical, observation-based knowledge of the physical *results* of the impact of his bodily movements upon the world. In this way, all that is really known without observation is contained in one's immediate proprioceptive awareness, and the action itself, as an efficacious event in the world, lies outside the scope of such awareness. If this general picture were correct, then there would be little reason left to insist on a basic difference between speculative knowledge and practical knowledge, since the idea of proprioceptive awareness, even if it is conceded to be 'non-observational', does not itself take us beyond the category of speculative knowledge. Anscombe, of course, rejects any such account, and for good reasons, as we shall see.

C—Further differences between the cases emerge when we consider the next category of the 'non-observational', what is sometimes called 'practical foreknowledge', which is the ordinary knowledge I may have that I will do something in the future because this is one of the options that is open to me and I have made up my mind to do it. This sort of knowledge is different, and differently based, from the sort of predictive, evidence-based, knowledge that another person may have of what I am going to do. This difference is illustrated by Anscombe's famous example of the man with the shopping list, and the different relations between *this* list and the items that actually end up in the shopping cart, and another list made by a detective following him and noting the items placed in the cart. (p. 56)

Although the phrase itself does not occur in this text, this example is the *locus classicus* for the idea of a difference in 'direction of fit' between an intention and a future action, and the 'fit' between a prediction or report and some future action. When intention and action fail to match, it is said, the mistake is in the *action*, whereas if the prediction or report fails to match the action then it is the report which is mistaken and must be corrected (as with the detective's list). So if we are willing to speak of 'knowledge' in both these cases, we can begin to see how observation would play a very different role for the detective than it does for the person making up the shopping list. Unlike theoretical or speculative knowledge, practical knowledge will not be passive or receptive to the facts in question, but is rather a state of the person that plays a role in the constituting of such facts. This is not to say that ordinary observation has no relevance here, but rather that it plays a different role than it does in the case of knowledge which *is* passive or receptive with respect to the facts in question.

D—This idea of a difference in 'direction of fit' is also clearly behind Anscombe's appeal later in the book to a phrase which Aquinas uses in distinguishing the operations of the practical intellect from those of the speculative intellect. Practical knowledge is said to be non-observational in that it is "the cause of what it understands", rather than being derived from objects known. (pp. 87–8) This might seem to be simply another way of making the point above (**C**). That is, if in the right circumstances my intention to pick up some milk at the store can be the basis of my practical knowledge that I *will* pick up some milk, then we may speak of my practical knowledge here, as embodied in my intention, as being "the cause of what it understands"; the cause, that is, of my getting some milk at the store. However, as we will see, it is important to the use Anscombe makes of this idea that the interpretation of 'cause' here in terms of *efficient* causes is at best a partial and misleading understanding of the sense in which one's intention to pick up some milk can be "the cause of what it understands". The point is not that the knowledge embedded in my intention helps to *produce* the movements that lead to the picking up of some milk, but rather that those movements would not count as my picking up some milk (intentionally) unless my practical understanding conceived of them in those terms. This will be important to understanding how the practical knowledge that I am, e.g., 'opening a window' can both extend to claims about windows and other ordinary observable objects and yet not itself be based on observation.

2. Delimiting the scope of non-observational knowledge

I share the sense of something phenomenologically apt in all of these cases of the putatively non-observational, but such aptness

Richard Moran

can be misleading both in encouraging us to amalgamate the different cases, and in obscuring the actual bases of Anscombe's argument about practical knowledge. Whatever is non-observational in the awareness of one's bodily position must on Anscombe's own account have a thoroughly different basis from, for instance, the practical foreknowledge of one's immediate plans, for the basic reason that such bodily awareness, however immediate or independent of particular sensations, remains an instance of *speculative knowledge*. What is known here is still 'derived from the object known', and the 'direction of fit' is still that of fitting the judgment to the independent facts. Even if immediate, and not grounded in observational evidence, the claim that one's knee is bent is still something corrected by the fact of one's straightened leg. Hence the immediate knowledge of one's bodily position cannot be an example of what Anscombe means by "practical knowledge", despite the intimate relation of such awareness to ordinary physical action, and despite the fact that both may be said to have a basis that is in some sense 'non-observational'.[2]

But the most basic difficulty one is likely to have with Anscombe's central claim is just in seeing how it could possibly be *true* of an extended action such as opening a window or painting a wall yellow, that the agent knows *that* he is doing this without observation. Surely, it seems, cases such as these are paradigms of observational knowledge. Even if we accept an account along the lines I suggested of the agent's practical foreknowledge that he will perform some action he has decided upon, and even if we accept that knowledge of bodily position is not based on awareness of corresponding sensations, it seems that the *only* way one could know the truth of a statement such as "I am (now) painting the wall yellow" is by looking at the wall and seeing what's happening there. Anscombe is fully aware of the provocative nature of her claim, and her defense of it is as forthright as it is obscure.

> Now, it may be, e.g., that one paints a wall yellow, meaning to do so. But is it reasonable to say that one 'knows without observation' that one is painting a wall yellow?" [...]
> My reply is that the topic of an intention may be matter on which there is knowledge or opinion based on observation, inference,

[2] This difference is often missed, but it is clearly made out in Rosalind Hursthouse's paper 'Intention', in Roger Teichmann, ed., *Logic, Cause, and Action* (Cambridge, 2000), where she credits Keith Donnellan's 'Knowing What I Am Doing', in *The Journal of Philosophy*, v. 60, n. 14; 1963.

hearsay, superstition or anything that knowledge or opinion ever are based on; or again matter on which an opinion is held without any foundation at all. When knowledge or opinion are present concerning what is the case, and what can happen—say, Z—if one does certain things, say ABC, then it is possible to have the intention of doing Z in doing ABC; and *if the case is one of knowledge or if the opinion is correct*, then doing or causing Z is an intentional action, and it is not by observation that one knows one is doing Z; or insofar as one is observing, inferring etc. that Z is actually taking place, one's knowledge is not the knowledge that a man has of his intentional actions. By the knowledge that a man has of his intentional actions I mean the knowledge that one denies having if when asked e.g., 'Why are you ringing that bell?' one replies 'Good heavens! I didn't know *I* was ringing it!'. [emphases added] (pp. 50–1)

What I gather from this is that various kinds of observation-based knowledge *are* presumed in the context of ordinary intentional action, including the knowledge of what is the case and what can happen if one does certain things. And when I am *mistaken* in such a presupposition, say the assumption that running this paint-brush along the wall will make it yellow, then I have mistaken opinion and therefore not knowledge of any sort. When I do know or believe empirically that pressing this button will produce the result of ringing this bell, then I *can have* the intention of ringing the bell by pressing the button, otherwise not. And when this empirical knowledge is in place, and can be presumed by me (when it is *true* and therefore genuinely *knowledge*), then I can have available to me the awareness that I am *doing Z*, e.g., that I am ringing the bell, when this is an intentional action of mine. And *this* awareness of what I am *doing* is not observational knowledge. It is something distinct from my observation-based knowledge that doing ABC can result in Z.

But if this is right, then it raises questions anew about what the philosophical *importance* could be of the idea of the non-observational defined in this way, for it now looks as though it is the *observational* knowledge that is doing all the epistemic work here. We might agree, that is, that if we add to my knowledge of my immediate bodily movement the empirical "knowledge concerning what is the case and what can happen if one does certain things", then I may indeed be credited with the knowledge, for instance, that I am ringing the bell. But accepting this much may still leave one with the feeling that the non-observational component to this knowledge

Richard Moran

is rather thin, not something really extending beyond our category **(A)** here, and not something to make the cornerstone of one's account of human action. Further, such a reconstruction would not take us all the way to non-observational knowledge such as the knowledge that I am opening a window or painting a wall yellow, knowledge that must include what is going on with the *window*, for instance, and not just with my own limbs. And yet Anscombe clearly does want to claim that knowledge of a complete, extended action of this sort is also known by the agent non-observationally. [category **(B)** here] I'll return to this question soon.[3]

At this point Anscombe notes the temptation to respond to these difficulties by restricting the scope of what is known in action so that it will make sense to speak of this knowledge as non-observational. She mentions two ways in which this might be attempted. We could cut out the external world altogether and say that what is known is only the intention (or the 'willing'), or we could cut out everything beyond the surface of the person's body and say that what is known without observation is only the bodily movement itself (in effect reducing practical knowledge to the proprioceptive awareness of my category **A**.) Anscombe rejects both of these options.[4] But at the same time, in the long passage just quoted (p. 50), she seems to make her own restriction on the scope of what is known, so that it may count as something known without observation. That is, *if* I have empirical knowledge of what can happen if I

---

[3] Anscombe's own worry at this point in the text is something different. *Her* worry at this stage of the argument is that "if there are two *ways* of knowing here, one of which I call knowledge of one's intentional action and the other of which I call knowledge by observation of what takes place, then must there not be two *objects* of knowledge? How can one speak of two different knowledges of *exactly* the same thing?" (p. 51) For now, I simply want to mark this question and leave it aside, since it is not clear just what kind of difficulty this is. For one thing, the position and movement of one's limbs has already been mentioned as something that can be known in two very different ways, without this raising issues of two different *objects* of knowledge. (This difficulty is also noted by Hursthouse, op. cit. p. 97.) Later we will consider a different version of Anscombe's question: If another person can often be said simply to *see* what I am doing, how can I know the very same thing *without* observation?

[4] "I think that it is the difficulty of this question that has led some people to say that what one knows as intentional action is only the intention, or possibly also the bodily movement; and that the rest is known by observation to be the *result*, which was also willed in the intention. But that is a mad account; for the only sense I can give to 'willing' is that in which I might stare at something and will it to move." (51–2)

do certain things, and if I know through observation (or otherwise) that Z can be the result of my doing ABC, *then* it is possible for me to have another sort of knowledge, the knowledge that *I am doing Z*. And *this* knowledge is not based on observation, although the intentional action that is its vehicle *does* presume the observation-based knowledge that Z can be the result of my doing ABC. Thus, the scope of what is known non-observationally includes 'what happens', but only insofar as this comes under the description of 'what I am intentionally *doing*'.

The idea of the restriction in scope here comes out one page later where she distinguishes between knowing without observation that I am writing something, and the observational role of the eyes as an *aid* in performing this action.

> Someone without eyes may go on writing with a pen that has no more ink in it [...] but the essential thing he does, namely to write such and such, is done without the eyes. So without the eyes he knows what he writes; but the eyes help to assure him that what he writes actually gets legibly written. In the face of this how can I say: I *do* what *happens*? If there are two ways of knowing, there must be two different things known. (53)

Aside from whatever is thought to be problematic in the idea of "two ways of knowing", I think we might see her real problem in the following way: If what she calls "the essential thing" known by the person writing is something he knows without observation, but what is known here is consistent with there being no ink in the pen and hence no writing being formed, then the worry is that this really begins to resemble the account she rejected as a mad one just a few paragraphs back: "That what one knows as intentional is only the intention, or possibly also the bodily movement; and that the rest is known by observation to be the *result*, which was also willed in the intention." (pp. 51–2)

So the conclusion she *wants* is that I know what I am doing without observation, and that *what I do* and *what happens* are one and the same: "I *do* what *happens*. That is to say, when the description of what happens is the very thing which I should say I was doing, then there is no distinction between my doing and the thing's happening." (pp. 52–3) But it keeps looking as if the conclusion she is actually steering toward is that as far as non-observational knowledge goes, this depends crucially on a *distinction* between 'what I do' and 'what happens'. That is, the *object* of my intention is a genuine resultant change in the world and not some purely interior happening. And *what* I end up doing is correctly described

Richard Moran

by naming some change in the world, e.g., washing the dishes. And my knowledge that I am *doing* this can be said to be non-observational only if we understand that this knowledge-of-doing depends on a background of *observation-based* knowledge of "what can happen—say, Z—f one does certain things, say ABC" (p. 50), *plus*, typically, the perceptual knowledge that serves as an *aid* in successfully carrying out this action. In this way, we could still say with Anscombe that "I *do* what *happens*," but it won't follow from this that my *knowledge* of what I am doing and my knowledge of what happens are the same. Hence the question I am trying to press here is not how it can *be* that "I do what happens", but how Anscombe can claim that my *knowledge* that I am doing something can be non-observational, when *what I do* includes, for example, the window I am opening or the words I take myself to be writing.[5]

The problem is not that Anscombe is unaware of the possibility of error, or that the idea of the non-observational must suggest something incorrigible by the facts of what is happening or failing to happen in the world.[6] An agent will have such awareness of 'opening a window' *only when* an actual window is getting opened, and similarly for her examples of pushing a boat out or writing with a pen. Hence if the pen has run out of ink and no actual writing is

[5] For this reason, I think that the issues she goes on to take up at this point in the text do not directly address this question. For it is directly after the discussion of the shopping list and the difference in 'direction of fit' that she introduces the idea of 'practical knowledge' as a corrective to the modern "incorrigibly contemplative conception of knowledge." (p. 57) But we should recall at this point that the shopping list and the analogy with commands seems most directly relevant to our category **(C)**, the case of 'Practical Foreknowledge', and not to the case of knowledge of what I am *currently* doing, where this is said to include non-observational awareness of some happening beyond my immediate physical movements, our category **(B)**. And yet it is these problems associated with the examples of opening the window and writing with one's eyes closed that Anscombe takes herself to be pursuing at this point in the text.

For criticism of Anscombe on Practical Foreknowledge, see D. Velleman, *Practical Reflection* (Princeton, 1989), especially pp. 18–22 and 102–5; and for a response to Velleman's account see George Wilson, 'Proximal Practical Foresight,' *Philosophical Studies* 99 (2000), 3–19.

[6] "Say I go over to the window to open it. Someone who hears me moving calls out: What are you doing making that noise? I reply 'Opening the window'. I have called such a statement knowledge all along; *and precisely because in such a case what I say is true*—I do open the window; and that means that the window is getting opened by the movements of the body out of whose mouth those words come." (p. 51, emphasis added)

getting done, then the agent's non-observational awareness is *mistaken*. This is all too easy to imagine. But as we've seen, Anscombe rejects the idea that in the *successful* cases, where a boat *is* getting pushed out, or writing *is* being produced, all that is really known by the agent immediately is something like the feelings of pressure in one's hands, or something else which excludes the actual boat or the window or the pen. She says two things in defense of this idea at this point (pp. 53–4). One is to point out that often the *only* way a person can describe what he is doing is by reference to objects and events beyond the confines of his body, as the person writing on the blackboard could say *what words* he is writing but could *not* describe this action in terms of any more 'immediate' motions of his hands and fingers.[7] In this way she seeks to undermine the idea that it is on the basis of this more immediate knowledge of the motions of one's hands that one knows what one is writing. Secondly, she appeals to the difference between knowledge of one's action being *based on* observation and being *aided by* observation. "Once given that we have knowledge or opinion about the matter in which we perform intentional actions, our observation is merely an aid, as the eyes are an aid in writing." (p. 53) Again, it is clear that whatever is known in practical knowledge will normally presume and depend on the observation-based deliverances of *speculative* knowledge. So one final way to put our question might be: if this is so, then in what way, if any, does 'what is known' in practical knowledge *go beyond* the observational knowledge that it requires? Without an answer to this question, Anscombe's appeal to the difference between knowledge *based on* observation and knowledge *aided by* observation will seem unhelpfully *ad hoc*. Anscombe needs an account of how the agent's 'practical knowledge' goes beyond his observational knowledge of what can happen and what is happening in order to avoid the charge mentioned earlier that, given the admitted dependence of successful action on empirical observations and assumptions, all the real epistemological work involved in the agent's knowing what he is doing is carried by his observational knowledge. What is still needed is a sense of practical knowledge that explains why its putatively non-observational character should matter to the account of intentional action, and which avoids the desperate measure of rescuing this character by restricting the scope of what is known to something that falls short of a genuine event in the observable world.

[7] "The only description that I clearly know of what I am doing may be of something that is at a distance from me. It is not the case that I clearly know the movements I make, and the intention is just a result which I calculate and hope will follow on these movements." (p. 53)

Richard Moran

3. What is done intensionally

In describing practical knowledge as "the cause of what it understands" Anscombe says: "This means more than that practical knowledge is observed to be a necessary condition of the production of various results [...] It means that without it what happens does not come under the description—execution of intentions—whose characteristics we have been investigating." (87–88) I take this to mean that if, for example, I do *not* have non-observational practical knowledge that I am clicking out a particular rhythm with the pump handle, then, as described this way *that* does not count as an intentional action of mine. It is something which I am indeed making *happen*, but it is not something I am *doing* in the sense of an intentional action of mine. This leads to a distinctive sense of practical knowledge as being 'the cause of what it understands', and it shows that the word '*what*' here must get special attention. For the 'what' that is the object of one's practical knowledge is not simply "the production of various results", or the event of my movements themselves, but rather the *fact* that I am doing this rather than that. The ascription of practical knowledge thus creates an intensional context, and will depend on the description under which the action is picked out. Hence, if I *know* what I'm doing under the description 'pumping water', then *that* description can count as one of the descriptions of my *action*, as opposed to all the other things my movements may be *affecting*, or making happen. Thus the sense in which my practical knowledge is 'the cause of what it understands' is not primarily in the sense that my intention to do a particular thing is a necessary causal antecedent for my making the movements I do. That would be a fully extensional understanding of the sense of 'cause' here and the sense of 'what' that is understood in practical knowledge. Rather, Anscombe's point is that practical knowledge, whose object is specified within an intensional context, determines which descriptions of 'what happens' may count as descriptions of what the person is intentionally *doing*. So the sense of the phrase from Aquinas is not about the efficient causal role of intention in producing movements, but rather concerns the formal or constitutive role of the description embedded in one's practical knowledge making it the case that *this* description counts as a description of the person's intentional action. If the agent didn't *know* this happening under *this* description, then as so specified it *would not be* 'what he is intentionally doing'. It is in this sense that 'practical knowledge is the cause of that which it understands'. What practical knowledge understands is an intentional action, and it would not be the action it is, or perhaps any action at all, if it were not known by the agent in this way.

This interpretation may seem to run against the grain of Anscombe's earlier gloss on practical knowledge, for 'doing' and 'happening' play very different roles on the reading I am suggesting now, whereas her formulation "I *do* what *happens*" (52) insists on an identity between the two. But the clash is more apparent than real. For her claim there can be put as saying that what I *do* and what I thereby have non-observational knowledge *of* is indeed "what happens", a genuine alteration in the world and not some subjective event. The crucial point to be added is that my practical knowledge comprises factual knowledge that I am performing such-and-such and action, which indeed involves something happening, but this fact will be known by me only as described in certain ways and not in others. This is confirmed by what she says on pp. 52–3 as a gloss on the phrase 'I *do* what *happens*': "That is to say, *when the description of what happens is the very thing which I should say I was doing*, then there is no distinction between my doing and the thing's happening." [emphasis added]

In one way it is right and in another it is not to say that in such a case "there is no distinction between my doing and the thing's happening". It is right insofar as one's doings are indeed happenings in the world, normally effectings of changes, such as 'opening the window', and the knowledge that one has in such a case is not something that stops short of the window itself. 'What I do' in such a case is not something restricted to the boundaries of my sensory body, nor is Anscombe concerned here with the claim that the agent's knowledge of his *intention* is something non-observational. Rather it is the actual accomplishment in the world that is said to be known in this way. But it is wrong or at best misleading here to say that there is "no distinction between my doing and the thing's happening" insofar as her claim that it is not by observation that I know that I am opening the window *depends* on the distinction between 'what I intentionally do' and 'what happens'. Understood, extensionally, I can know *what happens* only through observation, including the perception that serves as an aid in the execution of action such as writing on the blackboard (53), and the causal knowledge Anscombe refers to earlier as "knowledge or opinion concerning what is the case, and what can happen—say, Z—if one does certain things, say ABC" (50). With this empirical knowledge in place, I can form an intention to *do* something, such as opening a window, and then actually *do that thing*. But the event which is my action only counts as something I intentionally do only in virtue of some of its descriptions and not others, and my knowledge of it can be said to be 'non-observational' *only* under the terms of such descriptions. That is, Anscombe needs the difference between 'what I do' and 'what happens' in order that 'practical knowledge', which is said to be non-observational, not devolve into a kind of speculative knowledge of events, or a "very queer and special kind of seeing eye in the middle of acting" (57).[8]

4. The extent and the restriction of practical knowledge

Along these lines I see Anscombe's insistence on the intensional character of thought and discourse about action as doing considerably more work in her account of practical knowledge than is usually supposed. It enables her to maintain her formulation that "I do what happens", and avoid what she earlier characterized as the "mad account", according to which practical knowledge of what one is doing does not involve reference to actual changes in the world. But it also provides a way to say that what is claimed in practical knowledge is nonetheless something which goes beyond speculative, observational knowledge of what is the case. For the agent's practical knowledge commits itself not only to the obtaining of certain events in the world, but to the specification of the descriptions under which what happens counts as the execution of his intention. This knowledge depends on, but does not reduce to, the speculative knowledge of what can happen and what is happening, and in this way Anscombe may evade the charge mentioned earlier that the admitted dependence of successful action on ordinary observation must mean that the agent's knowledge of what he is doing is ultimately observational after all. And finally, it puts us in a position to say more about why the idea of the non-observational should matter in the first place to the philosophical understanding of action, for the thought is that if the agent had to *look* in order to find out what he is doing, nothing he could observe of his movements or their surroundings could itself specify the descriptions under which what is happening counts as an intentional action of his at all.

David Velleman begins his book *Practical Reflection* with consideration of cases where the person's ordinary practical knowledge of what he is doing momentarily fails: "You are walking up Fifth Avenue. All of a sudden you realize that you don't know what you're

---

[8] This section in particular has benefited from some comments from Helen Steward.

doing."[9] And, as he points out, in such cases where practical knowledge fails, the normal response to realizing this is to halt the movement one is engaged in until such knowledge can be recovered, as if intentional action could not continue when the agent realizes that he is missing the ordinary knowledge of what he is doing (and indeed this dependence is precisely what Velleman's book as a whole seeks to account for and develop further). For our purposes right now, such cases enable us to see how it can be true both that the agent will normally depend on observation of various kinds to carry through an action like walking up Fifth Avenue (Anscombe's "observational aids"), and also that the knowledge that is temporarily lost in such cases is nonetheless not made up for by further observations alone. The person stops and *looks around*, observing his position and his environment for clues to what he might have been up to, but this by itself does not deliver to him the knowledge of what he is or was doing, for it does not provide him with the particular set of descriptions of what he sees or the movements he is making, under which what he was doing counted as an intentional action of his.

There is an ordinary sense in which he *sees* the same things as he did when he was engaged in action (e.g., walking up Fifth Avenue). But there is also a sense in which what he sees is now blank to him, because he cannot articulate his own relation to it. The objects and scenes of his environment no longer have a role assigned to them in his ongoing action (as goal, obstacle, distraction, background, etc.). He sees Fifth Avenue, and he sees it from a particular perspective which indicates what direction he was heading in, but he does not see his goal. He does not see how his surroundings orient themselves with respect to his goal. Instead, he sees *everything* around him, the traffic going by, the meaningless street-signs, the strangers' faces, and nothing in those details enables him to discern a destination, a point to his being right here facing in this direction.

If the agent doesn't know what he's doing, looking around him may provide him with clues, but the knowledge he gains from looking around is not the same as the practical knowledge he has temporarily lost, and in this way we can begin to see how practical knowledge *could not* be observational, could not be perceptually derived from the world. For nothing the agent sees in the world could give him those descriptions, even though *what* is claimed in practical knowledge is a world-involving matter of fact. The person who loses his awareness of what he is doing still has a richly

[9] P. 15, *Practical Reflection* (Princeton, 1989)

intensionalist discourse available to him for describing his experience, for what he knows concerning Fifth Avenue, the storefronts, the people, etc. will itself be ascribable to him only under certain descriptions and not others. But he is nonetheless missing something that he had before, a kind of knowledge which involves the world around him (i.e., is not confined either to his mental interior or the surface of his body), but which further observation of the world around him does not provide him with (though such observation may prod him to *recall* what he was doing). In this way the knowledge he has temporarily lost is something that goes beyond his observational knowledge. It may depend on perception in various ways, but what he knew before he lost it was not something derived or inferred from perception.[10]

Anscombe's framework will thus involve an account not only of the *extent* of practical knowledge (beyond the agent's intention, beyond the agent's body), but also of the parallel *restriction* of such knowledge to the specificities of certain descriptions. The same considerations that allow her to describe what is known by the agent as genuinely world-involving will also require that what is known is restricted in ways that would not apply to the deliverances of an organ of sense. For instance, in writing the word 'cat' on the blackboard, what the agent accomplishes is as fully determinate as the event which constitutes it: he is writing at a certain speed, holding the chalk at a certain angle, in a certain particular colored chalk, in letters of a certain size. Many of these features, of course, will be ones to which the agent is indifferent, and hence do not form part of his intentional action. These descriptions and countless others are made true by the action he is performing, but the agent's practical knowledge does not extend to what happens when described in

[10] Early in *Intention* Anscombe briefly connects the non-observational character of practical knowledge, with the role of such knowledge in selecting from all the extensionally true descriptions of a person at a given moment: "Well, if you want to say at least some true things about a man's intentions, you will have a strong chance of success if you mention what he actually did or is doing. [...] I am referring to the sort of things you would say in a law court of you were a witness and were asked what a man was doing when you saw him. That is to say in a very large number of cases, your selection from the immense variety of true statements about him which you might make would coincide with what he could say he was doing, perhaps even without reflection, certainly without adverting to observation." (p. 8)
The person in Velleman's situation has available to him "the immense variety of true statements" about himself and his situation, but lacks what would enable him to say what he is doing.

those terms. That is because in referring to some event as an intentional action, we are constrained to descriptions that will capture 'what happened' as something the agent had a *reason* to make happen, and this provides us with a way to circumscribe the extent and the specificity of the agent's practical knowledge. For when an action is successful, it extends as far as the descriptions under which the agent has reason for pursuing the end which his action is aimed at realizing. If the reasons for writing on the blackboard require that the writing be legible but not that the chalk be of a particular colour (though of course the chalk will necessarily *be* of some particular color, and the agent may will know which color it is), then the agent's practical knowledge includes the legibility of the writing but not the particular color of the chalk. The range of descriptions under which the agent has practical knowledge that he is doing something (in the case of successful action) will be the same as the range of descriptions under which what happens is part of his aim in acting. Hence, the agent may be said to have practical knowledge that it is the word 'cat' which is getting written, but not the exact size of the letters in the word. It is these former descriptions which determine the content of the agent's practical knowledge, because these are the descriptions that figure in the reasons supporting the intention, and they are thus among the descriptions which the agent himself would give by way of explaining *what* he did (the identity of his action) and why he did it.

This does not mean that we must picture the agent as entertaining a whole range of intensionally-specified thoughts each time he acts in pursuit of some goal. If for no other reason, that would be a conclusion to avoid in light of the utter pervasiveness of intentional action, large and small, in our daily lives. During our waking moments, but not restricted to our reflective ones, we are more or less *always* engaged in intentional activity of one sort or another, both small and large, immediate and long-range. Some of these actions that are the result of explicit choosing and weighing between different options, but much of what we intentionally do involves no such prior planning or reflecting on reasons, but is more like something we find ourselves doing in the course of the stream of other activities. And yet, even for the less reflective and more spontaneous of our actions, the norm is for the person to know what he is doing, and to know this in knowing his reasons, and hence to know his action under some descriptions and not others. But the assumption that the person knows what he is doing at a given moment does not require anything like explicit consciousness of his reasons. We can see this by consideration of what happens to the person in Velleman's example when he temporarily loses his practical knowledge of what he is doing in walking up Fifth Avenue. In describing the change that leads him to stop in his tracks, it is not as if we are imagining that prior to this moment he must have any particular thoughts or descriptions in mind as he walked along. Instead he just 'knows what he is doing' in the ordinary, non-articulated sense. He knows his reasons for what he is doing, but not because he is thinking about them, or is describing his own behavior in some terms but not others. What changes is not that he goes from explicit awareness of his reasons to unawareness of them, but rather that before this he *could* become consciously aware of them by reflecting on what he is doing, and now when he reflects he finds that he cannot become so aware. The *recovery* of this knowledge will likely involve explicit reflection on his reasons, as well as the observation of his surroundings, but that doesn't mean that what he has temporarily lost is something either observational or explicit. Hence Anscombe's 'practical knowledge' does not involve some phenomenological vehicle, something containing a certain description, a "seeing eye in the middle of acting" (Anscombe, p. 57) which filters what it sees through the veil of some description. The knowledge thus attributed is non-observational, not because the agent is thought to have some non-observational awareness of these descriptions, but because these descriptions pick out an *aim* of his, and it is not by observation that one knows one's aims or knows what will count as the realization of one's aims.

5. Practical, speculative, and their possibilities of failure

The agent can, of course, be flatly wrong about what he takes himself to be doing, for instance when the wall is not getting painted yellow (p. 50), or when the pen runs out of ink without his noticing (p. 53), or more generally when the empirical conditions enabling a particular action fail to obtain. If he is wrong in assuming that writing is getting produced, then he cannot have practical knowledge that he is writing. In considering this sort of case, Anscombe herself seems to confuse the requirement of truth for knowledge, which applies to any knowledge, practical or speculative, with the question of whether it is the action or the (putative) knowledge that is to be corrected in the case of disparity:

> "That intention, for example, would not have been executed if something had gone wrong with the chalk or the surface, so that the words did not appear. And my knowledge would have been

the same even if this had happened. If then my knowledge is independent of what actually happens, how can it be knowledge of what does happen? Someone might say that it was a funny sort of knowledge that was still knowledge even though what it was knowledge of was not the case! On the other hand, Theophrastus' remark holds good: 'the mistake is in the performance, not in the judgement'." (p. 82)

But it is *not* a good answer to this problem of error and knowledge to advert to Theophrastus and the thought that the mistake here lies in the *performance* and not in what is *said*. To disqualify as knowledge, it doesn't matter where the error comes from so long as there is error; 'direction of fit' considerations are not to the point here. The distinction between practical and speculative knowledge does not concern the requirement of truth, but the question of what is to be corrected in cases of failure of fit.[11] But as with knowledge generally, while practical knowledge requires truth, it does not require being beyond risk of error. Observational aids and the general cooperation of the world will be necessary for the agent to be in a position to have practical knowledge of what he is doing, and when these fail then the claim to knowledge must fail as well. But this dependence does not by itself mean that the knowledge in question must really be observational after all, any more than the dependence of one's mathematical knowledge on the good working order of a calculator or a teacher or one's own brain means that such knowledge is really empirical and not *a priori*.[12]

However, I think that understanding Anscombe's emphasis on the intensional character of attributions of intentional action as well as attributions of practical knowledge enables us to see how the possibilities and consequences of error are importantly different for speculative and practical knowledge. Toward the end of *Intention* Anscombe says "It is necessarily the rare exception for a man's performance in its more immediate descriptions not be what he supposes" (p. 87), and this claim is followed immediately by the sentence, "Furthermore, it is the agent's knowledge of what he is doing that gives the descriptions under which what is going on is the execution of an intention." "It is necessarily the rare exception", I take it, because when the agent's practical knowledge *does* fail in this way, we may find ourselves unable to say what intentional action he

[11] I have been helped here by some remarks of David Velleman, although my way of putting this point may not be in line with his.

[12] See, for instance, Burge, Tyler, 'Content Preservation', *Philosophical Review* 102, No. 4 (October 1993).

is performing at all, even though the general form of action-description still seems to apply. For imagine one of Anscombe's cases where our agent is failing at making true one of these "more immediate descriptions" of what he is doing. Something has gone wrong with the chalk and no writing is appearing, or something has gone wrong with the paint brush and the wall is not getting painted yellow. (p. 53, p. 82) In such a case if we ask 'what is he doing?', an answer such as 'painting the wall yellow' is unavailable to us for the simple reason that it is not true. And, not being true, it is not something of which we, as observers, could suppose the agent to have practical knowledge. But in such a case it is not clear that there is any *better* answer that could be given to the question what intentional action he is then performing.

That is, let's suppose that in the event of success in action, one true description of what he is up to *is* 'painting the wall yellow'. Such a description counts as a true answer to the question not only by fitting the facts about what is happening there on the wall, but also only insofar as this description of what is happening there on the wall fits a certain structure. For, as we've seen, there are many other true descriptions of what is happening as a result of these movements that would *not* be truthful answers to the question 'What are you (intentionally) doing there?'. He may be dripping paint on the floor, or covering up an unseen inscription on the wall, aggravating the bursitis in his elbow, etc. If he is failing at painting the wall yellow, neither of us can simply retreat to one of these extensionally true descriptions of what is happening as an answer to the question 'What is he doing?'. To give one of *them* as a revised answer to the question would be as false as it would be now to say that he is painting the wall yellow.[13] An answer that gives the content of the agent's *practical knowledge* must conform to the structure under which what is happening is described as an *intentional action*, and this imposes requirements on the possible content of practical knowledge that do not constrain claims to speculative knowledge. Practical knowledge applies to only one domain: the agent's own intentional actions; whereas the possible objects of speculative knowledge are as unlimited as the range of knowable truths. Given this restriction of the domain of practical knowledge, it follows that what is thereby known must be something "to which a certain sense of the question 'Why?' is given application; the sense is of course that in which the answer, if positive, gives a reason for acting." (p.

[13] This is not to say that nothing a person *does* can fall outside of what he *intended*, that accidents are not possible, or that we don't sometimes respond to accidents by saying "Look what you've *done!*"

9). This question asks for some *point* to what the person is doing, even if that point is nothing involving some *further* end, but simply that of doing it for its own sake. And even here there will be such a point to what the person is doing only when that happening is described in certain terms and not in others. As described differently but no less truly, what the person has caused to happen may be something he has no reason to pursue, may be something from which he recoils in horror or embarrassment, and thus under such a description Anscombe's question 'Why?' is refused application. If there is nothing the person is making happen which can be described in terms of some aim of his, then nothing happening can be an object of his practical knowledge. What this means is that the range of descriptions under which what is happening is a possible object of practical knowledge may be quite narrow, certainly more narrow than the range of descriptions under which one might qualify a claim to speculative knowledge of something, and when some preferred description of the action (e.g., 'painting the wall yellow') is shown to fail, there may be no other true description of what is happening that would fall within the range of things being done of which the agent has practical knowledge.

If we are watching someone with a paint brush, the point of asking the question 'What is he doing?' depends on the assumption that the agent does know what he is doing. And it assumes as well that his epistemic position with respect to this question is different from ours or that of some other observer, for the observer, after all, can see as well as he can what is *happening* or not happening here. His question is asking for something which goes beyond this. And then we can express the problem this way. The agent is plainly doing something; it is not the case that these movements lie outside of action description altogether, if that means that either the agent or the observer confronts them as some kind of reflex. And yet he is also plainly not doing what he takes himself to be doing "in its more immediate description". So the observer knows that this person cannot be said to have practical knowledge of what he is then doing. And yet, in Anscombe's words, "it is the agent's knowledge of what he is doing that gives the descriptions under which what is going on is the execution of an intention" (p. 87). Here the observer can see that there is no description of what is happening that would count either as contributing to an aim the agent has, or as something he is pursuing for its own sake. There seems to be no weaker action description to fall back on, which would be a true answer to the question "What is he doing?" where the doing is meant to refer to an intentional action.

What I mean by a weaker description is a statement of what he is doing, where this statement is an expression of his practical knowledge; that is, we seem to lack a place for a claim of the *same form* as the claim that has just come to grief, but now a more circumscribed claim that will still count an expression of his practical knowledge of what he is doing. Such possibilities of qualification and retreat are part of the very texture of claims to *speculative* knowledge of one sort or another. I claim that there is a goldfinch at the bottom of the garden, but my companion corrects me. I then may say, "Well, it's either a goldfinch or a goldcrest", and then perhaps I have to retreat from this too, and so on. There is still quite some distance I may have to go before I'm willing to entertain the thought that I know *nothing* here (Well there's a bird there anyway", "I'm telling you I saw *something*"). In familiar ways, this process of retreat and recovery can become merely tedious, or it can be part of the ordinary process of actually getting more precise. The important point for now is that at each stage of revision, the person here is still entitled to make a claim of the same sort, a claim to speculative knowledge. But the situation of the person with the paint brush or the chalk seems different. In the event of failure of this kind (i.e., in the action's "more immediate" descriptions), although there are certainly things he can *say* about what is happening, we may arrive more quickly at the point where there is no weaker claim to practical knowledge of what he is doing to which he can retreat, a claim of the same form as the one he has been forced to withdraw.

If the wall is not getting painted yellow, it will not answer our question to say, for instance, "He is dripping paint on the floor", or "He is aggravating his bursitis." These would not answer our question, even assuming their truth and even assuming he was then and there aware of this truth. The reason for this is not only that we may assume that 'aggravating his bursitis' is not the description of an intentional movement of his. (It may be the *result* of an intentional movement of his, but so is digestion the result of the intentional movements connected with eating. But digestion is not an action.) For it would also not be an answer to our question for him to say: "I am moving my arm back and forth across this wall, can't you see?" —even though, unlike the other two examples, *this* might be thought to be one of the descriptions under which his movements count still as willed or voluntary (p. 89). For *this* to count as an answer to the question "What are you doing?", he would need to have practical knowledge either of some aim he has in moving his arm back and forth as such, or the fact that he is doing this simply for its own sake, which is also possible. This latter type of practical knowledge is *not* the same as having *no* answer to the question of why one is making some movement. It is not what is "left over" after any and all practical purposes have been ruled out. Rather, making this movement "for its own sake" would be specifically a positive answer to the question of what one is doing *in* making this movement, and as such is an expression of the agent's practical knowledge. But often neither of these types of answer will be available in the case of this sort of failure.

At this point it may be insisted that the person is at least *trying* to paint the wall yellow, and that this is a good answer to Anscombe's question 'What is he doing?' Sometimes, of course, that will certainly be the response, but it will not always serve as an answer to *this* question. If 'trying' is meant to refer to some more purely internal occurrence, then saying this may well be a way of making the person's movements intelligible to us, but it will not be a description of what the person is *doing* in the sense to which Anscombe means her claim to apply. It's important to recall that for her the expression of practical knowledge is a claim about what is *getting done*, a world-involving intensional description, and not a claim about one's intentions or tryings, when these are meant to be understood in a way that is independent of what happens. It is clear that, on her understanding of the terms, the claim to practical knowledge *fails* in the cases we are discussing, as it would *not* fail if it involved a claim only of what one is trying to do, in this purely internal sense. Practical knowledge is defined by her as knowledge of what one is *doing*, and "I do what happens" (p. 52). On the other hand, 'trying' need not be understood this way, of course, and commonly refers to the means employed to achieve some end. In the case of a more extended action-description, such as 'fixing a leak', the trying in question will itself consist in other describable actions, and the more immediate ones of these will be those to which Anscombe means her claim to apply (e.g., "I tried tightening it, and I tried taping it." See Anscombe's claim from p. 87). Here the person's trying to fix the leak consists in other describable actions, actions which can succeed or fail. If the leak is not in fact getting fixed, it will indeed still be true that the person is *trying* to fix it, and if so then he will have practical knowledge that he is, e.g., taping the pipe, or twisting the bolt. And if the action which constitutes this trying also fails, so that no tightening of the bolt is in fact taking place, he may still retreat to the claim that he is *trying* to tighten it (e.g., by holding the wrench this way and that, turning it, etc.). But this can be an answer to the original question 'What are you doing?', one that is on the same level as the claim that failed ('tightening the bolt') only because there is a straightforward way in which the person can see what he *is* doing (holding the wrench in place, pulling on it) as potentially contributing to the realization of the aim in question. This follows from the teleological structure of action. It is because the person can see what he is doing as contributing to an aim of his that it can be part of an intentional action of his and hence a possible object of his practical knowledge. And it is for this reason that an answer of this form ('trying to tighten the bolt') can be an answer to the question of what he is doing, an answer that is weaker than, but on the same level as, the original claim that failed. When we turn back to Anscombe's original cases of failure, however, it is much less clear that these conditions will always be fulfilled. If someone takes himself to be painting the wall yellow (p. 50), and discovers that either there is no paint on the brush or that it is red paint, he will not continue as before while retreating to claim "Well, I'm *trying* to paint the wall yellow, anyway", for that could only be an answer if he thought that moving the brush either with no paint or red paint on it could be a possible *way* of painting the wall yellow. Someone can be said to be *trying* to do X only if he can see what he is doing as potentially contributing to the achievement of X, and the cases Anscombe is concerned with fail in this regard. This kind of failure of knowledge of the action "in its more immediate description" may thus provide no weaker, substitute claim that is both a true description of what is happening and something which, as so described, the agent understands himself to have a reason to pursue. Without that there is nowhere to enter a claim to practical knowledge, and the agent's realization of this brings action to a halt.

By contrast, claims to speculative knowledge have greater resources for retreat and recovery when one's original claim has to be withdrawn, while maintaining the general claim to be in some relation of knowing to the way the world is. When my claim "There's a goldfinch in the bottom of the garden" fails, there are various weaker claims I can still insist on as expressing something that I *know*, and thus I can still maintain a claim of the same kind as the one that had to be withdrawn. For instance, there will normally be various more *general* descriptions of what I saw to which I can retreat and recover my claim to know something, whereas it will only be in special circumstances that a more general description of what I am doing will also satisfy the requirements of an object of practical knowledge (e.g., "All right, I may not be writing my name on the board, but I'm certainly making some marks."). If no writing is being formed by my movements, there may well be no other description of my movements that I could give, certainly no purely physical description, and not one that I could deliver without observation of myself and my surroundings. I knew my movements and could describe them only insofar as they contributed to my aim of writing on the blackboard. If they now do *not* contribute to any aim of mine that I recognize, they are not a possible object of my practical knowledge. And lacking an alternative description of those movements, according to which they would count as contributing to the realization of some aim, there will not be another weaker claim of the same sort (that is, a claim to practical knowledge) to which I might retreat and qualify my claim to know what I'm doing.

Speculative knowledge is not the cause, either formally or materially, of what it understands; and it follows from this that the failure of a speculative knowledge claim does not have the same consequences as a failure of practical knowledge. If a particular practical knowledge claim fails, then it is no longer the case that, within the specific terms of that knowledge, the event in question counts as an intentional action. Because of the relation of formal causality, a failure of practical knowledge means that the event in question no longer counts as a thing of a certain kind (an intentional action, as described in those terms). ("Without it, what happens does not come under the description—execution of intentions—whose characteristics we have been investigating." (p. 88)) An object of speculative knowledge, on the other hand, is independent, both formally and materially, of being known. No particular person stands in a relation to these facts such that they would not *be* the facts they are if they were not known by that person in a particular way. Because of this, a failure of some claim to speculative knowledge does not make any difference to the character of the object of that failed claim. Its being known in certain terms was not part of its character as a possible object of speculative knowledge, and hence when such a claim fails, the object in question remains intact, as it were, with all its properties, and stands ready to receive another more guarded attempt at a successful claim to knowledge.

* * *

This paper began by exploring the thought that there is some privileged relation (though not one of incorrigibility), within intentional action, between what an agent is doing and what he takes himself to be doing. A better way to put this now would be to say that Anscombe's conception of practical knowledge points to the place where *one* person's conception of the action does not bear only an epistemic relation to the action (that is, a theoretical or a descriptive relation), but rather also plays a role in constituting it *as* the action it is. For *practical* knowledge, on her account, is a necessary condition for the thing known to be the sort of thing it is, vis. the agent's intentional action. *This* sort of awareness of what I am doing is not just a kind of access to it which I have and which other people do not have, as in the case of awareness of the position of one's limbs.[14] The fact of my leg's being bent or straight is not dependent on, or in any way constituted by, my being aware of it as such. The person's non-observational awareness of this position is not "the cause of what it understands" either in the sense of an efficient cause or a formal cause.

The situation is different with respect to knowledge of what one is doing. An observer can be said to *see* straight off what someone is doing only if he is entitled to assume that the agent himself knows what he is doing *without* looking. The agent himself cannot know what he is doing intentionally by looking, if that means *only* by looking. For if he can't know this non-observationally, in the manner of practical knowledge, then there *is* nothing of the right kind for another person to *see* him doing. What the notion of 'privilege' comes to here is that if the agent doesn't know what he is doing, then no one else *can* know. This does not mean that the agent is always *right* about what he is doing, but that any observer's knowledge of what he is doing is dependent on the assumption that the agent himself does know, for "it is the agent's knowledge of what he is doing that gives the description under which what is going on is the execution of an intention." (p. 87) And moreover, what the observer can know is dependent on the assumption that the agent knows what he is doing *without* observation. When such practical knowledge is known to fail, then those descriptions are unavailable to both agent and observer, and yet falling back on one of the many extensionally true descriptions of what is happening will not tell either of them what intentional action, if any, he is performing.[15]

[14] For all I've said here, it may be that such non-observational awareness of the position of one's limbs is a necessary condition for ordinary agency. What I'm concerned to argue here is that such awareness does not play any constituting role for one's limbs being in a certain position.

[15] Earlier versions of this paper were delivered at the University of Edinburgh at the conference on 'The Will in Moral Psychology' in July 2002, and at the Royal Institute of Philosophy conference on 'Agency and Action' held at Oxford University in September 2002, and I'm grateful to the audiences on both those occasions. In the early stages of writing I had especially encouraging conversations with Martin Stone and Ed Minar. I also benefitted from the comments of Luca Ferrero, Richard Holton, Jennifer Hornsby, Adam Leite, Lucy O'Brien, Michael Smith, David Velleman, Bernard Williams, and George Wilson. Special thanks to the editors of this volume for comments at the final stages.

Action, the Act Requirement and Criminal Liability

ANTONY DUFF

1. The 'Act Requirement' in Criminal Law

The slogan that criminal liability requires an 'act', or a 'voluntary act', is still something of a commonplace in textbooks of criminal law. There are, it is usually added, certain exceptions to this requirement—cases in which liability is in fact, and perhaps even properly, imposed in the absence of such an act: but the 'act requirement' is taken to represent a normally minimal necessary condition of criminal liability.[1] Even offences of strict liability, for which no *mens rea* is required, require an act: thus to the familiar slogan that *actus non facit reum nisi mens sit rea* we can add the prior, more fundamental slogan that *mens non facit reum nisi actus sit reus*; before we ask whether a defendant acted with *mens rea* or fault, we must ask whether he committed a criminal act at all.

Two initial points should be noted about the act requirement as it is standardly conceived among criminal law theorists.

First, the requirement might be expressed in terms of 'an act', or of 'a voluntary act'. The reference to voluntariness, however, is not to a *further* requirement, beyond that of an act: it rather makes explicit what is taken to be implicit in the very notion of an 'act' in this context. It is as responsible agents that we are held criminally

---

[1] See e.g. P. H. Robinson, *Fundamentals of Criminal Law* (2nd ed., Boston: Little, Brown, 1995), 250; W. R. LaFave, *Criminal Law* (3rd ed., St Paul, Minnesota: West, 2000), 195–202; J. Dressler, *Understanding Criminal Law* (3rd ed., New York: Lexis, 2001), 81–93; G. Williams, *Criminal Law: The General Part* (2nd ed., London: Stevens, 1961), 1–16; W. Wilson, *Criminal Law* (2nd ed., London: Longman, 2003), 72–6; J. C. Smith & B. Hogan, *Criminal Law* (10th ed., by J. C. Smith, London: Butterworths, 2002), 30–68; G. H. Gordon, *The Criminal Law of Scotland* (3rd ed., by M. G. A. Christie, Edinburgh: Green, 2000), vol. I, 60–81. But contrast A. J. Ashworth, *Principles of Criminal Law* (4th ed., Oxford: Oxford University Press, 2003), 99–114; A. P. Simester and G. R. Sullivan, *Criminal Law: Theory and Doctrine* (2nd ed., Oxford: Hart, 2003), 71–86: what is required is not an 'act', but 'voluntariness'.

Antony Duff

liable, and only our voluntary, i.e. non-involuntary, behaviour can contribute to our responsible agency.[2]

Second, the act requirement serves both a descriptive and a normative role in criminal law theorizing. Our legal systems do in fact, it is said, typically require an act as an essential basis for criminal liability: so if our interest is in describing the criminal law, or in analysing its structure and key elements, we can properly cite the act requirement as a structural feature. However, the act requirement is also commended as a normative requirement of justice: it is unjust to impose criminal liability in the absence of an act, or so to define crimes that no act is required. When we find instances in which liability seems to be imposed in the absence of any relevant act, and which cannot be explained away as only apparent exceptions to the act requirement, theorists can therefore either condemn them as injustices which we should seek to remove (as qualifying the descriptive, but not the normative, slogan that criminal liability requires an act), or accept them as justified exceptions to the normative principle.

The act requirement does, I think, have a certain intuitive plausibility—a plausibility that largely derives from the kinds of liability it is standardly taken to exclude.

It is taken, first, to exclude criminal liability for mere thoughts: even if thoughts might be wrongful (for instance, entertaining sadistic fantasies about someone), they are surely not the proper business of the criminal law. We might disagree about just where we should draw the line between public matters which can properly concern the criminal law and private matters which concern only the individual's own conscience: but it is surely not controversial that the criminal law of a state that claims even a minimal respect for liberal values must not intrude into the private realm of thought. Citizens should be punished only for what they do, not for what they merely think, or think about doing.

It is taken, second, to exclude criminal liability for mere involuntary bodily movements. Dangerous driving is an offence of strict liability, in that a driver can be guilty of it although he did not realize that his driving was dangerous, or did not notice the features of his driving that made it dangerous: but it requires a 'voluntary act' of driving, and so is not committed by someone whose movements

---

[2] The 'voluntary', as legal theorists typically use the term, thus excludes the involuntary: what is done under duress, whilst not done 'voluntarily' in ordinary usage, counts as a 'voluntary' act in this sense.

(those that cause the car to move as it does) are involuntary—the result of an unforeseeable epileptic fit, for instance.[3]

It is taken, third, to exclude criminal liability for mere conditions or states of affairs. That is why the U. S. Supreme Court was right to declare to be unconstitutional a statute making it an offence to be addicted to narcotics:[4] the act requirement would permit the criminalization of actions such as acquiring or using drugs, or actions undertaken as a result of an addiction (such as theft); but we should not punish a person merely for the condition of being an addict. That is also why the Alabama Court of Appeal was right to overturn Mr Martin's conviction for appearing in a public place whilst manifestly intoxicated, since the police took him from his home, whilst he was drunk, into the street, where they arrested him.[5] The act requirement would permit the criminalization of actions such as going into a public place while drunk, or of disorderly drunken conduct, but not of the merely passive happening of being found drunk in public.

It is taken, fourth, to exclude general liability for omissions. We are of course sometimes criminally liable (and sometimes properly so) for what we fail to do, when the law imposes a special duty to act or to prevent harm: but whilst we can be criminally liable for any legally relevant harms that we cause by our voluntary acts, we are liable for legally relevant harms that we fail to prevent only if we are under such a special duty to prevent them. There is, we can say, a presumption that criminal liability requires a positive act, and that a mere omission is not sufficient: that presumption is defeated only by the existence of a special duty to act.[6]

In each of these cases, one who objects to being held liable in the absence of a voluntary act might express that objection by crying 'But I didn't *do* anything': the act requirement in criminal law gains its intuitive plausibility from whatever plausibility that natural protest has.

Whatever initial, intuitive plausibility it might have, however, the act requirement is far from clear in its meaning and implications. It is unclear partly because it is not yet clear what should count as an 'act' (an issue to which we will shortly return), but partly because it

[3] See *Hill v Baxter* [1958] 1 Q. B. 277.

[4] *Robinson v California* 370 U. S. 660 (1962).

[5] *Martin v State* 17 So.2d 427 (1944). Compare *Winzar v Chief Constable of Kent* (1983) The Times, 28 March (being found drunk in a highway); see Wilson, *Criminal Law* (n. 1 above), 73–4.

[6] See e.g. Wilson, *Criminal Law* (n. 1 above), 77–94; Dressler, *Understanding Criminal Law* (n. 1 above), 101–5.

is not yet clear whether an act is supposed to be required as the object of criminal liability, or only as a necessary condition of liability.[7] If an act is required as the object of liability, what we are held criminally liable for must be an act: as thus understood, the act requirement would exclude liability for thoughts, conditions, involuntary movements or omissions. But if an act is required only as a condition of liability, we could be criminally liable for things other than acts (including, perhaps, thoughts, conditions, involuntary movements or omissions), so long as they are suitably related to some act. I have presented the act requirement as if it concerned the objects of criminal liability, but it might seem more plausible, in at least some contexts, to interpret it as concerning the conditions of liability.

Consider first attempt liability. If I am to be guilty of a criminal attempt, I must intend to commit a crime, and commit some act in furtherance of that intention: for instance, in English law, 'an act which is more than merely preparatory to the commission of the offence'; under the American Model Penal Code, an act 'constituting a substantial step' towards the crime's commission.[8] On one reading, such an act partly constitutes the object of attempt liability: what the would-be criminal is liable for is an act done in furtherance of a criminal intention, which takes him far enough along the road towards completing that crime. On a different reading, however, the act serves merely as a condition of liability, and the role of the act requirement is evidential rather than constitutive. What the would-be criminal is liable for—what makes him criminally guilty—is his firm intention to commit a crime. The law requires an act which manifests that intention not because without such an act the defendant is not truly guilty, but because the act provides reliable and appropriate evidence of the intention that constitutes his guilt: the act requirement serves not to specify the substance of criminal guilt, but to protect us against oppressive police investigations and the danger of unreliable convictions. On this reading attempt liability is liability for a kind of thought, for a criminal intention, and the act requirement specifies not the substantive object, but a condition, of such liability: the would-be criminal is liable for his criminal intention, on condition that it is

[7] See D. Husak, 'Does Criminal Liability Require an Act?', *Philosophy and the Criminal Law: Principle and Critique*, R. A. Duff (ed.) (Cambridge: Cambridge University Press, 1998), 60, at 67–73.

[8] Criminal Attempts Act 1981, s. 1(1); *Model Penal Code* s. 5.01(1)(c).

manifested in a suitable act.[9] Now there is controversy about which of these readings makes better normative sense of the law of attempts. We cannot hope to settle that controversy merely by appealing to the act requirement, which is meant to specify an uncontroversial, minimal constraint on the criminal law; we therefore cannot assume that it requires an act as the object, rather than simply as a condition, of liability.

Consider, second, cases in which liability seems to be imposed for a condition rather than for an act. For instance, the criminal law includes various offences of possession: it is a crime to be in possession of controlled drugs, of an offensive weapon, of counterfeit currency, or of unlicensed firearms.[10] Now we might worry about how extensive the reach of such offences should be: we might think that in at least some cases what should be criminal is not the mere possession of something, but possession with intent to use in a way that would cause criminal harm;[11] we might think that it would certainly be unjust to hold a person criminally liable for 'possessing' something that he did not know he had.[12] But the mere fact—if it is a fact—that possession is not an 'act'[13] does not seem to constitute a fundamental bar to criminal liability for possession: the most that we could plausibly demand is that we be held criminally liable for possession only on condition that the possession resulted from some act of acquisition—i.e. that a suitable act be a condition, not the object, of liability.

[9] See H. Morris, 'Punishment for Thoughts', *The Monist* **49**, No. 3 (July 1965), 1; R. A. Duff, *Criminal Attempts* (Oxford: Oxford University Press, 1996), 63–4.

[10] See, respectively, Misuse of Drugs Act 1971, s. 5; Prevention of Crime Act 1953, s. 1; Forgery and Counterfeiting Act 1981, s. 16(2); Firearms Act 1968 s. 1(1).

[11] See, e.g., Explosive Substances Act 1883, s. 3 (possession of explosives with intent to endanger life or property); Firearms Act 1968, s. 16 (possession of firearms with intent to injure); Criminal Damage Act 1971 s. 3 (possession of something with intent to use it to damage property).

[12] This is an issue which has exercised English courts dealing with offences involving the unknowing 'possession' of drugs: *Warner v Metropolitan Police Commissioner* [1969] 2 A. C. 256; *McNamara* [1988] 87 Cr. App. Rep. 246; Smith & Hogan, *Criminal Law* (n. 1 above), 127–31.

[13] See, e.g., Wilson, *Criminal Law* (n. 1 above), 75–6; Ashworth, *Principles of Criminal Law* (n. 1 above), 109–10; Simester & Sullivan, *Criminal Law* (n. 1 above), 85–6; Smith & Hogan, *Criminal Law* (n. 1 above), 59; LaFave, *Criminal Law* (n. 1 above), 211. But contrast the stipulation in *Model Penal Code* s. 2.01(4), on which see Robinson, *Fundamentals of Criminal Law* (n. 1 above), 261–2.

Antony Duff

Consider, finally, the case of involuntary movements. A driver who is struck down by an unforeseeable fit is not guilty of driving through a red light, even though his car's movement through the red light was caused by the movements of his hands and feet on the controls: for there was no voluntary act of driving. If, however, he could and should have foreseen the fit, if he knew that he was liable to suffer such fits, he is guilty: for, we could say, there was then a voluntary act, of beginning to drive, which was suitably related to his car's passing the red light (as its cause).[14] Here again, the act requirement seems more persuasive as requiring an act as a condition of liability than as requiring an act as the object of liability: I can justly be held criminally liable for things other than acts, including involuntary movements, so long as they are suitably related to an act of mine—for instance as the effect of such an act.

However, if we are to decide whether the act requirement is plausible as specifying either the object or a necessary condition of liability, we must first resolve the other unclarity noted above, about what should count as an 'act' in this context. I have talked as if it is obvious that possession, for instance, is not an 'act', whereas acquisition can be; or that the movements of one who is suffering a fit are not 'acts', whereas starting to drive can be: but why is this so—what should we mean by 'act'?

It might seem that this is a question that philosophy ought to be able to answer, and that this is therefore one context in which philosophy can directly assist legal theory. For central to the philosophy of action, or to 'action theory' as a branch of philosophy of action,[15] is the question of what counts as an action. If we can then take it (not unnaturally) that the 'acts' or 'voluntary acts' that criminal liability is supposed to require will be actions, we can expect a philosophical account of the nature or the defining features of actions to clarify the meaning of the act requirement in criminal law: what is required is what counts, according to the best philosophical account, as an action.

This is the question that gives this paper its focus. Can philosophy of action provide an account of action, or of the concept

---

[14] See *Hill v Baxter* (n. 3 above). I leave aside here the problems that this argument raises, if driving through a red light is a strict liability offence for which no *mens rea* is required (on which see H. L. A. Hart, 'Acts of Will and Responsibility', in his *Punishment and Responsibility* (Oxford: Oxford University Press, 1968), 90), most notably the problem that a similarly voluntary act is found in the case of the unforeseeable fit.

[15] See J. Hornsby, 'The Poverty of Action Theory', *Philosophical Inquiry* **21** (Winter 1999), 1, at 1.

of an 'act', that will give plausible and unitary substance to the 'act requirement' in criminal law? The account, if it is to provide a solid foundation for the act requirement as orthodoxly portrayed, will need both to make it plausible that criminal liability should require an act, either as its object or as a necessary condition; and to show that that requirement is univocal in its different applications, that what it requires is the same kind of thing in each context. (The univocality of the requirement cannot be taken for granted: for we have seen that its initial plausibility derives from the four different kinds of liability that it is taken to exclude, and we cannot simply assume that 'act' carries the same meaning when it is contrasted with mere thought, with mere conditions, with involuntary movements, and with omissions.)

2. What is an Act?

*S*ome theorists and philosophers think that philosophy can indeed provide just what the law seems to need: an account of action that gives plausible, unitary sense to the act requirement in criminal law. I will focus here on Moore's argument to that effect.[16]

The criminal law's function, argues Moore, is to 'serve retributive justice' by punishing 'those who are morally culpable in the doing of some morally wrongful action'.[17] Criminal liability therefore requires an act (since there can be no wrong*doing* without an act), which Moore analyses as a bodily-movement-caused-by-a-volition; and criminal liability is for an act that has the further properties specified by the law's definition of a criminal *actus reus*.[18] The basic, general 'act requirement', that is to say, is that 'there can be no criminal offence without the doing of a voluntary act'.[19]

---

[16] M. S. Moore, *Act and Crime* (Oxford: Oxford University Press, 1993); *Placing Blame: A Theory of Criminal Law* (Oxford: Oxford University Press, 1997), especially chs. 1, 5, 6.

[17] *Placing Blame* (n. 16 above), 35. Moore actually says there that the law 'must punish all and only' those who are thus culpable: but it turns out in ch. 18 that a proper concern for liberty will on balance preclude the criminalization of many kinds of morally wrongful action, including at least most of those that liberals would not want to criminalise.

[18] *Act and Crime* (n. 16 above). The hyphenation makes the point that, for Moore, acts are to be identified neither with bodily movements, nor with volitions, but with the 'complex event volitions-causing-movements' (p. 113).

[19] *Act and Crime* (n. 16 above), 4.

However, what we are liable for are not mere acts as thus minimally defined, as bodily-movements-caused-by-volitions, but for acts that have the further properties that turn them into criminal *acti rei*: in the case of homicide, an act that has the property of causing a human being's death, for instance.[20] So possession is not an act, although there are acts of acquisition (and omissions to rid oneself of possession); nor are involuntary movements acts, although they may be caused by prior voluntary acts.[21]

What Moore offers us is thus not just an account of what constitutes an act, and thereby a determinate content to the act requirement, but an explanation of why the criminal law should include such an act requirement. That explanation, depending as it does on Moore's particular brand of metaphysical moral realism, is not one that many would accept, and I cannot discuss it here:[22] but textbooks of criminal law often adopt a volitionist account of action that, though perhaps cruder than Moore's, is of essentially the same kind—what is required by way of an act is a willed bodily movement.[23]

Now this is not the place for a discussion of the various objections to volitionist theories of action: I want instead to outline two critical responses to Moore's enterprise, and to others like it, and then to ask what room, if any, they leave for a substantive 'act requirement'.

The first response is Hornsby's.[24] Action theory can, she agrees,

[20] See *Act and Crime* (n. 16 above), ch. 7. Moore does allow one type of exception to the act requirement: we can properly be held criminally liable for some omissions, when we breach a stringent positive duty to act; see *Act and Crime*, 54–9; *Placing Blame* (n. 16 above), 262–86.

[21] See *Act and Crime* (n. 16 above), 20–2, 35–7; and text at nn. 10–14 above.

[22] However, although I do not share Moore's metaphysical views, or his conception of law as a functional kind (see *Placing Blame*, n. 16 above, 20–22), there is more to be said for the claim that conduct should be brought within the reach of the criminal law in order to provide for its retributive punishment than many would allow: see R. A. Duff, 'Crime, Prohibition and Punishment', Journal of Applied Philosophy **19**, No. 2 (Summer 2002), 97.

[23] See e.g. G. Williams, *Textbook of Criminal Law* (2nd ed., London: Stevens, 1983), 147–8; Smith & Hogan, *Criminal Law* (n. 1 above), 37; LaFave, *Criminal Law* (n. 1 above), 208–10; Dressler, *Understanding Criminal Law* (n. 1 above), 83–6.

[24] J. Hornsby, 'Action and Aberration', University of Pennsylvania Law Review **142**, No. 5 (May 1994), 1719; 'The Poverty of Action Theory' (n. 15 above); also her 'On What's Intentionally Done', *Action and Value in Criminal Law*, S. Shute, J. Gardner, J. Horder (eds.) (Oxford: Oxford University Press, 1993), 55; and B. Williams, 'The Actus Reus of Dr Caligari', University of Pennsylvania Law Review **142**, No. 5 (May 1994), 1661.

provide a philosophical account of action—of the identifying features of those events that are actions. That account is not Moore's: Hornsby's claim is, rather, that (with one crucial qualification) 'Every action is someone's moving [a bit of] her body', and that 'Every action is an event of an agent's trying to do something'.[25] But her account is of the same species as Moore's, in that it takes actions to form a class of events, whose defining features action theory should identify. However, she argues, in identifying the class of events that are actions we do not give an 'account of action which is suited to answering questions about the criminal law',[26] since that class of events is not one that interests the criminal law, or that includes all those events which could, as 'acts', ground criminal liability. Of course no one takes the category of *acti rei* to be identical to the category of acts, since many acts are legally innocent. But on Moore's account, the category of *acti rei* is a sub-category of that of acts: it includes those acts that have the further features specified in the law's definitions of criminal *acti rei*,[27] and their character as acts is essential to their criminality. This is what Hornsby denies: we cannot resolve issues about omissions liability, for instance, by focusing on the idea that omissions are not 'actions', or the problem of automatism by asking whether 'automatic' behaviour constitutes 'action'.

I will have more to say about this kind of objection to Moore's enterprise shortly, but we should first note a different response. If we are sceptical about the philosophical tenability, or the utility for criminal law theory, of an account of action like Moore's, we might search for a better account of the concept of action—one that will identify in a normatively plausible way that category of events for, or on the basis of which, we could justly be held criminally liable. We would then adjust our account of action to cope with counter-examples—cases in which liability is justly imposed in the absence of what that account would count as an 'action'; we would look for an account which enabled us to identify a relevant act in every case in which criminal liability is justly imposed. The trouble with this tactic, however, is that it is liable to lead us into vacuity: we allow

[25] 'The Poverty of Action Theory' (n. 15 above), 3, 6; and see p. 13—'an action is an event of someone's doing something intentionally'. The qualification is that there are things we can do without moving our bodies— 'just by thinking' or 'by staying still' ('The Poverty of Action Theory', n. 6): I discuss such cases in s. 3 below.

[26] 'The Poverty of Action Theory' (n. 15 above), 15; see 'On What's Intentionally Done' (n. 24 above), 69–73.

[27] See text at nn. 18–20 above.

our definition of action to be led by, rather than grounding, our judgments of when criminal liability can be justly imposed, with the result that we come to define action as something like 'events or states of affairs for which a person might be held responsible'.[28] This clearly cannot help us to explicate the grounds of criminal liability: to say that liability is for an event or state of affairs for which a person might be held responsible is to say nothing substantial about the question that should concern us—for what kinds of event or state of affairs should people be held responsible?

The difficulty of making plausible substantive sense of the act requirement has led some theorists to argue that we should abandon it, as either an analytical or a normative thesis. We should recognize, they argue, that instances in which liability is imposed for things other than acts (understood as essentially involving bodily movements), and in the absence of an act that could count as a necessary condition of liability, are neither exceptional nor obviously unjust, and that what matters normatively is not action, but control.[29]

We can see why it might seem more plausible to replace the act requirement by a control requirement by looking again at cases of liability for conditions.[30] In the case of possession, I noted earlier that it seemed more plausible to require an act as a condition of liability than to insist on an act as the object of liability: it did not seem to be at odds with the act requirement to criminalize the possession of something, so long as there had been an act of acquiring it. In the same way, it would not seem at odds with the act requirement to criminalize being found drunk in public, so long as there was an act suitably related to that being found, as its cause: if Mr Martin had taken himself into the street whilst drunk, or had acted in such a way as to give others good reason to put him into the street (for instance by drunken misbehaviour in a restaurant), it would not have been so obviously unjust, or so obviously inconsistent with the most minimal conditions of criminal liability, to convict him.

---

[28] H. Gross, *A Theory of Criminal Justice* (New York: Oxford University Press, 1979), 56; see D. Husak, *Philosophy of Criminal Law* (Totowa, N. J.: Rowman & Littlefield, 1987), 108; Moore, *Act and Crime* (n.16 above), 20–21.

[29] See Husak, 'Does Criminal Liability Require an Act?' (n. 7 above); also A. P. Simester, 'On the So-called Requirement for Voluntary Action', Buffalo Criminal Law Review 1, No. 2 (Spring 1998), 403; and P. R. Glazebrook, 'Situational Liability', in *Reshaping the Criminal Law*, P. R. Glazebrook (ed.) (London: Stevens, 1978), 108.

[30] See text at nn. 4–5, 10–13 above; Husak, *Philosophy of Criminal Law* (n. 28 above), 100–102.

However, once we require an act only as a condition, not as the object, of criminal liability, it becomes hard to see why we should require an act at all, rather than control. What matters both in cases of possession and in cases of 'being found' is whether the relevant condition was under the agent's control: it is fundamentally unjust to convict him if his possession of the relevant item, or his being found, was not within his control. Now if my possession of an item, or my being found somewhere, was the result of my prior act, it was within my control. But it was also within my control if, though no act of mine caused it, I could have acted in a way that would prevent or alter it: if, although the item came into my possession without any act on my part, I could have divested myself of it; or if, although I was passively brought into the place where I was found, I could have removed myself from it. If criminal liability for possession, or for 'being found', is just when those conditions resulted from the defendant's prior act, it is no less just when he could have averted or remedied those conditions, even if they did not result from a prior act by him.

So the suggestion is that the act requirement is not normatively plausible if it requires an act as the object of liability: there are too many cases in which liability is unexceptionally and unproblematically imposed for things other than acts. Nor is it plausible if it requires an act as a condition of liability: what matters as a basic condition of liability is not whether there was an act, but whether that for which liability is imposed was within the defendant's control. We should instead accept a control requirement which specifies not the object of criminal liability (we can be liable for a range of very different things), but a normatively necessary condition of liability: we should be liable only for what is within our control. That control requirement is related to the idea of action, since it is by acting that we typically exercise control over the kinds of event that concern the criminal law; but it does not require an action. Nor, therefore, does it require us to specify what counts as an action: criminal law theory can avoid reliance on controversial theses in the philosophy of action.

A control requirement clearly picks out an important condition of criminal liability: it is unjust to hold someone liable to a conviction that condemns him as a wrongdoer for what he could not control. But can it capture all that is normatively plausible in the act requirement: or is there still some force to the idea that criminal liability should depend not just on what we control, but on what we *do*—and thus on our acts or actions?

In what follows, I will provide further support for Hornsby's argument that philosophical accounts that identify action with moving one's body are of no help to criminal law theory: in particular, they cannot provide a plausible content for the 'act requirement'. I will also argue, however, that a rather different account of action as a social phenomenon can ground a more plausible, though modest and qualified, version of the act requirement, understood now as an 'action presumption'.[31]

3. Action as a Natural or as a Social Phenomenon

Action theorists who seek to explain actions as a natural kind,[32] or to identify that 'subclass of events which are actions',[33] seek an a- or pre-social account of action—an account which prescinds from the richly complex meanings that actions have in their social contexts.[34] It is not surprising that such theorists then make bodily movings central to their accounts: once we strip away the social dimension of action, nothing else is left to constitute our engagement as agents with the natural world in which we live.

My concern here is not with the familiar differences that one finds among action theorists who make bodily movings central in this way—with, for instance, the question of whether we should see such movings as basic actions that cannot be further analysed, or instead analyse them as bodily movements caused by volitions or acts of will;[35] or whether it is useful to say that every action involves trying.[36] The point I want to emphasize is rather that whatever form such theorists' accounts take, action as thus understood is not what interests the criminal law (nor indeed is it what interests history, or sociology, or moral thought, or other approaches to action as a social phenomenon).

[31] Compare Hornsby, 'The Poverty of Action Theory' (n. 15 above), 15, on the need for an account of action that 'combines suitably with an account of all the moral psychological notions and ... with an understanding of the social world'.

[32] Moore, Act and Crime (n. 16 above), 134–5.

[33] D. Davidson, 'Agency', in his *Essays on Actions and Events* (Oxford: Oxford University Press, 1980), 43, at 43–4.

[34] See A. C. Danto, *Analytical Philosophy of Action* (Cambridge: Cambridge University Press, 1973), ix.

[35] See e.g. A. C. Danto, 'Basic Actions', *The Philosophy of Action*, A. White (ed.) (Oxford: Oxford University Press, 1973), 43, as against Moore, *Act and Crime* (n. 16 above).

[36] See J. Hornsby, *Actions* (London: Routledge, 1980), as against Duff, *Criminal Attempts* (n. 9 above), 278–92.

Action, the Act Requirement and Criminal Liability

This is the force of Hornsby's objection to Moore's enterprise of using action theory to try to illuminate the objects or conditions of criminal liability. The force of that objection can be seen quite simply by looking at some of the many, unexceptional ways in which we can do things without moving our bodies. I am thinking here not of such purely mental activities as deliberating, contemplating and calculating (although we should not forget that, whilst we do in some contexts contrast action with 'mere thought', we also distinguish within the realm of thought those kinds of thought in which we are actively purposeful from those in which we are passive), but of ways in which we engage with and have an impact on our social world—but without having to move our bodies.

I can, for instance, insult someone by means that involve moving my body: by saying certain words, by making a certain gesture. But I can also insult someone without moving, or precisely by not moving in a particular way: by not rising from my chair when she enters the room, if politeness or deference requires me to rise; or by not acknowledging an acquaintance when she greets me in the street.

I can break a promise to someone in ways that involve moving my body: I promise not to reveal your secret, but then tell it to someone. But I can also break promises without moving: I promise to meet you at 6.00 for a drink, but at 6.00 I remain sitting in my chair.

Voting for a motion at a meeting often involves moving—I must raise my hand, or make a suitable mark on a piece of paper. But it need not involve moving: there could be meetings at which the convention is that when the motion is put, anyone who does not raise a hand to object to it thereby votes for it; at such a meeting, I vote for a motion by not raising my hand.

The crucial point to notice about each of these examples is that there is nothing abnormal about the cases in which I do something without moving, or by not moving. Such cases might be statistically unusual (although I doubt if even that is true in the case of promise breaking), but they are not in any way aberrant. Their status as doings is not doubtful, or secondary: it is just as much, and just as straightforwardly, an insult to fail to rise when the queen enters the room as it is to make a rude gesture at her (in both cases, of course, it counts as an insult only given certain conventions); it is just as straightforwardly a breach of promise to fail to turn up when I promised I would as it is to send an email revealing the secret that I promised to keep. We can call these cases of commission by omission if we like: the point is that they are clear cases of commission—of doing.[37] Indeed, it seems natural to call them actions: but, to avoid seeming to beg any questions, I will not yet talk of actions.

It might be said that none of these are examples of crimes—and that such examples are therefore not counter-examples to the claim that criminal liability requires an act understood as or as involving bodily motion.[38] However, there are ample examples in the criminal law of commission by omission—of ways in which crimes can be committed as straightforwardly by or without moving as they can be by moving.[39] It is, for example, a crime under s. 211.2 of the *Model Penal Code* recklessly to endanger another person, and I can endanger another not only in ways that involve moving, but also in ways that do not involve moving—for instance by doing nothing to stop a fire which starts in my house and threatens to spread to hers. For a second example, consider theft. Theft in English law requires the appropriation of another's property; appropriation is partially defined as 'any assumption by a person of the rights of an owner'.[40] Now suppose that someone leaves a book in my house, and I decide that I will keep it for myself. It might be argued that in making that decision I have already 'appropriated' the book:[41] but even if such a decision is not enough, I have certainly appropriated it if I lend it to a friend; and that lending could, given suitable conventions in our friendship, involve nothing more than not saying 'Yes I do' when she says 'You don't mind if I borrow this?'.

A further point will strengthen this argument. Suppose it is suggested that some kinds of promise breaking, or of insult, should be criminal.[42] There will be arguments, both principled and pragmatic, for and against such a suggestion—about whether promise breaking or insult can involve the kinds of wrongful harm that properly concern the criminal law, and about the practicability of criminalizing them. However, these arguments will not include the argument

[37] Of course they amount to doings or commissions, they have an impact on the world, only in virtue of their social settings of conventions, understandings or expectations: but such settings are crucial to action as a social phenomenon.

[38] Though voting could, for instance, make me liable on a charge of conspiracy.

[39] See generally Smith & Hogan, *Criminal Law* (n. 1 above), 61–3.

[40] Theft Act 1968, s. 3(1): see Smith & Hogan, *Criminal Law* (n. 1 above), 513–27.

[41] See Wilson, *Criminal Law* (n. 1 above), 415.

[42] 'Insulting behaviour' is criminal under English law, but only if it is intended or likely to cause immediate unlawful violence or the expectation of such violence: Public Order Act 1986, s. 4.

that only breaches of promise or insults that essentially involve bodily movings can properly be criminalized; or that the fact that such wrongs need not involve bodily movings is a reason against criminalizing them. Nor would it be appropriate to object to a proposal to criminalize them by saying that that the promise breaker or insulter has not *done* anything, since she has done something: she has broken a promise, or insulted someone.

All this shows that the kinds of exercise of our human agency that interest the criminal law (and morality, and history, and sociology) cannot be analysed in terms of a conception of action as consisting essentially in bodily movings. It is not essential to their identity as doings that they involve bodily movings; the fact that I Φ on this occasion without moving, or by not moving, does not render Φ's status as my doing doubtful or derivative in comparison with the occasions on which Φ-ing does essentially involve moving my body; from the perspective of a social understanding of agency, Φ-ing that requires no movement is not relevantly different from Φ-ing that essentially involves moving my body.

Those who define action in terms of bodily moving focus their account of human agency on our exercises of our capacity to move, and to control our movements, as embodied beings. We exercise that capacity (or that set of capacities) when we move; we also exercise it when we control movements that normally go on without such control—for instance if I control my breathing, or hold back a yawn or sneeze; and we sometimes exercise it in staying still, when that requires not merely not moving, but resisting a tendency to move— as with a guardsman who stays rigidly still at his post, or a twitcher who keeps still to avoid alarming the bird she is watching.[43] Given our nature, and the world in which we live, we usually have to exercise that capacity in engaging with the world as agents: we cannot usually have an impact on the world without moving, or without controlling our movements. Our responsibility for much that we do

[43] Moore argues that keeping still often essentially involves bodily movings (either muscle flexings to prevent the limbs from moving, or displacement movements of other parts of the body); and that if no such movings are involved, there is no action (*Act and Crime*, n. 16 above, 87–8, drawing on B. Vermazen, 'Negative Acts', *Essays on Davidson, Actions and Events*, B. Vermazen & M. Hintikka (eds.) (Oxford: Oxford University Press, 1985); *Placing Blame*, n. 16 above, 271–3). But our understanding of the guardsman's standing still as something to explain in terms of his reasons (and also to admire) is not affected by whether it involved any such movement: my understanding and my judgement are not altered if I find out that, contrary to my initial belief, such movement was involved.

or fail to do also depends on our having both that capacity and the opportunity to exercise it: this is the force of the 'control requirement', understood minimally as requiring control over one's movements. But none of this shows that our doings as social agents can be defined, or understood in their character as doings, in terms of our exercise of that capacity for movement: for we have seen that their identity and character as doings do not logically require movement.

That is why we should reject the claim (whether descriptive or normative) that criminal liability requires an act, if 'act' is understood as consisting in or necessarily involving bodily motion: even if it is true that in the majority of cases of criminal liability bodily movings are involved, they are not necessarily involved as either (parts of) the objects or as conditions of liability; to focus on bodily movings is not to focus on what interests the criminal law.

If this negative argument is right, the question then is whether we should simply abandon the 'act requirement', or look for some alternative account of the idea of 'act' or 'action' that might give such a requirement a more plausible focus and content. We might pursue the latter strategy by developing an account of action as a social, rather than a natural, phenomenon: an account that would identify as actions the kinds of doings that interest the law (and morality, and history, and sociology).

I cannot discuss the details of such an account here, but at its core lies the exercise of our capacity (which is itself a complex family of sub-capacities) to engage in practical reasoning and to actualize its results in ways that make a difference to the world.[44] Our status as human, social agents depends essentially on our possession of this capacity; we actualize ourselves as agents in exercising it. As we noted, the actualization of the results of our practical reasoning often depends on the exercise of our capacity to move and to control our bodily movements: but although that capacity is one that we must usually rely on as agents, it is not the defining or essential feature of our social agency. Our existence, our movements or lack of movement, can of course make various differences to the world without any exercise of our capacity for practical reasoning; we can also be properly held responsible not only for what we do in the exercise of that capacity, but also for our failures to exercise it—for omissions which simply display a failure to notice or to be moved by

[44] See further Duff, *Criminal Attempts* (n. 9 above), ch. 11, drawing on (among others) A. I. Melden, *Free Action* (London: Routledge, 1961); D. Gustafson, *Intention and Agency* (Dordrecht: Reidel, 1986).

the reasons for action that the situation presents. My suggestion here, however, is that the central, normal, straightforward cases of action as a social phenomenon essentially involve the exercise of the capacity to actualize the results of our practical reasoning.[45]

I have talked of giving an account of 'action' as a social phenomenon, and suggested that such an account can capture, in a way that an account focused on bodily movings cannot, the kinds of doing that interest the criminal law (I will say more about this point shortly). It might then be tempting to argue that this is how we should explain 'the concept of action', and that those who analyse actions in terms of bodily movings are simply wrong about the meaning of that concept or about the nature of human action. I have argued this myself:[46] but I now think it is wrong. Rather than laying claim to 'the concept of action' in this way, we should adopt a more pluralist stance that recognizes the legitimacy of two distinct philosophical enterprises in the philosophy of action, and thus of two distinct philosophical conceptions of action. One enterprise seeks to understand human action as a natural phenomenon that consists essentially in the exercise of our capacity to move and control our bodies; the other seeks to understand human action as a social phenomenon that consists in the exercise of our capacity to actualize the results of our practical reasoning. There are some interesting questions to be asked about the relationship between these two philosophical enterprises, but we should not assume either that they must form one unitary enterprise, or that one must depend on or be subordinated to the other: they are different enterprises, speaking to different interests that 'philosophers of action' may have.

(If I then say that, from the social perspective, such doings as appropriating property, or breaking a promise, are just as much *actions* when they do not essentially involve movement as when they do, I might be challenged by someone who thinks that actions must be events to say precisely when and where the appropriation or the breach of promise takes place—which it would be hard to do.[47] One response to this problem is to cede the concept of an action, as a particular, to the action theorists who take actions to be events that

[45] To avert some misunderstandings, I should perhaps add that by 'practical reasoning' here I do not mean only those rich kinds of reasoning that connect individual actions to larger conceptions of the right or the good, or only those kinds of reasoning that are manifested in some occurrent process of deliberation; any action that is done for a reason actualises the results of practical reasoning.

[46] See *Criminal Attempts* (n. 9 above), chs. 9–11.

[47] Al Mele pressed this point on me in discussion.

Antony Duff

essentially involve bodily movings: we could then talk of 'instances of action' or 'the phenomenon of action' in relation to doings that do not involve actions as particular, spatio-temporally locatable events.[48] I am, however, reluctant to cede the concept of an action in this way: although nothing of substance hangs on it (so long as we avoid misunderstanding by making clear the sense in which we are using the term), I see no good reason not to continue to count the agent's breach of promise, or his appropriation of another's property, amongst his actions even when no bodily movings were essentially involved.)

The question now is this: if we understand action in this way, as an engagement with the world involving the exercise of our capacity to actualize the results of our practical reasoning, can we give the 'act requirement' a more plausible, substantive content, as specifying either the object or a necessary condition of criminal liability? Can we claim either that the criminal law does normally require an action, as thus understood, or that it should do so?

4. Social Agency and the Act Requirement

The account of action I sketched in the previous section does at least focus on what properly interests the criminal law. The criminal law is concerned with the reasons we have for acting, or not acting, in certain ways, and is thus interested in us as beings who have and can exercise the capacity to actualize the results of our practical reasoning—the capacity to act for reasons, and to be guided by reasons that others offer us. What is defined as a crime is thereby defined as a wrong for which its perpetrator should be called to answer at a criminal trial: that is, it is defined as something that we should not do, that we have good reason not to do; and criminal trials call defendants to account for allegedly doing what they thus had good reason not to do. There is room for argument about how far the criminal law aims to offer us new reasons for action that we would not have in the absence of the law, or merely to remind us of the status and force of reasons that we already have. In the case of so-called *mala prohibita*, involving kinds of conduct that are wrongful only because they have been defined as criminal, it seems that the law is itself a source of reasons for action. *'Mala in se'* crimes, by contrast, involve conduct that is wrongful independently of its being defined as criminal: one could say that in criminalizing

[48] Hornsby, 'Action and Aberration' (n. 24 above), 1738–9.

such conduct the law aims not so much to offer the citizens any new reasons for refraining from it, but rather to declare that these are public wrongs that merit condemnation by the whole polity.[49] In both kinds of case, however, the criminal law addresses us as agents who can and should recognize and be guided by reasons for action— whether reasons that the law itself provides, or reasons of which it rather reminds us.

Is this then to say that what we are criminally liable for (the object of liability) either is in fact or should always be an action as thus understood; or that an action is always required as a necessary condition of liability?

Sometimes what we are criminally liable for is precisely the actualization of the results of practical reasoning, when a crime consists in successfully carrying out the intention to Φ: if I carry out an intention to wound someone, or to destroy their property (without their consent), or to deceive them into giving me their money, I am guilty of a crime unless I can plead some further defence; and what I am guilty of is the actualization of that criminal intention. In other cases, we are liable not for the actualization of the intention to Φ itself, but rather for the harm that we cause or the wrong that we do in actualizing our intention. I can be guilty of Ψ-ing (of wounding, for instance, or of rape) if I Ψ in or by carrying out my intention to Φ—if I cause a serious injury by carrying out my intention to burn down a building, or have non-consensual sexual intercourse in carrying out my intention to have intercourse. There are questions about the conditions under which I should be said to have Ψ-ed—in particular about the conditions under which I can be said to have caused the injury; there are questions about the conditions under which I can properly be held liable for the injury I caused—about whether I must have caused it knowingly, or recklessly or negligently; and there are questions about the extent to which the first two sets of questions are separable—about whether we can settle the issue of causation independently of considerations of fault or *mens rea*. But however we answer these questions, what we are held liable for in such cases is an action, whether for the actualization of an intention or for what is done in or by actualizing an intention; the questions concern the conditions

---

[49] See R. A. Duff, *Punishment, Communication, and Community* (New York: Oxford University Press, 2001), 56–66. The distinction between '*mala in se*' and '*mala prohibita*' is neither clear cut nor uncontroversial, but that problem need not concern us here.

under which such an action can be ascribed to an agent as one for which he can be condemned.[50]

Often, then, criminal liability is for an action: but can we say that this is always or should always be so; or, more modestly, that even if we can be criminally liable for things other than actions, an action is always required as a condition of liability? Or can we say no more than that criminal liability depends on our capacity for action—on our capacity to act for and to be guided by reasons? This would amount to a moderately rich, and normatively rather plausible 'control requirement':[51] we should be criminally liable only for what lies within our control as rational agents; it would be unjust to condemn a person for failing to conform her conduct to the reasons that the law declares to be authoritative if she lacked the capacity to guide her conduct by such reasons, or a fair opportunity to exercise that capacity. But such a 'capacity requirement' is quite different from an 'act requirement'; the question is whether we can also justify any kind of act requirement.

To see whether the conception of action I have sketched can ground an act requirement for criminal liability, we can look again at the four kinds of liability that the act requirement is taken to exclude: liability for thoughts, for involuntary movements, for conditions or states of affairs, and for omissions.

Liability for Thoughts

It is a merit of this account of action that it counts some kinds of thought as action, since our capacity to actualize the results of our practical reasoning is sometimes exercised simply in thinking. We can have reason to engage in thought—in deliberation, in contemplation, in structured imaginings, even in fantasizing; we can act for those reasons, by engaging in those kinds of thought; we can be held responsible, and be praised or blamed, for engaging or for failing to

---

[50] It should be obvious that I am drawing here on the Davidsonian idea that we can ascribe Ψ-ing to me as an action if I Ψ in or by intentionally Φ-ing (Davidson, 'Agency' (n. 33 above), 45–6), although in the service of a conception of action quite different from his. Note that, although I am now explicating the act requirement in terms of a conception of action that essentially involves intention, the satisfaction of the act requirement can still be separated, as theorists orthodoxly separate it, from the satisfaction of whatever *mens rea* requirements are specified for the offence: I Φ intentionally, but can unintentionally Ψ in or by Φ-ing.

[51] See text following n. 29 above.

engage in such thought, and for engaging in it well or badly. However, we do also contrast 'action' with 'mere thought', and in this context actions are exercises of that capacity that are apt by themselves to have an impact on or make a difference to the world. (Given the nature of the world and of our relations to it, we must often exercise our capacity to move if we are to have an impact on it: but, as we have seen, this is a contingent rather than necessary feature of action, and is not always involved.) But why should we not be criminally liable for thoughts in which we exercise our capacity for agency?

We must distinguish two kinds of active thought. First, there are those whose completion requires no overt or world-impacting action: fantasizing or contemplating, for instance, might lead to overt action, but they are not necessarily frustrated without it; they can be completed, perfected, whilst remaining within the realm of thought. By contrast, second, there are kinds of thought whose completion requires overt action. Obvious examples are deliberation and intention formation: whilst I can conclude a process of deliberation by reaching a decision, or form an intention, and not go on to do what I decide or intend to do, such lack of overt action frustrates my decision or intention; this kind of thought demands overt action in a way that the first kind does not.

There are familiar, liberal reasons for not criminalizing the first kind of thought, even if we allow that it can be wrongful, and can wrong other people (that, for instance, I wrong you if I make you the object of my sadistic fantasies). We might say that such thought can neither cause, nor make sufficiently likely, any kind of harm that could concern the criminal law: but even those who doubt the Harm Principle, and who might see reason to criminalize wrongful kinds of action that do not cause what advocates of that Principle would count as harm,[52] can see very good reason not to criminalize 'mere thought' of this kind. Quite apart from practical concerns about the impossibility of non-oppressive enforcement, any plausible account of the distinction between 'public' matters that properly concern the polity and 'private' matters that concern only the individual and those with whom he chooses to share them must count such thoughts, at least so long as they are not expressed to others, as 'private'.

The case of practical thought, which is oriented towards action,

---

[52] On which see J. Feinberg, *Harmless Wrongdoing* (New York: Oxford University Press, 1988), especially 1–38, 318–38; see R. A. Duff, 'Harms and Wrongs', Buffalo Criminal Law Review **5**, No. 1 (Fall 2001), 13.

Antony Duff

is less straightforward; as we have seen, some argue that such thought, for instance the formation of a firm intention to commit a crime, can be a proper object of criminal liability, even if they also require action in furtherance of that intention as a condition of liability.[53] There are powerful arguments for the opposing view that attempt liability should be for actions that come close enough to fulfilling a criminal intention to constitute an attack on a legally protected interest—but these need not detain us here.[54] The crucial point here is that whether a suitable act is required as the object, or only as a condition, of liability, the substantive work is not done by the 'act requirement'. For as far as that requirement is concerned, *any overt* action done in furtherance of a criminal intention would suffice; an attempt statute that laid down the most minimal 'first act' test for attempts would satisfy the requirement.[55] But those who object to criminalizing mere criminal intentions, however firm, would not be mollified by being told that, whilst a mere intention to commit forgery is not criminal, someone who opens his desk drawer to find a pen with which to commit forgery has committed an act in furtherance of that intention, and can therefore be held criminally liable. What is plausibly required, whether as the object or as a condition of liability, is not just *some* overt action, but an overt action that brings the agent close enough to the commission of the intended crime. There is controversy about how close that should be (and not just because theorists disagree about whether the requisite act is object or a condition of liability): but a bare 'act requirement' cannot help us to settle that controversy.

It might be said that I am expecting too much of the act requirement: all that it specifies is a minimal general condition of criminal liability; the further question of which acts should attract criminal liability, i.e. which should constitute the *acti rei* of criminal offences, is to be answered by different arguments about the scope and content of the criminal law.[56] But that response would miss the point. If the act requirement is to play a substantive normative role in precluding liability for mere thought, it must require something

[53] See text at nn. 8–9 above. Husak even casts doubt on whether an act should be required as a condition of liability for such firm criminal intentions, if sufficiently overwhelming evidence could be found without the kind of act that current attempt statutes require: see Husak, 'Does Criminal Liability Require an Act?' (n. 7 above), 89–90.

[54] See Duff, *Criminal Attempts* (n. 9 above), 385–95.

[55] See Duff, *Criminal Attempts* (n. 9 above), 35–7.

[56] This is Moore's approach, in distinguishing 'the act requirement' from 'the actus reus requirement'; see *Act and Crime* (n. 16 above).

that we could be expected to see as a more appropriate object or condition of liability than such thought: but opening a desk drawer is if anything less plausible, rather than more plausible, as an object or condition of criminal liability than is the formation of the intention to commit forgery.

The act requirement can thus be so formulated as to preclude liability for 'mere thought', even for active thought, but its normative weight is slight: it does not do very much to limit the scope of criminal liability.

Liability for Involuntary Movements

It might seem that the act requirement has more substantive force in precluding liability for merely involuntary bodily movements, which are not made in the exercise of the agent's capacity to actualize the results of his practical reasoning and are not susceptible to guidance by the provision of reasons. It is unjust to hold a person criminally liable for such movements (unless they can be attributed to his earlier voluntary act);[57] and it is surely unjust because the act requirement is not satisfied, since the identification of such an earlier voluntary act both satisfies the act requirement and rebuts that charge of injustice.

This is too swift, however, since it is not clear that it is the act requirement, rather than a control requirement, that does the work in this context. With strictly involuntary movements, the two requirements coincide: both preclude liability, unless an earlier voluntary act can be identified as the proximate cause of the movements. To see whether the act requirement has any independent plausibility, we must look at cases in which the requirements diverge: cases in which the movements are controllable, so that the control requirement is satisfied, but are not controlled (that is, are not the result of the exercise of the capacity for rational agency), so that the act requirement is not satisfied.

Here is such a case.[58] I am standing, innocently, by your valuable vase. A child playfully grabs my arm, and moves it towards the vase in such a way that it will clearly knock the vase over. I could easily resist the child, and withdraw my arm, but do not; the vase is broken. Can I be convicted of criminal damage? The act

---

[57] See text at n. 14 above; also Moore, *Act and Crime* (n. 16 above), 35–7.

[58] See also Simester, 'On the So-Called Requirement for Voluntary Action' (n. 29 above), 407–8.

requirement would preclude liability: though the knocking over of your vase involved my arm, it was not something that I did as an exercise of my capacity for rational agency; nor can we attribute the movement of my arm to any earlier act of mine. The control requirement does not preclude liability, since the relevant movement of my arm was within my control: I could have averted the damage (but if my arm had been irresistibly moved by a stronger person, the control requirement would preclude liability).

The only reason for preferring the act requirement to the control requirement in this kind of case lies in the distinction between acts and omissions. As between a case in which I knock your vase over by an extravagant gesture which I realized was risky, and one in which a child moves my arm so that it knocks the vase over, the key difference is that in the former I knock your vase over in or by gesturing, so that knocking your vase over can be attributed to me as an action; whereas in the latter case I simply omit or fail to control the movement of my arm. The question then is whether, although I have no general legal duty to prevent harm occurring to others' property (as distinct from a duty not to harm it), I do or should have a special duty to prevent harm occurring through the movements of my body: but that is just one aspect of the general question of whether and under what conditions we are properly held liable for our omissions, on which I comment shortly.

Liability for Conditions or States of Affairs

It might be tempting to deal with instances in which liability is apparently imposed for a condition or state of affairs, rather than for an action, in the way that Moore deals with crimes of possession. Section 2.01(4) of the Model Penal Code declares that

> [P]ossession is an act [in relation to the rule that liability requires a voluntary act] if the possessor knowingly procured or received the thing possessed or was aware of his control thereof for a sufficient period to have been able to terminate his possession.

So, argues Moore, what is being punished is not 'the *state* of possessing' but 'either the act of taking possession or ... the omission to rid oneself of possession'—in which case liability for possession is no more problematic than other kinds of liability for omissions.[59] Similarly, we might argue that in any case in which liability is apparently imposed for a condition or a state of affairs, it is as consistent

[59] *Act and Crime* (n. 16 above), 21.

with the act requirement as is any other case in which we can be liable on the basis of omissions, just so long as liability requires either an act of bringing the condition or the state of affairs into existence or a failure to terminate it.[60] This would replace the act requirement with the control requirement: for to say that a condition or state of affairs was under someone's control is just to say that it was something that she could have avoided, either by not acting in a way that would bring it about, or by acting so as to remove it once it had come about.

A conception of action as a social phenomenon would, in principle, allow us to reconcile some liability for conditions or states of affairs with a more robust act requirement than this. Possession, for instance, can constitute action, as an exercise of our capacity to actualize the results of our practical reasoning, even when there was no initial act of acquisition (and when there is no bodily motion): if I decide to retain something (a stolen picture, or drugs, ...) that someone leaves in my house, the actualization of that intention might not require me to move (though it might involve being ready to move if I have to), but constitutes keeping the object; and keeping falls within the realm of action—as much when it requires no bodily motion as when it involves motion. Can we then plausibly maintain that possession and other conditions should be criminalized only when they involve action: i.e. either that we should be liable only for actions of acquiring or maintaining the condition, or that we should be liable for being in the condition only if it is suitably related to an action of acquiring it?[61]

Such a requirement would preclude liability for mere failure to terminate a condition that I did not actively acquire, thus giving the act requirement some substantive bite. The question of whether such an act requirement is plausible is one aspect of the larger question of when, if ever, omission-based liability is justified, which I discuss shortly: for the only cases in which the act requirement is

[60] Moore seems to assume that an act (or omission) is required as the object of liability: that is what 'is being punished'. But one might as plausibly require a suitable act or omission simply as a condition of liability for a condition or state of affairs.

[61] There would then be further questions about what should count as acquiring a condition, when the agent did not intend to acquire it. Should we attribute Mr Martin's condition, of being drunk in public, to his prior action of getting drunk in his home; or should we treat the police intervention as 'the cause' (see text at n. 5 above; Moore, *Act and Crime* (n. 16 above), 36–7)? Should we take a different view if he was drunk in public because he had got drunk in someone else's house and been forcibly ejected (see Wilson, *Criminal Law* (n. 1 above) 73–4)?

not satisfied, but in which it could be plausible to impose liability (and in which the control requirement is satisfied), are those in which the agent can be said to have failed or omitted to terminate the condition or the state of affairs.

A brief discussion of crimes of possession will illustrate some of the central points here, although an adequate discussion would need to attend to a range of different examples.[62]

Possession is criminalized not because it itself constitutes the kind of wrongful harm that primarily concerns the criminal law, but because it is liable to lead to, or increases the danger of, some such wrongful harm. The occurrence of that consequential harm depends, typically, on further actions undertaken either by the possessor or by others: controlled drugs, offensive weapons, firearms, and counterfeit currency notes will harm legally protected interests only if they are (ab)used in certain ways.[63] We must therefore ask whether, and how and how far, the criminal law should be stretched to cover not just the harmful (ab)use of such things, but their very possession: what scope, if any, should this particular kind of pre-emptive law have? One possibility is to criminalize not the possession by itself, but possession with intent to use the thing in some criminal way;[64] another is to criminalize the mere possession.[65]

The first of these strategies is a way of extending the law of attempts to capture intending criminals whose criminal enterprise has not yet advanced far enough to bring them within the scope of the general law of attempts. Crimes of possession defined in this way satisfy the act requirement as understood here. Whether or not

---

[62] See Glazebrook, 'Situational Liability' (n. 29 above) for a useful collection of examples. For an incisively critical discussion of possession offences, see M. D. Dubber, 'Policing Possession: The War on Crime and the End of Criminal Law', *Journal of Criminal Law and Criminology* **91** (Summer 2001), 829.

[63] See n. 10 above, and accompanying text. Sometimes, of course, what is possessed can be dangerous in and of itself, without further human action: unstable explosives, or various kinds of poisonous substance that might leak, for instance. These kinds of case usually involve corporations rather than private individuals, and are dealt with under health and safety or environment laws; they could also, in principle, fall under endangerment laws in jurisdictions that have general offences of endangerment—see Model Penal Code s. 211.2; Gordon, *The Criminal Law of Scotland* (n. 1 above), vol. II, 427–30.

[64] See n. 11 above, and accompanying text.

[65] See n. 10 above. There are other strategies that fall between these two extremes; see, e.g., Explosive Substances Act 1993, s. 4 (possession of explosives that the defendant cannot show he had for a lawful purpose).

I was active in acquiring an object, if I now have it with intent to use it my possession of it is an exercise of my agency: it figures in my practical reasoning as a means towards my ends, and my keeping it (which I might do simply by not surrendering it or disposing of it) is an exercise of my capacity to actualize the results of my practical reasoning.

The second strategy, of criminalizing mere possession, is more controversial: should we really subject someone to criminal conviction and punishment, not because his conduct poses a direct threat to legally protected interests, or because he intends to attack such interests, but just because he has in his possession something that could be used to attack such interests?[66] However, first, what makes this controversial is not that it flouts the act requirement, since as we have seen, mere possession can satisfy the act requirement: we can distinguish the person who keeps an object from one who simply fails to divest herself of it; and that distinction can still be drawn when keeping the object does not involve moving it, or hiding it, or touching it. Second, if the act requirement has plausible normative force, we should see stronger reason to object to criminalizing possession that amounts to no more than failing to divest oneself, than we do to criminalizing possession that amounts to keeping: the former faces all the objections that there are to the latter, and the further objection that it flouts the act requirement.

I am not sure whether it is more objectionable to criminalize mere passive non-divesting than to criminalize active keeping (leaving aside questions raised by the difficulty of proving that a defendant was keeping, rather than merely failing to divest himself). Suppose we agree that given the dangers that firearms (or their improper use) pose, we should criminalize their unlicensed possession. If I decided to keep a gun that someone has left in my house, I would be guilty of this offence: but what if I simply fail to do anything about it? Should we say that in this case too I am guilty—which would again be to replace the act requirement by a control requirement; or that I am not guilty, since I do not actively *keep* the gun?[67] The

---

[66] See Ashworth, *Principles of Criminal Law* (n. 1 above), 51–2; and more generally A. von Hirsch, 'Extending the Harm Principle: "Remote" Harms and Fair Imputation', in *Harm and Culpability*, A. P. Simester and A. T. H. Smith (eds.) (Oxford: Oxford University Press, 1996), 259.

[67] One could portray the question here as that of whether failure to divest myself of the gun constitutes 'possession' of it: but an answer to that question (which cannot be reached by a simple examination of the ordinary meaning of 'possession') would reflect, rather than grounding, the decision about criminalization.

answer to this question will depend on our view of householders' responsibilities in relation to this kind of danger: but any normative force that the difference between these two cases has clearly flows from the general distinction between acts and omissions—to which we must now turn.

Liability for Omissions

It seems that the substantive force of the act requirement lies in precluding liability for or on the basis of omissions. I cannot here try to resolve either the question of whether there is an intrinsically significant moral difference between acts and omissions, or the related and no less difficult question of how we should distinguish 'acts' from 'omissions'. All I can do is to note that I share the view that there is a significant moral difference, in terms of responsibility as well as of culpability, between actively doing wrong or harm and failing to prevent wrong or harm being done; that that difference has to do with the difference between intervening in or making a difference to the world, and not intervening so that things happen as they would have happened without me;[68] and that that difference must be reflected in our categorization of behaviour as constituting act or omission. But if this is right, what are its implications for the act requirement?

Since even the most fervent advocates of the act requirement allow that liability for or on the basis of omissions is sometimes justified, we should perhaps talk of an 'act presumption', rather than of an act requirement—of a presumption against omission-based liability: we can be criminally liable for relevant harms that we actively cause, but we are not generally liable for those we merely fail to prevent, unless we were under a special duty to prevent them.[69]

Even this way of putting the point is not quite accurate. There are what Smith and Hogan call offences of 'mere' or 'pure' omission, involving liability not for or in virtue of outcomes that the defendant failed to prevent, but simply for not doing what she was legally required to do: for instance, for failing to provide a breath specimen when required to provide one, or for failing to report a road accident one was involved in.[70] Such offences are clearly incon-

[68] See L. Katz, *Bad Acts and Guilty Minds* (Chicago: Chicago University Press, 1987), 143.

[69] See at n. 6 above.

[70] See Smith & Hogan, *Criminal Law* (n. 1 above), 60; for some other clear examples, see e.g. the duties imposed on bankrupts by ss. 353–5 and 361 of the Insolvency Act 1986.

sistent with the act requirement, and can be justified only as exceptions to it: to determine which are justified, we must ask what kinds of duty it is reasonable for the law to impose on us, on pain of criminal liability if we fail to fulfil them. On the other hand, there are offences that involve a determinate result, and that typically involve an action that produces that result, but that one might also be able to commit 'by omission': if a parent does not feed his child, intending that the child should suffer serious bodily harm, he is guilty of murder if the child dies.[71] If we are to get clear about the force of the act requirement, we must focus on this second kind of case: could we plausibly maintain that there should be at least a presumption against liability, if not a complete bar to liability, when the result that would complete the crime is not the result of the defendant's action, but she could have prevented its occurrence?

So-called 'Bad Samaritan' laws, which criminalize unreasonable failure to help or rescue those who are in grave peril, show the importance of this distinction.[72] Such laws criminalize 'pure' omissions: someone who fails to provide help that she is legally obligated to provide is guilty whether the victim is harmed or is saved by others (and whether or not she *intends* that the victim should suffer harm); she is convicted simply for that failure; and her sentence will be lighter than the punishment imposed for homicide or wounding. By contrast, a parent who fails to feed his child is guilty of murder only if the child dies because she is not fed, and only if he intended that the child should at least suffer serious bodily harm; but he is then guilty of murder, and is sentenced as a murderer.[73] To justify Bad Samaritan laws, we therefore do not need to deny the significance of the distinction between acts and omissions: all we need argue is that, while failing to save life is not morally equivalent to killing, we have a general moral duty, which the criminal law should enforce, to aid those in peril. Indeed, Bad Samaritan laws presuppose that there *is* a significant moral distinction between acts and omissions:[74] if there were no such

[71] See *Gibbins and Proctor* [1918] 13 Cr. App. Rep. 134.

[72] See J. Feinberg, *Harm to Others* (New York: Oxford University Press, 1984), ch. 4; also Robinson, *Fundamentals of Criminal Law* (n. 1 above), 424–5.

[73] The same distinction holds if the duty to act is special rather than general. A parent who fails to feed his child is guilty of neglecting the child (an offence of pure omission) even if the child is not harmed (because someone else intervenes), and whatever his intent: see Children and Young Person's Act 1033, s. 1(2)(a).

[74] *Pace* Feinberg, *Harm to Others* (n. 72 above), ch. 4.

distinction, bad Samaritans would be guilty of homicide if the victim died, and of attempted homicide if he did not; we would have no room for distinct Bad Samaritan laws.

To discern the normative force, if any, of the act presumption, we should therefore focus on the question of 'commission by omission': should there be a presumption that liability for offences involving the causation of harm requires an act that causes the harm; should it only be in special cases, when a person is under a special duty to act, that failure to act can ground liability?[75]

Even this question is misleading, however, given the account of action with which we are working: for we saw (in section 3) that there are straightforward examples of 'commission by omission'— of Ψ-ing precisely by omitting to Φ. I insult you by not rising when you enter the room, i.e. by omitting or failing to rise; I break my promise by not turning up to our meeting; I vote by not raising my hand. These are not special cases, in which failure to act is treated as, or as if it were, an action; they are as straightforwardly cases of insult, or breach of promise, or voting as are those in which some active bodily motion (making a gesture, telling someone your secret, raising a hand) is essentially involved.

The position is, I think, as follows. We begin with a class of action terms that describe a range of wrongful harms which should properly concern the criminal law: murder, rape, theft, wounding, damaging property, defrauding are obvious examples, as are perjury, driving when unfit through drink or drugs, and many others. The first role of the 'action presumption' is to declare that at the core of the criminal law should indeed be kinds of action—things we do as exercises of our capacity to actualize the results of our practical reasoning, or things we do in or by such exercises, that make a difference to or have an impact on the world; mere failures to act or to prevent harm, even when the harm is of a kind whose active causation is criminal, are not presumptively criminal, though we may criminalize them in special cases, either when the harm is very great (as with Bad Samaritan statutes) or when we should create or recognize a special duty or responsibility.[76]

---

[75] I leave the question of liability for inchoate offences of attempt or endangerment aside here; we must answer the question about complete offences first.

[76] Though the very idea of an omission, or of a failure to act, presupposes some expectation that the person would act—an expectation that is often a normative matter of the person's duties or responsibilities (see J. Casey, 'Actions and Consequences', *Morality and Moral Reasoning*, J. Casey (ed.) (London: Methuen, 1971), 155). The question then is: which of these expectations should the criminal law enforce?

Action, the Act Requirement and Criminal Liability

There will be a wide variety of ways in which, or means by which, these kinds of action can be done. As we have seen, some actions can be done by not doing things—by omissions. This reminds us that, though we distinguish 'acts' from 'omissions', omissions can be active exercises of our capacity for agency: we can omit or refrain from an action because we decide to do so, i.e. as an actualization of an outcome of practical reasoning, and what we omit to do can figure in our deliberation and our activity as a means to a further end. I can decide not to turn up to a meeting that I promised to attend, and so decide because I see that this will serve my ends (it will give me more time to prepare my lecture): my failure to attend the meeting is then not mere forgetfulness, or a failure to do something that it never occurred to me to do, but an exercise of my capacity for agency: I act, that is, precisely by not doing something.

If we are to get clear about the implications and the normative plausibility of an 'action presumption', we must therefore ask whether and under what conditions the actions that are criminalized can be done by omission. Sometimes the answer to this question will be at least strongly suggested by ordinary, extra-legal usage: if breach of promise was criminal, then unless there was some reason for the law to diverge radically from morality, that crime could surely be committed by the failure to do what was promised. But in other cases, there will be more room for debate, and a clearer need for decision: under what conditions, for instance (if any), should a failure to do what is known to be needed to save or preserve life count not just as a letting die, but as a method of killing?

There is no fact of the matter to be discovered in such cases: what is required is a careful consideration of the responsibilities that are or should be involved in different cases, and the moral implications that should attach to their breach. If I do not save someone to or for whom I have no responsibility (if there are any such people), I have not even failed to save him; if I do not save someone to whom I owe the kind of responsibility that we owe to strangers, then most of us would say that I have, at most or at worst, failed to save him or let him die; but if a parent fails to feed his child, and the child dies, we would naturally switch into the language of action. He does not just let the child starve, or let her die; he starves her, and kills her. We would say this because of the very stringent responsibility that we think parents must have for their children's well-being, and relatedly because of the young child's complete dependence on the parent; whereas we can say of ordinary omissions that the harm would have ensued if the omitter had not been present or had not existed, we would not think it apt to say that the child would still have starved even if the parent had not been present or had not existed. The parent's failure therefore does, unlike a mere omission, make a difference to the world,[77] and if that failure also actualized the outcome of the parent's practical reasoning—a decision not to feed the child—this is a straightforward case of action by omission.

But what if a parent's failure did not thus actualize his practical reasoning: what if he was so callous, or so ignorant, or so distracted, that he did not even decide not to feed the child? If he was still a responsible agent,[78] we should still say that he killed his child: but how, on the account I am working with, can we say this, if his failure did not involve the exercise of his capacity for agency? To say this is indeed to stretch the notions of action and agency beyond their core meaning; this is not a straightforward, paradigm case of commission by omission.[79] What motivates that stretching is, I suppose, the thought that the reasons for feeding the child are so obvious and so stringent (that they would loom so large in the practical reasoning of a 'reasonable person') that we insist on judging the parent as if he attended to them and decided not to feed his child.

The discussion in this section should have suggested that an action presumption can do some modestly substantive work in determining the proper bounds and grounds of criminal liability. It puts a question mark over liability for mere omissions, even when they involve a failure to prevent harm that would, had it been actively procured, ground criminal liability; and it requires us to identify the particular conditions under which the law should hold that a substantive crime can be committed by an omission. However, first, we have already noted that this is no longer an act *requirement*: not even Moore thinks that liability can never justly be based on omissions, or that such liability always marks a pragmatic compromise between the demands of justice (as reflected in the act requirement) and the consequentialist demands of effective harm reduction. Second, an action presumption as thus understood will not help us to determine the proper boundaries of criminal liability in controversial cases.

We can say that people should be guilty of homicide (as distinct from a separate, lesser Bad Samaritan offence) only if they kill, and

[77] See at n. 68 above.

[78] If he is not a responsible agent, the ascription of agency becomes more complicated: for whilst we can ascribe agency without ascribing full criminal or moral responsibility, the ascription itself is liable to be qualified.

[79] See text at n. 37 above.

of criminal damage only if they damage others' property; this points towards a relevant distinction between killing and letting die, or between damaging and failing to prevent damage. But if we ask what counts as killing, and under what conditions people can kill by omission, an action presumption cannot give us the answer: a finding that there was an action of killing, not just a failure to save, marks the conclusion of the argument about whether we should attribute this death to this agent as a homicide that he committed, rather than a ground for such a conclusion.

5. Concluding Comments

I have argued that there is little to be said for the act requirement as it has been understood by most legal theorists, in either its descriptive or its normative form: what such theorists count as an 'act', a moving of (some part of) one's body, is not in fact required as either a condition or the object of criminal liability; nor is there good reason to insist that it should be required; nor does such a conception of an act specify a phenomenon that is of particular interest to the criminal law. We can identify a plausible 'control' requirement—it is a condition of criminal liability that one has the capacity to control one's bodily movements (and a fair opportunity to exercise that capacity): but this is a long way from an act requirement.

I have also argued that we can make some progress by adopting a different understanding of acts or actions, as engagements with a social world in which we exercise our capacities for actualizing the results of our practical reasoning. A conception of this kind does pick out what interests the criminal law, which addresses us and judges us as agents who have and exercise that capacity. It also defines a richer control requirement: it is a condition of criminal liability that one has this capacity for rational agency and a fair opportunity to exercise it. It does not, however, identify a plausible substantive act requirement. In the contexts in which some such requirement appears plausible, i.e. in which it precludes types of liability that we would agree are illegitimate, it is not clear that this requirement is what does the substantial work: whilst it precludes liability for mere thought, the distinction it draws between thought and action is not one that carries real weight in determining the bounds of liability; whilst it precludes liability for purely involuntary movements, and for conditions and states of affairs not suitably related to action, in most contexts the control requirement seems to offer a better explanation of why liability should not be imposed.

An act requirement would do substantive work in precluding liability based on omissions as distinct from actions, since it is here that it is distinguishable from the control requirement: but it is not plausible to argue that omission-based liability is generally illegitimate, or that it marks only a rare exception to the act requirement.

I suggested that we might talk of an action presumption rather than of an act requirement, to make the point that while omission-based liability is often legitimate, its justification needs to overcome the general presumption that liability should be based on what we do rather than on what we merely fail to do. We should talk of an 'action presumption' rather than of an 'act presumption' to make clear that what is presumptively required is not an act of the kind that legal theorists have sought, but action as an exercise of our capacity for rational agency that makes a difference to the world.

However, such a presumption does not specify either an object or a condition of criminal liability that could be identified in advance of, and that could thus provide an independent ground for, attributions of responsibility or liability in difficult cases. For, as I noted above, a decision about whether someone brought x about as an action, or merely failed to prevent x occurring (as well as a decision about whether she failed or omitted to prevent x, or merely did not prevent x), depends on what we take her responsibilities to be in relation to x; it will reflect, and thus cannot provide an independent ground for, a decision about whether and in what way she should be held responsible for x.

It might now seem that neither the act requirement nor an action presumption should play any significant role in criminal law theorizing, but that would be premature. Though an action presumption cannot generate a set of distinctive and independent criteria for the ascription of criminal liability, it can help to structure our understanding of criminal liability (an analytical understanding of our existing legal doctrines, and a normative understanding of how criminal liability should be determined), especially if we take the presumption to be not merely that an action is presumptively required as a condition of liability, but that what we are liable for, the object of liability, should presumptively be an action of a suitable type. We can then see the law's central definitions of crimes as definitions of actions that constitute public wrongs, and its various doctrines of responsibility and excuse as doctrines concerning the conditions under which a wrongful action can be legitimately attributed to an agent; this will, I believe, help us to get clearer (in part by drawing on the resources of a rich moral philosophy of action) about the proper form and content of those definitions and doctrines.

Action, the Act Requirement and Criminal Liability

That is, of course, no more than a promissory note or gesture, whose fulfilment will take a lot of further, detailed work. I will end, however, with a further equally gestural suggestion: that by taking seriously the claim that criminal liability is, presumptively or paradigmatically, for actions, vague as that claim might still be, we will also be able to see what is wrong with the recurrently popular idea that the true basis of liability lies in the defective character traits or vices that offenders' conduct reveals.[80] The act requirement was often taken to hold that *at least* an act is required as either an object or a condition of criminal liability: mere thought, or mere involuntary bodily movements, or mere conditions or states of affairs, were not enough. We can read the action presumption, however, as also holding that *nothing more* than action is required or relevant as the object of liability: that, in particular, the criminal law should not be interested in our character traits, in our virtues or vices, except insofar as they are manifest in our actions, as contributing to the legally relevant character of those actions. But this too is a large topic, and one for another occasion than this.[81]

[80] See, e.g., M. D. Bayles, 'Character, Purpose, and Criminal Responsibility', Law and Philosophy **1** (1982), 5; C. Finklestein, 'Duress: A Philosophical Account of the Defense in Law', Arizona Law Review **37** (1995), 251; K. Huigens, 'Virtue and Inculpation', Harvard Law Review **108** (1995), 1423. For critical discussion, see R. A. Duff, 'Virtue, Vice, and Criminal Liability', Buffalo Criminal Law Review **6** (Spring 2003), 101.

[81] This paper was written during my tenure of a Leverhulme Major Research Fellowship; I am very grateful to the Leverhulme Trust for this support. I am also grateful to Jennifer Hornsby, and to participants in the Royal Institute of Philosophy Conference on *Action and Agency* at which an earlier version of this paper was given, for helpful comments and suggestions.

Emotion, Cognition and Action

DAVID CHARLES

1. Introduction: cognitive theories of the emotions

Contemporary philosophers have not, at least until very recently, been much concerned with the study of the emotions. It was not always so. The Stoics thought deeply about this topic. Although they were divided on points of detail, they agreed on the broad outline of an account. In it

> emotions are valuational judgments (or beliefs) and resulting affective states.

Thus, for example, fear was understood as the judgment that some object is harmful followed by a desire to avoid it. When a person is afraid, the relevant desire and belief are (typically) accompanied by some further physiological reaction. Both desire and physiological reaction count as types of affective state.

The Stoics did not need to say that emotions cause the resulting affective states or that emotions are valuational judgments. For the emotions could, in their view, include both the valuational judgment and the resultant affective states.[1] For them, the judgments or beliefs in question were of the same genus as judgments or beliefs about matters unconcerned with action. According to them, the relevant beliefs could be differentiated as stronger or weaker (in terms of degrees of belief), but in no other salient respect. Whatever their disagreements, they were united in rejecting the older Aristotelian idea that some emotions are based on states more primitive and less rational than belief (or judgment).[2]

Why did the Stoics hold this view? There were several reasons. [A] It gave them a way of representing an agent's action as

---

[1] On these issues, see Martha Nussbaum, *The Therapy of Desire*, Princeton 1994, Richard Sorabji, *Emotion and Peace of Mind*, Oxford 2000.

[2] Aristotle discusses imagination (*phantasia*) in *De Anima* Γ.3. In one of his examples, he describes a person for whom the moon looks a foot across, even though he believes that it is the size of the inhabited world (428b2ff). Imagination, unlike belief, is not subject to rational argument (428a18ff). Aristotle's canonical description of fear is as arising from the imagination of some imminent pain or harm (*Rhetoric* B.5, 1382a21–3).

reasonable: the agent has considerations which he/she sees as favouring his/her acting as he/ she does, considerations which make her so acting justified by her own lights. These considerations are encapsulated in the beliefs and desires which provide reasons for their action.

[B] It enabled them to understand how emotions can be open to rational persuasion and criticism. Thus, if the original beliefs are shown to be false, or to be inadequately supported, the agent has good reason to reject them and give up the relevant emotion. If he does not do so, he is guilty of a form of irrationality: he holds on to a belief in the face of overwhelming evidence that it is false.

[C] It allowed them to depict the agent's judgments as an essential part of the story of why she acts as she does. On their account, her emotions are not merely epiphenomenal additions to a more basic physiological or behavioural explanation of her behaviour.

Even if contemporary philosophers have not paid sustained attention to the study of the emotions, contemporary psychologists and psychiatrists have. Here, one important model has been presented by its originators as an extension of the Stoic account. According to the cognitive account (developed by Aaron Beck and his colleagues in a series of influential books and papers)[3] an individual's affect and behaviour are largely determined by the beliefs, judgments and assumptions he makes about (eg) himself, his environment, and his future. This cognitive model has gained considerable support from the success of cognitive therapy in treating a range of psychiatric conditions, such as panic, depression, and a variety of phobias (eg: spider phobia). As Rachman recently remarked:

> 'the cognitive explanation of results of cognitive therapy is the best supported at present. Indeed, there is no plausible alternative explanation for the effects of cognitive therapy at present. ...'[4]

What is more, the successful results of cognitive therapy have been substantiated by randomized controlled treatment trials in a number of areas. I shall begin by considering a case in which this type of therapy has proved strikingly successful.

[3] See for example, A. T. Beck, *Cognitive Therapy and Emotional Disorder*, New York 1976, Beck A. T., Rush A. J., Shaw B. F., and Emery G., *Cognitive Therapy for Depression*, New York 1979, Alford B.A. and Beck A. T., *The Integrative Power of Cognitive Therapy*, New York 1997.

[4] J. Rachman, Introduction to *The Science and Practice of Cognitive Therapy*, Essays in Honour of Michael Gelder, ed. D. M. Clark and C. G. Fairburn, Oxford 1997.

2. Cognitive therapy in action: panic.

Panic disorder, as investigated in the current psychiatric literature, is a narrowly defined phenomenon. It consists in recurrent unexpected panic attacks, involving physical symptoms (such as a racing heart) and anxiety focussed on the possibility of experiencing similar future, life threatening, attacks.

The cognitive treatment for this disorder is to suggest to the patient alternative, non-life threatening, hypotheses distinct from the one which he has formulated (eg: the chest pains are brought on by some non life threatening condition). The therapist points out to the patient that all these hypothesis (his and the less drastic ones) are (at least) equally well-confirmed by the evidence so far at his disposal, and encourages him to view them all as possible hypotheses open to subsequent testing. He also urges the patient to test these hypotheses without falling back on the types of 'safety behaviour' (things people do to avoid the feared consequences) he may have devised in the past. The therapist points out (as time goes by) that either the pains have not recurred or that (if they have) they have but not been followed by catastrophic cardiac collapse. He may also note the presence of other factors which could have precipitated the onset of chest pains in these conditions. If all goes well, the patient comes to reject his earlier hypothesis about the causal origin of his chest pains and ceases to experience panic if they recur.[5]

Research evidence shows that cognitive treatment of this disorder is particularly successful, more successful in terms of recovery and avoidance of further onset than treatments which are purely behavioural or drug based. This suggests that, in an account of pure panic, cognition has a central role to play. Why is this so?

In cases of pure panic, the basis of the condition is not the experience itself (the chest pain), but rather a belief about the cause of the pain (eg: interpreting it as a sign of a life threatening cardiac illness). Panic is grounded in a theoretical belief about the cause of one's pain, not directly in the experience of pain itself. This disorder appears fundamentally belief based, depending (as it does) on the patient's misinterpretation of his (or her) painful sensations.[7]

---

[5] See, for example, D. M. Clark, 'A Cognitive Approach to Panic', *Behaviour Research and Therapy*, 1986, 24, pp. 461–70.

[6] See *A Guide to Treatments That Work*, ed. P. M. Nathan and J. M. Gorman, Oxford 2002, pp. 315–6.

[7] The phrase 'belief-based' is intended to encompass two different types of cognitive theory. In one, beliefs account for the origin of the condition, in another for its maintenance. Cognitive theorists do not always clearly distinguish between these two very different types of account.

The patient's theoretical belief is central to cognitive treatment of this condition. The cognitive therapist seeks to lead him to see that it disconfirmed both by the absence of evidence to confirm it (eg: the patient does not suffer a life threatening cardiac attack) and the presence of evidence which supports some alternative hypothesis (eg the onset of the chest pains occurred in such and such conditions/ after food of type A etc.) The therapist aims to ensure that the patient focuses on evidence (some of it experiential) which disconfirms the belief that his/her chest pain is a sign of a life threatening disease.

There are, no doubt, other disorders which are fundamentally belief based. Perhaps certain eating disorders are of this type, those whose origin lies in the thought that (eg) the only valuable thing is being as slim as possible or that control of one's weight is the only way to happiness and personal success. Such disorders (if they exist) will be grounded, as panic is, in theoretical beliefs about the cause of one's dissatisfactions. The relative success of cognitive methods in the treatment of *bulimia nervosa* may suggest that this is a case in point. For these methods are directed at undermining and dismantling the beliefs just mentioned. Relapse will occur if these are not tackled.[8]

If the cognitive account is correct for panic, it is plausible to suppose that it will apply also to a range of (non-pathological) emotions. While it would be a lengthy task to establish which these are, one might speculate that, for example, certain kinds of pride (eg: pride in one's achievements) and anger (eg: anger at injustice) fall within this category.[9]

3. Cognitive therapy in action: two less successful cases.

[A] Specific phobias, such as spider phobia (arachnophobia)

In the simplest case, the cognitive therapist aims to challenge the patient's belief that spiders in the immediate vicinity are dangerous

---

[8] In the case of eating disorders in general, purely behavioural treatment does not work as well. The research evidence is summarized in *A Guide to Treatments That Work*, p. 569.

[9] D. Davidson: 'Hume's Cognitive Theory of Pride', in *Essays on Actions and Events*, Oxford 1980 and R. Wollheim *On the Emotions*, New Haven 1999. Wollheim focuses on sophisticated emotions which arise after one has been drawn to or repelled by something and involve awareness of one's own relation to the appealing and the repellent.

or harmful. The aim is to prove to the patient that this is not the case and thereby to remove the anxiety which they experience as a result of their (erroneous) belief that the spiders they encounter are dangerous. Once this belief has been changed, the patient will (if all goes well) not engage in the elaborate types of avoidance behaviour characteristic of spider phobics.

Beck and his colleagues outline this general method with considerable clarity:

'Once the patient learns to test her cognitions against the available reality-based evidence, she will have a chance to assess her assumptions.' (Beck, Rush....p. 154)

'The basis or evidence for each thought should be subjected to the scrutiny of reality testing, with the application of the kind of reasonable standards used by [non-phobic] people in making judgments...' (Beck, Rush,....p. 153)

However, perhaps not unexpectedly, cognitive therapists have encountered considerable difficulties in treating some patients in this way. One major problem is that some persist in their fear even when they have come to agree that spiders (in their area) are harmless, and are no longer even disposed to believe that they are harmful. This is the manifestation of a general difficulty. As Poseidonius long ago remarked, it is possible to fear without believing that the object feared is dangerous or harmful, still less that one is in danger of being harmed by it. Thus the therapist can change these beliefs without changing the emotion. More generally, possession of one of these beliefs does not seem to be necessary either for the onset or for the persistence of the relevant fear.

In this area, cognitive methods have not proved more successful than traditional behavioural ones (eg: exposure treatment). As a result, cognitive theorists have modified their account of the beliefs which lead to fear and also their methods for treating the phobia itself. We shall consider these modifications of the cognitive approach to spider phobia below. (See Section 8).

[B] Depression/ mood disorders

The study and treatment of depression has been a central preoccupation of cognitive theorists and cognitive therapists. In their view, the clinically depressed have stable background beliefs (or 'schemata') to the effect that they are inadequate, inferior, and/or unable to deal successfully with the situations they encounter. When they confront a stressful situation, such as taking an examination, getting a less good grade than expected, or the loss of a loved one, they are prone to negative thoughts such as 'I am so stupid that I shall fail the course', 'I shall never be able to survive her death...', thoughts which arise automatically and generate a variety of affect (feeling sad, miserable....). In the cognitive account, the background schema serves to direct the individual's attention to current experiences in such a way as to generate specific beliefs about them (eg: 'my getting a less good than expected grade means that I shall fail the course/ not get into university' etc). These specific beliefs are rationalized (for the agent) by their possession of the relevant stable background beliefs. Their onset leads the patient to feel sad and miserable, rendering him unable to maintain relations with others and undermining his interest in activities that usually engage him. These consequential states (including those involving affect) can further sustain the beliefs that precipitated them in a vicious circle (belief leads to affect/ affect leads to and sustains belief) characteristic of sustained depression.

The classical cognitive model for the treatment of depression is set out by Beck and Emery. The following passage gives the flavour of their approach:

Therapist: Why do you think that you will not get into the University of your first choice?

Patient: Because my grades are not really not so hot.

Therapist: What was your grade average?

Patient: Well, pretty good until my last semester in high school.

Therapist: What was your grade average in general?

Patient: A's and B's.

Therapist: How many of each?

Patient: I guess all were A's except for the terrible ones last semester.

Therapist: What were your grades then?

Patient: 2 A's and 2 B's.

Therapist: Since your grade average would seem to me to come out as almost all A's, why don't you think you won't get into University.

Patient: Because the competition is so tough.

Therapist: Have you found out the average grade for Admission?

Patient: Someone told me that B+ average would suffice.

Therapist: Isn't your average better than that?

Patient: I guess so.

Beck and Emory claim that, in this case, the patient came to see (through what they call the 'Socratic questioning' of the therapist) that she had reached an erroneous conclusion about her Admissions prospects on the basis of a cognitive error in her thinking. When this error is exposed, one of the beliefs that sustain her depression will have been removed. If other such beliefs can be dislodged in this way, including some quite general ones (known as 'schemas'), she will (if all goes well) cease to be depressed.

It may come as no surprise to learn that this type of cognitive therapy works no better than either interpersonal therapy (where no attempt is made to modify beliefs of this type) or behavioural therapy.[10] Further, none of these psychological treatments work better than standard drug treatments. What is more, the problems encountered by the cognitive therapists in this area have been of a systematic kind.

[A] *Causal primacy*: it has been found that dysfunctional general thoughts ('schemata') themselves vary with mood. That is, when a previously depressed patient recovers from their depression, they are no longer prone to think of themselves as inadequate or inferior. There is no evidence that those who are subject to depression have a permanent background belief of this type. Rather, the available evidence supports an alternative hypothesis: so far from background thoughts and beliefs generating mood (or affect) in the ways indicated in Beck's classical cognitive theory, the relevant moods themselves generate the thoughts in question.[11] When the mood passes, the thoughts themselves also disappear. If so, it might seem that the relevant notion of depressed mood cannot be analysed in the Beck's way (as a result of general schema+specific incident..), since we need to employ the notion of mood to account for the occurrence of the relevant background thought or schema. It seems that some further ingredient is required to account for the onset of the relevant general beliefs.

[B] *Valuational judgment not sufficient for emotion*: people can endorse the general judgment that they are inadequate or inferior, and agree that their position is hopeless, but still not experience depressed mood. Clinically, people can sometimes think of themselves as useless etc without experiencing the relevant affect.[12] And this result conforms to general experience: one can accept that one

[10] See N. S. Jacobson, C. R.Martell, T. Dimijdan, 'Behavioral Activation Treatment for Depression', *Clinical Psychology: Science and Practice 2001*, pp. 264–70. S. D. Hollon, 'Behavioral Activation for Depression: A Commentary,' *Clinical Psychology: Science and Practice 2001*, pp. 271–4.

[11] On this, see J. Teasdale and P. Barnard., *Affect, Cognition and Change*, Hove 1993, pages 8ff.

[12] J. Teasdale and P. Barnard., *Affect, Cognition and Change*, p. 216.

is useless or inadequate in some area (or quite generally) but do so calmly and coolly with a 'mental' shrug of the shoulders. 'That is just how things are, I'll never be able to solve these intellectual/emotional/ political problems, but I'll not let that fact get me down. The fact that I am a failure (eg: in mathematics) won't make me despair...etc....'

These two problems, together with the possibility of suffering fear without the relevant valuational judgments about spiders noted above, suggest there are systematic difficulties in the classical cognitive account of moods and emotions. Indeed, the research programme based on that account seems to be in crisis. As theoreticians, we need to understand why cognitive methods work in some cases and not in others. Further, we may need to consider whether there are alternatives to the cognitive account which better explains some of the relevant phenomena. Before beginning on this task, it may be helpful to review some recent responses to these problems.

4. Contemporary responses: overview

[A] *Practical response*: therapists have responded to these difficulties by adding experienced-based techniques to the purely cognitive ones recommended by the classical cognitive model. Indeed, the combination of traditional behavioural and cognitive methods has led the treatment to be redescribed as 'cognitive behavioural therapy' (or sometimes 'cognitive-behavioural therapy') rather than 'cognitive therapy.' This response is, no doubt, justified on the basis of clinical practice and clinical judgment. But its success raises its own problems: what explains the comparative success of such methods in some areas when compared with those of traditional cognitive therapy? In particular, what understanding of the relevant moods and emotions accounts for the increased success of cognitive behavioural therapy? One great merit of classical cognitive therapy (as its practitioners rightly emphasized) was the close fit it suggested between clinical practice and the cognitive theory of the emotions. The change in clinical practice away from purely cognitive methods requires a reassessment of the underlying account of the moods and emotions themselves. What is needed is an account of these (at the theoretical level) which explains why cognitive behavioural (or cognitive-behavioural) methods work where they do (and fail where they do).

[B] *Theoretical response*: it is possible to distinguish two types of theoretical response to the problems sketched above.

One (the more conservative) has searched for other beliefs to underpin the purely cognitive approach. The underlying assumption is that the cognitive account is correct, and it is only a matter of finding the right beliefs to complete that story. Thus, in the case of spider-phobics, it might be suggested that the patient need not actually believe that spiders are dangerous or harmful. They may rather believe that they themselves will panic in the presence of spiders, lose control of themselves, and/or be unable to cope with the situation when it arises. Others, no doubt, will attempt to find different stable background beliefs to underlie the onset of depression (although so far this research strategy has failed to produce any plausible candidates).

There is a second, more innovative, approach to be found in the writings of two Cambridge based psychologists: John Teasdale and Philp Barnard.[13] Their assessment of the problems in classical cognitive theory led them to characterize emotional beliefs (or 'hot beliefs' as they call them) in terms other than those applied by Beck and his school. They have proposed that we should distinguish different types of belief, only some of which are involved in emotions and in the generation of affect. While Beck held that the relevant beliefs were to be distinguished solely in terms of degrees of belief (subjective probability), Teasdale and Barnard proposed that there are different types of belief involved corresponding to 'hot' and 'cold' cognition. In the next section, I shall investigate their proposal in more detail. It seems the most interesting of the responses currently on offer.

[C] *Philosophical views*: those who have rejected cognitive accounts have appealed to such notions as 'irreducible psychic feelings'[14] or 'moods' to account for the relevant phenomena.[15] But this approach does not help us to explain why purely cognitive (or cognitive-behavioural) methods work in some cases and not in others. Nor does it offer much insight into what is to have the relevant emotion or mood. We appear to need richer conceptual resources to pinpoint the way in which certain emotions (or moods) are distinct from the favoured combination of beliefs and desires.

---

[13] See their *Affect, Cognition and Change*, esp. pp. 65–96 and 209–23.

[14] Michael Stocker, 'Psychic Feelings' in *Australasian Journal of Philosophy*, 61, 1983, pp. 5–26.

[15] Peter Goldie, *The Emotions*, Oxford 2000, Geoffrey Madell, *Philosophy, Emotion and Music*, Edinburgh 2002.

5. Teasdale and Barnard: *Affect, Cognition and Change*

Teasdale and Barnard's view is complex and I shall offer only a thumbnail sketch (which may to some seem a caricature). Their basic move is to separate two types of meaning and two corresponding types of belief. In addition to the meaning of ordinary factual propositions, they introduce what they describe as 'implicational meaning.' The latter is to be explained as follows.

1. In given stressful situations, features in information attached to past situations that have produced the emotion are processed to generate generic (or implicational) meanings.

2. Generic (or implicational) meanings are higher order regularities involving such ideas as ' I am useless', which Teasdale and Barnard characterize as 'core themes characteristic of the relevant emotion'.

3. When these generic (or implicational) meanings are generated, the relevant emotion is produced.

In describing generic (or implicational) meanings, Teasdale and Barnard make two basic claims.

(a) Generic meanings are more abstract representations of the contents of specific propositions

Thus, there can be the same generic meaning expressed in different sentences or different languages.

(b) Generic meanings involve information drawn from a variety of 'informational codes': they involve the integration of sensory information and information drawn from the effector system (how the abstract proposition impacts on me)

Thus, they write of 'implicational meaning' as abstract and holistic, and represent it as integrating in a abstract or schematic model information taken from specific propositions, specific sensory information and the specific effects such information has on us. They describe information thus integrated as 'an implicational schematic model'(I.C.S.).

Depression provides their favoured case study. In their view, the immediate antecedent to this condition is not the negative automatic thoughts proposed in the cognitive model, but rather the 'processing of accessible depression-related schematic models.' These can be thought of as abstract pieces on information, such as 'I am useless', processed in such a way as to involve simultaneously sensory and effector information. Such information is 'hot' in virtue of its connections with sensory and effector information (or codes). It is not merely believed to be true by the subject. Further, in their view, such schemata will only be accessible if we can simultaneously process information from these varied sources of information. If we cannot do this (eg: if our present state is not of the right kind to summon up the relevant sensory and effector information), we will not be able to process the relevant (depression-related implicational schema) and so will not be in possession of the relevant depression-thoughts* (where the * describes hot information). In this way, Teasdale and Barnard can explain the periodic nature of depressive *thoughts.

Much more could be said about this theory, but enough detail has (I hope) emerged to allow us to assess some aspects of its basic structure. I shall note four problems with it.

1. *Why insist on generality?* It is far from clear that high levels of generic meaning are required for all cases of emotion or emotional disorder. In some cases, it certainly appears that the emotion experienced is a direct response to particular situations or objects ('I am afraid of that spider') and does not involve a highly abstract representation of myself drawn from many similar cases and combined with sensory information drawn from a wide variety of similar situations. At best, the Teasdale-Barnard model may apply to some cases of emotional disturbance, such as those involving the onset or maintenance of general mood disorder. It does not appear to offer a general model for all emotions or all emotional disturbances (even if it could be applied successfully to their favoured case of depression).

2. *How does the holism work?* Even if we grant that it is characteristic of certain emotions (or moods) that they involve information drawn from several codes (sensory and effector codes), we need to understand why invoking this further information produces the relevant mood. Why cannot one be aware of the relevant memories, sensory experiences, their impact in the past, and still view all this in a detached and unemotional way? Why should introducing more information of this type by itself generate 'hot cognition' out of an assembly of (potentially) 'cold' information? Conversely, if some of this information cannot be viewed in the relevant 'cold' or 'detached' way, we need to know which this is and why. An answer to this question is a a possible key to an account of the relevant type of heat in the 'hot' cognition that * I am (eg) useless.

The present point could be sharpened as a dilemma: either the additional information invoked by the implicational system is of the same kind as that captured in 'cold' propositional meaning or it is not. If it is, how does it generate 'hot' cognition? If it is different, we need to examine the nature of the difference if we are to account for what is distinctive of emotion and emotional reaction. (In the present vocabulary, what is distinctive about the 'sensory and effector codes' and how are they involved in the relevant mood or emotion?).

3. *Explanatory gap?* Why is information from past situations of the appropriate type invoked in some cases and not in others? What is it about my present state or experience of this situation that makes the abstract informational schema relevant in this case and not in others? Teasdale and Barnard note that sometimes the background schemata are invoked and sometimes not. But why? Is there a psychological explanation of why this occurs in some cases and not others? It is certainly natural to think that it is the nature of one's present experience (as, for example, sad or miserable) which accounts for one's calling up general informational schemata of this type. But, if so, the basis for the explanation lies with the character of this type of emotional experience. It is this we need to understand, and it cannot be explained (on pain of circularity) by invoking the general informational schema.

4. *Remoteness from practice?* Teasdale has emphasized the importance of experience in discussing the therapeutic strategy he wishes to support (on the basis of his model). Thus, in considering Beck's depressed student mentioned above, who does not believe that she will get into college, he makes three points.

1. The belief that she will not get into college is best seen as the product of the thought of oneself as useless or incompetent, not as its cause.

2. Treatment should consist not in challenging the basis for the student's beliefs, but by 'fostering non-depressogenic models' of oneself as ' competent, but with doubts in my competence.'

3. This is to be done by arranging for actual experiences in which new or modified models are created.

Indeed, in his subsequent work, Teasdale has focused on the importance in therapy of the recall of past successful experiences which allows one to re-experience past positive affect and on the need to develop skills for 'the intentional use of attention and awareness'[16] However, these interesting therapeutic ideas about experience and attention have not, as yet, been successfully integrated into the general theoretical model which he and Barnard developed.

While Teasdale and Barnard have argued convincingly for the need to account for some moods and emotions in a way different from that proposed in the classical cognitive model, their own proposal stands in need of supplementation in several respects. In what follows, I shall develop their idea that certain fears and phobias are to be understood in terms other than those of judgment and ('cold') belief, but not do so in the way they suggested. Rather, I shall offer a general sketch (indeterminate in many important respects) of some differences between experience and judgment and then use the resulting account of experience in characterizing the nature of certain specific fears. I shall argue for this account by suggesting that it provides a satisfying account of why certain types of treatment for these conditions are more effective than others. It is no part of my contention that this style of account applies to all emotions, let alone to (the quite different phenomenon of) moods and mood disorders. My focus is specifically on the importance and distinctive role of experience in certain fears and phobias.

6. Emotion: an analogy with experience

6.1 A first approximation

The Müller-Lyer lines look to be of unequal length even when you know that they are of equal length. They can look like this, even when you know that the reality is different. In the latter case, one may not even be disposed to believe that the lines are of equal length.

It has recently been argued that the type of experience involved in the Müller-Lyer case cannot be or be grounded in a kind of belief. If it were, the experience would changeable by rational persuasion. It would be possible to affect how things look to you by rational argument. One should be able to exploit the fact it is irrational to believe that things are of unequal length when you know (or believe) that they are not in an attempt to alter your belief about

[16] See his 'The relation between Cognition and Emotion: The Mind in Place in Mood disorders' in *The Science and Practice of Cognitive Therapy*, ed. D. M. Clark and C. G. Fairburn, Oxford 1997, and also *Mindfulness Based Cognitive Therapy*, Z. V. Siegel, J. M. G. Williams and J. D. Teasdale, New York 2002.

how things look to you. At very least, you would be subject to rational criticism if you experienced the lines as of unequal length when you knew that they are of the same length.[17]

However, as things are, it is not possible to affect how things look to you by rational argument. One cannot exploit the fact that it would be irrational to believe that the lines are of unequal length in this situation to alter how things look to you. Nor are you even *prima facie* subject to rational criticism if the lines do appear to be of unequal length even when you know that they are not. It may be irrational to act on your experience in such a case, but that is a different matter.

According to this view, certain types of experience should not be analysed in terms of belief (or even disposition to believe). Can this style of account be applied to the experience of fear? Take the case of the spider-phobic: something can seem dangerous or harmful to him even when he knows that it is not so (and is not even inclined to believe that it is so). Here too, as noted above, it does not seem possible (in some cases) to affect how things seem to the patient on the basis of rational argument. One cannot exploit the fact that it is irrational to think of A as dangerous to alter the fact that A seems dangerous to you. In such a case, one might say:

'The spider seems dangerous even though it is not really so.'

If one cannot analyse how things look in terms of belief, it seems plausible to suggest that one cannot explain the nature of emotional experience in terms of belief either. The fact that A can seem dangerous even when one is not inclined to believe that it is suggests that the experience of A as dangerous cannot be analysed in terms of belief. On this model, one's fear cannot be analysed in terms solely of belief or of belief plus (eg) desire or some additional phenomenological or physiological elements. For there need be no such belief present.

Can this account of fear be sustained? It is important to note that not all fears involve things seeming dangerous or harmful to the subject. Here are some other characteristic expressions:

That spider seems frightening
That spider scares/frightens me
It will be frightening to be in the presence of a large black spider

In these cases, there is no attempt to represent the spider as dangerous or harmful. It need not even seem dangerous or harmful.

[17] For discussion of this case, see Gareth Evans's *The Varieties of Reference*, Oxford, 1982, pp. 123ff.

The subject focuses rather on the impact of the spider on him: that it strikes him as frightening. No amount of pointing out that the spider in question is neither harmful nor dangerous can rationally affect his experience of it as frightening. How are these expressions to be understood? What is the state involved?

The immediate response in the case of the present tense cases just noted is as follows: to experience something as frightening or terrifying (fear) is to be in a state in which one is disposed to react in a given way, whether the reactions be actions (such as flight), physiological reactions (such as being sick/ autonomic responses) or psychological affects (such as being anxious). Indeed, what makes the experience an emotional experience is its tendency to guide our reactions in this way.[18]

A similar story can easily be told about present tense cases of experiencing something as (for example) annoying or provoking (anger), depressing or distressing (feeling sad or dejected), as nauseating or disgusting (feeling upset), as attractive or repulsive, as amusing or funny (being amused). Examples come easily to hand:

'it makes me wild/ angry/'mad'/ sad/ fed-up/ worried/ 'sick'/ gloomy/ dejected/ amused/ excited/ calm/, or in more colloquial style

'It turns me on/off, it really gets to me...etc...'

In these cases, to experience something as sad is to be in a state in which one is disposed (in normal circumstances) to be dejected or gloomy, and (in some cases) to cry. Indeed, what makes an experience one of sadness is the fact that, in experiencing it, one is disposed to react in this type of way.[19] Of the reactions mentioned, those

[18] For an interesting account of relevant internal reactions, see A. Damasio's discussion of 'background feelings' such as excitement, calmness, dread, tension and malaise (sickness) in *The Feeling of What Happens*, London 1999, p. 286. Damasio helpfully distinguishes these from what he calls 'primary emotions' such as fear, anger, disgust, surprise and sadness, and 'secondary' (more sophisticated) emotions such as jealousy, guilt, embarrassment and pride. There is need for further investigation of Damasio's trichotomy. If it can be sustained, there can be no one theory of all the emotions. (Perhaps my present proposal is correct for certain primary, Richard Wollheim's for certain secondary emotions. Neither seems to work for background feelings or moods).

[19] These cases, so understood, present an interesting analogy with a certain view of spatial experience. According to this account, as developed by Gareth Evans in his 'Molyneux's Problem', *Collected Papers*, Oxford 1984, pp. 364–99, to experience something as being to my left or within my

119

connected with action seems less important. One can experience something as sad but not be inclined at all (given one's cultural formation) to cry. Similarly, one can experience something as frightening even if one is so overwhelmed, numbed or mesmerized by the experience as to be unable to flee (or even think of fleeing).

What is the connection between this style of account and beliefs? One can, of course, believe that the spider now seems frightening. But this belief appears to register the fact that the spider is now frightening me rather than to constitute it. Further, I may on occasion be frightened of an object but not believe that I am being frightened by it. Perhaps I only realize later that I was being made anxious or frightened by it. I may even lack (perhaps temporarily) the conceptual sophistication required to have beliefs about this type about my mental states or fail to classify my internal states correctly. But none of these failures in belief undermine the fact that I am now experiencing the spider as frightening (provided that I am, in reality, now appropriately affected by it). For similar reasons, I can experience the object as frightening without thinking of it as being disposed to frighten me. (For I need have no view about its having dispositions which impact on me or misclassify the disposition in question). In these cases, I (or even simpler organisms) may experience something as frightening without having any beliefs about the cause of my present experience. Rather, what makes the experience one of something's seeming frightening to me is my being disposed (in having this experience) to react in a given way. In having such an experience, one is not simply registering the features of the object; rather one is being affected by it.[20]

If this is correct, the experience of something as frightening cannot be accounted for (in cognitive terms) merely as seeing the

---

[20] It is important to distinguish the case in which something *looks* frightening to me (as distant rocks might do at sea) from that in which it *seems* frightening to me. The expression 'it seems frightening to me' serves to indicate (at least in the use on which I am focussing) the presence of some fear in me.

---

reach is to be disposed (in normal circumstances) to act (or react at the sensorimotor level) in a given way. On this account, what is essential to the experience of something as to my left is my being disposed to act in a given way. Indeed, Evans suggested that is its ability to guide actions in this way that gives our conscious experience its distinctive spatial *content*. Here, too, there is room for debate as to whether the relevant reactions are best conceived as bodily movements or (more internally) as ways of attending to the object. (I shall simply assume, for present purposes, that a zombie could not have Evansian spatial experience.)

object as frightening (if this is understood as simply registering the features of the object independently of their impact on us). For, on the view just outlined, one cannot account for what it is to experience the object as frightening without essential reference to its impact on us (and our being disposed to respond in a given way to it in normal conditions). One is not simply observing in a reaction-independent way the features of the object.[21] Nor is the observational account rectified if one adds as further ingredient the suggestion that the agent desires to escape the object or that he is seriously concerned about it. For both desire to escape and serious concern can be present along with a relevant perception but without fear.[22]

6.2: Fear of the future

In the cases so far described the impact of fear is directly perceptual. But this need not always be the case. In some cases, what is feared may be in the future. Is there a cognitive component in this case? Someone, afraid of meeting spiders and engaging in aversive behaviour, says:

'It will be frightening to be in the presence of a large black spider', or

[21] There may be uses of the phrase 'seeing as' which allow us to see things as frightening only when they have a given impact on us. But such accounts would not be cognitive accounts as I construe them. For I am taking 'cognitive accounts' of my seeing something as frightening to be ones which do not essentially involve my being disposed to react in a given way to the object.

[22] For an account along these lines, see R. Roberts: (*Phil Review* 1988 and *Philosophy* , 71, 147–56, 1996). In Roberts'account, to fear A is (1) to construe A as something dangerous or harmful which is coming one's way, and (2) to be seriously concerned about it. But this account faces several serious problems:

1. the object feared may not even *appear* harmful or dangerous, let alone be seen as actually dangerous or harmful (see the plight of the spider-phobics);
2. what counts as having a serious concern in this case other than taking A as frightening? Roberts' account will not (in my view) be rescued simply by replacing (1) with (1)*: to see as (or construe) A as frightening. For an experienced sailor can construe or see nearby rocks as frightening but not be frightened by them. What would make him frightened is not how they appear to him, but how they affect him: how they seem to him to be.

'I shall lose control and make a fool of myself if there is a large spider around..'

Are these really just predictions or beliefs about what one will experience in the future? It seems not. One can coolly predict that one will experience fear, or lose control, in the future without now being afraid. Nor is the emotion regained if one adds that the agent has a desire to avoid the future presence of the spider. For this he may have in a cool and unemotional way. Nor is it enough that the agent feels some appropriate physiological reaction. For that might be caused by a deviant internal causal chain initiated by the presence of the desire to avoid the spider (or from the prediction). Further, one can be afraid of being in the presence of something in the future even though one knows that when the situation comes along they will not be frightened. It seems, as before, that the presence of these beliefs is neither sufficient nor necessary to account for the onset of the relevant emotion.

What is required (if the sentences quoted are to be expressions of fear) is that the agent be currently afraid of getting into a situation in which spiders are present or in which he loses control, and so is prone (on this basis) to takes avoidance measures. In this case, the sentence expresses the current impact on the subject of the imagined (or envisaged) future state and is not merely a prediction about what will happen. The subject is currently affected by the prospect of what will happen. As Aristotle once said, he has the future 'before his eyes', and it is this that affects him.[23]

In this case, the fear is not based on how things look perceptually to the subject, but on what the future seems to hold. As in the earlier cases, how it seems to him to be is not to be accounted for in terms of what he believes or is inclined to believe. In both, what is

[23] See *De Anima* Γ. 7, 431b7f. The sentence

'It will be pleasant to be in Cardiganshire in April.'

may be understood in two different ways: as a prediction about what how it will be if one is in Cardiganshire in April, and as the expression of a desire to be in Cardiganshire in April. In the former, the prediction may lead to a desire to be in Cardiganshire in April. In the letter, one is actually expressing one's current desire to be there at that time. What happens in the case represented by (2)? The agent imagines being in Cardiganshire then and this affects her in a way analogous to that in which the present perceptual scene might do. She is currently affected by the envisaged future scene. Indeed, what it is to envisage the future state as pleasant is to be attracted towards it. There is no need for a further or additional desire to be present (over and above his imagining it as pleasant) to explain her aiming to be in Cardiganshire in April.

important is the impact the imagined or perceived scene makes on the subject: the relevant states cannot be understood except by reference to the subject's disposition to act or react physiologically in given ways. This will be the case whether the agent's state is to be described as one in which things look or seem to him a given way. (For the type of seeming is not one in which the agent is inclined to believe that something is the case.)[24]

In both cases of perception and future directed imagination, things can go on seeming (or looking) frightening when one knows that there is nothing harmful or dangerous in one's vicinity. They can still go on seeming frightening even when you have been convinced by others that nothing really bad will happen if you touch the spider. You may have even touched spiders and found out that this is not disturbing and still be afraid when in their presence. Spiders can go on seeming frightening even when you know that they will not adversely affect you if you touch them. This is just how they seem to you to be.

In the cases considered, how things seem or look to you is not subject to rational persuasion or rational control. The statement

'The spider seems frightening'

expresses one's immediate reaction to the situation (or envisaged situation) at a level which is not immediately sensitive to the power of truth-based reasons pro and con. For anxiety, dread and tension are reactions that are not a species of judgment or belief.

6.3: Fear and normativity

In the case of the Müller-Lyer illusion, there is no irrationality (or so it is claimed) in the lines looking a given way even when you know that they are not really so. But can things go on looking harmful or seeming frightening to you even when you know they are not actually harmful or such as to give you bad / distressing experiences without your being guilty of irrationality? While you may not be guilty of holding inconsistent judgments or holding judgments in the face of overwhelming countervailing evidence, you still appear to be criticizable: you are not reacting to the objects around you as you ought to! While the fact that the spider looks frightening (or looks harmful) is not rationally challenged (in any way) by one's

---

[24] Some spider-phobics may agree that spiders (in their present perceptual field) seem frightening to them but deny that they look frightening. If so, in their case, the type of seeming is one which captures how they are emotionally affected by the spider, and not something they are inclined to believe.

knowledge that the spider is not harmful or that experience of it will not be at all adverse, there is still some irrationality in the case in point. One can recognize that one's experience is not as it should be.

What is the basis for this adverse criticism? One is not reacting as one should to the environment around one because one's reactions do not constitute the basis for a successful way of navigating one's way through it. They lead one to avoid or make one feel anxious about objects which there is no need to avoid or feel anxious about. One's actions and reactions are affected by things which should not do so. Indeed, avoidance or anxiety of this type can undermine one's ability to do what one thinks one ought to. It is dysfunctional. One is experiencing fear in ways one should not rationally do so (whether because one's fear is excessive or because it is directed at things that one should not fear at all).

In the cases of emotional experience, the relevant norm appears not to be that of truth but rather that of appropriate action (or reaction) in the environment in which one finds oneself. This is why dysfunctional fears can be criticized as irrational even though they are not alterable by truth-based rational persuasion. At this point, there is a disanalogy between this case and that of the ordinary perceptual illusions (such as the Müller-Lyer). For in the latter, the subject is not subject to rational criticism if the equal lines look to be unequal, even though he may be irrational if he acts on that experience. What is the basis for this disanalogy? One possible explanation is that, in the Müller-Lyer case, the disposition to act is not part of the experience itself but is something added to it. This is why it may be irrational to act on how things look to you, even though there is no irrationality in their looking that way to you. By contrast, in emotional experience the relevant disposition is part of the experience itself. An alternative explanation is that there is nothing dysfunctional in our experiencing the Müller Lyer lines as being of unequal length. Indeed, we are built (perhaps for evolutionary reasons) to respond to these situations in these ways. By contrast, certain fears, such as those of harmless spiders, are irrational because they undermine one's ability to function properly (eg: by refusing to leave one's room). Since we are not built to fear spiders in this way, we are subject to criticism when we fear them in ways which are dysfunctional.[25] Both of these explanations suggest ways

[25] One could, of course, (*pace* Evans) think that norms of successful action are also relevant to the content of spatial experience. For this view, see Adrian Cussins' 'The Connectionist Constuction of Concepts', 1990, reprinted with additional material in (ed) Y.H. Gunther, *Essays on Nonconceptual Content*, Cambridge Mass. 2003, p. 133.

in which the norm of appropriate action (or reaction) is relevant to emotional but not spatial experience. We do not need to decide between them here.

How does the norm of appropriate action apply to emotional experience? There are, once again, at least two types of account on offer. In one, the norm applies to the *content* of the experience:

A seems frightening.

This content will be appropriately accepted provided that it is appropriate to react with fear to A. Things can be experienced as frightening in the same way as they can be experienced as to my left or to my right: one sees them as such. Their repulsiveness (or frightening aspect) is part of the world as we experience it (in the same way as I am currently experiencing the left-sidedness of my left hand), and it is this which is the basis for my being disposed to react to them with revulsion or fear. Things are correctly experienced as repulsive or frightening when (and only when) it is appropriate to react to them in this way. The norm to invoke in assessing what is seen as frightening is not truth but rather the appropriateness of the relevant reaction.[26] Perhaps (as in one traditional version of this account) it is appropriate to fear what the virtuous agent would fear (if she is to live the virtuous life etc). In an alternative style of account, the content of the experience:

A seems frightening

will be appropriate provided that A is, in reality, frightening, but it will be appropriate to *accept* that A seems frightening when (and only when) it is appropriate to react with fear to A. Here, the norm of appropriateness governs the mode of acceptance rather than the content accepted.[27] In one extension of this account, it will be appropriate to react with fear to A when and only when the virtuous would do so. The virtuous will be governed in what they fear not only by what is, in fact, frightening but also by what they should fear (e.g.) in order to live the virtuous life. If so, the virtuous should accept as frightening what they should fear given their aims. Thus, they may hold that (in certain conditions) some dangers that they see as frightening are nonetheless not to be accepted as such (given their goals and commitments).

[26] For further development of this style of view, see, for example, the paper by Adrian Cussins mentioned in the previous footnote.

[27] For this style of view, see for example Paul Grice's *Aspects of Reason*, Oxford 2001, chapters 2 and 3. I attribute a version of this view to Aristotle in my *Aristotle's Philosophy of Action*, London 1984, pp 84–96.

David Charles

Both alternatives share several features. In both, there is a norm of assessment at work other than that of truth, and in both things in the world can be experienced as frightening. Further, in neither is it merely a causally necessary condition for one's experiencing A as frightening that one is frightened. While there are important differences between these two accounts, it is not necessary to adjudicate between them here. The present proposal is, or so it seems to me, consistent with both.[28] I shall now suggest that this general view of experience is applicable to the case of certain types of fear.

7. Spider-phobia and therapy

7. 1 Spider-phobia and experience.

The proposal in the previous section gives one a way to address some of the difficulties raised for the cognitive theory raised in Section 4. Thus, one can have beliefs of the form

1. This object is disposed to produce frightening experiences in me/ this object is harmful,
2. This object is disposed to harm me...

without experiencing fear. Similarly, one can change one's beliefs about what is harmful/ dangerous or about the nature of the experience one is going to have if one touches the spider without removing the emotion of fear: for the person can still experience the spider as frightening ('It looks/seems frightening') even when she knows that it is not harmful/ does not merit fear/will not produce bad experiences etc. But can this proposal be sustained. Does it provide the basis for an account of why cognitive treatment works in some cases but not in others? As we noted above, cognitive therapy

[28] There is a striking analogy between the present proposal and Mark Johnston's discussion of affect in his excellent essay 'The Authority of Affect' in *Philosophy and Phenomenological Research* Vol. LXIII, No 1, 2001, pp. 181–214. I am indebted to Ralph Wedgwood for bringing Johnston's essay to my attention (after I had read my paper at the Oxford Conference on Action in 2002). Both of us aim to understand (what Johnston describes as) 'affective experience' as involving experience of the world around us. We differ, however, in several ways. (1) Johnston denies that his account of 'affective perception' applies to the emotions (op.cit p.182 fn1). (2) Johnston's view appears consistent with thinking of the appropriate affect as merely a causally necessary condition for experiencing what is (e.g) alluring or frightening. (3) Johnston does not connect his discussion of affect with the idea of norms of assessment other than truth.

seems to work as well as more traditional forms of behaviour therapy for spider-phobics.[29]

7.2 Cognitive-behavioural therapy for spider-phobia

A favoured form of cognitive-behavioural therapy works like this:[30]

You encourage patients to catch spiders under a glass. This involves directing the spider towards the glass with a pen and (after a while) your finger. The treatment begins with small spiders and is repeated with larger ones for one session only. According to the cognitive theory, what happens here is that patient tests the hypothesis that (eg) spiders are harmful and comes to realize that it is false (ie: spiders are not harmful). The primary focus of the treatment is to ensure that the patient comes to realize that the hypothesis in question is false.

This form of treatment is often successful. The cognitive account of what happens is that the patient amasses evidence for the conclusion that the spider is not harmful. (In cognitive terms, he comes to grasp a new belief: eg that spiders are harmless.). But how does this happen: what is it about this episode that generates this conclusion? How does he come to see spiders differently under these conditions?

One explanation runs as follows: the patient in testing the hypothesis does so by being encouraged to approach, closely observe and finally touch the spiders. When he does so, his experience is tolerable. His anxiety level eventually drops and this results in the spider seeming less frightening to him than at the initial stages of the encounter. In the end, the spider does not generate the levels of anxiety which it did at the outset. It is this change which produces the differing assessment of the threat posed by the spider at the end of the treatment. With his new experience of acting on spiders, they cease to seem frightening to him.

In successful cases, the patient will no longer fear the spiders he encounters. The therapy is completed at this point. He may go on

---

[29] Nor is this result confined to spider-phobics. For similar results in the treatment of certain cases of obsessive-compulsive disorder, see P. D. McLean, M. L. Whittal, D. S. Thoradson and S. Taylor, 'Cognitive versus Behavior Therapy in the Group Treatment of Obsessive-Compulsive Disorder', *Journal of Consulting and Clinical Psychology*, 2001, vol. 69, no. 2, pp. 205–14.

[30] This method is discussed in detail by Susan Thorpe in *Cognitive Processes in Specific Phobias and their Treatment*, Oxford D.Phil 1994

to note that he has disconfirmed some hypothesis he initially held on the basis of his experience. He may no longer predict that it will be horrible to be in contact with spiders. But, even if he did not take this further step, he would still be cured. The refutation of his original hypothesis does not seem required for his treatment. It is not as if, in this case, experience is serving merely as powerful evidence to be considered in checking his hypothesis as a means to the cognitive discovery of the falsity of his original claim. It is rather that when his experience of spiders has changed in the relevant respects, he is already cured. He feels happier in the presence of spiders. The crucial factor seems to be the change in the nature of the relevant experience, not the subsequent change in belief.

7.3. Behavioural treatments

One favoured form of behavioural treatment runs like this:

Expose the patient to spiders and you will find that (after several successful episodes of exposure) that the patient (if all goes well) is far happier in the presence of spiders. He has become habituated to spiders through immersion therapy.

This type of method (no doubt) works well in many cases. But why? One obvious explanation is that the patient in being exposed to spiders comes to experience them as not being as frightening/threatening as he/she first feared. What changes, once again, is the nature of the relevant experience, the new type of experience leading him/her to submit happily/less reluctantly to further exposure. Anxiety is reduced.

Behavioural treatments work as well without a cognitive component. The obvious explanation for this datum is that it is the experience of the objects involved that is altered in these treatments, and that it is this change which is the decisive one.

7.4 Purely cognitive therapy

It is fully consistent with the account so far given of emotional response that pure cognitive therapy (exposing certain beliefs as ill-founded/ illogically supported) can, on occasion, play some role in treatment of certain patients who suffer from experience based disorders.

As has been frequently remarked, emotional response generates beliefs which may well in turn support the emotional response in question. There may be, as Beck and others have noted, a spiral (or circle) of mutually supporting beliefs and emotions involved in the maintenance of emotional states and disorders. In these cases, the beliefs will help to maintain and rationalize the emotional reaction, and their being called into question may render the maintaining cycle less resilient. If so, the original emotional basis for the circle may be more open to attack by experience based means.

There is a further point. Visual illusions (such as the Müller Lyer case) are to some degree permeable by reason. While we cannot persuade ourselves by argument that the lines do not look to be of unequal length, we can train ourselves to use techniques for looking at these lines which influence how we see them. Thus, if one makes oneself look at the lines and ignore the arrows (or attend more to the lines than to the arrows), one can affect how the lines look to you. Some claim that, after training of this type, the lines look to them to be of equal length. Others say that after such training the lines look to be of equal length (if one focuses on the lines) and of unequal length (if one focuses equally on the arrows). While these techniques do not work in all cases, they do in some.

In the successful cases, how things look can be guided by techniques inspired by our rational understanding of the situation, even though we cannot persuade ourselves by rational means or argument that things do not look a given way to us. If the situation involved is one which regularly occurs and is one where it is important for us to get it right, we can be fairly criticized for not succeeding in guiding our experiences in this way. (eg: a sportsman who regularly fails to spot a certain type of spin or is deceived in the flight). Although there is no irrationality if

Things look a given way to me, even when I know that they are not so

I can be criticized (in certain cases) for not training my visual system to focus in such a way as to see things differently (so as to spot the spin etc).[31]

[31] Our visual system can be influenced in other ways by our understanding. Our cognitive grasp of what is in our environment often leads us to experience things differently. We can learn to see and group things differently as we acquire new concepts and a new understanding of the situation. To this extent our visual system is influenced by our cognitive grasp of our environment. In some cases, we can free ourselves from one way of looking at objects when we grasp new concepts and apply them to our experience. (See P. F. Strawson: 'Imagination and Perception' in his *Freedom and Resentment and Other Essays*, London 1974). In this way certain important aspects of our visual experience can be correctly described as conceptual.

David Charles

In the case of emotional experience, there may be a similar phenomenon. Perhaps one can develop techniques which affect how things seem: focussing on some aspect of the situation, avoiding others. It may even be that for some the clear perception that spiders are not to be feared is by itself enough to alter the nature of their emotional experience. But in any such case cognitive treatment will work by changing the nature of the experience itself and not by rationally persuading the patient that the spider does not seem frightening. It should be no surprise that techniques which work directly on the experience itself are more successful.

7.5 Failures of various types of therapy

In some cases neither cognitive-behavioural nor behavioural methods work. In these cases, the spider still goes on seeming frightening even when you have experienced it several times without adverse affect. (In similar ways, for some fairground rides or public speaking can go on seeming frightening even when they have tried them out several times without bad experiences and believe that the next time will be just like previous ones.) In these cases, how the thing seems is not affected for the better by what we experience. The best the therapist can do (in many such cases) is to encourage the patient to go on repeatedly trying out the relevant experience. But, in some instances the anxiety level may be so high that whatever happens cannot dispel (or even reduce) the fear the patient feels at the prospect of being in the same room as a spider. Such a patient is not making a cognitive error in experiencing such fears. It is rather the case that how things seem to him cannot be influenced by his reason or experience in the way the therapist (and he) may hope.

Summary:

1. It seems that one can account for the successes and failures of certain types of therapy by distinguishing sharply between experience and belief. Some emotional conditions, such a panic, are more responsive to cognitive (or cognitive behavioural) methods than to purely behavioural ones because they involve an essential cognitive component. Other experience based emotions, like fear of spiders, are not. Here, experience (as we characterized it in Section 6) appears to play a major role.

2. It is a merit of the proposal that it explains why cognitive-behavioural and behavioural therapies work equally well in the

treatment of spider phobics, and why both are preferable to purely cognitive means. It also explains why none of these methods work in certain types of case. There does not seem to be one model which applies to all emotions and emotional disorders.[32]

3. The present proposal suggests a modification in the aim of therapy. Confronted with a spider-phobic, and armed with this account of the relevant emotion, the therapist should proceed as follows:

> [T] 'You know is that this object is not dangerous, but you still believe that you will experience it as frightening/ terrifying, even though you do not think that you should do. Now, I see how you feel about things, and can easily imagine what it is like to have these fears. Perhaps one route is try out the experience again using distancing techniques, or attending especially to certain features of the spider (eg: how small it is....) Also, we can employ simulation techniques to recreate the experience in advance and try to develop techniques for dealing with it. Patients often find that their initially high levels of anxiety are reduced through repeated exposure.'

The aim of this therapist is not to lead the patient to test a hypothesis about what is harmful or about what will happen in a given situation nor to generate an alternative general 'hot' schema. Her target is rather to enable her patient to experience the phenomenon in a less anxiety-involving way. If she can bring him not to see an object as threatening or nauseating, nothing more needs to happen to change his emotional reaction to it. In this account, conscious experience plays a crucial role in successful therapy. What is sought is a way of changing the patient's experiences of (and reactions to) objects and situations.

8. Emotion and action

The view just presented has (I believe) important consequences for our understanding of action explanation. I shall conclude by out-lining some of these, although (as I readily acknowledge) much more needs to be done to secure the points at issue.

One motivation for the Stoic view was that it offered a way of representing the agent's action as reasonable: the agent has considerations which she sees as favouring her acting as she does,

[32] There are significant differences between phobia and mood disorders (such as depression) which need to be investigated further.

David Charles

considerations which make her so acting justified by her own lights. These considerations are encapsulated in the valuational beliefs and desires which together provide reasons for their action.

However, the Stoic account of the emotions seems flawed. In the case of intentional actions motivated by fear, the agent need not see her attempts to avoid the object as justified in this way. Standardly, she will lack the valuational belief (eg) A is harmful (or bad *qua* harmful) that (in the Stoic account) rationalizes her desire and subsequent action. She might even say 'there is no justification at all for my acting in this way. I just have these fears of spiders, fears which I can see are not justified by how things really are (or by how my experience turns out to be). Given that (as I can see) my fears are unjustified, the action that follows from my fears is also unjustified.' She can act without the proposed valuational belief.

An alternative to the Stoic view of action on emotion runs as follows: the fear in question generates a desire to avoid the object and this together with the belief about how to do so leads to (and rationalizes) her avoiding it.[33] From this perspective, the agent has at least this to say in favour of her action: it was what I wanted to do. In the case of the spider-phobic, the desire to avoid the object may arise without a good reason to support it. However, given that it is present, the agent still has something to say in favour of her action. If she looks solely at her desire to avoid the spider (and lays aside issues of how well founded that desire is), she still has a reason to offer to answer the question 'Why did you do that?' This may be all that is required for the 'anaemic sense of justification' required to rationalize the action in question.[34] The agent in

[33] For a view of this type of the role of claustrophobia, see Donald Davidson, *Essays on Actions and Events*, Oxford 1980, p. 7. Davidson appears to see emotions as inputs to (or sources of) pro (or con) attitudes not as instances of such attitudes (note their absence from his list of such attitudes: *ibid* p. 4.) One motivation for this view may be that emotions are primarily object-related (fear is of (eg) enclosed spaces, jealousy is of one's rival...) while Davidson's attitudes are directed to actions of a certain type (*ibid*. p.4)

[34] Rosalind Hursthouse. (*J. Phil* 1991, pp. 57–9) attempted to refute this aspect of Davidson's account by analysing a dramatic example in which Jane so hates Joan that, when she sees Joan's photograph, she tears at it with her nails in an attempt to gouge out Joan's eyes. Hursthouse plausibly notes that Jane's action is not to be explained by saying that she wanted to tear out Joan's eyes and believed that damaging the picture was the (or a) way to achieve this goal, and concludes that there is no Davidsonian desire-belief pair which can be invoked in explaining her action. But Davidson's own remarks (op. cit. p. 7) suggest a different model in which

question has no justification beyond the fact that she wants to avoid the object which looks frightening to her. But, it will be suggested, this is justification enough. While her reason is not as good as the one offered in the Stoic view, she still has a reason for her action.

In this influential account, how the object seems (or looks) to the agent gives her a desire to act in a given way. The presence of the latter is what provides her with a minimal justification for her action. On this view, the desire is a self-standing entity. Perhaps she should not have this desire, but given that she does it provides some justification for her action. Its justificatory role is not completely undermined by its questionable antecedents. She can focus on the fact that she wants to avoid the spider, and cite this fact as a *prima facie* reason for her action (even if it is rationally outweighed by other more powerful considerations against avoiding it). In this account, emotions (or emotional experiences) are understood as causes of the desires which (together with beliefs about how to avoid the object) rationalize the relevant action.

One part of this suggestion is at odds with the account of fear sketched above. For, if that is defensible, to experience something as frightening essentially involves being disposed to react to it: eg to be repelled by it. There is no need to postulate a further desire over and above the emotion to account for the resulting action. The experience of the object as frightening or repulsive is enough (together with one's beliefs about how to avoid it)[35] to make that

---

[35] Is there always a belief of this type present? In some simple actions (such as moving or turning away from the threatening object), there may be a direct connection between the experience and our sensorimotor responses, unmediated by the presence of a further belief about how to achieve one's goal. In Davidson's account of intentional action, one requires beliefs to connect a generalized pro-attitude (eg: to avoid this spider) to the specific action to be undertaken (moving away in a given fashion from it right now) But this requirement seems to result from insisting on the presence of a generalized pro-attitude in the explanation of all intentional action. If one begins one's account with a specific experience of this object as frightening now, there seems less reason to invoke a further belief to account for one's attempts to avoid it: one just moves away from it. (This issue requires further discussion.)

Jane's anger makes her want to destroy Joan's picture and she believes that ripping it up is a (or the) way to do this. After the episode, Jane can (according to Davidson) say this: I did what I wanted to do (however irrational the source of my want may have been). Successfully to pursue Hursthouse's goal one needs to challenge the role Davidson assigns to the emotions as causal sources of desire.

David Charles

action intelligible. The spider-phobic saw the spider as repulsive, realized that leaving the room was the best thing to do to get away from it and so left the room. Her 'con-attitude' to the spider was not a separate state generated by her fear, but an essential part of what it was for her to be frightened of it.[36]

In many standard explanations of intentional action, the experience of objects is sharply distinguished from the attitudes (pro and con) which lead to action. Experiences register how things are; pro-attitudes aim to change the world in a certain ways. On these accounts, experiences may (with other factors) produce separate pro (or con) attitudes, and need to do so if they are to lead to action. However, if the picture proposed here is correct, the experience of something as frightening cannot be decomposed into two separate phenomena: an experience of the object as being a certain way and a separate pro-attitude towards actions of the avoidance type. For one cannot, I have suggested, characterize the relevant experience as of a frightening object without referring to the fact that the experiencer is repelled by it. Indeed, part of what it is to experience something as frightening is to be affected in this way. There is no need for a separate con-attitude to the spider (still less one to being in the presence of the spider) to account for the resulting action.

Why invoke a separate factor, desire, to account for the actions in question? Sometimes fear leads us to escape, sometimes it does not. Surely, there must be a further state present to explain what happens when fear leads to action? It is natural to suggest that there must be a separate desire to escape present in those cases where fear leads to action. But this line of thought is not conclusive. Experiencing the spider as repulsive may by itself lead to action unless something intervenes (eg: the presence of a contrary reason, 'mental paralysis' induced by the presence of the fear. ...). If so, what explains why action sometimes but not always results from emotion may be the presence (or absence) of countervailing factors of this type. There is no need to introduce a further state, e.g.desire for flight, to account for the cases where the emotion leads to action. In the absence of countervailing factors, the fact that she is repelled by the spider seems enough (perhaps when combined with a belief about how best to avoid the repulsive object) to account for her action. If so, the desire-belief model of action explanation is not required for all intentional action.

[36] This con-attitude to the spider (being repelled by it) should not be confused with a desire to escape it (or its presence). For one can be repelled by something but be so overawed as to have lost one's desire for flight!

134

If this account is correct, is there anything capable of providing 'from the agent's point of view ... something to be said for the action'? The agent can, of course, answer the question: 'Why did you do that?' by pointing to the fact that the spider seemed frightening to her. But while this makes her action readily intelligible, it is less clear that it justifies her in acting as she does. In the case of the Müller-Lyer lines, the fact that they look unequal does not provide one who understands his situation with any reason at all (by his own lights) to believe that the lines are unequal. By analogy, how the spider seems should not provide the spider-phobic (if she understands her situation) with any reason at all (by her own lights) to avoid it. In both cases the possible rational grounds for acting (or believing) are undermined by their understanding of their situation. The consideration cited can no longer provide any evidence (or justification) for their belief (action). It is not that these considerations are outweighed (or counterbalanced) by other factors. It is rather that, quite literally, for the subject such considerations no longer count as justifying reasons at all.[37]

If this sketch proves defensible, some intentional actions will be intelligible to us (as to the agent) without their being justified or rationally explainable by our lights (or her's). Our sympathetic understanding of her actions will not be a species of rational explanation.[38] In some cases, however, we appear to understand why an agent acts on how he experiences things as being, without regarding his action as rationally explainable. If so, we may be able sympathetically to understand why an acratic agent acts as he does, even though his action is not (even by his lights) *prima facie* a reasonable thing to do. Some cases of acratic action may be intentional but not action on a reason (since the agent may have nothing to say in

[37] One might say that, in this situation, such considerations are 'silenced' as reasons. For this terminology, put to different use, see John McDowell's 'Are Moral Requirements Really Hypothetical?' *P.A.S.S.* vol. 52, 1978, pp. 13–29.

[38] This comment, if correct, offers a way of undermining the first premiss in an argument sometimes used to call into question the possibility of *acrasia*. The argument, as developed by Davidson in 'The Paradoxes of Irrationality' (*Philosophical Essays on Freud*, Cambridge 1982, ed. J. Hopkins and R.Wollheim, pp.289-305) runs as follows:

[1] Intentional action is action on reason (Premiss) .
[2] If intentional action is action on a reason, it is rationally explainable (from 1).
[3] If action is rationally explainable, it is rational (from 2).
[4] *Acratic* action is irrational but intentional action (Premiss).

justification of what he does). For while such actions may be intentional (because they arise from how things seem to her), they are not ones which are justified (in even the most anaemic sense) from her own point of view. The agent just finds herself acting on fears, some of which she may see as baseless or even counterproductive![39]

Study of the emotions and of actions expressive of emotion rightly calls into question paradigms that have been for too long part of conventional philosophical and psychological wisdom. There is still need for systematic study of this area.[40]

---

[39] David Velleman ('What Happens When Someone Acts?' in his *The Possibility of Practical Reason*, Oxford 2000, pp. 126ff) focuses on actions motivated by certain emotions and criticizes the standard (Davidsonian) model for not separating these adequately from actions in which the agent is genuinely involved, in which he acts on 'a desire of his own'. While Velleman is right (in my view) to distinguish between these two classes of action, it remains unclear why the agent fails to be involved in his emotion-based actions or why these motivations are not 'his own.' The alternative, sketched briefly here, is to separate those actions which the agent sees as justified from those which he does not. While the latter may be intelligible to him ('I get angry easily'), they are not rationalized by his lights.

[40] I was assisted in writing this essay by helpful questions and criticisms from several participants at the Oxford Conference on The Philosophy of Action (September 2002) and at a subsequent Helsinki workshop on the emotions. I am indebted to them and to John Campbell, Jennifer Hornsby and especially Adrian Cussins for their subsequent comments. My greatest debt is to Zafra Cooper for many discussions of the relevant psychological and philosophical issues and for her continuing dissatisfaction with my attempts to address them.

Kantian Autonomy

TERENCE IRWIN

1. The role of autonomy

Kant takes autonomy to be recognizably valuable. In claiming that non-Kantian views of morality treat the morally good will as heteronomous, he intends to present an objection to these views. He expects proponents of these views to recognize that the implication of heteronomy is a serious objection; his task is not to convince them that heteronomy is bad, but to convince them that their views imply heteronomy.

If this is the right way to understand the dialectical role of Kant's claims about autonomy and heteronomy, we need to be convinced that his concept of autonomy is a concept of something that we can recognize as valuable even if we have not already accepted Kantian moral theory as a whole. We ought to be able to grasp this concept, and see why autonomy is good, without having already been convinced that, for instance, the autonomous will cannot be determined by any temporally prior events or states. We discover that the autonomous will is noumenal, once we combine our previous grasp of autonomy with Kantian metaphysics; but we must have this previous grasp if Kant's argument is to begin in the right place.

According to Kant, 'autonomy of the will (Wille) is that property of it, by which it is to itself (independently of any property of objects of volition) a law' (*Grundlegung* 440). Heteronomy results if the will 'goes outside itself and seeks the law in the property of any of its objects' (441). In this case 'the will does not give itself the law, but the object through its relation to the will gives the law to it'. He takes autonomy to be a central element in freedom. If the will is heteronomous, we are not free; and so if a conception of the good will involves heteronomy, it is thereby open to serious objection. We ought to be able to see that we are free only if we follow a law that is the will's own law, and that a will meets this condition only if it satisfies the further conditions that Kant imposes on autonomy.

In taking autonomy to be essential for some kind of free agency, Kant relies on his rather complex view of freedom. The freedom that consists in autonomy is 'positive' freedom; agents who lack this positive freedom still have 'negative' freedom.[1] We are positively free in so far as we are determined by the legislation of the rational will (*MdS* 225).[2] Negatively free agents who act heteronomously are not compelled to accept maxims that come from some other source than the will itself; even when they accept these maxims, their will has the capacity to give itself the law. Hence, our permanent negative freedom is a permanent capacity for autonomy.[3] The difference between heteronomy and autonomy does not consist in the difference between compulsion and free acceptance, but in the source of the principles that we freely accept. We become evil not by being overcome by an evil principle, but by freely incorporating such a principle in our maxim.[4]

Does Kant rely on conditions for autonomy that his opponents can be expected to accept? And does he show that their theories deny autonomy to the good will? In his view, non-Kantian accounts of moral principles imply heteronomy 'because the will does not give itself the law but only directions for a reasonable obedience to pathological law' (*KpV* 33). How many conceptions of morality are open to the objection that they prevent the will from giving itself the law?

[1] 'The freedom of the Willkür is this independence from sensuous impulse in the determination of the Willkür. This is the negative concept of freedom. The positive concept of freedom is that of the power of pure reason to be of itself practical. But pure reason can be practical only if the maxim of every action is subjected to the condition that it qualifies as a universal law.' (*MdS* 213-14)

[2] Hereafter I will use 'will' or 'rational will' to indicate Wille, and 'choice' or 'elective will' for Willkür. Kant also introduces a negative and a positive conception of freedom at *G* 446. But here these seem to be two ways of conceiving the same condition, rather than two distinct conditions; at least Kant does not insist on their distinctness as sharply as he needs to.

[3] I am assuming some controversial points that need further discussion. In particular, I assume that it is possible for a rational will (Wille) to be heteronomous, by failing to give itself for the law; in these cases the matter of volition is a determining ground of the Wille. See *KpV* 36, 39, 41. I doubt whether this view can be reconciled with *Groundwork*, ch. 3, but I take it to be the most plausible account of Kant's position in *KpV* and *MdS*. On this point, I generally agree with the position of Henry Allison, *Kant's Theory of Freedom* (Cambridge: CUP, 1990), 94–106.

[4] ... freedom of choice is of a wholly unique nature in that an incentive can determine choice to an action only so far as the individual has incorporated it into his maxim (has made it the general rule in accordance with which he will conduct himself); only thus can an incentive, whatever it may be, co-exist with the absolute spontaneity of choice (i.e. freedom). (*Religion*, 23f)

2. Aspects and degrees of autonomy

Kant's claims about autonomy catch our attention because we agree with him in recognizing autonomy as something worth having. We also agree with him in connecting autonomy with freedom in three different areas: freedom of the will, freedom of action, and political and social freedom. It does not follow that we mean the same as Kant means in speaking of autonomy in these different areas. But it will be helpful to recall some familiar aspects of our views on freedom and autonomy, to see that they both clarify Kant's claims and raise useful questions about them.

Freedom and autonomy, understood as giving oneself the law on which one acts, might be taken to come in degrees:

1. *Acting on our desires.* Minimally, we give ourselves the principle of our action when our action results from our representing some desirable feature to ourselves. Free agents, on this test, are all those whose actions are caused in the usual way by their own appearance of something preferred.

2. *Acting on our higher-order desires.* This minimal test captures the agency of all conscious animals, together with young children, incontinent, and wanton agents. But we think they lack some kind of freedom. Agents in whom the law comes from themselves, and not just from their impulses, have selves distinct from their impulses. Hence freedom requires action to come from ourselves giving the law. Hence it requires action from whatever aspect of us is properly identified with ourselves. We might explain this demand by identifying the free agent with the agent acting on higher-order desires endorsing lower-order desires.

3. *Acting on our rational evaluations.* This way of capturing freedom, however, does not explain how we ourselves act. If the desires directed to desires are simply desires of the same sort as the desires of the wanton, it is not clear why they should be more strongly identified with the self. Perhaps, then, we ourselves determine our actions by acting on our rational evaluations. The outlook of the self does not consist simply in higher-order desires, but in the rational evaluative outlook on the basis of which one considers the merits of actions and the appropriateness of satisfying desires. This outlook generates higher-order desires, but the presence of such desires is not its essential feature.

4. *Acting on our own reasoned principles.* But we may still doubt whether agents acting on their rational evaluative outlook are autonomous, if we consider how the outlook has been formed and is

maintained. Agents who act on outlooks that are in fact rational, but who neither have exercised nor can exercise their rational capacities in forming, modifying, or sustaining this outlook, seem to lack some element of autonomy. They do not seem to give themselves the law, but simply to take it over from somewhere else. They are autonomous only if the principles of their action come from their own reason. Agents might satisfy this condition if they recognize certain principles as the correct ones to act on, understand why they are correct, and act on that understanding. In this respect we might think autonomy is exercised in the first-hand understanding and application of (for instance) a scientific theory.

5. *Acting on principles we have made*. But perhaps even these agents are not autonomous. The law they act on is not their own; for if it is objectively correct, they do not create it, but it comes from somewhere else. Autonomy requires acting on principles that one has created or constructed for oneself.

We might regard these conditions as marks of a property that comes in degrees, so that the more of these conditions we satisfy, the more autonomous we are. Perhaps the first three conditions mark degrees of free agency, whereas the last two mark not only degrees of freedom, but degrees of autonomy. But I do not want to insist on this distinction. I have arranged these five conditions in this sequence to suggest that discussion of freedom naturally leads to discussion of autonomy.

3. Kant's interest in these aspects of autonomy

I have just collected these aspects of autonomy from common conceptions. If we compare Kant's claims about autonomy with the features I have mentioned, do we find any connexions?

Kant believes that the development of autonomy involves making up one's own mind about what to believe and how to act. He explains the title of the First Critique by connecting it with the demands of contemporary society and contemporary thought for thorough criticism through 'free and public examination' by reason.[5] The demand for the free and public use of reason expresses the attitude

---

[5] 'Our age is the genuine age of criticism, to which everything must submit. Religion through its holiness and legislation through its majesty commonly seek to exempt themselves from it. But in this way they excite a just suspicion against themselves, and cannot lay claim to that unfeigned respect that reason grants only to that which has been able to withstand its free and public examination.' (*KrV* Axi)

that Kant calls 'enlightenment'. In his essay 'What is Enlightenment?' he argues that enlightenment requires freeing oneself from the 'minority' and 'immaturity' that is 'inability to make use of one's own understanding without direction from another' (Ak. viii 35).[6] It requires independent thinkers who 'will disseminate the spirit of a rational valuing of one's own worth and of the calling of each individual to think for himself' (Ak viii 36).

If the result of the free and public use of reason is our acceptance of a principle that we have examined, we may claim to be autonomous in relation to that principle. We have not simply accepted it on authority; we have also come to accept it for reasons of our own. Hence we ourselves give the law, since we do not simply take over a law given by someone else. And we give our own law, since it is a law that we accept for our own reasons, not because we go along with someone else.

This conception of autonomy may arouse suspicion. The fact that we can find it in Kant's essay on enlightenment may itself lead us to suspect that it is part of a questionable 'Enlightenment' outlook. Is it always important or desirable to refuse to take over a law from someone else? Ought we to reject every sort of authority external to ourselves, so that we never accept anything for which we have not weighed the evidence ourselves?

One might understand the demand for individual judgment so that it leads to anarchism. This is how Godwin understands it, arguing that one's own individual conviction is the only legitimate basis for any action.[7] Application of this anarchist standard would leave us believing very little, since our capacity to weigh evidence is very limited in relation to the number of things we tend to believe. We have to rely on testimony and authority for many of our beliefs.

If reliance on testimony and authority conflicts with autonomy, autonomy is not a reasonable aim in all areas of belief, and we have to identify the areas to which it applies. But if reliance on testimony allows autonomy, autonomy cannot require completely first-hand assessment of everything we believe.

This second way of conceiving autonomy is preferable. For even

---

[6] See *Practical Philosophy* (ed. Gregor), 17.

[7] 'If a man be in some cases obliged to prefer his own judgment, he is in all cases obliged to consult that judgment, before he can determine whether the matter in question be of the sort provided for or no. So that from this reasoning it ultimately appears, that the conviction of a man's individual understanding is the only legitimate principle imposing on him the duty of adopting any species of conduct.' (Godwin, *Enquiry concerning Political Justice*, ii 6 (ed. Priestley, 181).)

in cases where we inevitably rely on authority, we can distinguish mere acceptance from critical first-hand assessment. Minimally, this means that we have some basis for distinguishing the area within which we have to accept the word of an authoritative expert from the area in which we may legitimately doubt. Scientific claims about the alleged links between race, heredity, intelligence, and criminality offer obvious illustrations of this point.

We need not, then, interpret Kant's demand for enlightenment as an expression of an extreme demand for a completely first-hand outlook that completely abandons reliance on authority. Whether or not the demand for such an outlook is even coherent, it does not follow from the demand for criticism and reflexion through the public use of reason.

With this explanation understood, we may take Kant to endorse Rousseau's claim that only self-legislation guarantees freedom.[8] But what does self-legislation involve? Does it require only the fourth condition I mentioned or also the fifth? Can we be autonomous in accepting principles that are true independently of our acceptance of them, or must the principles also be the product of our own will?

The demand for autonomy does not apply only to practical in contrast to theoretical beliefs. As I suggested in referring to Kant on enlightenment, the demand may be applied to one's beliefs in general. But to ask how far autonomy ought to go, or what is needed for genuine autonomy, does not seem sensible independently of reflexion on a given subject-matter. If the sort of critical and first-hand outlook I have roughly described is appropriate both in a physicist and in an artist, it still does not seem reasonable to expect the very same attitude in both. While we expect some first-hand critical understanding from physicists, we do not expect them to abandon all the theories recognized as most plausible and to begin again from views they have thought out entirely for themselves. It is not so obviously inappropriate to admire an artist who makes this sort of fresh start, or to say that such an artist represents an ideal of artistic freedom.

These views about autonomy in different areas remind us that we cannot fix the appropriate conception of freedom and autonomy in a moral agent without also considering the character of morality. Even though the fifth condition I mentioned may be regarded, from

---

[8] L. W. Beck, *Commentary on Kant's Critique of Practical Reason* (University of Chicago Press, 1960), 200 cites Rousseau, *Social Contract*, i 8: '... moral freedom, which alone makes a person truly master of himself. For the impulse of appetite alone is slavery, and obedience to the law that one has prescribed to oneself is freedom.'

some points of view, as a higher degree of autonomy than the fourth condition, it is not necessarily the sort of autonomy that is appropriate to morality.

If, then, we want to investigate what Kant means in speaking of the will giving itself the moral law, we should not investigate this question independently of his views about the status of morality. Nor should we simply assume that his views on autonomy ought to determine his views about the status of morality. If Kant believes this is the right direction of argument, his belief is open to question.

4. Autonomy and Kantian constructivism

These questions allow me to introduce an account of Kantian autonomy that I want to examine and eventually to reject. This account attributes a constructivist position to Kant. Rawls takes Kant to be committed to constructivism primarily because of the demands of autonomy, as Kant conceives it.[9]

To fix the relevant aspect of constructivism, it is useful to distinguish two doctrines: (1) We might hold a constructivist account of method in moral theory, arguing that we will reach morally correct results by following a certain procedure. Rawls ascribes this method to Kant in speaking of 'the Categorical Imperative procedure'. (2) We might hold a constructivist metaphysical doctrine, claiming that moral truth is constituted by a certain constructive procedure whose correctness does not depend on its reaching true results.

A constructivist method does not obviously imply a constructivist metaphysical doctrine; hence the mere fact that Kant's method may be described as a 'Categorical Imperative procedure' does not make him a metaphysical constructivist. Metaphysical constructivism is the position that Rawls has in mind in claiming that autonomy requires constructivism.[10] As Rawls understands Kant, autonomy precludes the recognition of any objective moral truths

[9] It is convenient to call this position 'Kantian constructivism'. To be more precise, I have in mind the moral constructivism that Rawls ascribes to Kant at *Political Liberalism* (NY: Columbia UP, 1993), 99–101. This is distinct from the political constructivism that Rawls defends.

[10] In discussing Kantian constructivism as Rawls understands it, I am not taking a position on other views that have been called 'constructivism' and are inspired by Kant. One such view is described by Onora O'Neill, *Constructions of Reason* (Cambridge: CUP, 1989), 188n: 'I use the term [sc. 'constructivist'] to cover approaches that seek to justify ethical principles by reference to an account of agency and rationality, without relying on claims about desires or preferences.' It is not clear, without further

independent of how rational agents view themselves.[11] Moral principles depend on what Rawls calls 'our conception of ourselves as
reasonable and rational persons'. They depend on our activity of
conceiving ourselves this way; they do not depend on the fact that
we are reasonable and rational persons.[12] Moral principles are

[11] 'Yet in Kant's moral constructivism it suffices for heteronomy that first
principles obtain in virtue of relations among objects the nature of which is
not affected or determined by our conception of ourselves as reasonable and
rational persons (as possessing the powers of practical reason), and of the
public role of moral principles in a society of such persons. Of particular
importance is the conception of persons as reasonable and rational, and,
therefore, as free and equal, and the basic units of agency and responsibility. Kant's idea of autonomy implies that there exists no moral order prior to
and independent of these conceptions that is to determine the form of the
procedure that specifies the content of first principles of right and justice
among free and equal persons. Heteronomy obtains not only when these first
principles are fixed by the special psychological constitution of human
nature, as in Hume, but also when they are fixed by an order of universals,
or of moral values grasped by rational intuition, as in Plato's realm of forms
or in Leibniz's hierarchy of perfections'. (Rawls, 'Themes in Kant's moral
philosophy', in *Collected Papers*, ed. S. Freeman [Cambridge, Mass.:
Harvard UP, 1999], 512.) A similar statement appears in 'Kantian constructivism', in *Papers* 345, and in *Lectures on the History of Moral Philosophy*
(Cambridge, Mass.: Harvard UP, 2000), 236. It is clarified at *Lectures* 72, 229.

[12] Further comments by Rawls clarify his view: 'In contrast with rational
intuitionism, constitutive autonomy says that the so-called independent
order of values does not constitute itself but is constituted by the activity,
actual or ideal, of practical (human) reason itself. I believe this, or something like it, is Kant's view.' (*Political Liberalism*, 99.) 'Rational
intuitionism says: the procedure is correct because following it correctly
usually gives the correct (independently given) result. Constructivism
says: the result is correct because it issues from the correct reasonable and
rational procedure correctly followed.' (*Lectures* 242.)

argument, whether a 'constructivist' in this sense must be a metaphysical
constructivist (in the sense that excludes moral realism). Similarly, Hill,
Dignity and Practical Reason (Ithaca: Cornell UP, 1992), 231, has a doctrine
of method in mind. He identifies Kantian constructivism with Rawls's use
of the original position: 'The choosers are not seen as seeking to *discover* a
moral order, Platonic, natural, or divine, which exists independently of
their reasoned choices; rather, we are to view principles as justifiable by
virtue of their being what persons with the specified values would choose
in the defined situation.' This is a description of a constructivist method,
without any explicit commitment to a constructivist metaphysics; one
might agree with Hill that the people in the original position are not
conceived as metaphysical realists about morality, while still maintaining
that this constructive method is correct because it matches moral truths.

correct because they are the product of the appropriate procedure of practical reasoning; the procedure is not correct because it achieves some specific conclusion. This argument from autonomy to metaphysical constructivism is the one I want to discuss.[13]

The ascription of constructivism to Kant partly depends on Rawls's presentation of two other positions: (a) The sentimentalist position of Hume, which makes morality depend on the specific sentiments of human beings. (b) The perfectionism and rational intuitionism of Plato, Leibniz, and Clarke. If these are the only other options besides constructivism, Kant is committed to constructivism; for he takes both of these positions to exclude autonomy. But are these in fact the only non-constructivist options, and does Kant think so?

Rawls's constructivist interpretation may appear plausible in any case, whether or not these are the only non-constructivist options. Kant's discussions of autonomy often refer to the internal connexion between the rational will and the moral law. Heteronomous views go 'outside' the rational will to an object, so that the rational will does not give its own law to itself. We might suppose that these remarks about the internal law imply that Kant takes the fourth condition I mentioned to fall short of moral autonomy. If I rely on my own first-hand rational understanding of a theory whose truth is independent of my rational understanding, do I not take the law from 'outside' my understanding? If autonomous agents cannot take the law of their actions from 'outside' their practical reason, does this not exclude dependence on objective facts?

We might, therefore take Kant's remarks about internality and about the will giving itself the law to exclude any objectivist account of the law. Autonomy, on this view, requires the agent to be the author, not merely the recipient, of the law.[14] Hence the truth of the

---

[13] The argument from autonomy is not the only argument for taking Kant to be a constructivist. Hence, even if I am right about this argument, it does not follow that Kant is not a constructivist about morality. But it will be reasonable to re-examine other arguments for taking him to be a constructivist.

[14] See J. B. Schneewind, 'Autonomy, obligation, and virtue', in *Cambridge Companion to Kant*, ed. P. Guyer (Cambridge: CUP, 1992), ch. 10, at 316: 'Suppose that a kind of state of affairs is intrinsically good because of the nature of that state of affairs. Then the goodness occurs independently of the will of any finite moral agent, and if she must will to pursue it, she is not self-legislating. Suppose the goodness of states of affairs comes from some standard. Then the standard is either the outcome of someone's will—say God's—or it is self-subsistent and eternal. In either case conformity to it is not autonomy. Conformity would be what

law cannot be independent of the activity by which the rational will gives itself the law.

This argument from the internal relation between the will and the moral law to the falsity of objectivism about the moral law seems to me neither a sound argument nor a Kantian argument.[15] I will therefore need to explain how Kant's claims about how the moral law is internal to the will do not exclude the independence of the law from the activity of rational willing.

5. Laws v. imperatives

The argument from autonomy to constructivism rests on claims about the relation between the rational will and the moral law. It is useful to examine these claims by recalling some of Kant's views about different possible relations between a rational will and a law. He distinguishes a 'holy' will, a will necessarily determined by practical reason, from our imperfect will. He relies on this division in contrasting practical laws with categorical imperatives. Practical laws reveal practical necessities, but they are not necessarily imperatives. They are imperatives, and introduce an 'ought', only in finite rational agents whose practical reason does not necessarily determine the will.[16] A holy will does not conceive the practical law as an imperative, or as prescribing a duty.

[15] I use 'objectivist' to refer to the view that Rawls rejects on Kant's behalf. 'Realist' is often used in the same sense. Rawls notes (*Lectures*, 243–7) that the constructivism he ascribes to Kant also allows a conception of objectivity.

[16] 'In natural science the principles of what occurs ... are at the same time laws of nature, for there the use of reason is theoretical and determined by the constitution of the object. In practical philosophy, which has to do only with the grounds of determination of the will, the principles

---

Kant calls heteronomy.' At 315 Schneewind seems to impose less extreme anti-objectivist conditions for self-legislation.

In 'The use of autonomy in ethical theory' (in *Reconstructing Individualism*, T. C. Heller, M. Sosna, and D. E. Wellbery (eds.) [Stanford: Stanford UP, 1986], 64–75.), 66, Schneewind contrasts Kant with Butler: 'The defining feature of an autonomous agent, in Kant's view, is its ability to guide its own action by the choice of a will that is such that whatever it wills is good simply because it is willed by it. The point is not that the autonomous will unerringly hones in on what is independently and antecedently good, as Butler's conscience does. The point is rather that when something is chosen or pursued by such a will, that very fact makes the object of the will good. An agent so guided is not led by anything outside himself.' Schneewind goes on to compare and contrast Kant with Pufendorf.

Imperatives and duty, therefore, belong only to wills that have other motives besides those that automatically conform to practical reason.[17] Kant's discussion of the formulae of the Categorical

take place according to the rule.' (*KpV* 19f)

[17] 'If reason infallibly determines the will, then the actions of such a being which are recognized as objectively necessary are subjectively necessary also, i.e., the will is a faculty to choose that only which reason independent of inclination recognizes as practically necessary, i.e., as good. But if reason of itself does not sufficiently determine the will, if the latter is subject also to subjective conditions (particular incentives) which do not always coincide with the objective conditions; in a word, if the will does not *in itself* completely accord with reason (which is actually the case with human beings), then the actions which objectively are recognized as necessary are subjectively contingent, and the determination of such a will according to objective laws is obligation, that is to say, the relation of the objective laws to a will that is not thoroughly good is conceived as the determination of the will of a rational being by principles of reason but which the will from its nature does not of necessity follow. The conception of an objective principle, in so far as it is obligatory for a will, is called a command (of reason), and the formula of the command is called an imperative. All imperatives are expressed by an *ought*, and thereby indicate the relation of an objective law of reason to a will that from its subjective constitution is not necessarily determined by it (an obligation). They say that something would be good to do or to forbear, but they say it to a will which does not always do a thing because it is conceived to be good to do it.' (*G* 412f) 'Now this principle of morality, ... includes the Infinite Being as the supreme intelligence. [In finite beings], ...the moral law is an imperative that commands categorically, because the law is unconditioned; the relation of such a will to this law is dependence under the name of obligation, which signifies a necessitation to an action, though only by reason and its objective law; and this action is called duty, because a choice subject to pathological affections (though not determined by them, and, therefore, still free), implies a wish that arises from subjective causes and therefore may often be opposed to the pure objective determining principle; whence it requires the moral necessitation of a resistance of the practical reason, which may be called an internal but intellectual, constraint. In the supreme intelligence choice (Willkür) is rightly conceived as incapable of any maxim which could not at the same time be objectively a law; and the notion of holiness, which on that account belongs to it, places it, not

that one makes for oneself are not yet laws by which one is inexorably bound, because reason, in practice, has to do with a subject and especially with its faculty of desire, the special character of which may occasion variety in the rule ... This rule, ... is an imperative for a being whose reason is not the sole determinant of the will. It is a rule characterized by 'ought', which expresses the objective necessitation of the act and indicates that, if reason completely determined the will, the action would without exception

Imperative is really about the supreme practical law, which is an imperative only in finite rational agents.

Kant's division between practical laws and imperatives defines his position in a long dispute about the character of natural law and its relation to morality. Naturalists and voluntarists disagree about the relation of moral rightness to laws, obligations, and commands. Their different views mark disagreements about the possibility of 'intrinsic' morality—rightness and wrongness that follows from the existence of human beings in the world, without reference to any further choice, will, command, or legislation.

Some of the relevant differences are these: (1) One naturalist view, held probably by Aquinas and certainly by Vasquez, takes rightness to imply law and obligation, but not to imply commands. Hence it recognizes intrinsic moral rightness, and takes it to imply natural law. (2) A voluntarist view, held by Pufendorf, takes moral rightness to imply law, obligation, and commands. Hence it denies intrinsic moral rightness. (3) The intermediate position of Suarez separates moral rightness and duty (debitum) from law, obligation, and commands. Hence it recognizes intrinsic moral rightness without natural law.[18]

[18] The use of 'without' over-simplifies Suarez's position. A few passages indicating Suarez's position: 'This will of God, prohibition or prescription, is not the whole character of the goodness and badness that is present in the observance or transgression of natural law, but it assumes in the actions themselves some necessary rightness or wrongness, and joins to indeed above all practical laws, but above all practically restrictive laws, and consequently above obligation and duty. This holiness of will is, however, a practical idea, which must necessarily serve as a type to which finite rational beings can only approximate indefinitely, and which the pure moral law, which is itself on this account called holy, constantly and rightly holds before their eyes.' (*KpV* 32–4) 'That will whose maxims are necessarily in accord with the laws of autonomy is a holy, or absolutely good, will. The dependence upon the principle of autonomy of a will that is not absolutely good (i.e., moral necessitation) is obligation, which cannot therefore be applied to a holy being. The objective necessity of an action from obligation is called duty.' (*G* 439) 'An imperative differs from a practical law in that a law indeed represents an action as necessary but takes no account of whether this action already inheres by an *inner* necessity in the acting subject (as in a holy being) or whether it is contingent (as in the human being); for where the former is the case there is no imperative. ... A categorical imperative, because it asserts an obligation with respect to certain actions, is a morally practical *law*. But since obligation involves not merely practical necessity (such as a law in general asserts) but also *necessitation*, a categorical imperative is a law that either commands or prohibits ...' (*MdS* 222f)

Kant does not agree verbally with any of these three positions. He agrees with voluntarists against naturalists in connecting the moral 'ought' with obligations and imperatives. But he agrees with naturalists in accepting moral rightness and law without imperatives. In substance, he is close to Suarez, despite the verbal differences; for he recognizes intrinsic rightness without any acts of commanding or obliging. Moral principles present intrinsic rightness apart from obligations and commands, as Suarez supposes, though, contrary to Suarez, they also present law. In Kant's view, commands and acts of binding are relevant to limited rational agents, who are also subject to other incentives and so have to be instructed and urged to follow the moral law. But commands and acts of binding are unnecessary for the existence of the moral law, which is the law for all rational wills, whether wholly rational or subject to non-rational impulses.

For some purposes it may not matter to distinguish features of holy wills from features of the wills of finite rational agents. But it matters for understanding autonomy. For Kant believes that a holy will is also autonomous, since its maxims are 'necessarily in accord with the laws of autonomy' (*G* 439). A will can therefore be guided autonomously by its own law without any imperative, obligation, or duty; for 'obligation contains not only practical necessity (which law in general asserts), but also constraint' (*MdS* 223), and a holy will observes a practical law without constraint. Hence imperatives, obligations, or duties are not needed for autonomy. Not surprisingly, Kant normally discusses agents for whom practical laws are imperatives, since all human agents belong to this class. But his claims about reasons and about moral goodness do not require the possibility of internal conflict that is the source of imperatives.

6. Is legislation necessary for autonomy?

Kant claims that we are autonomous only in so far as the will legislates for itself, or 'gives' itself the law.[19] In his discussion of the Categorical Imperative, he often speaks of rational agents giving

---

[19] '... this legislation of its own by pure and thus practical reason is freedom in the positive sense.' (*KpV* 33).

them a special obligation of divine law.' (*De Legibus*, ii 6.11) 'In this opinion, I take to be true the teaching that it assumes in its foundation about the intrinsic rightness or wrongness of actions, by which they fall under the natural law that forbids or prescribes ...' (ii 5.5). I hope to discuss Suarez's position more fully elsewhere.

themselves the law, and of being legislators in a kingdom of ends. But what is it to legislate for oneself?[20]

Kant clarifies his claim about legislation, by distinguishing the legislator from the author of a law.[21] A morally practical law contains a categorical imperative. The legislator is the author of the obligation in accordance with this law, but not necessarily the author of the law. We ought, therefore, to be able to understand Kant's claims about legislation for oneself by understanding the difference between the legislator (the author of the obligation) and the author of the law.

But before we can use Kant's distinction to clarify legislation for oneself, we must correct an error—or at least an over-simplification—in the discussion. The error lies in the assumption that a practical law contains a categorical imperative. This is an error because a holy will recognizes and follows a practical law without treating it as an imperative and without being obliged to follow it.

A holy will, therefore, follows the moral law without any legislation, since legislation introduces obligation. The moral law is an imperative only in relation to an imperfect will. In an imperfect will, a legislator commands and is the author of an obligation; but a holy will is not subject to commands or obligations. Since legislation imposes obligation, a holy will does not legislate for itself, because it does not impose obligation on itself.

We must therefore question Kant's account of autonomy as self-legislation. He seems to accept all of these mutually inconsistent claims:

1. A holy will is free and autonomous.
2. A holy will follows the moral law, without imperatives and obligation.

[20] Andrews Reath discusses many of the relevant issues helpfully in 'Legislating the moral law' *Nous* 28 (1994), 435-64, and in 'Legislating for a realm of ends', in Reath, A., Herman, B., and Korsgaard, C., eds., *Reclaiming the History of Ethics*. (Cambridge: CUP, 1997), 214–39. At some places he seems to suggest that one gives the law to oneself simply in so far as the law is the law of the will. See 'Legislating' 456: 'The fundamental law regulating moral deliberation is a principle derived from the nature of rational volition; it is thus the law which the rational will gives to itself.' In that case, the will need not choose what the content of the law will be.

[21] 'A law (a morally-practical one) is a proposition which contains a categorical imperative (a command). He who commands (imperans) through a law is the lawgiver (legislator). He is the author (auctor) of the obligation (Verbindlichkeit) in accordance with the law, but he is not always the author of the law. If he were so, the law would be positive (contingent) and arbitrary (willkürlich).' (*MdS* 227)

3. Legislation imposes obligation.
4. A holy will does not require legislation.
5. Autonomy consists in self-legislation.

Though Kant distinguishes holy wills from the imperfect wills of human beings, and therefore distinguishes practical laws from categorical imperatives, his discussion of autonomy does not observe these distinctions. Given his views about holy wills, he is wrong to claim that autonomy consists in self-legislation; for holy wills are autonomous without any legislation by themselves or for themselves.

To resolve this inconsistency in Kant's claims, we should (a) reject either the third or the fifth of these claims, or else (b) limit these claims to imperfect rational agents.[22] Different resolutions leave us with different questions to answer: (i) If autonomy is self-legislation, what sort of legislation does not impose obligation, contrary to Kant's official account? (ii) If autonomy does not require self-legislation, what does it require? (iii) If legislation and obligation are needed for autonomy only in imperfect rational agents, what does autonomy itself consist in?

7. The author of the law v. the author of the obligation

We have not yet examined everything that Kant says in this passage of *MdS* about laws and legislation. He notices that an act of legislation may include two elements: (1) Deciding what the content of the law is to be. (2) Making it the law. A particular legislator may be competent over both elements or only over the second. In the second case, the legislator is only authorized to accept or to reject proposed laws that the author of the law presents. The author of the law fixes its content; the legislator is the author of the obligation. If the legislator is also the author of the law, the law is positive and arbitrary.[23]

[22] These resolutions are preferable to those that would abandon the division between holy and imperfect wills; for Kant insists that the moral law is not only relevant to the distinctively human aspects of human rational wills. We would do serious damage to his whole position by abandoning this element in it. The preferable resolutions do not involve such serious damage.

[23] Rousseau draws a somewhat analogous contrast between the legislator (corresponding to Kant's 'author of the law') and the person or body who adopts the laws for a given state. See Rousseau, *Social Contract* ii 7. Cf. R. Grimsley's edition (Oxford: OUP, 1972), 30.

Terence Irwin

We saw earlier that Kant's distinction between law and imperative takes a position in disputes between naturalists and voluntarists about morality and natural law. These same disputes clarify his distinction between the author of the law and the author of the obligation. Voluntarists about natural law claim that God not only commands observance of the natural law, but also decides on the content of the law; in Kant's terms, God is both author of the obligation, as legislator, and author of the law itself. Naturalists argue that, though God commands observance of the natural law, God does not decide on its content; its content is fixed by intrinsic morality, independent of divine commands. In Kant's terms, naturalists claim that God is the author of the obligation, but not the author of the law.[24]

Kant endorses the naturalist position on the relation of God's legislative will to the moral law.[25] He accepts God as legislator, and hence as author of the obligation of the law. But he denies that God could be the author of the law. God does not decide on the content of the moral law.[26]

---

[24] As I mentioned earlier, this is not how Suarez puts it, since he disagrees with Kant about necessary conditions for law. I mean only that Kant's division captures the substance of Suarez's distinction in other terms.

[25] 'The law which obliges (verbindet) us a priori and unconditionally through our own reason can also be expressed as proceeding from the will of a supreme lawgiver, i.e. of one who has only rights and no duties (accordingly, from the Divine Will). But this only signifies the idea of a moral being whose will is law for all, without his being conceived as the author of the law.' (*MdS* 227.)

[26] Allen Wood, *Kant's Ethical Theory* (Cambridge: CUP 1999), 161, takes this passage to show that the rational will must be the author of the moral law: 'He distinguishes the *legislator* of a law, the one who issues a command and may attach positive or negative sanctions to it, from the law's author, the one whose will imposes the obligation to obey it. In these terms Kant has no objection to regarding God's will as the legislator of the moral law, but thinks only the rational will of the person obligated can be its author.' The passage, however, offers no support for 'but thinks only ...'. If Wood were correct, it would imply that the law by which we are obliged is 'positive and arbitrary'.

As further evidence of Kant's holding the view he ascribes to him, Wood cites two other passages: (1) *G* 448: 'Reason must regard itself as the author (Urheberin) of its principles, independently of alien influences.' It is not clear that being the author of its principles implies being the author of the moral law that its principles embody. (2) *Rel.* 99: 'But neither can ethical laws be thought of as proceeding *originally* merely from the will of

Kant's distinction between two aspects of legislation raises a question about his analysis of autonomy. If we concede for the moment that autonomy requires legislation, which aspect of legislation has Kant in mind? Does the will decide both on the content of the law and on whether it will be its own law, or does it decide only the second point?

The autonomous will, according to Kant, is not the author of the law; for no one fixes the content of the moral law. When we think of God as the supreme legislator, we do not make God the author of the moral law. Nor is God is the author of a law that God imposes on himself. By the same token, moral agents are not the authors of any law that is a categorical imperative; for if they were the authors, the law would be 'positive and arbitrary' and so could not be a categorical imperative.

Kant does not always seem to observe this important distinction between the legislator and the author of a law. In the *Groundwork*, he suggests that the will both legislates universal law and is the author of the law.[27] If 'author of the law' is taken in the strict sense explained in the *Metaphysics of Morals*, Kant implies that rational agents decide on the content of the law, and that therefore the law is 'positive and arbitrary'. Probably, however, he is simply using 'author' loosely in this passage of the *Groundwork*, so that he does not distinguish the author of the law from the legislator who is the author of the obligation. The rest of his discussion of autonomy and the Categorical Imperative supports this suggestion; he speaks of rational wills only as legislators, and does not suggest that they choose the content of the law. Probably, then, he does not mean to affirm what he denies in the *Metaphysics of Morals*.

[27] 'The will is thus not merely subject to the law, but is subject to the law in such a way that it must be regarded also as legislating for itself and only on this account as being subject to the law (of which it can regard itself as the author).' (*G* 431)

this superior (as statutes that would not be binding without his prior sanction), for then they would not be ethical laws, and the duty commensurate to them would not be a free virtue, but an entirely enforceable legal duty. Therefore only such a one can be thought of as the supreme lawgiver of an ethical community, with respect to whom all *true duties*, hence also the ethical, must be represented as *at the same time* his commands.' This passage says nothing about the will of the person obliged being the author of the law. On the contrary, it suggests that ethical laws do not proceed from anyone's will. Kant's remark about the supreme lawgiver suggests that something's already being a true duty is presupposed by its being one of his commands.

8. Autonomy without legislation?

This discussion of laws and legislators in the *Metaphysics of Morals* clarifies Kant's claims about autonomy, but the clarification is mostly negative. Autonomy does not consist in legislating to oneself and thereby imposing obligation on oneself; for holy wills are autonomous, but do not impose obligation on themselves. We have also found that it cannot consist—either for holy or for imperfect wills—in being the author of the moral law; for the moral law has no author. What, then, does autonomy require?

In beings who need obligation, practical reason obliges and legislates. But what is its role in beings who do not need obligation and legislation? Kant's remarks are puzzling. Though he speaks of pure reason legislating for human beings, he also infers that the 'universality of the lawgiving' makes the principle of morality a law for all rational beings, and hence not only for human beings who are subject to obligation, but also for holy wills that are not subject to obligation.[28] If 'universal lawgiving' applies to them, we must understand 'lawgiving' so that, contrary to Kant's explicit account, it does not involve obligation and imperatives.

Kant alludes to non-obligatory lawgiving. Though for human beings obligation is involved, the universality of the lawgiving makes the law applicable to all rational agents, and practical reason 'declares' this. 'Declaring' a law is the residue of legislation that is left when its obligatory and imperative aspect is removed. A declaration is different from an imperative because it does not include the imposition of any obligation. The content of the law and its appropriateness for rational beings are independent of the declaration by practical reason. Kant does not suggest that it is the act of declaration that makes the law a law for rational agents.

---

[28] 'Pure reason is of itself alone practical, and gives (to the human being) a universal law, which we call the moral law. ... Now this principle of morality, just on account of the universality of the lawgiving that makes it the formal supreme determining ground of the will regardless of all subjective differences, reason declares (erklärt) to be at the same time a law for all rational beings in so far as they have a will, i.e., faculty of determining their causality through the conception of a rule, and consequently in so far as they are competent to determine their actions according to principles and thus to act according to practical a priori principles, which alone have the necessity which reason demands in a principle. It is thus not limited to human beings, but extends to all finite beings having reason and will; indeed it includes the Infinite Being as the supreme intelligence. In the former case, however, the law has the form of an imperative.' (*KpV* 32)

If Kant were to claim that the act of declaration is necessary for the existence of a moral law, he would contradict a further claim about the relation between acts of legislation and underlying moral laws. In the passage of the *Metaphysics of Morals* that we examined earlier, Kant alludes to disputes about natural law, intrinsic morality, and divine commands. He alludes further to these disputes in his most explicit remark about natural law in this context.[29] He argues that positive laws—those that exist only because of acts of legislation—presuppose a natural non-positive law that provides the ground of the authority of the legislator. This natural law is recognized by reason as obligatory independently of any act of legislation. If we modify Kant's claim so that it applies to holy wills, we need to say that natural law is recognized by reason as being law and as being necessary.

If, then, we were to claim that practical reason makes the moral law a law because of its act of declaring the law, we would make the moral law a special kind of positive law. We would then have to postulate a further moral law that authorizes practical reason to legislate. This further moral law could not itself be made law by some act of practical reason. Practical reason, therefore, can declare a moral law only by recognizing some law that exists apart from its act of declaration

Autonomy, therefore, cannot depend on our acknowledging only those laws that are made laws by our own acts of legislating or declaration. On the contrary, autonomy requires us to recognize at least one practical law that is a law apart from any act of legislation or declaration.

From this discussion we can extract an account of autonomy that observes the distinctions that Kant draws, but sometimes blurs: (1) Taken generally, so as to apply to all rational agents, autonomy consists in the recognition of the moral law as the universal law for all rational agents. (2) In its specific application to finite rational agents, autonomy consists in the legislation that consists in making the moral law obligatory for us. In the second case, but not the first, rational agents are legislators, as authors of obligation. In neither

---

[29] 'Those external laws whose obligation can be recognized a priori by reason even without external legislation are natural laws; those, on the other hand, which without actual external legislation do not bind (and so without it would not be laws) are called positive laws. Hence it is possible to conceive of an external legislation which contains only positive laws; but then it would have to be preceded by a natural law providing the ground of the authority of the legislator (i.e., his authorization to obligate others by his mere choice).' (*MdS* 224)

155

case are they authors of the law itself; they do not decide the content of the moral law.

9. Autonomy without construction?

I have examined Kant's claims about laws, legislation, and autonomy, in order to fix the relation of his views to constructivism about morality. So far we have found nothing to support the view that Kant takes autonomy to require the construction rather than the recognition of moral principles. We would have an argument for a constructivist interpretation if we had found that, in Kant's view, autonomy requires the moral law to be our own in the sense that we are its authors. But Kant rejects this view. He does not even take the imposition of obligation on oneself to be necessary for autonomy; for holy wills are autonomous without imposing obligations.

This account does not make Kant indifferent to the aspects of autonomy that reflect the demand for enlightenment.[30] Autonomous individuals do not assume uncritically that something is the moral law. They act on their individual rational understanding that a principle with this content is the universal law for rational beings, and hence they act on their individual reason. If they are finite rational agents, they must act on this rational understanding by assenting to the moral law and seeking to conform their other impulses to its demands.

If this is Kant's view of autonomy, he does not believe that all the five conditions for autonomy that we distinguished earlier[31] are appropriate for morality. I distinguished the fourth condition, requiring us to act on our own rational understanding, from the fifth, requiring us to act on principles that are the product of our own will. The fifth condition may appear to be Kant's position, if we take self-legislation to involve determination of the content of the moral law by my choice. But this is not his view of self-legislation. Hence he does not agree that moral autonomy makes moral principles depend on my choice.

---

[30] See Wood, intro. to *Practical Philosophy*, xxii: 'The principle of autonomy is also a principle of *enlightenment*, because it locates the source of moral legislation in the reason of human individuals who think for themselves, locating the ultimate criterion of morality in "the moral judgment of every human being in so far as he makes the effort to think [the moral law] clearly" (A807/B835).'

[31] See §2 above.

10. Heteronomy and the spurious principles of morality

Even if I have shown that Kant's explication of the concepts related to autonomy does not connect autonomy with construction, I have not refuted all the arguments to show that he ought to have connected them. Rawls appeals to Kant's claim that heteronomy is the source of all spurious principles of morality (*G* 441). If, as Rawls asserts, the principles Kant regards as spurious include all non-constructivist accounts of morality, Kant commits himself to the view that autonomy requires construction. In that case we must say either (1) that his claims about autonomy and spurious moral principles conflict with his explications of autonomy, or (2) that we have misunderstood his explications of autonomy.

In Kant's view, spurious sources of morality lead to heteronomy because in some way they lead us outside the rational will, and seek the law in a property of the possible objects of the will (*G* 441). In this case 'the matter of volition, which can be nothing other than the object of a desire that is connected with the law, enters into the practical law *as a condition of its possibility*' (*KpV* 33). If this reference to an 'object' of willing or desiring includes everything that exists independently of a rational will, the demand for autonomy excludes all forms of objectivism and leaves only constructivism as an acceptable view of the status of the moral law. This contrast between the will and its object opposes everything within the will to everything outside it, and hence opposes everything dependent on the will to everything independent of it.

But this is too simple an account of Kant's use of 'object of willing'. He treats the object as part of the matter of volition, in contrast to the form; this matter is an empirical condition. That is why 'a practical precept that brings with it a material (hence empirical) condition must never be reckoned a practical law' (*KpV* 34). The object of a volition is an empirical feature of it, because it distinguishes one volition from another, and so is not a necessary feature of all volition.

Moral principles that depend on the matter of volitions give us the wrong sort of reason for following morality. Since they depend on possible objects of volition that are not required for all rational agents, they give us a reason only if we have the appropriate antecedent motive. According to one view, actions are right in so far as they accord with our moral sense. This view gives reasons only if we find the appropriate sorts of pleasures and pains in morally good and bad actions. But no argument has been given to show that all rational agents have reason to feel the appropriate sorts of pains and pleasures. The only way to show that they have reason to feel these pains and pleasures would be to show that they have reason to take morally right and wrong actions seriously. Hence an appeal to the moral sense either is useless or gets the issues the wrong way round.

Kant, therefore, suggests a weakness in the sentimentalist position. For if the moral sense does not rest on some prior belief about the rightness of the action being approved of, it seems capable of giving a reason for action only in proportion to the strength of the sentiments connected with it. In approving of an action I do not imply (in the sentimentalist view) that it deserves the approval of anyone else, or that anything in it deserves approval apart from my favourable feeling. Kant notices this feature of the moral sense. A purely sentimentalist account that avoids Kant's allegation of circularity makes moral reasons a matter of comparative strength.[32]

Since sentimentalism does not attribute to the moral sense any judgment that the action in question deserves a favourable reaction, it cannot offer other people a reason for approving the action if they do not already share our own reaction to it.[33] A moral judgment sets out to 'judge validly ... for other men', since it claims to offer reasons for other people, apart from what they may happen to want or to feel. Even if everyone has the desires presupposed by moral judgment and criticism, people have them to different degrees. Hence, if reasons depend on the strength of the relevant desires, moral criticism cannot offer reasons to other people apart from the strength of their specific desires. Since we believe that moral criticism offers such reasons, sentimentalism cannot be true if we are right about moral criticism.

Kant's objections to Leibnizian perfectionism are more difficult to describe.[34] He argues that it agrees with sentimentalism in relying

[32] '... The concept of duty cannot be derived from it (sc. a feeling of satisfaction), for we would have to presuppose a feeling for law as such and regard as an object of sensation what can only be thought by reason. If this did not end up in the flattest contradiction, it would destroy every concept of duty and fill its place with a merely mechanical play of refined inclinations, sometimes contending with the coarser.' (*KpV* 38-9) In the last sentence, the apodosis ('it would destroy ...') seems to refer to an attempt to offer a non-circular sentimentalist account.

[33] '... the appeal to the principle of moral feeling is superficial, since men who cannot think believe that they will be helped out by feeling, even when the question is solely one of universal law. They do so even though feelings naturally differ from one another by an infinity of degrees, so that feelings are not capable of providing a uniform measure of good and evil; furthermore, they do so even though one man cannot by his feeling judge validly at all for other men.' (*G* 442)

[34] See Rawls, *Lectures* 228–30, 235–7.

on an end that is an empirical object of the rational will. If Leibniz's conception of perfection is non-moral—'the fitness or adequacy of a thing for all sorts of ends' (KpV 41), it does not seem to give a reason to all rational wills. It seems, on the contrary, to give a reason only to those rational wills that happen to take some antecedent interest in that sort of perfection. One might try to defend Leibniz by saying that Kant is wrong in ascribing this purely non-moral idea of perfection to him. But if we add enough to make it moral perfection, the second part of Kant's criticism of sentimentalism becomes relevant; to find that moral perfection gives us a reason, we must already see a reason to care about morality, so that perfectionism assumes what it seeks to prove.

This objection to perfectionism also applies to rational intuitionism as defended by Clarke.[35] According to Clarke, moral facts consist in relations of fitness, and these relations of fitness do not depend on facts about rational agents. The fitness between making a promise and keeping it is a relation between these two states of affairs themselves; the nature of the agents who make, receive, keep, and break promises is not a term of the relation of fitness.[36] It is therefore appropriate to ask: What is it about relations of fitness that gives reasons to rational agents? Clarke's appeals to contradiction do not seem adequate to answer these questions.

These objections to sentimentalism and perfectionism are meant to show that both positions fail the fourth condition for autonomy. The moral outlooks that they describe do not really proceed from one's own reasoned principles. Ultimately they must proceed from something other than one's reasoned principles. This is clear in the case of sentimentalism, which explicitly appeals to something other than practical reason as the source of moral principles. It is less clear, but none the less true, in the case of rationalist perfectionism as well.

11. Objectivity, independence, and externality

More discussion would be needed to evaluate Kant's arguments fully, and to separate weaker from stronger elements. But I do not need to go into these details in order to make my main point.

---

[35] Rawls mentions Clarke at 'Kantian constructivism', in *Papers*, 343, and discusses him in *Lectures*, 77–81.
[36] See Clarke's *Discourse of Natural Religion*, in *British Moralists*, ed. D. D. Raphael (2 vols, Oxford: OUP, 1969), § 225f.

Examination of Kant's arguments suggests that heteronomy results from conceptions of morality that allow only a contingent connexion between morality and the reasons that are necessarily reasons for rational agents. They do not provide a universal law for rational agents, but only a law for those particular agents who have the appropriate cognitive or affective relation to this or that principle.

Kant's refusal to go 'outside' the rational will does not imply any denial of objective moral principles that are true independently of any acts of will. When he speaks of principles or objects that are external to the will, he means that they are only contingently connected to the will.

This is a familiar conception of the internal. Examples of 'internal relations' or 'internal connexions' are easy to find in functional contexts. A sausage-making machine is internally related to sausages; it would not be what it is unless it were appropriately related to that product, but the sausage may none the less be made and exist without the machine. More controversially, we might consider the relation of senses to their objects. Colour is not externally related to sight; since (let us suppose) sight is essentially the sense that is aware of colour, it is not a contingent fact that we see colours as opposed to sounds. None the less, colours are external to sight, if they exist independently of it and are not the creation of sight. Some have suggested a similarly internal relation between thought and the Principle of Non-Contradiction. The fact that PNC is in some way a 'law of thought' does not make it a law about thought, or a law that depends on thought. One might say that the dependence goes the other way; an activity is not rational thought unless it refrains from simultaneously denying every property that it affirms of a given subject. In these cases, x's being internal to y does not make x dependent on y.

Might Kant intend such a connexion between the rational will and the moral law? If he intends it, he should believe that a rational will is not the sort of will it is unless the sorts of reasons that are provided by the moral law are reasons for it. This connexion between the will and the reasons provided by the moral law does not imply that the moral law is not true independently of the will's acknowledgment of it as true.

I do not see why we should not attribute such a view to Kant. If it is his view, a constructivist account of moral principles is not the only account consistent with his views on autonomy and heteronomy.

12. Objections to constructivism

I have tried to show that we can explain Kant's claims without imputing constructivism to him. I have not yet asked whether his views exclude constructivism. I now turn to that question.

We would have a good reason for denying that Kant is a constructivist if we could identify constructivism with the position that he rejects in his discussion of legislation. This identification might seem legitimate. For interpreters who treat Kant as a constructivist appeal to his remarks about legislation. I have argued that such appeals do not succeed. Kant denies that we ourselves are the authors of the moral law. If we suppose that we are the authors of the law, we face two objections: (1) We must acknowledge that the law is positive and arbitrary. (2) In any case, if it is to be genuine law, it must rest on a natural law 'providing the ground of the authority of the legislator' (*MdS* 224).[37]

Still, we might argue that Kant could be a constructivist without making us authors of the moral law. Constructivism differs from voluntarism in so far as it dispenses with any explicit commands and acts of legislation. Moral principles might depend on, and be constituted by,'the activity of practical reason itself' (as Rawls puts it)[38] without our actually being their authors. Even if we do not decide that some specific principles rather than others are to be principles of morality, our rational activities may make them the principles.

To find a partial parallel, we might consider rules that are derived from shared practices. An account of the rules of a deliberative assembly may record the practice that has grown up over time. The members of the assembly must accept this practice, but they need not have made any deliberate decision that these are to be the rules. If the practice of the assembly changes, again without any further deliberate decision, these rules will no longer be correct.

Though this is not a complete parallel to the relation between practical reason and moral law that Rawls has in mind, it helps to identify some features of a constructivist view. We must be able to describe the relevant activities of practical reason without essential reference to the truth of the moral law or to belief in the moral law; if either of these is introduced, we no longer have the sort of independence that a constructivist view requires. It would not be plausible, for instance, to claim that scientific laws are constituted by our scientific activities, if we refer to those scientific activities that presuppose the truth of these laws; on the contrary, such

[37] Quoted more fully above at n. 29.
[38] An abbreviated quotation from the passage quoted in full at n. 12 above.

activities are themselves legitimate only if the relevant laws are true.[39]

If we agree that a coherent constructivist position is possible and that this position is different from voluntarism, does this matter from Kant's point of view? Is a constructivist position subject to his two criticisms of the view that the moral law is the product of our legislation?

Suppose we claim that the moral law is constituted as such by our activities of practical reason. If these activities are understood so that they do not essentially presuppose the truth of the moral law, it is difficult to see how a law constituted by them, even if not deliberately legislated, could fail to be positive and arbitrary in the ways that Kant objects to. For what gives us a moral reason to accept the law that underlies, and is constituted by, the activities that we do not initially regard as morally required? We must apparently appeal to some further moral principle that entitles us to act on principles constituted by our activities of practical reason. This is the natural law that underlies a positive law by giving the legislator the right to legislate.

We do not avoid Kant's criticisms, therefore, if we substitute 'constitution' or 'construction' for 'legislation'. For we can still legitimately ask for the moral credentials of the constituted or constructed principles. If these depend on the actions that constitute or construct the principles, we can ask the same question about these actions. To avoid an infinite regress, we must recognize some non-constructed principles. This is just a variation on Kant's argument about positive law presupposing natural law.

Suppose we reject this argument about a regress, and claim that the constituting activities are neither morally right nor morally wrong. In that case, we are open to Kant's arguments about heteronomy. If the constituting activities cannot be shown to be reasonable for every rational agent as such, it is not clear why we should engage in them, unless we have some inclination that does not give a reason for every rational agent. But if we rely on such an inclination, we act heteronomously; for our will does not act on its own law.

For these reasons, Kant's conception of autonomy not only does not require constructivism, but positively excludes it. A constructivist account of moral principles implies that we act on them heteronomously; hence it must introduce one of the spurious principles of morality.

[39] I will set aside the difficult issues that arise in deciding whether Rawls's own theory meets this test for being genuinely constructivist

13. A reasonable conception of autonomy?

I began this discussion with a more or less 'intuitive' or 'ordinary' conception of autonomy, and I suggested that Kant's initial claims about autonomy do not express his stipulations about a technical notion of his own, but his views about how to capture some intuitive assumptions about autonomy. I now return to that ordinary conception, with a further question: Has Kant any good reasons for believing the claim I have attributed to him, that morality requires the fourth condition for autonomy, but precludes the fifth?

If Kant is wrong, and if we are authors of the moral law, moral autonomy requires the fifth condition; one's own law is the law whose content one decides for oneself. But, in Kant's view, if we decide the content of the moral law for ourselves, we do not act on a law—in the sense in which the principles of morality constitute a law. Though pure reason 'announces itself as originally lawgiving' (*KpV* 31), as the author of the obligation of the law, it does not announce itself as the author of the law. It claims to be correct in imposing this law on us; since this is a reason for accepting the imposition, it cannot simply be a feature of any imposition, but must be a feature of this specific law. Hence the law must be correct for some reason other than the fact that practical reason has imposed it. As Kant says, positive law presupposes natural law that is prior to acts of legislation.

Kant does not merely say that in the case of morality, the fifth condition for autonomy need not be satisfied. In this case the fifth condition is incompatible with autonomy. If we are autonomous, the principles of our action come from our own reason. But they come from our own reason only if they meet the rational standards that make them correct; our choosing them does not make them correct.

The fourth and fifth conditions, therefore, do not mark a lower and a higher degree of autonomy. In the area of morality, the fifth condition marks a lower degree of autonomy; for instead of having our action guided by practical reason, meeting the appropriate standards for correctness, we have to be guided by a choice that falls short of these standards. Hence, in Kant's view, we return to a heteronomous condition if we think of ourselves as authors of the moral law.

This does not mean that the fifth condition can never be an element of autonomy. In an area in which no questions arise about the correctness of the principles we act on, it is not irrational to choose them for ourselves. The fact that we are basically guided by inclination rather than by laws that meet some further test for correctness does not mean we are less completely guided by reason than we should be. In such an area, then, we can be autonomous by being the authors of our own law. But since morality is an area in which legitimate questions arise about the correctness of imposing this law rather than another on ourselves, autonomy does not consist in being the authors of our own law. It consists in being guided by our ration al grasp of the independently correct law.

Such an account of moral autonomy leads us to a further question. We might agree with Kant's judgment that morality is an area in which questions about the correctness of a specific act of legislation seem to be legitimate, and that this is why it seems to be an area in which we cannot be the authors of our own law. But if we become convinced that the questions that seem to be legitimate are really illegitimate, because we cannot give any reasonable answers to questions about the correctness of this or that legislation, we will conclude that our initial conception of moral autonomy rested on an illusion.

In saying this I am repeating the earlier point that our conditions for autonomy in a given area must reflect our views about the sort of law that is available in that area. I have avoided discussion of Kant's account of the correct law in the area of morality; but we cannot avoid discussion of it if we want to decide about his account of moral autonomy.

The Structure of Orthonomy*

MICHAEL SMITH

According to the standard story of action, a story that can be traced back at least to David Hume (1740), actions are those bodily movements that are caused and rationalized by a pair of mental states: a desire for some end, where ends can be thought of as ways the world could be, and a belief that something the agent can just do, namely, move her body in the way to be explained, has some suitable chance of making the world the relevant way. Bodily movements that occur otherwise aren't actions, they are mere happenings (Davidson 1963, Davidson 1971).

The feature that bodily movements have that makes them especially suitable to count as actions, as distinct from (say) the ends that agents desire, is that they are the events in the world over which agents are supposed to have direct rational control: agents' abilities bottom out with movements of their bodies (Danto 1963). This is why the occurrence of an action, as distinct from a mere happening, does not depend on whether the agent's bodily movement causes and rationalizes the end she desires. That merely affects whether that which she directly controls, the movement of her body, can be redescribed as the action of intentionally bringing about the desired end (Davidson 1971).

We can therefore sum up the roles of the different elements in this Humean story of action in the following terms. When desires for ends and means-end beliefs combine to cause and rationalize bodily movements in the way required for direct control by an agent—this is what the 'DC→' signifies in figure 1—then those bodily movements count as actions of that agent.

Much has been said both to clarify and to defend this standard Humean story (Hornsby 1980, Peacocke 1979, Smith 1987, Wilson 1989, Mele 1992, Smith 1999). Though more doubtless needs to be

* An earlier version of this paper was presented at the Royal Institute of Philosophy conference on *Action and Agency*, St John's College, Oxford, September 2002, and as one in a series of three Erskine Lectures delivered at the University of Canterbury, Christchurch, March 2003. I would like to thank Jonathan Dancy, Jennifer Hornsby, John Hyman, Cynthia Macdonald, Graham Macdonald, Philip Pettit, John Tasioulas, Jay Wallace, Ralph Wedgwood, and Bernard Williams for their many useful comments.

Michael Smith

Figure 1. The standard Humean story of action

means-ends
belief

+	DC→	**bodily**	desired
		movement	end?

desire for
an end

The crucial elements are in bold.

said, my aim here is not to add anything further by way of clarification or defence. Rather, taking the story for granted, I wish to raise a question concerning the status of actions themselves. If the rational etiology of a bodily movement—its genesis in desires for ends and means-end beliefs—is what turns a mere happening into an action, an event under the control of an agent, then does the rational etiology of those desires for ends and means-end beliefs turn an action into something which is under the control of an agent in some more significant way still?

More specifically, does the rational etiology of the desires for ends and means-end beliefs that produce an action turn a *mere action* into an *orthonomous action* (Pettit and Smith 1990, Pettit and Smith 1993, Pettit and Smith 1996, Smith 2003)? In other words, does the rational etiology of these desires and beliefs show the extent to which the action was performed by an agent who exercises his *orthonomy*, that is to say, his distinctive capacity to get things *right* or *correct* (this is the 'orthos')? As we will see, philosophers of quite different persuasions can and should agree that the rational etiology of the desires for ends and means-end beliefs that produce action in the standard Humean story does indeed have this kind of import. Moreover, as will emerge, this fact about the rational etiology of desires for ends and means-end beliefs provides us with an illuminating picture of both responsibility and control. Interpreted ecumenically, it provides a framework in which we can recognize, and in terms of which we can make sense of, a whole range of cases in which people act correctly, thereby displaying their responsibility.

The alternative and more standard account of responsibility and control asks whether an agent manifests his capacity for *autonomy* (Christman 1989). But, as a casual glance at the literature on autonomy reveals, such value as we place on autonomy looks to be entirely derived from the value we place on orthonomy (Watson

1975, Wolf 1990). Autonomy is the mere capacity an agent has to rule himself (this is the 'autos'). But we value agents ruling themselves to just the extent that, in so doing, they thereby manifest their capacity to get things right (Pettit and Smith 1993). The main aim of the present paper is thus to lay out the structure of orthonomy. My hope is to encourage philosophers to think in terms of this structure—to think in terms or orthonomy, not autonomy—when they engage in further theorising about the nature of responsibility and control.

The paper is in four main sections. In the first I describe a minimal conception of orthonomous action. In the second section I explain why, at least according to common sense, we must go beyond this minimal conception. In the third section I argue in favour of the more expansive, common sense, conception of orthonomous action by showing how it can be underwritten in both realist and irrealist terms. And then, in the fourth and final section, I show how the common sense conception of orthonomous action provides us with framework in which we can recognize, and in terms of which we can make sense of, a puzzling case of responsibility and control that has been much discussed in the recent literature.

1. Radical Humeanism

As I said, the standard Humean story tells us that actions are the product of a desire for some end and a belief that something the agent can just do has some suitable chance of bringing that end about. So far, however, this story tells us nothing about the rational etiology of the desires and means-end beliefs themselves. That requires a supplement to the standard Humean story.

According to the most minimal supplement, the one that Hume himself would presumably have accepted, the desires and means-end beliefs that produce actions differ significantly in their rational etiology (Milgram 1995). Because means-end beliefs are representations of how things are, the radical Humean view is that they are evaluable in terms of truth and falsehood, and, as a consequence, that they are also evaluable in terms of how well or ill justified they are, given the evidence available to the subject. This means that, assuming that rational subjects have the capacity to grasp the evidence available to them and to form beliefs that accord with that evidence, the justification of subjects' beliefs turns on whether or not they have exercised such evidence-grasping and belief-forming capacities as they have. The exercise of these capacities, in turn, is what underwrites the possibility of rational criticism of the actions they perform. Actions are rationally criticizable to the extent that the beliefs that produce them are rationally criticizable.

Of course, since agents differ in their capacities—since some are more capable than others of evaluating evidence, for example—it follows that there is another dimension to the evaluation of subjects as well, namely, an evaluation in terms of how capable they are. But an evaluation of subjects of this kind does not constitute criticism of them because such an evaluation does not suggest that the subjects fail in respects in which they could have succeeded. Though 'ought' implies 'can', 'acted badly' does not imply 'could have done better'. What makes criticism apt is thus a subject's failure to exercise such capacities for grasping evidence and forming beliefs as she has.

By contrast, however, at least according to the most radical version of the Humean story, the desires for ends that produce actions—that is to say, those desires that are not themselves derived from further desires for ends and beliefs about means (Smith 2004: more on this later)—are, in Hume's memorable phrase, 'original existences' (Hume 1740, 415). This means not just that they elude evaluation in terms of truth and falsehood, but also, and supposedly as a consequence, that they are not evaluable in terms of how well or ill justified they are either. Agents may have conflicting desires for ends, of course, but not even these conflicts are supposed to be resolved via recourse to rational principles. Rather they are resolved more or less mechanically by the causal force of the desires involved. Unlike beliefs about means-ends, then, desires for ends are supposed to elude rational criticism altogether (Smith forthcoming).

Spare though it is, this account of the rational etiology of desires for ends and beliefs about means to ends provides us with all we need in order to provide an account of the structure of fully orthonomous action, at least by the lights of radical Humeanism. It provides us with an interpretation of the claim that an agent manifests his capacity to get things correct. When an agent acts in a fully orthonomous way—when he manifests his capacity to get things correct—the following conditions must all obtain: facts about which of the means available to the agent are means to which of the ends he desires must impact, in the right kind of non-accidental way, on the evidence available to him; this available evidence must in turn fix, in the right kind of non-accidental way, his beliefs about which of the means available to him are means to which of his desired ends; these means-end beliefs must then join together, in the right kind of non-accidental way, with a desire for an end to rationalize the appropriate bodily movement, that is, a bodily movement picked out as an available means to that desired end; and this bodily movement must produce the desired end, again in the right sort of non-accidental way.

What exactly does it mean to say that all of these things must come about in the 'right kind of non-accidental way'? Facts produce evidence in the right kind of non-accidental way when they produce evidence in the way required for beliefs formed on the basis of that evidence to count as knowledge (this is what the 'K→' signifies in figure 2), and bodily movements cause desired ends in the right kind of non-accidental way when they produce desired ends in the way required for the bringing about of those desired ends to count as intentional conduct: that is, roughly speaking, when they come about in the way specified in the agent's pattern of practical reasoning (this is what the 'PPR→' signifies in figure 2). An agent's possession of the capacity to get things correct may therefore require that he be situated in a suitably obliging world, where a world is suitably obliging if it is one in which agents can have knowledge and act intentionally. Plainly not all worlds are suitably obliging in this sense: think of the myriad examples of wayward causal chains that undermine both agent's having knowledge and their acting intentionally.

But for other events to happen in the right kind of non-accidental way what is required is not so much that the agent be situated in a suitably obliging world, but rather that the agent himself meets a certain condition of ideal rationality. Available evidence produces belief in the right kind of non-accidental way, for example, when the formation of the belief, in the light of that evidence, counts as an exercise of the ideal capacity to rationally believe in accordance with the evidence available to him (this is what the 'IR→' signifies in figure 2), and the agent's desires for ends and means-end beliefs cause his body to move in the right kind of non-accidental way when the movement of the body counts as an exercise of the capacity to directly control his body (this is what the 'DC→' signifies in figure 2). The question we must ask is thus whether the agent has and exercises these rational capacities.

We can picture the radical Humean conception of fully orthonomous action in the following way (see figure 2).

The radical Humean conception of fully orthonomous action thus plainly allows that various things can go wrong when an agent acts. For example, some of the connections required for an action's being the upshot of the agent's distinctive capacity to get things

Michael Smith

Figure 2. The radical Humean conception of fully orthonomous
action

facts about   K→ available   IR→ means-ends
means to   evidence   belief
desired ends   about means to
                  desired ends

                              +   DC→ bodily PPR→ desired
                                        movement   end
                                   desire for
                                   an end

The crucial elements are again in bold.

right might not be in place. The available evidence about means-
ends might be misleading, say, because not appropriately related to
the facts about means-ends. The agent might fail to form beliefs
about means-ends in the light of the evidence available to him. The
agent's desire for an end and means-end belief might fail to cause a
bodily movement. Or the events caused by the agent's bodily movement might not be the agent's desired ends. Alternatively, though
all of these connections are in place, some of them might be in place
by fluke or accident. For example, though the agent's beliefs about
means-ends might accord with the available evidence, perhaps he
doesn't have that belief as a result of having exercised his belief-
forming capacities. Or though the desired end is caused by the
agent's bodily movement, it might happen via a wayward causal
chain. In that case, though the agent gets things right, his action
would not be a manifestation of his distinctive capacity to get things
right.

With this catalogue of things that can go wrong before us, it
becomes clear that there is a natural division within this class. For
whereas some of the things that can go wrong are things for which
it makes sense to hold the agent himself responsible, at least assuming that he has the requisite rational capacities, others plainly aren't.
Whether an agent forms appropriate means-end beliefs in the light
of the available evidence, for example, is plausibly a failure for
which he could, in principle, be held responsible. For all that is
required for the formation of appropriate beliefs, given that the evidence for forming those beliefs is available, is that the agent fully
exercises his rational belief-forming capacities, again, assuming he
has such capacities.

But other things that can go wrong are plainly not things for which it would make any sense at all to hold the agent responsible. Whether the facts about means to ends manifest themselves in the evidence available to an agent is plausibly an example of a failure of this kind. The mere exercise of an agent's rational capacities may be insufficient to ensure that such facts manifest themselves to him. Good luck is required: location in a suitably obliging world. Likewise, whether or not the bodily movement that is caused by an agent's desires for ends and means-end beliefs produces the desired end may not be something that the agent can control once that bodily movement has been performed. The mere exercise of his rational capacities will have no effect on interference that occurs beyond his body when such interference can't be anticipated. Again, good luck is required: location in a suitably obliging world. (The reason for the qualifications—the 'may's—is that (say) the failure of the facts to manifest themselves in evidence could be the result of some prior action of the agent's of hiding the facts from himself, in which case he would be responsible. Likewise for the failure of his bodily movement to cause and rationalize the desired end.)

It thus follows that fully orthonomous action itself turns out to be, in part, a matter of good luck. But it also follows that we can define a more partial kind of orthonomy, a kind that will always be a legitimate aspiration for an agent given that agents are, by definition, capable of the exercise of such rational capacities as they have. This more partial kind of orthonomy—let's call it 'narrow orthonomy'—is a matter of agents' getting things right to extent that it is up to them whether or not they get things right: that is, to the extent that they fully exercise such rational capacities as they have. This is a capacity an agent has whether or not he is situated in a suitably obliging world and no matter how impoverished his rational capacities are. All that matters is that he fully exercises such capacities as he has to rationally manage his own psychology.

Narrow orthonomy thus looks like it will be of the greatest significance in philosophy, as it promises to provide a relatively straightforward and uncontroversial account of the nature and scope of responsible conduct. For, according to this account, the concept of responsible conduct simply piggy-backs on the concept of responsible believing and desiring. Responsible conduct is a matter of an agents' controlling their behaviour in the sense of acting after having exercised such rational capacities as they have, capacities they have to get things correct rather than incorrect independently of whether they are in a suitably obliging world. In order to produce such an account of responsible conduct all we need to do is to provide a fully spelled out story of the nature and scope of an agent's rational capacities.

Importantly, however, and especially in the light of the potential significance of narrow orthonomy for the understanding of responsible conduct, radical Humeanism suggests that there is a further natural division within the class of things that can go wrong. For whereas there are various ways in which things can go wrong in the way in which means-end beliefs and desires for means are produced—the beliefs formed may not be true, or they might not be formed in the light of the available evidence, or the agent might irrationally fail to form a desire for the believed means to his desired end—and whereas some of these are the agent's own responsibility— it is up to the agent to exercise such capacities as he has to believe what is supported by the available evidence, and it also up to him to exercise such capacities as he has to desire the believed means to his desired ends—there is simply no way in which things can go wrong as regards the production of an agent's desires for ends. This is not to deny that desires for ends are caused in various ways, for of course they are. It is simply to say that, at least according to radical Humeanism, it does not matter to the narrow orthonomy of the resulting action how an agent's desires for ends are caused. This is the cash value of Hume's claim that such desires are original existences. Because desires for ends are not the product of a rational capacity, they are not subject to a correctness condition. Desires for ends are not subject to rational control.

When the point is put as bluntly as this it will doubtless raise eyebrows. 'Surely', it will be objected, 'the fact that an agent's desires for ends are not the product of a rational capacity doesn't suffice all by itself to show that they are not subject to a correctness condition. To think that it does is to be taken in by the ambiguity of the phrase "correctness condition". The existence of a correctness condition for desires for ends turns on whether or not there is some standard or other by which we can assess such desires. But while it might be agreed that *rationality* does not provide such a standard, that is consistent with there being some other system of norms that does provide such a standard: norms of *morality*, say.' The objection is a good one, as it forces us to sharpen the point.

Though it is true that we could relativize orthonomy to a system of norms, we mustn't lose sight of the fact that what makes orthonomy of such special interest is its potential to provide an account of responsible conduct. This constrains our choice of a system of norms relative to which orthonomy can be judged. Being responsible is, after all, an inescapable feature of the circumstances we face

172

as rational actors. But it follows from this that we must therefore evaluate orthonomy relative to a system of norms to which we are subject, as rational actors, in a similarly inescapable way. Given that being subject to norms of reason is constitutive of being a believer and desirer, and given that such norms provides a natural interpretation of what it means to get things right, this makes the norms of reason the obvious choice. Conversely—at least if the norms of morality do not reduce to the norms of reason (see Smith 1994 for the alternative view)— given that being subject to norms of morality is not similarly constitutive of being a believer and desirer, it follows that the norms of morality would be a very poor choice of norms relative to which we should judge orthonomy. For in that case there would be no grounds on which to base the inescapability of responsibility: no basis for the universal expectation that people do in fact get things right, at least to the extent that they can.

We can represent this radical Humean conception of narrow orthonomy in the way suggested in figure 3. According to this conception, it is irrelevant to the narrow orthonomy of an agent's action whether the evidence available to him is misleading, and whether the end the agent desires fails to result from his bodily movement due to some unforeseeable interference. All that matters is that the agent exercises such rational capacities as he has: his actual rational capacities (this is what the 'AR→' signifies in figure 3).

However, and to repeat, the distinctive feature of the radical Humean conception of narrow orthonomy is that though it insists that the exercise of such rational capacities as an agent has will have all sorts of effects on which means-end beliefs he has, it tells us that it will have no similar effect on which desires for ends he has. This is because desires for ends are not the product of an agent's rational capacities. In assessing the radical Humean conception of narrowly orthonmous action, the question we must ask is thus whether this is really credible.

Figure 3. The radical Humean conception of narrow orthonomy

facts about means to desired ends?	**available evidence about means to desired ends**	**AR→ means-ends belief**		
			+ DC→ bodily movement	desired end?
		desire for an end		

Michael Smith

2. Common sense

As we will see, the problem with the radical Humean conception of narrow orthonomy is that it is inconsistent with a widely accepted and common sense view about the relationship between two kinds of reasons for action: motivating reasons and normative reasons (Woods 1972, Smith 1987, Smith 1994). The point will take a little explaining, however, so let me begin by making the distinction itself.

It is now familiar that we can distinguish between two kinds of reasons for action: normative reasons and motivating reasons. Motivating reasons are psychological states that teleologically explain what an agent does (Wilson 1989). If, as many think, such teleological explanations reduce to a kind of causal explanation, then this amounts to the claim that motivating reasons are psychological states that cause and rationalize an agent's doing what he does (Davidson 1963). Unsurprisingly, these psychological states are thus the desires for ends and means-end beliefs that we have been talking about so far in spelling out the standard Humean story. Normative reasons, by contrast, are the considerations to which we appeal when we construct a justification of an agent's conduct (Nagel 1970, Dancy 2000). The difference is that captured by the following pair of claims, both of which are true at the moment of my writing:

(i) My reason for tapping on the keys to my laptop is that I want to write a paper about philosophy of action and believe that I can do so by tapping on the keys to my laptop (this is the motivating reason)

and

(ii) My reason for tapping on the keys to my laptop is that people are counting on me to write a paper about philosophy of action (this is the normative reason).

To repeat, the distinction is that between psychological states that teleologically explain and considerations that justify.

The importance of making this distinction in this way becomes clear when we ask whether all actions must be done for reasons. For though this question gets answered resoundingly in the affirmative when reasons are understood to be motivating reasons—as we saw at the outset, what makes an action an action is the fact that there is a desire-belief pair that causes and rationalizes it—the question gets answered just as resoundingly in the negative when reasons are understood to be normative reasons. An agent can act without there being any considerations at all that justify his doing what he does (and, just to forestall any concern about equivocation, let me clarify that from now on all talk of justification will be talk of rational justification). He can, after all, be mistaken about which considerations provide a rational justification of his conduct, and he can be mistaken about whether or not such considerations obtain in the circumstances in which he acts.

Moreover, and perhaps even more strikingly, an agent can act without believing that there are any considerations that rationally justify his doing what he does, and even while believing that the considerations that bear on what he is doing all dysjustify (to borrow an excellent term of Michael Stocker's (2004)), rather than justify. For example, though I am tapping on the keys to my laptop because I want to write a paper about philosophy of action and believe that I can do so by tapping on the keys to my laptop, I may yet believe, perhaps correctly, that I am required *not* to write such a paper: that everything is to be said against, and nothing in favour, of my doing so. Of course, to continue writing a paper about philosophy of action in such circumstances I would have to be rather perverse and irrational. But some people clearly are perverse and irrational in exactly this way (Stocker 1979, Smith 1999).

The distinction between motivating and normative reasons needs to be handled with some care, however. For, as Bernard Williams has pointed out, facts about considerations that rationally justify cannot be divorced entirely from considerations of explanation (Willliams 1980). When someone has a normative reason to act in a certain way this must be the sort of consideration that could figure in an explanation of her conduct, if not on that occasion, then at least on others. In the light of the huge gulf between the two sorts of reason, however—motivating reasons are psychological states that explain, normative reasons are considerations that justify—we must ask how that connection gets forged.

The obvious answer to give is that the connection gets forged by a rational requirement of response upon recognition of a normative reason (Pettit and Smith forthcoming). What makes a normative reason a normative reason is, inter alia, the fact that, when agents recognize that they have such a reason, they are rationally required to respond appropriately by acquiring corresponding motivations. In other words, reason requires those who judge that they have a normative reason to act in a certain way to be motivated to act in that way. A failure to be so motivated indicates that the agent suffers from weakness of will, or compulsion, or some other such

Michael Smith

form of practical unreason. This explains the possibility of perverse agents who act on considerations that dyjustify.

This common sense view of the distinction between normative reasons and motivating reasons and their relations is widely accepted in the philosophical literature. Indeed, it is common ground among both those who are sympathetic to a Humean conception of human psychology, and those who are hostile such a conception. Here, for example, is Williams, a Humean.

> Does believing that a particular consideration is a reason to act in a particular way provide, or indeed constitute, a motivation to act? ... Let us grant that it does—this claim indeed seems plausible, so long at least as the connexion between such beliefs and the disposition to act is not tightened to that unnecessary degree which excludes *akrasia*. (Williams 1980, 107)

On the plausible assumption that Williams takes akrasia to be a form of practical unreason, this amounts to the claim that the norms governing practical reasoning require that those who believe that such-and-such provides a reason to act in a certain way are motivated to act in that way.

Christine Korsgaard, a Kantian, puts forward a similar view.

> Thus, it seems to be a requirement on practical reason claims that they be capable of motivating us. ... Practical-reason claims, if they are really to present us with reasons for action, must be capable of motivating rational persons. (Korsgaard 1986, 11)

and she elaborates on what she means by this in the following terms:

> ...if a person did know [about the existence of a reason] and *if nothing were interfering with her rationality*, she would respond accordingly. (Korsgaard 1986, 14, footnote 9)

Her idea is thus the same as Williams's. In so far as people are rational they are motivated to do what they believe that there is a normative reason for them to do.

Thomas Scanlon, who has misgivings about both Humean and Kantian conceptions of human psychology, makes much the same point.

> Rationality involves systematic connections between a person's judgments and his or her subsequent attitudes. ... [A] rational person who judges there to be compelling reason to do A normally forms the intention to do A, and this judgment is sufficient explanation of that intention and of the agent's acting on it (since

176

this action is part of what such an intention involves). (Scanlon 1998, 33–34)

In other words, according to Scanlon, people who judge themselves to have a normative reason to act in a certain way are rationally required to be motivated to act in that way. But if these theorists are right then it follows that, contrary to radical Humeanism, desires for ends are subject to a correctness condition. For reason requires that agents' desires for ends covary with their judgments about what they have normative reason to do.

This, in turn, tells us something important about fully orthonomous action. If desires for ends are indeed subject to such a norm of reason then it follows that, when agents act in a fully orthonomous way, their desires for ends must be the product of a capacity to have motivating reasons that accord with their judgments about what they have normative reason to do. Agents whose desires for ends do not covary with their judgments about their normative reasons in this way violate a norm of practical reason. Moreover it also follows that when agents act in a fully orthonomous way their judgments about normative reasons must meet their own correctness condition.

Agents' judgments about their normative reasons look, after all, like they can be true or false, and more or less sensitive to the available evidence. I might think that I am required to write a paper about philosophy of action, but I might be mistaken, as I am not in fact required to write such a paper. Or, abstracting away from whether or not I am required to write such a paper, my judgment that I am subject to such a requirement might bear no relation to such evidence as regards what I am and am not required to do as is available to me. To be completely correct, then, agents' desires for ends must not only covary with their judgments about what they have normative reason to do, but their judgments about their normative reasons must in turn be the product of the evidence available to them, evidence that is itself a manifestation of the facts about their normative reasons.

It thus follows that, at least according to common sense, radical Humeanism quite dramatically misrepresents the structure of fully orthonomous action. Common sense tells us that the desires for ends and means-end beliefs that produce fully orthonomous action must be understood in a far more symmetical fashion (see figure 4).

According to common sense, fully orthonomous action requires not just that agents be in a position to have and act on knowledge of means to ends, but also that they be in a position to have and act on

Michael Smith

Figure 4. The common sense conception of fully orthonomous action

```
facts about    K→available    IR→ means-ends
means to       evidence           belief
desired ends   about means to
               desired ends

                       +   DC→ bodily    PPR→ desired
                                movement        end
                           desire for
                           an end
                             ↑
                           IR
facts about    K→available    IR→ judgments
what there is  evidence about     about what
normative      what there is      there is
reason to do   normative          normative
               reason to do       reason to do
```

knowledge of what there is normative reason to do. In this respect, common sense tells us that fully orthonomous action requires that we live in a doubly obliging world—facts of both kinds must make themselves manifest—and it also requires that we have and exercise ideal belief-forming capacities about means to ends in the light of our evidence, ideal judgment-forming capacities about the normative reasons we have in the light of our evidence, and ideal desire-forming capacities in the light of the judgments we make about the normative reasons that we have. Fully orthonomous action is paradigmatically virtuous action (Pettit and Smith 1993).

Correspondingly, common sense also entails that narrowly orthonomous action is a much more substantial accomplishment than radical Humeanism suggests. For narrowly orthonomous action commonsensically requires that an agent's beliefs about means-ends are the product of such belief-forming capacities as she has—her actual rational capacities—given the evidence available to her, that her judgments about what she has normative reason to do are the product of such judgment-forming capacities she has given the evidence available to her, and that her desires for ends are the product of such capacities as she has to form desires in the light of the judgments she makes about what she has normative reason to do (see figure 5).

The glaring differences between this common sense conception of narrow orthonomy and the radical Humean conception are

178

Figure 5. The common sense conception of narrowly orthonomous
action

facts about	available	AR→	means-ends
means to	evidence		belief
desired ends?	about means to		
	desired ends		

+ DC→ **bodily**   desired
           movement   end?

desire for
an end
↑
AR

facts about	available	AR→	judgments
what there is	evidence about		about what
normative	what there is		there is
reason to do?	normative		normative
	reason to do		reason to do

striking. Moreover the common sense nature of the common sense
conception reveals the truly revisionary nature of radical
Humeanism.

3. Realist and irrealist interpretations of common sense

The mere fact that radical Humeanism is a revisionary doctrine is
no objection to it. For if there are compelling reasons to revise common sense then we have no choice but to embrace those revisions.
But are there such reasons?

The obvious grounds for revising common sense in the direction
of radical Humeanism would be that we can make no sense of the
key elements in the common sense conception of orthonomous
action. To repeat, these key elements are:

(i) the idea that there are facts about what we have normative
reason to do;
(ii) the idea that these facts manifest themselves in the form of
evidence about what we have normative reason to do;
(iii) the idea that, via the exercise of our rational capacities, we
can arrive at judgments about what we have normative
reason to do;

and

(iv) the idea that, via the exercise of our rational capacities, we can acquire corresponding desires.

The question we must ask next is whether we can give a plausible interpretation of these four key ideas.

There is, of course, one completely straightforward interpretation of these key ideas. Realists hold that there are indeed facts about what we have normative reason to do, and hence that judgments about what we have normative reason to do are none other than expressions of our beliefs about this domain of facts (see figure 6).

Figure 6. A realist interpretation of the common sense conception of fully orthonomous action

facts about	**K→ available**	**IR→ means-ends**
means to	**evidence**	**belief**
desired ends	**about means to**	
	desired ends	

$$+ \quad \text{DC→ bodily} \quad \text{PPR→ desired}$$
$$\text{movement} \quad \text{end}$$

desire for
an end
↑
IR

facts about	**K→available**	**IR→ beliefs about**
what there is	**evidence about**	**what there is**
normative	**what there is**	**normative**
reason to do	**normative**	**reason to do**
	reason to do	

Fully orthonomous action is a matter of an agent's being suitably placed to have knowledge of both means-ends and normative reasons, of her having and exercising idealized capacities for the formation of rational beliefs about both means-ends and normative reasons in the light of the evidence available to her and the formation of desires in the light of her beliefs about her normative reasons, of her having and exercising the capacity to move her body in the way required to realize her desired ends, and of the world obliging her by allowing that desired end to come about in a manner that corresponds to her pattern of practical reasoning.

There is also a corresponding realist picture of the structure of narrowly orthonomous action (see figure 7).

Figure 7. A realist interpretation of the common sense conception
of narrowly orthonomous action

facts about means to desired ends?	**available evidence about means to desired ends**	**AR→ means-ends belief**		
		+ DC→ bodily desire for an end ↑ AR	**desired movement end?**	
facts about what there is normative reason to do?	**available evidence about what there is normative reason to do**	**AR→ beliefs about what there is normative reason to do**		

As before, narrowly orthonomous action abstracts away from the assumption that the agent is located in a suitably obliging world, and of her having idealized rational capacities. According to the realist, it simply requires that she exercises such belief-forming capacities as she has about her normative reasons, and such capacities as she has to form desires and act in the light of these beliefs. Such capacities may, of course, be very limited. But the crucial point is that, since this is all we could possibly expect of an agent, it follows that this is all that there could be to holding her responsible.

Now it might be thought that this realist alternative is a non-starter. After all, how could we take seriously the idea of there being facts about normative reasons for action, facts belief in which are subject to a requirement of reason to pair up with a desire to act accordingly? Isn't the radical Humean right that, since desires cannot be true or false, it follows that there is no way to make sense of such a rational requirement? And doesn't this entail that desires are not subject to such requirements of reason? There are, however, two quite different ways in which this realist option can be developed.

On the one hand, there is non-reductive realism of the kind that is argued for by Jonathan Dancy (1993, 2000), Derek Parfit (1997), and Thomas Scanlon (1998). In defending realism these theorists take the high road. They offer no analysis of facts about normative reasons (i), and hence no account of either how such facts manifest themselves in evidence (ii) or of how, on the basis of such evidence, we are capable of arriving at rational beliefs about what we have normative reason to do (iii). Nor, therefore, do they offer any account of why our beliefs about our normative reasons, understood as beliefs about an unanalysable domain of facts, rationally require us to have corresponding desires (iv). Instead they simply proceed on the confident assumption that the existence of normative reasons with such features can be taken for granted in all their theorising. In other words, they take these assumptions about normative reasons to be basic: assumptions which require nothing by way of justification or defence. In so doing they do not so much refute the radical Humeans' claim that desires are original existences as turn their backs on it.

Though not everyone has this sort of brazen confidence, it is, I think, instructive that at least some philosophers do. For it forces the rest us to ask why we feel the need to respond to the radical Humean's view that desires are original existences, and hence not subject to rational control. Why shouldn't we take the fact that desires are subject to rational control, in precisely the way described in the realist conception of orthonomy, as a rock bottom assumption? But there is, I think, an obvious answer to this question: the one given at the outset. Radical Humeans insist that we explain the source of the rational requirements to which desires for ends are subject because, given that desires for ends cannot be true or false, it is unclear to them what the source of such rational requirements could be. For those of us who feel the force of this radical Humean challenge there is, fortunately, a low road, more reductive, realist alternative (Williams 1980, Smith 1994).

As Williams has pointed out, even the most radical Humeans usually admit that desires are subject to certain sorts of rational requirements (though see Millgram 1995). Most obviously, for example, they admit that desires are subject to the means-end requirement: reason requires that when agents desire to ϕ and believe that they can ϕ by ψ-ing, they desire to ψ (Smith 2004). But it follows immediately from this that desires for means, at any rate, are subject to rational control in at least the following sense: agents may have, but fail to exercise, the capacity to desire the believed means to their ends. Moreover it also follows that desires for means are subject to control in the light of information. Agents must, it seems, be criticizable if they have desires for means that are based on less than a full and frank assessment of the evidence about means to ends that is available to them, given such capacities as they have to provide such an assessement.

Once this much is agreed, however, it seems irresistible to

suppose that desires are subject to other rational requirements as well. For example, desires for ends look like they must also be subject to an informational requirement. A desire for an end that is poorly understood looks like it is rationally criticizable if the agent whose desire it is would lose that desire if he were to reflect and gain that better understanding. And desires for ends look like they must be subject to other, more demanding, requirements. For example, sets of desires that include desires for very specific things and desires for very general things look like they can, and so should, be brought into a coherent and unified relationship with each other, a relationship not unlike that which Rawls describes in his famous account of reflective equilibrium (Rawls 1951).

Crucially, however, once it is agreed that desires are subject to at least some of these rational requirements, it seems that we have said all we need to say to vindicate realism. For there are facts about what agents would desire if their desires satisfied these rational requirements, and these facts look like they are proper objects of belief. Moreover agents who have such beliefs look like they will be subject to a distinctive rational requirement. After all, agents who are capable of reflecting on the rational status of their beliefs and desires, and so of forming beliefs about the ways in which their beliefs and desires could be rationally improved, would seem to be in an incoherent state of mind if they find themselves believing that they would have certain beliefs or desires if they had an ideally rational set of beliefs and desires, and yet also find themselves failing to have those beliefs or desires. For their failure indicates a failure to exercise a quite general capacity rational agents possess to rationally manage their own psychologies, that is, to impose coherence upon them.

On this alternative, more reductive, approach, the suggestion is thus that facts about what we have normative reason to do are analysable in terms of idealized psychological facts: facts about what we have normative reason to do are facts about what we would want ourselves to do if we had a maximally informed and coherent and unified desire set (i). Equipped with such an analysis of facts about normative reasons we have a ready-made account of both how such facts could manifest themselves to us and how the beliefs we form in the light of such manifestations can be more or less justified (ii and iii). For the epistemology of facts about normative reasons turns out to be no more problematic than the epistemology of counterfactuals in general. Finally, we also have a ready-made explanation of why our beliefs about such facts rationally require us to have corresponding motivations (iv). The explanation lies in the fact that desiring a certain end coheres better with believing that we would desire that end if we had a maximally informed and coherent and unified desire set than does either having an aversion to that end or being indifferent towards it (Smith 1994, Smith 1997, Smith 2001). In having such a desire we manifest a capacity we possess, as rational creatures, to regulate our psychologies by reflecting on the normative requirements to which they are subject. In other words, we acquire such desires by exercising a quite general capacity we possess, as rational creatures, to have a more, rather than a less, coherent psychology.

Of course, not everyone will be willing to go along with either of these realist interpretations of the common sense conception of orthonomy. In an ecumenical spirit, it is therefore important to note that there is also an irrealist interpretation. As irrealists see things, talk of normative reasons should be interpreted not as the expression of our beliefs about a domain of facts, but rather as a projection of certain non-belief attitudes we have towards certain ways of acting. Thus, for example, an irrealist might hold that when an agent makes the realist-sounding claim that she has a normative reason to act in a certain way—in other words, when she appears to be making claims about what the facts are as regards what she has normative reason to do—she thereby expresses not a belief she has, but rather a higher-order desire of some sort, a desire about which of her first-order desires for ends is to lead to action, say (Blackburn 1998).

Unsurprisingly, irrealists therefore have a ready-made account of why we are rationally required to have desires for ends that accord with our judgments about what we have normative reason to do. For it is the role of higher-order desires that certain of our first-order desires for ends result in action to bring those first-order desires about so that they can indeed result in action (iv). Moreover, since such higher-order desires may fit more or less coherently with the rest of an agent's higher-order attitudes, irrealists can give an interpretation of the claim that an agent's judgments about what she has normative reason to do must tally with the evidence available to her. We suppose that such judgments are evidentially well-based, irrealists might say, when they cohere well with the rest of an agent's higher-order attitudes, and we say that they are poorly based on evidence otherwise (iii).

Moreover, once this much is agreed it seems that the irrealist can even offer an account of what it means to say that the evidence available to an agent is a manifestation of the facts about what there is a normative reason to do. For when someone, a theorist say, insists that an agent's evidence about what there is normative reason to do is a manifestation of the facts about what there is normative reason to do, irrealists will insist that that theorist thereby expresses his own higher-order attitudes. In other words, he thereby endorses the contents of the agent's higher-order attitudes (ii). In this way the irrealist can even provide an interpretation of the realist-sounding claim that fully orthonomous action is possible only in an obliging world. For, irrealists will insist, each of us will suppose that worlds are obliging for other agents to the extent that we endorse acting on certain first-order desires ourselves (i), desires that accord with the objects of other agents' higher-order desires. These, irrealists will say, are the circumstances in which we will be prepared to call the judgments that other agents make about what there is normative reason to do 'knowledge'.

We thus have the following irrealist picture of fully orthomomous action. An agent is fully orthonomous, the irrealist will say, just in case she has and exercises her capacity to have a set of higher-order desires about which ends are to result in action and first-order desires for ends that fit together in a coherent way (this is what 'IR→' signifies in figure 8). In this picture, to repeat, higher-order desires play the roles of judgments and evidence about what there is normative reason to do. Moreover, the irrealist will say, for an agent's actions to be fully orthonomous—that is, for us, as theorists, to suppose that the expression of such higher-order desires counts as knowledge—we theorists must endorse the contents of those higher-order desires (hence the 'quasi-facts' and the 'QK→' in figure 8).

The picture of narrow orthonomy that emerges on this irrealist interpretation is then the following (see figure 9).

Figure 8. An irrealist interpretation of the common sense conception of fully orthonomous action

facts about means to desired ends	K→ available evidence about means to desired ends	IR→ means-ends belief		
		+ DC→ bodily movement	PPR→ desired end	
		desire for an end ↑ IR		
quasi-facts about what there is normative reason to do	QK→ desires that certain other desires for ends are to result in action	IR→ desire that this desire for an end is to result in action		

Figure 9. The irrealist interpretation of the common sense conception of narrowly orthonomous action

facts about means to desired ends?	**available evidence about means to desired ends**	**AR→ means-ends belief**		
			+ DC→ bodily	**desired**
			movement	**end?**
		desire for an end ↑ AR		
quasi-facts about what there is normative reason to do?	**desire that certain desires for ends are to result in action**	**AR→ desire that this desire for an end is to result in action**		

For the irrealist, when we assess the narrow orthonomy of an agent's actions we abstract away from our own endorsement of the contents of her higher-order attitudes. We limit our attention to such capacities as the agent has—her actual rational capacities—to make her higher-order desires about which ends are to result in action and her first-order desires for ends fit together in a coherent way (this, again, is what 'AR→' signifies). Such capacities may be limited. But, the irrealist will hold, since the exercise of such capacities is all that we can legitimately expect of a rational agent, so this is all that can be at issue when we hold her responsible.

Let me summarize the argument of this section. Common sense provides us with a rich conception of orthonomous action, a conception that stands opposed to that suggested by radical Humeanism. The common sense conception has four crucial elements (i-iv). Because radical Humeans can give no interpretation of these elements, they insist that we have grounds on which to revise common sense. But I have argued that since, contrary to the radical Humeans, we can give a variety of interpretations of these crucial elements—as we have seen, we can give non-reductive and reductive realist interpretations, and we can give an irrealist interpretation—it follows that we have no need to revise common sense. Instead we should suppose that common sense provides us with an ecumenical framework in which to think about both fully orthonomous and narrowly orthonomous action.

4. Novel cases

Having thus established the credentials of the common sense conception, it is time to put it to work. A striking feature of the common sense conception of orthonomous action is the way in which it forces us to think of agents as exercising a whole range of rational capacities that they possess, capacities that forge connections between different elements in their psychology. Though we have so far focussed on the ways in which three such elements get combined in fully orthonomous and narrowly orthonomous action—available evidence about what there is normative reason to do, judgments about what there is normative reason to do, and desires for ends—in what follows I want to describe two further ways in which these three elements can be combined.

The fact that these elements in the common sense conception can be combined in all manner of different ways should hardly be surprising. Indeed, given that both fully orthonomous and narrowly orthonomous action assume a significant degree of idealisation—fully orthonomous action is explicitly an idealisation, but it is almost as hard to imagine someone who is consistently narrowly orthonomous, given that this would require his constant exercise of such rational capacities as he has—it is a fair bet that most of us, most of the time, display psychological structures rather different to those described so far. If we succeed in acting correctly none the less, and if we are responsible for so acting, then the explanation of why looks like it is yet to be given.

In this spirit, consider the following combination of the three elements (see figure 10).

Figure 10. Motivation accords with judgment about normative
  reasons independently of available evidence

facts about means to desired ends	**K→ available evidence about means to desired ends**	**AR→ means-ends belief**
	+	**DC→ bodily** desired **movement** end?
		desire for an end
		↑
		AR
facts about what there is normative reason to do?	available evidence about what there is normative reason to do ?	**judgments about what there is normative reason to do**

187

In this case, the agent's desires for ends result from an exercise of such capacities as she has to have desires that accord with her judgments about her normative reasons, but her judgments are formed without regard to the available evidence. In other words, she exercises certain of her rational capacities, but she fails to exercise others.

Next consider the following combination (figure 11).

Figure 11. Motivation accords with available evidence about normative reasons independently of judgment

facts about means to desired ends	K→ available evidence about means to desired ends	AR→ means-ends belief		
		+ DC→ bodily movement	desired end?	
		desire for an end		
	↗ AR			
facts about what there is normative reason to do?	available evidence about what there is normative reason to do?	judgments about what there is normative reason to do?		

In this case, the evidence available to the subject causes and rationalizes the agent's desire for an end, but the agent's judgment about what there is normative reason to do is formed independently of that evidence, and the agent also fails to exercise such capacity as she has to have desires for ends that accord with her judgment. Once again, this is a case in which the agent exercises certain rational capacities, but fails to exercise others.

Cases much like these have, in fact, been much discussed in the recent literature on responsibility (Bennett 1974, McIntyre 1990, Arpaly 2000, Jones 2003). Here, for example, is an example of Nomy Arpaly's.

Emily's best judgment has always told her that she should pursue a PhD in chemistry. But as she proceeds through a graduate program, she starts feeling restless, sad, and ill motivated to stick to her studies. These feelings are triggered by a variety of factors which, let us suppose, are good reasons for her, given her beliefs and desires, not to be in the program. The kind of research that she is expected to do, for example, does not allow her to fully exercise her talents, she does not possess some of the talents that the program requires, and the people who seem most happy in the program are very different from her in their general preferences and character. All these factors she notices and registers, but they are also something that she ignores when she deliberates about the rightness of her choice of vocation: like most of us, she tends to find it hard, even threatening, to take leave of a long-held conviction and to admit to herself the evidence against it. But every day she encounters the evidence again, her restlessness grows, her sense of dissatisfaction grows, and she finds it harder to motivate herself to study. Still, when she deliberates, she concludes that her feelings are senseless and groundless. One day, on an impulse, propelled exclusively by her feelings, she quits the program, calling herself lazy and irrational but also experiencing a (to her) inexplicable sense of relief. Years later, happily working elsewhere, she suddenly sees the reasons for her bad feelings of old, cites them as the reasons for her quitting, and regards as irrationality not her quitting but, rather, the fact that she held on to her conviction that the program was right for her as long as she did... Emily, I would like to argue, acts far more rationally in leaving the program than she would in staying in the program, not simply because she has good reasons to leave the program, but also because she acts for these good reasons. (Arpaly 2000, 504–5).

As Arpaly describes her, Emily's psychology has the structure depicted in figure 11. Her feelings of alienation from the graduate program, and ultimately her impulse to leave it, result from the evidence available to her that the graduate program is not for her, evidence to which she is insensitive in forming her judgment about what she has normative reason to do. Moreover, in the possible world Arpaly has us imagine at the end of the passage, the possible world in which Emily sticks by her resolve to get a PhD in chemistry, her psychology has the structure depicted in figure 10. Her desire to stay in the program squares with her judgment about what she has normative reason to do, but her judgment is insensitive to the overwhelming evidence to the contrary.

It is, I think, a great virtue of the common sense conception of orthonomy that it predicts the possibility of these structures. Moreover, it is also a great virtue of the common sense conception that it provides us with the tools with which to understand them. The fundamental point, at least according to the common sense conception, is that an agent's global rationality is a function of her exercise of capacities that can be assessed for their rationality on a more local basis (Smith 2004). An agent's global rationality depends, inter alia, on whether various rational connections hold between the different elements in her psychology. Are her beliefs about means to ends formed in response to available evidence about means to ends? Are her judgments about what there is normative reason to do formed in response to the evidence available to her about what there is normative reason to do? Are her desires for ends formed in response to her judgments about what there is normative reason to do? And, even, are her desires for ends formed in response to the evidence available to her about what there is normative reason to do? To repeat, according to common sense, each of these connections is ripe for local assessment.

The upshot is thus that even if, in the end, we agree with Arpaly that Emily is more globally rational for leaving the program than she would have been if she had stayed—in other words, even if we agree that a desire to leave the program is what is required for Emily to get things right—what thinking about this case in terms of the structure suggested by the common sense conception forces us to acknowledge is that she thereby purchases her global rationality at the cost of local irrationality (see also Jones 2003). Emily's impulse may be well-sourced in her evidence about what she has normative reason to do, and this fact about her impulse might be of overwhelming significance when it comes to assessing her global rationality. For a real-world, fallible, creature like Emily, a creature who, 'like most of us, ... tends to find it hard, even threatening, to take leave of a long-held conviction and to admit to herself the evidence against it', having such well-sourced impulses might even be as close as she will ever get to approximating narrow orthonomy. But, if so, then it seems that the global rationality of real-world, fallible, creatures like Emily—that is, her exercise of such global capacity as she has to get things right—requires nothing less than local irrationality. That is to say, it requires a failure on her behalf to exercise a local capacity she possesses to get things right. There is no paradox here. But, as I said, it is a great virtue of the common sense conception that it makes the point transparent.

Moreover, thinking about Emily's case in terms of the structure suggested by common sense forces us to face up to a thorny question about her responsibility. The question is whether, notwithstanding the global rationality of her decision to leave to the program, it is appropriate to hold her responsible for that decision. Can we really see her acquisition of her bad feelings about the program, and ultimately her impulse to leave it, as having resulted from her exercise of a capacity to respond in these ways to evidence? This is what the 'AR→' in figure 11 suggests, but is that really plausible? Can we really suppose that Emily exercises a rational capacity to acquire these feelings in response to the evidence available to her, or should we suppose instead that, in such cases, the evidence simply causes these feelings in her, where that causal sequence is one which happens to accord with reason's dictates? I do not wish to take a stand on this issue here. For the record, my hunch is that such cases show that there is a certain indeterminacy in our concept of a rational capacity, and hence a corresponding indeterminacy in our concept of responsibility and control. But, once again, it is, I think, a great virtue of the common sense conception that it forces us to face up to such thorny questions, and that it equips us with the critical tools with which to attempt an answer.

References

Arpaly, Nomy 2000: 'On Acting Rationally against One's Best Judgment' in *Ethics*, 110, 488–513.

Bennett, Jonathan 1974: 'The conscience of Huckleberry Finn' in *Philosophy*, 49, 123–34.

Blackburn, Simon 1998: *Ruling Passions* (Oxford: Clarendon Press).

Christman, John. 1989: ed., *The Inner Citadel: Essays on Individual Autonomy*, (Oxford: Oxford University Press).

Dancy, Jonathan 1993: *Moral Reasons* (Oxford: Basil Blackwell).

—— 2000: *Practical Reality* (Oxford: Oxford University Press).

Danto, Arthur C. 1963: 'What We Can Do', *Journal of Philosophy*, 60, 434–45.

Davidson, Donald 1963: 'Actions, Reasons and Causes' reprinted in his *Essays on Actions and Events* (Oxford: Oxford University Press, 1980).

Hornsby, Jennifer 1980: *Actions* (London: Routledge and Kegan Paul).

Hume, David 1740: *A Treatise of Human Nature* (Oxford: Clarendon Press, 1968).

Jones, Karen 2003: 'Emotion, weakness of will, and the normative conception of agency' in Anthony Hatzimoysis, ed, *Philosophy and the Emotions* (Cambridge: Cambridge University Press).

Korsgaard, Christine 1986: 'Skepticism about Practical Reason', *Journal of Philosophy*, 83, 5–25.

McIntyre, Alison 1990: 'Is Akratic Action Always Irrational?' in Owen Flanagan and Amelie Rorty, eds, *Identity and Moral Character* (Cambridge: MIT Press), 379–400.

Mele, Alfred 1992: *Springs of Action* (New York: Oxford University Press).

Michael Smith

Millgram, Elijah 1995: 'Was Hume a Humean?' in *Hume Studies* 21, 75–93.

Nagel, Thomas 1970: *The Possibility of Altruism* (Princeton: Princeton University Press).

Parfit, Derek 1997: 'Reasons and Motivation' in *Proceedings of the Aristotelian Society* Supplementary Volume 71, 99–130.

Peacocke, Christopher 1979: *Holistic Explanation* (Oxford: Oxford University Press).

Pettit, Philip and Michael Smith 1990: 'Backgrounding Desire', *Philosophical Review*, 99, 565–92.

—— 1993: 'Practical Unreason' in *Mind*, 102, 53–79.

—— 1996: 'Freedom in Belief and Desire' in *Journal of Philosophy*, 93, 429–49.

—— forthcoming: 'External Reasons' in Cynthia Macdonald and Graham Macdonald, eds, *McDowell and His Critics* (Oxford: Blackwell)

Rawls, John 1951: 'Outline of a Decision Procedure for Ethics', *Philosophical Review*, 60, 177–97.

Scanlon, Thomas 1998: *What We Owe to Each Other* (Cambridge: Harvard University Press).

Smith, Michael 1987: 'The Humean Theory of Motivation' in *Mind*, 96, 36–61.

—— 1994: *The Moral Problem* (Oxford: Blackwell).

—— 1997: 'In Defence of *The Moral Problem*: A Reply to Brink, Copp and Sayre-McCord' in *Ethics*, 108, 84–119.

—— 1999: 'The Possibility of Philosophy of Action' in Jan Bransen and Stefaan Cuypers, eds, *Human Action, Deliberation and Causation* (Dordrecht: Kluwer Academic Publishers), 17–41.

—— 2001: 'The Incoherence Argument: Reply to Schafer-Landau' in *Analysis*, 61, 254–66.

—— 2003: 'Rational Capacities' in Sarah Stroud and Christine Tappolet, eds, *Weakness of Will and Varieties of Practical Irrationality* (Oxford: Oxford University Press).

—— 2004: 'Instrumental Desires, Instrumental Rationality' in *Proceedings of the Aristotelian Society* Supplementary Volume 78.

—— forthcoming: 'Is there a Nexus between Reasons and Rationality?' in Sergio Tenenbaum, ed., *Poznan Studies in the Philosophy of Science and Humanities: New Trends in Moral Psychology* (Amsterdam: Rodophi).

Stocker, Michael 1979: 'Desiring the Bad: An Essay in Moral Psychology', *Journal of Philosophy*, 76, 738–53.

—— 2004: 'Raz on the Intelligibility of Bad Acts' in R.Jay Wallace, Philip Pettit, Samuel Scheffler, and Michael Smith, eds, *Reason and Value: Themes from the Moral Philosophy of Joseph Raz* (Oxford: Oxford University Press).

Watson, Gary 1975: 'Free Agency' reprinted in Gary Watson, ed., *Free Will* (Oxford: Oxford University Press, 1982).

Williams, Bernard 1980: 'Internal and External Reasons' reprinted in his *Moral Luck* (Cambridge: Cambridge University Press, 1981).

Wilson, George M. 1989: *The Intentionality of Human Action* (Stanford: Stanford University Press).

Wolf, Susan 1990: *Freedom Within Reason* (New York: Oxford University Press).

Woods, Michael 1972: 'Reasons for Action and Desire', *Proceedings of the Aristotelian Society* Supplementary Volume 46, 189–201.

Normativity and the Will

R. JAY WALLACE

If there is room for a substantial conception of the will in contemporary theorizing about human agency, it is most likely to be found in the vicinity of the phenomenon of normativity. Rational agency is distinctively responsive to the agent's acknowledgment of reasons, in the basic sense of considerations that speak for and against the alternatives for action that are available. Furthermore, it is natural to suppose that this kind of responsiveness to reasons is possible only for creatures who possess certain unusual volitional powers, beyond the bare susceptibility to beliefs and desires necessary for the kind of rudimentary agency of which the higher animals are arguably capable.

But what exactly is the relation between normativity and the will? In this paper I want to discuss two contemporary answers to this question, both of which draw their inspiration from Kant. The first answer, due to Christine Korsgaard, holds that normativity itself must be accounted for in terms of the movements of the will. On the constructivist position that Korsgaard favours, what makes a given principle normative for me is my volitional commitment to comply with it in action. The primary role for the will in understanding rational action is thus to serve as what she calls the "source" of normativity, providing an account of what makes principles binding on us in the first place, as reasons for action. The second answer departs from Korsgaard's position in accepting a realist rather than constructivist framework for thinking about the normative principles that specify what we have reason to do. According to this approach, such principles are not made normative for us by our commitment to comply with them, rather their normative force is taken to be prior to and independent of our particular decisions about what to do. The distinctive role for the will, on the second approach, is to explain the striking capacity of rational agents to be guided in their activity by their conception of what they have reason to do.

I myself reject the first, constructivist conception of the work that is done by the notion of the will, and accept the second, realist approach to this question. My aim in this paper, which will of necessity be sketchy and incomplete, will be to adduce some considerations that motivate these conclusions.

R. Jay Wallace

1. Constructivism about the Normative

In a series of influential recent writings Christine Korsgaard has developed a constructivist approach to the fundamental issues in moral philosophy, which includes a distinctive and important account of the sources of normativity in our volitional activity.[1] Korsgaard presents her approach as an alternative to realism in ethics. I want to begin by considering some interpretations of moral realism, in the hope that this will provide an illuminating foil for the reflections that follow about the relation between normativity and the will.

It sometimes seems as if there are as many versions of moral realism as there are moral realists. But one thing that most realist positions have in common is the following. They can be understood as attempts to give expression to the idea that discourse in a certain domain is answerable to a reality that is in some sense prior to and independent of us. Korsgaard herself endorses a similar thought when she characterizes moral realism as 'the view that propositions employing moral concepts may have truth values because moral concepts describe or refer to normative entities or facts that exist independently of those concepts themselves' (2). The difficulty is that talk about the concept or agent independence of entities or facts is rather dark, and admits of a variety of incompatible interpretations.

One way to make out the independence and priority of moral reality would be to take seriously Korsgaard's reference to 'normative entities'. That is, we might adopt an objectual paradigm of the real, assuming that discourse is realistic if it makes reference to objects or events that are both independent of us, and capable of standing in causal relations to us. To be a moral realist, on this conception of realism, would be to hold that the furniture of the world includes, in addition to the ordinary physical objects with which our senses put us in contact (medium-sized dry goods and the like), an array of concrete normative entities or values, conceived perhaps as particulars of some kind or other. Actually, I believe that the objectual conception of realism underlying this position is more often adopted by opponents than by proponents of realism in ethics.

[1] Korsgaard's reflections on this topic are presented most recently in a paper written for a special APA session on the state of moral philosophy at the turn of a new century; see Christine Korsgaard, 'Realism and Constructivism in 20th Century Moral Philosophy,' forthcoming in the *Journal of Philosophical Research*. Page numbers in the text to follow refer to passages in Korsgaard's manuscript.

196

Thus anti-realists often assume the objectual interpretation of real-ity, and then proceed to argue that realism is not a tenable position in ethics, because of the utter implausibility of the view that moral discourse makes reference to a realm of concrete normative entities that are anything like the physical objects and events with which we make causal contact in experience.[2] Nevertheless, we may agree that if a defender of realism in ethics wished to adopt this objectual interpretation of reality, the resulting position would not be very plausible. Moral discourse, on this objectual construal of it, would be conceived basically as a way of characterizing a peculiar set of normative entities, whose independence from us is modeled on the independence of ordinary physical objects.

There is a second class of positions in ethics that more interest-ingly develop the basic realist idea. This class of positions is distin-guished by the following two commitments. There is, first, a factive as opposed to an objectual conception of independent reality. That is, moral realists of this stripe would claim that the reality to which moral discourse is answerable is not a realm of concrete particular entities or objects, but a set of distinctive facts about what is the case. The independence of moral reality, on this conception of it, finds expression in the idea that moral facts obtain in a way that is prior to and independent of our judging that they obtain. Second, the class of realist positions I am envisaging is further distinguished by what is sometimes referred to as an externalist conception of the relation between moral facts and reasons for action. According to this kind of conception, the question of whether a given moral fact does or does not obtain is strictly independent from the question of whether any given agent has reason to act accordingly. Even if moral facts are conceived in such a way that their linguistic characterization requires apparently normative vocabulary (as in: 'It is wrong to torture the innocent'), it does not follow from the truth of such claims that any particular agent has reason to comply with them. Instead, the legitimacy of talk about an independent realm of moral facts might be established by making out the explanatory significance of such facts (for instance, in accounting for large-scale processes of social change).

This variety of factive moral realism seems a good bit more plausible than the objectual version sketched earlier. It is, for one thing, a view that a number of actual philosophers have been

<hr/>

[2] Cf. Gilbert Harman, *The Nature of Morality* (New York: Oxford University Press, 1977), chap. 1 and J. L. Mackie, *Ethics* (Harmondsworth: Penguin Books, 1977), chap. 1.

tempted to hold and to defend (examples might be Richard Boyd, David Brink, and Peter Railton[3]). What this position shares with objectual moral realism, however, is its rejection of the practical conception of ethics that Korsgaard—in common with others influenced by Kant—have advocated. Korsgaard herself presents the practical conception by contrasting two different accounts of the function of moral concepts: as serving to describe an independent reality, on the one hand, and as working out solutions to practical problems, on the other. I must confess that I am a little uncomfortable with talk about the 'function' of 'concepts'. But I think I understand well enough what Korsgaard is driving at. On the practical conception she favours, the normativity of moral discourse has to do with its suitability to answer the questions that we pose in the first-person standpoint of practical deliberation. A claim is normative, in this sense, insofar as it identifies a reason, a consideration that speaks for or against a given agent's acting in some specific way or other.

In these terms, the practical conception of ethics interprets moral discourse as discourse about an autonomous domain of reasons for action. Of course, we must leave open the possibility that ethics comes to nothing, insofar as there might turn out to be no distinctively moral reasons for acting one way or another. But the practical conception interprets moral discourse as essentially aspiring to identify a distinctive class of normative considerations, in the sense sketched above. It follows that an account of moral reality or objectivity that leaves open the question of whether anyone ever has reason to comply with moral demands would fail to capture the kind of normativity that is essential to and distinctive of moral discourse, as the practical conception conceives it. In this respect, the second kind of moral realism sketched above resembles the first version that we considered: both forms rest on an 'essentially theoretical' conception of ethics (cf. 36).

Let us now consider a third variety of moral realism, one that accepts the factive rather than the objectual interpretation of the real, but that abandons the thesis that questions about the obtaining of moral facts are independent from questions about their standing

[3] See Richard Boyd, 'How to be a Moral Realist,' as reprinted in Stephen Darwall, Allan Gibbard, and Peter Railton, eds., *Moral Discourse and Practice* (New York: Oxford University Press, 1997), pp. 105–35; David Brink, *Moral Realism and the Foundations of Ethics* (Cambridge, England: Cambridge University Press, 1989); and Peter Railton, 'Moral Realism,' as reprinted in Darwall et. al., *Moral Discourse and Practice*, pp. 137–63.

as reasons for action. Thus, a factive moral realist might agree with Korsgaard that moral discourse essentially aspires to normativity in her sense, characterizing or purporting to characterize a domain of distinctive reasons for action. According to this kind of realist position, the priority and independence of moral facts is a matter of their obtaining prior to and independent of our judging that they obtain. But the appropriate kind of moral fact will obtain only if (say) rightness and wrongness are genuine reasons for action, considerations that can and should count for and against prospective courses of action in the perspective of practical deliberation. I believe that a position of roughly this shape—we might refer to it as normative moral realism, or NMR for short—is implicit in the work of a number of contemporary philosophers, including Thomas Nagel, Derek Parfit, Joseph Raz, and T. M. Scanlon.[4]

As I said above, it would seem to be a touchstone of realist positions that they take our discourse to be answerable to a reality that is in some sense prior to and independent of *us*. This is an idea that NMR accepts. It holds that when we project ourselves into the practical point of view, and set our minds to the question of what we ought to do, our deliberation is an attempt to get clear about an objective and appropriately independent fact of the matter, namely what an agent in our deliberative situation has most reason to do. Offhand, the assumption that the will is answerable to independent and irreducibly normative facts of this kind would seem neither metaphysically extravagant, nor otherwise implausible. To paraphrase Thomas Nagel, some unchosen constraints on choice may be among the conditions of its possibility.[5]

If NMR is a promising approach to the relation between

[4] See Thomas Nagel, *The View from Nowhere* (New York: Oxford University Press, 1985), chap. 8; Derek Parfit, 'Reasons and Motivation,' *The Aristotelian Society*, Supplementary Volume 77 (1997), pp. 99–130; and T. M. Scanlon, *What We Owe to Each Other* (Cambridge, Mass.: Harvard University Press, 1998), chap. 1. Actually Scanlon is a constructivist of a sort about moral reasons, and a realist about normative reasons of other kinds; one could also be a realist about normativity, but a sceptic about morality, denying that moral considerations constitute genuine reasons for action. For my purposes in what follows, the more important position is general realism about the normative, rather than the specific view that moral reasons are prior to and independent of the will, since it is the more general position that fundamentally contrasts with Korsgaard's brand of constructivism. I shall understand NMR in what follows in this more general sense.

[5] See Thomas Nagel, *The Possibility of Altruism* (Princeton: Princeton University Press, 1970), p. 23.

normativity and the will, why does Korsgaard reject it in favour of her constructivist alternative? She seems to hold that NMR does not come to grips with the fundamental philosophical problem of normativity, and that in this respect constructivism is distinctly superior. Korsgaard's most fundamental complaint about NMR is that it doesn't in the end *explain* the normativity of the concepts and judgments to which it applies. NMR says that there are independent normative truths about what we have reason to do (including truths about our moral reasons), and that deliberative reflection is an attempt to get clear about this independent normative realm. But NMR does not itself provide any global account of why the normative considerations it countenances are genuine reasons for action, considerations that advance a justified claim to govern our deliberative reflections. Thus Korsgaard represents the moral realist as postulating normative rules or standards that are to be applied by us when we engage in practical deliberation. But this way of conceiving of normativity, she argues, is unable to account for the authority of the postulated rules to tell us what we must do. 'If we think of rules of action as something we may or may not *apply* when we deliberate about what to do, then either we are obligated to apply them or we are not' (23). In the first case, the realist will have to suppose that 'the notion of obligation [is] prior to the existence of the rule' (22); this is tantamount to giving up the suggestion that normativity is fixed by independent rules that are potential objects of knowledge. In the second case, the realist will have abandoned the idea that the postulated rules are genuinely normative principles, and the fundamental problem of practical philosophy will remain unsolved.

Actually, this dilemma seems to be escapable by the proponent of NMR, as I have presented it. We should concede that the normative principles that the theory postulates are ones that we may or may not apply in practice. To admit this much is to acknowledge what is in any case extremely plausible, namely that people are only imperfectly rational, and that we often fail to do what we ourselves see to be normatively required. (This is a point I shall return to later.) It doesn't follow from this, however, that there is a further normative question that can be raised in regard to any given normative principle, of whether we are obligated to comply with it. The normativity or bindingness is built into the content of the principle, its standing as a principle that specifies what we have reason to do. The question whether we are obligated to comply with a given principle is already settled by whatever considerations establish it, in the first place, as an expression of the independent truth of the matter about what there is reason to do. These considerations, I take it, will primarily be the deliverances of first-order deliberative reflection about action. Thus, if it is not incoherent to suppose that there can be independent normative truths about what we have reason to do, then there is nothing implausible about supposing that knowledge of those truths might guide our deliberative reflection.

Nevertheless, I think I have some idea of what Korsgaard is objecting to in this realist picture. Her complaint must be that the realist assumes that there are independent normative facts or truths, without doing anything to explain philosophically how the normative truths it postulates are possible. And indeed, if we conceive realism in ethics as an attempt to provide a unified philosophical *account* of normativity, then we must agree with Korsgaard that it does not succeed in shedding much light on the matter. If realism is to yield an explanation of this kind, then we should expect its distinctive feature—the postulation of a body of truths that are prior to and independent of us—to illuminate the capacity of those truths to legislate to us how we are to act and to live. But Korsgaard is surely correct in thinking that the independence of the moral truths does not itself explain their normative grip on us. On the contrary, in the context of the search for a global explanation of how normativity is possible, the postulation of an independent body of moral truths threatens to multiply questions rather than to answer them. Morality will start to look like an objective structure that is completely independent of the will, and consequently presumptuous in its aspiration to prescribe to us how we are to behave.

Let us now turn to Korsgaard's constructivism, to see whether it offers a more satisfactory approach to this explanatory issue. The idea that is central to constructivism is that we, as agents, construct or bring about a reality that is not prior to and independent of our volitional activity, but rather its product. If this is to help with the present problem, then the reality that is constructed must be the realm of the normative. Thus, whereas a realist view such as NMR has it that there are normative truths that are prior to and independent of the will, a constructivist position might hold that such truths are distinctively the result of our volitional activity. The question is, can we really make sense of the idea that the realm of the normative is itself constructed through our deliberative activity as agents?

There is one class of positions in moral and political philosophy that offers a comparatively clear account of the idea of constructing a normative realm, namely contractualist positions. These accounts represent the basic normative principles of justice or morality as the result of the choices of hypothetical agents under carefully-circumscribed conditions. Thus Rawls defines justice by reference to principles defining the basic structure of society that a self-interested chooser would select from behind a veil of ignorance. Similarly, Scanlon takes morality to be specified by principles for the general regulation of conduct that could not reasonably be rejected by persons who are informed about their situation, and motivated by the concern to arrive at a set of principles that no-one could reasonably reject. But it is striking that these theories attempt to construct only a part of the larger realm of normative concepts: in Rawls's case, the realm of justice, and in Scanlon's the morality of right and wrong.[6] The contractualist apparatus that gives a content to the metaphor of construction is in each case embedded within a larger context of normative concepts that are not themselves explicated in terms of a hypothetical choice situation, including reasons for action that are grounded in agents' projects, life plans, relationships, aspirations, conceptions of the good, and so on.

Korsgaard herself acknowledges this feature of contractualist views. She raises the interesting question of whether a form of constructivism can be conceived that goes all the way down, or whether instead constructivist approaches always presuppose more basic normative notions that are to be understood in realist rather than in constructivist terms. She does not herself return a definite answer to this question. But for my part, it seems that constructivism has to go all the way down if it is to represent a genuine alternative to the kind of position in ethics represented by NMR. So long as a constructivist theory takes for granted normative notions that are not themselves accounted for in constructivist terms, it loses its title to be the approach that is uniquely adequate to make sense of the characteristically *practical* dimension of normative thought and concepts. At the same time, so long as contractualism provides our paradigm for a constructivist approach, it is unclear that constructivism really could go all the way down. For I doubt that we can really make sense of the idea that *all* normative principles are the result of a hypothetical choice under specified conditions. To render this idea coherent, we would need to imagine agents making choices under parameters that can be represented without recourse to any normative concepts whatsoever, and our ideas of agency and

---

[6] Thus as I mentioned above, Scanlon's NMR is a form of realism about normativity in general (including what he would call morality in the broader sense), within which his constructivism about the 'morality of right and wrong' (or morality in the narrower sense) is embedded. I discuss this aspect of his position in my paper 'Scanlon's Contractualism,' *Ethics* 112 (2002), pp. 429–70, sec. 4.

choice would arguably give way under those conditions. Again, some unchosen normative constraints on choice would seem to be among the conditions of its possibility.

If I understand Korsgaard's position, it would seem to move in a rather different direction from these familiar contractualist accounts. Her version of constructivism rests ultimately on the idea that the normative principles that govern the will are the very same principles that are constitutive of the will in the first place. In a sympathetic discussion of Kant's views on freedom and morality, Korsgaard writes that 'the categorical imperative is a principle of the *logic* of practical deliberation, a principle that is constitutive of deliberation, not a theoretical premise applied in practical thought' (30). The idea seems to be that the normativity of practical principles is to be accounted for by showing that we necessarily commit ourselves to complying with them whenever we undertake to act; commitment to such principles is, indeed, constitutive of willing anything at all. The element of construction in this account is to be understood not in terms of the hypothetical choice of principles (as in contractualist theories). It refers, more basically, to the fundamental role of practical activity in grounding the principles that regulate that very activity. Principles of practical reason are not principles whose normative force is prior to and independent of the will. Rather they are principles that are rendered normative for us *by* our act of willing itself, insofar as they describe constraints that we aspire to comply with in willing anything at all.

This is, of course, a bracingly audacious philosophical program. Korsgaard may be correct in thinking that it is the only approach that stands a chance of providing a unified account of the source of normativity, and she herself has done more than anyone to articulate its merits as an option in contemporary moral philosophy.[7] But I am sceptical that the normative force of all principles of practical reason can be accounted for by showing that we are committed to complying with them through the very act of willing. I shall mention two reasons for doubt on this score. First, there is the striking diversity of considerations that appear to have normative weight when people deliberate about what to do. Taken together, the things that can recommend or speak in favour of (or against) the potential actions of any given agent form a remarkably heterogeneous group. They include, to take only a few examples, considerations about the

---

[7] Especially significant in this connection is her book *The Sources of Normativity* (Cambridge, England: Cambridge University Press, 1996), and her 2002 John Locke lectures on 'Self-Constitution: Action, Identity and Integrity.'

R. Jay Wallace

bodily and mental states of the agent (that a prospective action would be harmful, or cause pleasure or pain); considerations about the agent's relationships and status (that it would be unbecoming to do x, given one's professional role); and considerations of an aesthetic and moral nature that are themselves highly diverse and multifaceted. Korsgaard's constructivist thesis is that the normativity of all these different reasons can be accounted for in the very same way, by appeal to the basic idea of volitional commitment. But the project of providing a unified account of the normativity of such a heterogeneous range of considerations seems implausible on its face. It is far more natural to suppose that there is no unified account to be given of what renders the variety of considerations that count as reasons for action normative, what makes them significant for our practical deliberation.

Second—and more importantly—there are problems surrounding the interpretation of the notion of the will, as it figures in Korsgaard's constructivism. The unitary source of normativity, according to that account, is the commitment to comply with such normative requirements as the instrumental principle and the categorical imperative, a commitment that is in turn built into all concrete determinations of the will. But how are we to understand this important idea? There seem to be two possible interpretations, and neither of them is very plausible. We might take volitional commitments to be brute motivational tendencies of some kind to comply with the principles whose normativity is in question. According to this interpretation, a basic tendency to act in accordance with those principles is partly constitutive of willing or choosing to do any particular action. But how can a brute tendency to comply with a given principle render that principle normative for me, a source of *reasons* for doing that which I am committed to doing? It could do so, I should have thought, only if some antecedent normative principle is operative that tells us that we have reason to comply with those principles that we are ineluctably inclined to act in accordance with. But a normative principle of this kind would not seem very plausible—it hardly seems to follow from the fact that I have a brute inclination to do something that it would be good or valuable to do so.[8] More to the point, postulation of such a principle would anyway explode the framework of constructivism, introducing at a crucial juncture in the account a principle whose normative force is not after all explained in terms of the idea of volitional commitment.

[8] I assume, here and in what follows, that an agent will have reason to do x only if their doing x would be good or valuable in some way.

Alternatively, we might try to interpret such commitments not as brute motivational tendencies, but rather in essentially normative terms. Thus, Korsgaard might understand the commitments that are necessary to any individual determination of the will as states with normative content rather than as mere tendencies to act. But this proposal seems to introduce normativity at the wrong place. We need an account that shows how the commitment to comply with a principle can render that principle normative for the agent. For these purposes, it would seem necessary to attach normativity to the stance or state of commitment itself, and not merely to the content of that stance or state. From the fact that I am, say, committed to the normative principle that it would be good to thwart my enemy, it cannot be inferred that it really would be good for me to thwart my enemy. This would follow only if the stance of commitment is normative not merely in its content but in its essence. The problem is that there seems to be no way to make out the latter claim without presupposing some normative principle of the sort that the constructivist was supposed to be accounting for in terms of the idea of commitment itself.

Korsgaard might respond that this argument fails to take seriously the first-personal character of the perspective of deliberation. The normative commitments that are constitutive of individual acts of willing are commitments of the first-personal standpoint of practical reason. The objection broached in the preceding paragraph is that those commitments, even if necessary, might turn out to be false. But to affirm the falsity of such a first-order normative claim is itself to make a move from within the deliberative point of view. Korsgaard might contend that a move of this kind is ruled out by her argument for the necessity of the commitment to the normative principles that determine what we have reason to do (such as the categorical imperative and the principle of instrumental reason). If these commitments are genuinely constitutive of the standpoint of practical reason, there is no position from which we could intelligibly challenge them—any attempt to do so will lead to a performative contradiction.

This interpretation treats constructivism as a kind of transcendental argument, about the conditions for the possibility of willing. When we recall that the approach is meant to provide a unified explanation of the normative force of *all* reasons for action, it becomes clear just how ambitious it really is, and how unlikely it is to succeed on its own terms. But even putting this problem to the side, a difficulty remains concerning the interpretation of the notion of commitment. We have been supposing that commitments are normative in their content, and this amounts to treating them in essentially cognitive terms, namely as commitments to *believe* or *accept* that it would be good or valuable to act in compliance with certain principles. But this interpretation leaves unexplained the *motivation* of rational agents to comply with their reasons for action. Korsgaard covers over this problem by using ambiguous terms like 'commitment' to present her constructivist position, terms that can be understood either in a cognitive or in a conative sense. This encourages us to suppose that the states that are implicit in all deliberation and choice can explain at once the truth of normative claims about what we have reason to do, and our determination to comply with those truths in practice. But when we put pressure on this notion, and start to consider more carefully what exactly it might mean, an interpretation capable of discharging these dual tasks appears elusive. At the very least, more needs to be said about the notion of the will before we can make sense of the constructivist idea that it functions as the unified source of normativity.

2. Normative Realism and the Will

The considerations adduced above make me sceptical about the prospects for Korsgaard's constructivism about normativity. The alternative approach that I myself favour is NMR. This approach holds that there are normative truths that are prior to and independent of the individual human will. In the version of NMR that I am attracted to, no attempt is made to provide a unified account of the normative force of the variety of reasons that are relevant to practical deliberation; in particular, there is no assumption that the postulated priority and independence of the normative truths is the common feature that makes them all normative. NMR should therefore not be construed as aspiring to rival Korsgaard's unifying explanation of the sources of normativity. It is rather a framework for thinking about practical normativity, one within which the aspiration to trace all normativity to a unified source is eschewed.

Among the advantages of this framework, to my mind, is the way it promises to illuminate the structure of rational agency. Agency of this kind, as I understand it, exhibits precisely the feature that Kant singled out when he characterized practical reason as the capacity to act not only in accordance with laws, but in accordance with one's conception of laws. This feature goes beyond the bare capacity for intentional action, construed as bodily movement that is both aimed at some goal, and causally sensitive to the agent's conception of the goal, as that which the agent is aiming to bring about. Activity can be intentional in the latter sense without being rational, and it is natural to locate the difference in the idea of responsiveness of action to the agent's conception of distinctively normative 'laws' or principles. By postulating that there are independent normative truths of the matter about what agents have reason to do in the situations they encounter, NMR secures a condition for the possibility of rational agency in this sense. Rationality in action can be understood as a matter of thinking clearly about the independent normative facts regarding one's reasons, and acting in a way that is both in accordance with and guided by one's grasp of those independent normative truths.

If this picture is to have application, however, then normative knowledge alone will not suffice. In addition, rational agents will require capacities that enable them to translate their normative insights into action, and to do so in ways that are genuinely guided by their normative understanding of what it would be best to do. This, in my view, is where the will comes in. The role that the will should play in relation to normativity is not as the unified source of normative principles, but rather as that which enables agents to act in the light of their grasp of such principles. The will, in this sense, is part of what sets distinctively rational creatures apart from other creatures that are capable only of more rudimentary intentional agency. In the remainder of this paper I want to discuss this way of thinking about the will. I shall first contrast my conception of the rational will with the popular Humean approach to the explanation of intentional action; I shall then distinguish two different ways of conceptualizing the rational will, and marshal some considerations that speak in favour of one of those models.[9]

The Humean approach that is familiar to all of us treats action as the causal result of concrete first-order desires and beliefs. This approach, I want to say, can perhaps make sense of the primitive phenomenon of intentional or goal-directed agency; but it is not adequate to account for the phenomenon of rational agency, as I have characterized it. According to the Humean, intentional action is causally influenced by the agent's beliefs, but the beliefs in question are not normative beliefs about what it would be good or desirable to do, but beliefs about the availability of things that, as a

---

[9] The ideas presented in this section are developed more fully in my paper 'Three Conceptions of Rational Agency,' *Ethical Theory and Moral Practice* 2 (1999), pp. 217–42.

matter of contingent psychological fact, one happens to want.[10] Consider an example that is couched in terms of the Humean model—a case in which, say, you go to see a movie, as a result of thinking about what would make for an entertaining evening. Deliberative reflection is here exclusively a matter of specifying a substantive end that is taken as given. As far as the generation of motivation and action is concerned, there is no role to be played by distinctively normative thoughts to the effect that it would be *good* to go in for some entertainment, or that this is what one *ought* to be up to. Rather we are to picture you as equipped with a substantive disposition to do something entertaining, which gets engaged causally by your thoughts about what would count as an entertaining evening in the circumstances. Under this scenario, your action is perhaps controlled by your grasp of considerations that count as reasons for action, but not by your grasp *that* they have this normative status, recommending or speaking in favour of what you end up doing. The result, I would contend, does not do justice to your standing as a rational agent, capable of determining what you do as the result of your own deliberative reflection. Rational deliberation is precisely reflection on the normative reasons that bear on your alternatives for action, and it turns out that there is no room for practically effective reflection of this kind on the Humean approach.

If we are to improve on the Humean account, then, we must suppose that rational agents are equipped with volitional resources that go beyond the basic susceptibility to concrete first-order desires and the beliefs that interact with them causally. Following Kant, I will call these special volitional resources the will, understanding by this expression those powers, whatever they are, that make possible distinctively rational agency. To say this much, however, does not yet tell us what exactly the will is like, for there are a number of different ways of conceptualizing the distinctive volitional powers that make rational agency possible. I now want to sketch two different approaches to understanding the rational will, which I have elsewhere called meta-internalism and volitionalism, respectively.

Meta-internalism assumes a variety of forms, but the basic idea common to them all is that there is an abstract or second-order

---

[10] Another way to put this point would be to say that the Humean interpretation of rational motivation seems to imply a kind of noncognitivism about the normative judgments arrived at through practical deliberation. These function not to ascertain independent truths about (say) what we have reason to do, but rather to express our motivating attitudes.

disposition or desire, subjection to which is constitutive of our being rational or (alternatively) of our being agents, and that it is this abstract disposition or desire that ultimately both makes possible and explains action in accordance with our conception of our reasons. Thus it has been suggested that we are rational only to the extent we exhibit a disposition to coherence in our attitudes, or to do what we believe we ought to do;[11] while our status as agents has been identified with the desire to be autonomous, or to act for reasons, or to do what makes sense to us.[12] For ease of exposition I shall focus on the version that holds that the second-order desire that is constitutive of the rational will is the desire to do what we believe we ought to do; let us look briefly at how this approach can help us to make sense of rational agency.

Meta-internalism shares with the Humean approach the apparently empiricist idea that motivation can be accounted for by appealing to combinations of beliefs and desires or dispositions. It departs from straightforward Humeanism by construing the desires or dispositions that are operative in rational agency not as concrete first-order states (such as the desire to do something entertaining this evening), but as abstract or second-order states: in the version we are considering, for instance, as a disposition to do what one ought to do. This feature in turn makes possible an appealing interpretation of the basic idea that rational agents are guided by their grasp of independent normative truths about what they have reason to do. To say that we are in this way guided by our recognition of

[11] The tendency to coherence is appealed to by Michael Smith, most fully in 'The Definition of "Moral",' in Dale Jamieson, ed., *Singer and his Critics* (Oxford: Blackwell, 1999), pp. 38–63; see also his *The Moral Problem* (Oxford: Blackwell, 1994), sec. 5.10, and his 'In Defense of *The Moral Problem*: A Reply to Brink, Copp, and Sayre-McCord,' *Ethics* 108 (1997), pp. 84–119, secs. 5–6. The disposition to do what one believes one ought is discussed by John Broome, in 'Reasons and Motivation,' *The Aristotelian Society* supplementary volume 77 (1997), pp. 131–46.

[12] These proposals are all due to J. David Velleman. See his *Practical Reflection* (Princeton: Princeton University Press, 1989), for the desire to do what makes sense; his 'What Happens When Someone Acts?,' *Mind* 101 (1992), pp. 461–81, for the desire to act in accordance with reasons; and his 'The Possibility of Practical Reason,' *Ethics* 106 (1996), pp. 694–726, and 'Deciding How to Decide,' in Garrett Cullity and Berys Gaut, eds., *Ethics and Practical Reason* (Oxford: Clarendon Press, 1997), pp. 28–52, for the desire for autonomy. The basic strategy of postulating a tendency to rationality that is causally responsible for rational action is anticipated in C. G. Hempel, 'Rational Action,' *Proceedings and Addresses of the American Philosophical Association* 35 (1961–62), pp. 5–24.

normative considerations is apparently to offer a certain kind of explanation; it is to hold that we did, say, x, *because* we recognized that we ought to do x. Meta-internalism offers a straightforward account of the idea of normative guidance, in causal terms. According to this position, our normative beliefs succeed in guiding our behaviour when, in combination with the standing disposition that makes us (rational) agents in the first place, they cause us to act in an appropriate way. Rational guidance is thus interpreted in a way that coheres with the popular causal approach to the workings of the mind.

The ability to account in such clear and familiar terms for the idea of normative guidance is undoubtedly the strength of the meta-internalist approach. It has, however, what is to my mind a serious weakness. This emerges most clearly when we think about cases of practical irrationality, in which we do intentionally what we ourselves believe we do not have most reason to do.[13] In situations of this kind, meta-internalism entails that the agent must have lacked the basic capacity to act in accordance with reason. This in turn undermines the important assumption that the requirements of practical reason apply even where they are violated.

Consider a familiar example of practical irrationality in the above sense: a case of *akrasia,* in which I believe (say) that I ought to get to work on the stack of student papers sitting on my desk, but I choose instead to watch a football game on television. Let us assume that this really is a genuine, hard case of *akrasia,* where my practical judgment that I ought to start on the papers is not interpreted in an 'inverted commas' sense, but instead expresses my sincere assessment of what I have most reason to do under the circumstances. What can the meta-internalist say about a case of this kind? The distinctive claim of the meta-internalist is that the operations of practical reason can be traced back to the causal effects of the basal desire or tendency that makes us (rational) agents in the first place, such as the desire to do what we ought.[14] In the case under consid-

---

[13] Some might prefer to characterize *akrasia* differently, as involving action contrary to one's judgment about what it would be best to do. I shall assume, however, that these formulations are equivalent: in the context of practical deliberation, judgments about what it would be good to do are, in effect, judgments about what one has reason to do.

[14] The remarks that follow apply most directly to the versions of meta-internalism proposed by Broome and Smith. Velleman's variant is more complicated, since the higher-order desires he postulates are meant to be constitutive not of rational agency in particular, but of agency across the board. (The desire to act for reasons might seem to be a constitutively

eration, however, this basal disposition is by definition not strong enough to motivate me to act rationally. I sincerely judge that I ought to grade the student papers, but watch the football game instead. If we interpret the basal disposition to do what one ought as an ordinary psychological state that competes with other states of the agent's for causal influence, then we must conclude that my desire to watch the game was stronger than the disposition to do what I ought. It follows that in acting *akratically*, I was—in a quite straightforward sense—incapable of acting rationally under the circumstances. This in turn calls into question the important assumption that I really ought to have graded the papers in the first place. For how can it be required rationally that I do what I lack the basic capacity to do? Doesn't 'ought' imply, in this sense, 'can'?

There is of course much more to be said about this issue.[15] Rather than dwell on the resources that are open to the meta-internalist for making sense of irrationality in action, however, I would like to turn now to a second way of conceptualizing the rational will that is in my view more promising. On this *volitionalist* approach, as we may call it, there is an important class of motivating attitudes that are directly subject to our immediate control. Familiar examples from this class of motivations are such phenomena as decision and choice. Ordinarily we think of decisions and choices not merely as states to which we happen to be subject. Rather they are attitudes for which

---

[15] Thus the interpretation of 'can' in contexts such as the present one is notoriously controversial. Proponents of meta-internalism might draw on the empiricist tradition, contending that *akratic* agents could have complied with their better judgment just in the sense that they would have so acted had their basal disposition to do what they ought been stronger under the circumstances. Accounts of 'can' that take this form suggest a kind of psychological determinism that, I believe, cannot be reconciled with our sense of our own agency. For discussion of this point, see my 'Moral Responsibility and the Practical Point of View,' in Ton van den Beld, ed., *Moral Responsibility and Ontology* (Dordrecht: Kluwer Academic Publishers, 2000), pp. 25–47.

---

rational desire that one acts against in cases of *akrasia,* but only if it is given a *de dicto* interpretation, which Velleman himself rejects.) *Akratic* action, on his account, will be motivated by the desire(s) constitutive of agency, and what makes this possible is the fact that the agent's normative beliefs about what it would be best to do fail to engage properly with those constitutive desires. I suspect that this strategy for explaining *akrasia* ends up tracing it to defects in the agent's normative understanding, in a way that is false to the potential perversity of the phenomenon; but there is not the space to go into this problem here.

211

we are ourselves directly responsible, primitive examples of the phenomenon of agency itself. It is most often in our power to determine what we are going to do, by deciding one way or another. Furthermore, when we exercise our power of self-determination by actually making a decision, the result is something we have done, not something that merely happens to us. The idea is not that decisions or choices play a role that is analogous to that of higher-order dispositions on the meta-internalist account, serving as states to which agency or rationality can be reduced. Rather, these attitudes seem at home in a conceptual context that includes, primitively, *agents*, whose activity is expressed in quotidian episodes of deciding or forming an intention to do something.[16] Examples of these kinds suggest that in the first-person perspective of practical deliberation, we cannot help assuming that there is a kind of motivation that is directly subject to our own control. My suggestion is that we need to take this deliberative point of view on action seriously if we are to make sense of the realist idea that there are independent normative truths about action, capable both of guiding our activity through deliberation and of retaining their normative force when such guidance breaks down.[17]

[16] Talk of an unreduced ontology of agents and their choices or decisions is likely to raise the puzzling specter of agent-causation, suggesting that we launch our decisions into the world from a position curiously outside of it, as a kind of 'unmoved mover' of the things we do. The mistake in this picture, as I see things, is not the failure to reduce agents to congeries of psychological states or attitudes, but the suggestion that the relation between agents and their choices is a causal one. To say that agents cause their decisions or choices is to say that we can *explain* these attitudes by citing the agent; but the relation between agents and their choices is fundamentally attributional rather than explanatory. For more on this issue, see my 'Moral Responsibility and the Practical Point of View.' I would further suggest that this whole conceptual scheme of agents and their choices or decisions has application only to creatures who are capable of practical reason and deliberation, the kind of reflection on normative considerations that is my subject in this part of the present paper.

[17] Compare my *Responsibility and the Moral Sentiments* (Cambridge, Mass.: Harvard University Press, 1994), sec. 5.2. Similar ideas are interestingly developed in Korsgaard, 'The Normativity of Instrumental Reason,' in Garrett Cullity and Berys Gaut (eds.), *Ethics and Practical Reason*, pp. 215–54—with the important difference that Korsgaard interprets the stance of volitional commitment in *essentially* normative terms, whereas I do not. I discuss this difference in my paper Normativity, Commitment, and Instrumental Reason, *Philosophers' Imprint* 1, no. 3 (December 2001): http://www.philosophersimprint.org/001003.

Thus it is plausible to maintain that the capacity for this kind of volitional self-determination is a condition for the normativity of rational requirements that we deliberately flout. Agents who are equipped with this basic capacity can retain the ability to comply with reasons that they knowingly act against. When they act *akratically*, for instance, it is not merely true of them that they would have done what they believe they ought had they been subject to a different configuration of desires and dispositions. It is true, more strongly, that they could have done what they ought, holding fixed the desires and dispositions to which they were subject when they chose to do otherwise. For the volitionalist capacity for choice is precisely a capacity to determine what one shall do in ways independent from one's merely given psychological states. In this way, the volitionalist conception represents an improvement over meta-internalism. That approach pictures rational agency as a system consisting wholly of causally interconnected beliefs, desires, and desire-like dispositions, and a system of this kind leaves no room for the kind of rational powers that our subjection to requirements of practical reason presupposes.

But what about the idea of guidance by one's grasp of normative principles? We saw above that it is the strength of meta-internalism that it offers an appealing causal interpretation of this phenomenon; how does the volitionalist hope to make sense of it? The basic volitionalist idea, I take it, is that when we are rational we ourselves determine what we shall do, in a way that is guided and controlled by our conception of what we have reason to do. More specifically, the volitionalist approach places attitudes such as choices and intentions at the centre of our conception of rational agency. These are not states with respect to which we are merely passive, but rather direct expressions of our agency, and they are criterially connected with appropriate bodily movements. Attitudes of these kinds, however, admit of sophisticated forms of intentionality. In the Kantian tradition (with which I would associate volitionalism), the content of the intentions that are expressed in our actions are specified by maxims. These may be thought of as having, potentially, the following, schematic form: 'I shall do x, in circumstances C, in order to y/as a way of y-ing.' By filling in the slots in this schematic representation of a maxim, we provide information about what agents take themselves to be up to in acting as they do. Above all, the last slot in the maxim-schema can be filled in ways that specify the agent's conception of the reason on which they are acting. This suggests an intentional rather than a causal interpretation of the image of rational guidance. Agents are guided by their conception of their reasons when that conception is reflected in the content of the intention on which they act; in that case, one will be able to understand what the agents are doing only by grasping what speaks in favour of so acting, from the agents' own point of view.

An example may help to illustrate how this might work. Consider the situation discussed by Kant in the first section of the *Groundwork*, in which actions of a single kind are performed for different reasons.[18] Agent A may act beneficently because it is the right thing to do, whereas B does so in order to collect a financial reward. The causal theorist would treat this situation as one in which two agents perform an action of the same type—an act of helping someone, say—which is rationalized and caused by different sets of attitudes in the two cases: in A's case, by the desire to do what is morally required, together with the belief that it would be wrong not to help, and in B's case by the desire for financial gain, together with the belief that helping the needy person will most likely bring a reward. Indeed, the causal theorist will insist that it is only by thinking of acting for reasons along these lines that we can make sense of a possibility that seems real enough, namely that there is a fact of the matter about what one's reasons for action are, although several competing sets of rationalizing attitudes are present.[19] Agent A, for instance, might have the same desire for financial gain that motivates agent B, and the same belief that the helping action will prove lucrative, without it being the case that A performs the helping action for these reasons. How else to account for this possibility, if not by supposing that the reasons on which we act are causally responsible for bringing those actions about?

On the alternative I have sketched, this possibility is captured by assuming that there is a fact of the matter about the content of the intentions with which the agent acts. Those intentions, I have suggested, can incorporate information about the agent's conception of their reasons for acting as they do. Thus in the original example we may suppose that A's intention is to provide assistance as a way of doing what is morally required, while B acts on the different

[18] In discussing this example I sketch the straightforward Humean style of causal explanation rather than the kind to which meta-internalism is committed; but the example could equally be developed in meta-internalist terms. Doing so, we would treat the two agents A and B as motivated by the same formal desire (e.g. to do what they ought), but as differing in their beliefs about what it is they ought to do.

[19] The classic statement of this line of thought is Donald Davidson, 'Actions, Reasons, and Causes,' as reprinted in his *Essays on Actions and Events* (Oxford: Oxford University Press, 1980), pp. 3–20.

intention of providing assistance as a way of collecting a financial reward. In just the same way, we can also make sense of the thought that A's real reason for performing the helping action is that it is the right thing to do, even though A believes the action would also prove lucrative, and wants to acquire more money. We need only suppose that A might act on the first of the two intentions specified above—the intention to help as a way of doing what is morally required—despite the presence of the desire for financial gain. It need hardly be added that in granting this possibility, we do not for a minute need to think that it is necessarily a simple matter, even for agents themselves, to ascertain what their real intentions in acting are.[20] In this respect, the intentional account I have sketched is in no worse shape than the causal account of guidance by one's conception of reasons. At issue is not the epistemological question of the conditions under which one can have knowledge of the true reason on which one acts; it is whether the volitionalist approach to reason explanations has the conceptual resources to make sense of the phenomenon of rational guidance. I believe the answer to this question is clearly yes, once we have a suitably sophisticated understanding of the content of an agent's maxims of action.

Crucial to this reconstruction of rational guidance is the assumption that our understanding of what we are doing as agents can reflect our implicit conception of the reasons that support the action we are performing. Rational action is in this way an inherently intelligent phenomenon. Indeed, once the possibility of this kind of account is brought into focus, it begins to seem obscure how any other approach could do justice to the idea that we are guided by our conception of our reasons, while also leaving appropriate room for the kinds of irrationality in action manifested by *akrasia*. On the volitionalist account I have sketched, the relation between reason and action is internal, in the sense that one's intentional representation of what one is doing incorporates as well an understanding of one's reason for acting in that way.[21] When this internal relation is

---

[20] Compare Kant's remarks at the beginning of the second section of the *Groundwork* (p. 407 in the Akademie edition) about the impossibility of knowing with certainty the true motive on which one acts.

[21] I find myself in agreement here with some points made by Annette Baier in 'Actions, Passions, and Reasons,' as reprinted in her *Postures of the Mind* (Minneapolis: University of Minnesota Press, 1985), pp. 109-134. I should like to stress, however, that it is no part of volitionalism as I understand it to deny that the intentional states that incorporate our understanding of our reasons can *cause* the bodily movements we make in act-

present, our choices acquire an inherently normative content, and in terms of this kind of normative content we can make sense of the idea that rational agents are guided by their conception of their reasons.

The volitionalist conception thus offers an appealing account of rational agency, showing how such activity can be controlled by the normative reflection of the agent. I myself believe that it represents the most promising interpretation of the distinctive capacities that enable agents not merely to grasp independent normative truths about action, but to translate their normative understanding into appropriate behaviour. At the same time, I am well aware that I have not said enough to justify completely my confidence in the volitionalist approach. I will be content for now if I have convinced my readers that NMR represents a more promising framework than constructivism for thinking about the relation between normativity and the will, and that within this context there is a need to go beyond the resources of the Humean picture to make sense of the phenomenon of rational agency. There is still plenty of work to be done by the idea of the rational will, and my discussions of both meta-internalism and volitionalism point in directions that future treatments of this issue may find it promising to follow[22]

[22] I received helpful feedback on earlier versions of this paper from audiences present at the following occasions: an APA session on the future of moral philosophy in December 2001, the 2002 Riverside Conference on the history and future of the will, and the 2002 Royal Institute of Philosophy conference on action and agency. I have particularly benefited from written comments by Michael Bratman, Christine Korsgaard, and Helen Steward.

ing. What volitionalism denies is not the causal efficacy of such attitudes as choice or decision, but the idea that those attitudes are in turn caused by our antecedent desires and beliefs.

Can Libertarians Make Promises?

ALFRED MELE

Libertarians hold that free action and moral responsibility are incompatible with determinism and that some human beings occasionally act freely and are morally responsible for some of what they do.[1] Can libertarians who know both that they are right and that they are free make sincere promises? Peter van Inwagen, a libertarian, contends that they cannot—at least when they assume that should they do what they promise to do, they would do it freely.[2] Probably, this strikes many readers as a surprising thesis for a libertarian to hold. In light of van Inwagen's holding it, the title of his essay—'Free Will Remains a Mystery'—may seem unsurprising.

Although, as I will explain, van Inwagen's effort to motivate his contention about promising is problematic, an interesting challenge to libertarians that is focused on promise making can be motivated. In this essay, I will motivate a challenge of this kind, identify three ways libertarians may try to answer it, and develop one of the answers.

1. Van Inwagen's Predicament

As part of an argument against the theoretical utility of agent causation, van Inwagen asks his readers to imagine an indeterministic world in which he knows, perhaps because God told him, that there are 'exactly two possible continuations of the present': in one, he reveals a damaging fact about a friend to the press; in the other, he keeps silent about his friend.[3] He also knows that 'the objective, "ground-floor" probability of [his] "telling" is 0.43 and that the objective, "ground-floor" probability of [his] keeping silent is 0.57.' Van Inwagen says that, given what he knows, he does not see how he can 'be in a position to' promise his friend that he will keep silent.

[1] I understand determinism, with van Inwagen, as 'the thesis that there is at any instant exactly one physically possible future'. See Peter van Inwagen, *An Essay on Free Will* (Oxford: Clarendon Press, 1983), 3.

[2] Peter van Inwagen, 'Free Will Remains a Mystery', *Philosophical Perspectives* 14 (2000), 1–19.

[3] 'Free Will Remains a Mystery', 17.

This last assertion is a premise of an argument that plays an important role in van Inwagen's attack on agent causation. Attention to his use of the premise will shed light on why he takes the position he does on promising. With the premise in place, van Inwagen adds the following: 'if I believe that I am able to keep silent, I should, it would seem, regard myself as being in a position to make this promise. What more do I need to regard myself as being in a position to promise to do X than a belief that I am *able* to do X? Therefore, in this situation, I should not regard myself as being able to keep silent. (And I cannot see on what grounds third-person observers of my situation could dispute this first-person judgment.)'[4] This, he says, is an 'argument for the conclusion that it is false that I am able to keep silent'.[5]

Two sources of distraction should be eliminated. First, some people understand sincere promising as one species of promising and insincere promising as another. If the distinction is granted, van Inwagen's claims about promising should be understood to be about *sincere* promising. Second, there may well be a significant difference in many cases between the probability that an agent will keep silent and the probability that he will keep silent given that he sincerely promises to do so. I will assume that the 0.57 probability van Inwagen has in mind is the probability of the latter. After all, even if the unconditional probability that an agent will keep silent about a friend is 0.57, the probability that he will keep silent given that he sincerely promises to may be 1.[6] An agent who knows that conditional fact about himself certainly seems to be in a position sincerely to promise to keep silent, other things being equal.

Many readers are likely to deem van Inwagen's assertion that he is not *able* to keep silent obviously false. Such readers have a reason to think that he does not understand 'able' as they do. Elsewhere, I have distinguished among three kinds or levels of ability to act.[7] One, I called *simple* ability to A (S-ability), a kind of ability that is entailed by an agent's A-ing. Just now, I tossed a five with a single

---

[4] 'Free Will Remains a Mystery', 17–18.

[5] 'Free Will Remains a Mystery', 18.

[6] That a world is indeterministic does not entail that no future events have a probability of 1. The following is possible. A certain radioactive particle decayed at t, and that event was not deterministically caused; but the particle had been recruited as a randomizing trigger for a bomb, and once it decayed, the bomb was deterministically caused to explode. At t, when the particle decays, the probability that the bomb will explode at $t+n$ is 1.

[7] Alfred Mele, 'Agents' Abilities', *Noûs* 37 (2003), 447–70.

toss of a fair die. I was able to do that, in a straightforward sense of 'able', one in which it is a truism that we never do anything at any time t that we are not able at t to do at t. Another kind or level of ability is the ability to A *intentionally* (I-ability). Although I am not able to throw a five intentionally with a single toss of a fair die, I am able now to tie my shoes intentionally now. A third I called *promise-level* ability (P-ability). I was led to my view of it partly by reflection on the point that, in utterly normal circumstances, some things that we believe ourselves to be able to do intentionally we take ourselves not to be in a position sincerely to promise to do. For example, Ann is an excellent free-throw shooter. She sinks 90% of her attempts. Assuming normal conditions, it is very plausible that Ann is able intentionally to sink the free throw she is about to attempt. But given that, despite her best efforts, she has not been able to reduce her 10% margin of error, and given her knowledge of her own success rate and of her level of skill, it also is very plausible that she is in no position sincerely to promise to sink the shot. On a simplified version of my view, X is a P-ability to A only if X is a sufficiently reliable ability to ground, in an agent who understands what promising is and knows her own abilities, complete confidence that, barring unexpected excusing factors (including, prominently, unexpected substantial obstacles and unexpected future beliefs that one was tricked into making one's promise or mistakenly made it), if she sincerely promises to A, she will A.[8] I dub this *the grounded confidence condition* on P-ability. (I have no need to insist on this condition in this essay, as will soon become clear. I state it to provide guidance about the sort of ability van Inwagen might have in mind.)

Given the supposed 0.57 probability that van Inwagen will keep silent if he sincerely promises to do so, it certainly seems that he is at least S-able to keep silent. Some readers may think that this probability is too low for van Inwagen to be I-able to keep silent, and others may disagree. Is a basketball player whose success rate at the free-throw line is 57% and who now, owing primarily to her pertinent skills, has a 0.57 'objective ... probability' of sinking the free throw she is about to attempt able to sink it intentionally? Readers' opinions may diverge; some may have higher standards than others regarding levels of control or reliability required for intentional

[8] My actual statement of this condition qualified agents of the kind at issue further: they have 'no abnormal source of beliefs about what they will do ... and disbelieve all of the following: that they will A unintentionally; that they will A nonintentionally; that they will A but perhaps intentionally and perhaps not'.

action. However, for my purposes, disagreements of this kind can be set aside. Van Inwagen's argument, if it succeeds at all, should succeed even when the probabilities are significantly altered—for example, from 0.57 vs. 0.43 to, say, 0.95 vs. 0.05. Few people would deny that an extraordinary player with a success rate of 95% and a 0.95 probability of sinking the free throw she is about to attempt is able to sink it intentionally, other things being equal; and my guess is that few would deny that van Inwagen is able to keep silent intentionally in a version of the case with the new probabilities I mentioned.

I should explain my claim about conditions under which van Inwagen's argument should succeed, if it succeeds at all. A central plank in his argument against the theoretical utility of agent causation is the claim that an agent who knows that 'it is undetermined'[9] whether he will A is not able to A. That is the claim he defends with the portion of the argument I have been discussing. If the claim is true, it is true of an agent who knows that it is undetermined whether he will keep silent about a friend even if he promises to do so and knows that the objective probability of his keeping silent given that he promises to is 0.95.

Van Inwagen's claim about agent causation in particular is that the further knowledge that he 'will be the agent-cause' of his conduct in a scenario of the sort he describes would not undermine his belief that he is not able to keep silent.[10] The claim is that agent causation does not help with a certain problem that *all* libertarians face, including those who shun agent causation. How impressed should libertarians be by van Inwagen's argument? In my scenario with the altered probabilities, even if van Inwagen is S-able and I-able to keep silent, perhaps he is not in a position sincerely to promise to keep silent and is not P-able to keep silent. Is that so? And if it is, is that a serious problem for libertarians?

2. Libertarian Abilities

A proper investigation of these questions requires additional background on libertarianism. Typical libertarians contend that an agent freely A-ed at a time only if, at that time, he was able to perform an alternative intentional action.[11] Libertarians and other

[9] 'Free Will Remains a Mystery', 17.
[10] 'Free Will Remains a Mystery', 18.
[11] See e.g. Robert Kane, *The Significance of Free Will* (New York: Oxford University Press, 1996), 110-11 and van Inwagen, 'Free Will Remains a Mystery'.

incompatibilists also contend that an agent was able to act otherwise than he in fact acted only if determinism is false, and they typically hold that an agent who did not *A* at *t* was able at *t* to *A* at *t* if and only if in another possible world with the same past (i.e. up to *t*) and laws of nature, he *A*-s at *t*. Similarly, on a view of this kind, an agent who did not intentionally *A* at *t* was able at *t* to *A* intentionally at *t* if and only if in another possible world with the same past and laws, he intentionally *A*-s at *t*. I dub this package of libertarian theses *PL*.

Suppose that Ann *A*-ed at *t*, that her *A*-ing was a free action, and that she *A*-ed in order to keep a promise she made—a promise to *A* at *t*. According to *PL*, Ann was able to perform an intentional alternative to *A*-ing at the time. Imagine that what Ann promised was to toss, in one minute, at high noon, the coin she was holding. No unexpected substantial obstacles arose, no excuses for not tossing the coin came to mind, and she intentionally tossed it at noon. According to *PL*, that she freely tossed the coin entails that she was *I*-able at noon to act otherwise then, which in turn entails that in another possible world with the same laws and with the same past right up to the moment at which the coin toss begins, Ann performs some alternative intentional action. For example, in such a world Ann might, at noon, decide to hold the coin for another minute— that is, perform the momentary mental action of forming an intention to hold the coin for another minute—and she might act accordingly.[12]

My choosing an example featuring deciding is no accident. The intention expressed in Ann's promise persists until she tosses the coin, at noon. Ann also has no intention not to toss the coin then, no intention to wait until later to toss it, and so on. According to *PL*, any relevant possible world is the same in all these respects until noon. But it seemingly is conceptually impossible that, for example, Ann *intentionally* holds on to the coin at noon in the absence of any pertinent *intention*, and libertarians certainly do not want our alleged *I*-abilities for alternative actions to rest on conceptual impossibilities. Somehow, a relevant intention emerges at the right time in a relevant world in which Ann intentionally holds on to the coin at noon. In deciding to *A*, one forms an intention to *A*. Perhaps the intention at issue emerged in that way—that is, in an act of

---

[12] On deciding to *A* as a momentary mental action of intention formation, see Alfred Mele, *Motivation and Agency* (New York: Oxford University Press, 2003), ch. 9. Also see Harry Frankfurt, *The Importance of What We Care About* (Cambridge: Cambridge University Press, 1988), 174–76 and Hugh McCann, 'Intrinsic Intentionality', *Theory and Decision* 20 (1986), 254–55.

deciding. Libertarians, including proponents of *PL*, can claim that there is no conceptual impossibility in Ann's *deciding* at noon to hold on to the coin, even holding the laws and the past fixed. If deciding to *A* were to require a prior intention to decide to *A*, libertarians would fail here, since Ann had no intention before noon to decide to hold on to the coin at noon. But there is good reason to believe that decisions to *A* normally are not preceded by such intentions.[13]

In 'Agents' Abilities', I argued that a version of the grounded confidence condition includes grounds for confidence about the persistence of the intention expressed in a sincere promise. Setting aside certain complications, it is plausible that in order to make a sincere promise to *A*, reflective agents who have a firm grip on what promising is must believe or presuppose something to the following effect: (*B*) barring occurrences that they would reasonably take to warrant abandoning their intention to *A*, if they sincerely promise to *A*, they will not abandon their intention to *A*.[14] In sincerely promising to *A*, agents typically express an intention to *A*, and suitably reflective agents expect, or are disposed to expect, the intention to persist.[15] *B* is a way of fleshing out the expectation. If, having promised to toss the coin at noon, Ann were to become persuaded that *PL* is true, were to believe that, at noon, she will be able to toss the coin freely, and were to believe what these propositions entail, could she be fully confident in a straightforward instance of *B* that features her intention to toss the coin at noon?

From *PL* and the proposition (*Pf*) that, at noon, she will remember her promise and be able to toss the coin freely, Ann infers that, at noon, she will be able intentionally to refrain from tossing the coin then. She expects (*Pn*) that she will neither be nor take herself

[13] See *Motivation and Agency*, ch. 9. If it is conceptually impossible to decide to *A* in the absence of a prior relevant intention to decide what to do, an intention that persists until the decision is made, and if Ann has no such intention before noon in the actual world, the problem arises again. (In the actual world, Ann made up her mind a minute before noon to toss the coin at noon and did not reopen the question.) However, it is debatable whether the phenomenon at issue is conceptually impossible.

[14] For a reference to some complications, see n. 8. Another complication is the possibility of a prior intention to bring it about that one intends to *A* (for a fanciful illustration, see *Motivation and Agency*, 203–04). An agent with this higher-order intention would, in certain circumstances, be able to promise to *A* even though he does not yet intend to *A*.

[15] Two points need to be made here. First, as I use 'express an intention', one may express an intention that one mistakenly believes one has. Second, I say 'typically' owing to the possibility mentioned in the preceding note.

to be warranted in abandoning the intention expressed in her promise, and she takes Pn to be consistent with the conjunction of PL and Pf. So Ann infers that at noon, while neither being nor taking herself to be warranted in abandoning her intention to toss the coin, she will be I-able to refrain from tossing it then. And she understands this to entail that there is a possible world with the same laws and past (relative to the time at which she has this thought) in which at noon, under the expected conditions, she intentionally does otherwise than toss the coin. In light of this, Ann is not fully confident that her intention to toss the coin at noon will persist through the intended time of the tossing, even in circumstances in which she is convinced at noon that nothing warrants her abandoning her intention. She believes that there is a real chance that she will abandon that intention at noon despite being convinced at noon that nothing warrants her abandoning it. Ann concludes from this that she is not an agent of a kind fit to be in the business of making promises.

That is how Ann sees it. I turn now to a third-person perspective on her situation. In Ann's case, no relevant obstacles occurred. So none occurred in the pertinent counterfactual scenarios in which she decides at noon to hold the coin a while longer. Ann's constitution as an agent is such that, in some relevant possible world, despite her sincere promise and the intention expressed in it, despite her remembering her promise, and despite there being no unexpected substantial obstacles to her acting as she promised and nothing that she takes to warrant not keeping her promise, she decides at noon not to toss the coin then and behaves accordingly. Consequently, Ann's ability to toss the coin at noon is not sufficiently reliable to ground, in an agent who understands what promising is and knows her own abilities, complete confidence that, barring unexpected excusing factors, if she sincerely promises to toss the coin at noon, she will toss it at noon. That is, Ann does not satisfy the grounded confidence condition on having a promise-level ability to toss the coin at noon.

How might a libertarian who wishes to retain the claim that freely A-ing at t entails being I-able at t to do otherwise than A at t react to the preceding two paragraphs? I sketch two predictable reactions here and return to them in Section 5. One is a move to protect libertarian promise-level ability. A libertarian may claim that if the chance of Ann's going off the rails and deciding for no good reason not to toss the coin is minuscule, her ability to toss the coin at the promised time deserves the designation 'promise-level ability'. I dub this the *close enough* view. Alternatively, a libertarian may claim

Alfred Mele

that agents freely A-ed only at times at which there was about an even chance that they would perform some other intentional action instead, or (more modestly) only at times at which they had significant reasons or motivation for doing otherwise than A. It may be claimed accordingly that although Ann might have freely decided to toss the coin and might have freely promised to do so, she did not freely toss it. A libertarian who takes this line may accept an account of P-ability that is compatible with determinism. Such a libertarian may hold, for example, that having a promise-level ability to A is inconsistent with the degree or kind of chanciness about one's A-ing that freely A-ing requires and that promise-level ability therefore is not a *freedom*-level ability.[16] This view may be termed *restrictivism*.

Another possible libertarian reaction is to see the apparent problem I raised as grounds for rejecting my positive claims about P-ability. However, even if those claims are rejected, a version of the problem remains. Imagine that Ann's actual condition at the pertinent time includes her being convinced, rightly, that she has no significant reason for not tossing the coin nor for deciding to do anything other than toss it. An agent who is able to decide, under these conditions, to do something that she knows would break her promise—an agent who, in another possible world with exactly the same past and laws, makes such a decision—arguably should not be making promises. Of course, the first two libertarian reactions I described may be directed at this worry too.

3. Conferred Freedom Introduced

I have tried to motivate a worry about libertarianism that resembles van Inwagen's. His critics will say that he has not shown—or even made it plausible—that no agent who knows that 'it is undetermined' whether he will A is able to A. I agree, if what they mean by 'able' is 'S-able', or 'I-able', or something similar. But it is arguable that honest, reflective agents who were to become persuaded that their internal indeterministic workings (or abilities) are such that there is a real chance that, despite promising to A and despite being convinced, at the time of action, that they have no good reason to break that promise, they will break it would feel very uncomfortable

[16] Freedom-level ability may be understood as a kind of ability such that if, setting aside ability conditions, everything necessary for an action's being free were present, adding a suitably exercised ability of this kind would yield sufficient conditions for the action's being free.

about making promises, and would even conclude that they are not in a position to make sincere promises. It also is arguable that this reaction reveals something problematic about agents' practical abilities on standard libertarian views and that these views have the result that free agents lack robust practical abilities associated with sincere promising.

Although I myself am not a libertarian, that does not prevent me from wondering how libertarians should respond to the kind of worry about abilities that van Inwagen tried to raise.[17] Here, again, are the elements of *PL*, a common libertarian package of theses:

1. An agent freely *A*-ed at a time only if, at that time, he was able to perform an alternative intentional action.
2. An agent was able to act otherwise than he in fact acted only if determinism is false.
3. An agent who did not *A* at *t* was able at *t* to *A* at *t* if and only if in another possible world with the same past and laws of nature, he *A*-s at *t*; and an agent who did not intentionally *A* at *t* was able at *t* to *A* intentionally at *t* if and only if in another possible world with the same past and laws of nature, he intentionally *A*-s at *t*.

Thesis 2 separates libertarians from traditional compatibilists.[18] Thesis 3 explicates two kinds of incompatibilist ability. Libertarians should be happy with it—at least, those who do not mind talking in terms of possible worlds and who do not believe that an agent's exercising freedom-level ability in acting at *t* entails that there is no possible world with the same past and laws in which he performs an alternative (intentional) action at *t*.[19] A theorist who worries that

[17] I am officially agnostic about compatibilism. See Alfred Mele, *Autonomous Agents* (New York: Oxford University Press, 1995).

[18] A nontraditional compatibilist view is discussed in Section 4.

[19] Kane contends that 'Exact sameness or difference of possible worlds is not defined if the possible world contains indeterminate efforts or indeterminate events of any kinds' (*The Significance of Free Will*, 172). For example, when an agent makes an indeterminate effort to resist temptation, we cannot 'imagine the same agent in two possible worlds with exactly the same pasts making exactly the same effort and getting lucky in one world and not the other'. According to Kane, in addition to the falsity of determinism, such indeterminacy is required for free action (172–74). For criticism of the idea identified in the first two sentences of this note, see Timothy O'Connor, *Persons and Causes* (New York: Oxford University Press, 2000), 40-41. For an argument that even if Kane is granted the idea, it does not benefit him, see Alfred Mele, 'Ultimate Responsibility and Dumb Luck', *Social Philosophy & Policy* 16 (1999), 274–93.

reflection on promising and associated abilities makes trouble for *PL* should take a close look at 1.

A theorist who holds that 1 is true and holds, as well, for example, that an agent cannot perform an intentional action while having no reason and no motivation for performing it cannot consistently hold that an agent freely *A*-s at *t* in a case in which he has, at *t*, no reason and no motivation to do anything else instead. Theorists who assent to the first two theses mentioned in the preceding sentence had better be sure that they do not count as free any actions the alternatives to which the agent is not in a position to perform intentionally at the time. Frankly, I do not see why it should be denied that I freely turn down requests that I have no reason, and no motivation, to accept—for example, requests from salespeople to purchase items that I have no interest in owning or giving away, in (utterly normal) situations in which I also have no reason and no motivation to please the salesperson, to impress anyone with a purchasing act, and so on. Of course, as I mentioned, I am not a libertarian; if I were, I might have a different attitude about this. But libertarians can, in principle, agree with me about cases of the kind in question. They can claim that a free action, *A*, does not depend for its freedom on the agent's being able to perform an alternative intentional action at the time, if *A* is suitably linked to an earlier free action or actions of the agent performed at a time or times at which he was *I*-able to do otherwise.[20] *I*-ability to act otherwise would still be required for free action, but it would not be required at the time of each and every free action.

Accepting this idea would weaken worries associated with promising and promise-level ability. If Ann freely promised and decided to toss the coin at noon at a time at which she was *I*-able to do otherwise than make that promise and decision, perhaps her intentionally tossing the coin at noon and her intentionally keeping her promise can be counted as free largely in virtue of their connection to the earlier actions of promising and decision. These earlier actions may be freedom-conferring free actions, free actions that confer freedom on suitably related subsequent actions of the agent; and the subsequent coin tossing and promise keeping can be free without the troublesome requirement that Ann be able at the subsequent time to perform alternative intentional actions. I dub this *the conferred freedom idea*.

[20] See *Autonomous Agents*, 208–9

4. Three Issues

Before I develop the conferred freedom idea, three issues require attention. The first is the status of the thought that rejecting thesis 1 displays conceptual confusion. The second and third issues— about what it is to do something intentionally and about action times—concern the idea that an agent cannot intentionally A while having no reason and no motivation to A.

Harry Frankfurt used a well-known thought experiment in an attempt to falsify the thesis that 'A person is morally responsible for what he has done only if he could have done otherwise'.[21] I and others have used similar thought experiments in attempts to falsify theses about free action like thesis 1: An agent freely A-ed at a time only if, at that time, he was able to perform an alternative intentional action.[22] In the pertinent cases, the agent A-s 'on his own', and it is claimed that he is morally responsible for A-ing and A-s freely even though, owing to the presence of a potential controller of a certain kind, he could not have done otherwise at the time than A. I lack the space for an examination of Frankfurt-style cases here. However, some observations about the literature on them are in order.

In a recent paper, David Robb and I constructed a Frankfurt-style case that we argued falsifies a thesis like 1.[23] Although that paper has attracted considerable critical attention, no critic has claimed that the article failed to present a successful counterexample to a thesis like 1 *because* freely A-ing at t entails being able to do otherwise than A at t.[24] It is a truism that being free at t to do otherwise than A at t entails being able—more precisely, S-able—at t to do otherwise than A at t, but whether freely A-ing at t entails being free at t to do otherwise than A at t is a topic of debate. I take the Mele/Robb paper I mentioned and a sequel (see n. 24) to show that there is no such entailment, but I will not argue about that here.

[21] Harry Frankfurt, 'Alternate Possibilities and Moral Responsibility', *Journal of Philosophy* 66 (1969), 829.
[22] See *Autonomous Agents*, 140–42; Alfred Mele, 'Soft Libertarianism and Frankfurt-Style Scenarios', *Philosophical Topics* 24 (1996), 123–41; Alfred Mele and David Robb, 'Rescuing Frankfurt-Style Cases', *Philosophical Review* 107 (1998), 97–112; and John Fischer, *The Metaphysics of Free Will* (Cambridge, Mass.: Blackwell, 1994), ch. 7.
[23] 'Rescuing Frankfurt-Style Cases'.
[24] For references to our critics' work and a reply, see Alfred Mele and David Robb, 'BBs, Magnets and Seesaws: The Metaphysics of Frankfurt-Style Cases', in *Freedom, Responsibility, and Agency*, M. McKenna and D. Widerker (eds.) (Aldershot: Ashgate, 2003), 127–38.

Alfred Mele

A related point about the literature is that it includes *semi-com-patibilism*, a position motivated partly by Frankfurt-style cases.[25] John Fischer describes his semi-compatibilism as the view that 'moral responsibility is compatible with causal determinism, even if causal determinism is incompatible with freedom to do otherwise'.[26] It also is a view about free action. Fischer asserts that 'guidance control is the freedom-relevant condition necessary and sufficient for moral responsibility',[27] and he reports that his 'account of guidance control (and moral responsibility) . . . yields "semi-com-patibilism"'.[28] Thus, I take semi-compatibilism to encompass the thesis that free action is compatible with determinism (as tradition-al compatibilists assert), even if 'determinism is incompatible with freedom to do otherwise' (which traditional compatibilists deny). Semi-compatibilism is a live option, and this would not be so if specialists generally agreed that someone had proved that it is a conceptual truth that freely A-ing at t requires being able at t to do otherwise than A at t.

I turn to the two issues about action that I mentioned. Occasionally, claims made in the literature on double effect entail that some agents intentionally A while having no reason and no motivation to A. Gilbert Harman, for example, contends that 'in firing his gun', a sniper who is trying to kill a soldier 'knowingly alerts the enemy to his presence. He does this intentionally, think-ing that the gain is worth the possible cost.'[29] Harman says that this is so even though the sniper 'certainly does not intend to alert the enemy to his presence'; and one can add, in the same spirit, that the sniper has no reason and no motivation to alert the enemy. Steven Sverdlik and I have criticized this view of double effect, but there is no need to argue about it here.[30] Alleged unmotivated intentional actions in double effect cases—call them 'intentional side-effect actions' (e.g. the sniper's alerting the enemy)—are parasitic on motivated intentional actions (e.g. the sniper's 'firing his gun'). If all intentional side-effect actions are related in this way to

[25] See Fischer, *The Metaphysics of Free Will*, and John Fischer and Mark Ravizza, *Responsibility and Control: A Theory of Moral Responsibility* (New York: Cambridge University Press, 1998).

[26] *The Metaphysics of Free Will*, 180.

[27] *The Metaphysics of Free Will*, 168.

[28] *The Metaphysics of Free Will*, 180.

[29] Gilbert Harman, 'Practical Reasoning', *Review of Metaphysics* 79 (1976), 433.

[30] Alfred Mele and Steven Sverdlik, 'Intention, Intentional Action, and Moral Responsibility', *Philosophical Studies* 82 (1996), 265–87.

motivated intentional actions, an agent's I-ability to do otherwise than A, where A is a motivated intentional action, will never be *non-derivatively* secured by an intentional side-effect action in another possible world with the same past and laws. And since any free intentional side-effect actions would presumably depend for their freedom on the freedom of actions on which they are parasitic, if A is a *side-effect action* and the agent is not able to do otherwise than perform the motivated intentional action(s) on which A is parasitic, the possibility of his being I-able to do otherwise than A is a mere curiosity.

Tiny actional parts of larger intentional actions also pose an apparent problem for the idea that an agent cannot perform an intentional action while having no reason and no motivation for performing it. It is arguable that at least some of these tiny actions are intentional and that the agent has no motivation to perform them and does not perform them for a reason. Elsewhere, I have suggested that they derive their intentionality from that of the larger, motivated intentional actions.[31] If that is right, these tiny actions seem to have no special importance for freedom.

It is very plausible that, at least setting aside intentional side-effect actions and intentional tiny actional parts of larger intentional actions, an agent cannot intentionally A while having no reason and no motivation to A. And if what I said in the preceding two paragraphs is correct, possible actions of the two kinds set aside in this claim—which actions are assumed for the sake of argument to be performed in the absence of any reason and any motivation for performing them—can be set aside entirely for the purposes of this article.

Now, for the issue about action times. The libertarian view under consideration asserts that an agent was I-able at t to do otherwise than he did at t if and only if in another possible world with the same past and laws, he performs an alternative intentional action at t. Obviously, some actions take more time than others to perform. Running a marathon takes a lot longer than flipping a coin. An agent who intentionally ran a marathon might have performed an alternative intentional action by intentionally quitting after several miles, or several yards, or by intentionally watching the whole race from the sidelines. In the case of extended intentional actions, relevant possible worlds for the purposes of testing libertarian I-ability to do otherwise than A are the same as the actual world up to the

---

[31] Alfred Mele, *Springs of Action* (New York: Oxford University Press, 1992), 113–14.

moment at which the agent's intentional conduct first diverges from his actual action, A. This initial divergence can happen at a moment at which the agent is A-ing in the actual world or at the moment at which his A-ing begins in the actual world.

Given the plausibility of the idea that overt intentional actions (i.e. intentional actions essentially involving peripheral bodily motion) are explained partly by intentions that come on the scene at least some fraction of a second before the actions begin, decisions or choices—momentary mental actions of intention formation—naturally receive a lot of attention in the free will literature. Libertarians who say that an agent who, in executing a hand-raising decision he made, intentionally raised his hand at t was I-able at the time to do otherwise at the time may mean, more precisely and more fully, that shortly before t, when he decided to raise his hand straightaway, he was I-able to make an alternative decision, and if he had made such a decision he would not have raised his hand at t and would have performed an intentional alternative then.[32] In this case, the moment at which the agent decides to A is the moment of initial action divergence. In the actual world, he decides at that moment to A; in some relevant possible world, he performs, or begins performing, an intentional alternative action. For example, it may be that in some relevant possible world he decides at that moment not to A.

Presumably, all decisions are at least partially based on or influenced by some psychological states or other—beliefs, desires, recognitions of reasons, or whatever. Anything of this kind that emerges simultaneously with a decision made at t arrives too late for that decision to have been based, even partly, on it, and too late for the decision to have been influenced by it. The upshot is this: In the case of a decision to A that an agent makes at a moment t, her having libertarian I-ability to do otherwise requires that there be a possible world that does not diverge from the actual world before t in which she does otherwise than make that decision at t.

5. Conferred Freedom and Some Alternatives

I return to the conferred freedom idea (CFI) and the two alternatives mentioned in Section 2. I will not attempt to eliminate

[32] On the view I favor, overt actions begin in the brain (see Frederick Adams and Alfred Mele, 'The Intention/Volition Debate', *Canadian Journal of Philosophy* 22 (1992), 323–38.) But this is another point on which there is no need to insist for my purposes in this article.

competitors to *CFI*. That would require a detailed comparative examination of the various options on free action open to libertarians. It is a project for a book. In the present section, I comment on the trio of competing libertarian ideas under consideration. In the following section, I will develop *CFI* further.

Some libertarian readers who initially find *CFI* attractive may begin to worry that they cannot do much with it, given that free agents operate indeterministically. They may worry that given this indeterminism, there is always a chance that free agents will decide to break a promise and behave accordingly, even if they have no reason and no motivation to (decide to) break it.[33] However, if it is a conceptual truth that, with the possible exception of intentional side-effect actions and tiny intentional actional parts of larger intentional actions, agents cannot intentionally *A* at a time at which they have no reason and no motivation to *A*, this worry is ill-founded.

A libertarian reader who initially finds comfort in this point may start worrying that, given the indeterministic nature of free agency, motivation to break a promise can emerge at any time as a matter of chance, even when nothing in the agent's situation would even tend to excuse her for breaking her promise. However, the assumption of indeterministic agency certainly does not *entail* this possibility. And if it were to be claimed that the assumption of indeterministic *free* agency does entail it, that claim would certainly require an argument.

The conferred freedom idea should be attractive to libertarians inclined to hold that we can freely keep promises that we have no motivation and no reason not to keep—*unopposed promises*, for short—provided that they are willing to loosen up on thesis 1. Some such libertarians who are reluctant to loosen up on this thesis may search for grounds for the idea that some agents are able intentionally to break unopposed promises, while others may critically examine their inclination to hold that we can freely keep unopposed

---

[33] Perhaps, in normal cases, one's reasons for deciding to *A* are limited to one's reasons for *A*-ing. (For discussion, see Alfred Mele, 'Intending for Reasons', *Mind* 101 (1992), 327–33 and Thomas Pink, *The Psychology of Freedom* (Cambridge: Cambridge University Press, 1996).) But whatever the truth is about normal cases, there are unusual scenarios—for example, the scenario in Gregory Kavka's toxin puzzle—in which one has a reason to decide to *A* that is not a reason to *A* (Gregory Kavka, 'The Toxin Puzzle', *Analysis* 43 (1983), 33–36). In these cases, there is a (potential) payoff for deciding to *A* that is not a (potential) payoff for *A*-ing. Hence, the parenthetical inclusion of 'decide to' in the sentence to which this note is appended.

promises. (Some might pursue both the search and the critical examination.) Some libertarians of the former kind may toy with the idea that an agent who intentionally kept an unopposed promise was nevertheless *I-able* to break it in virtue of the fact that, at the relevant time, he *could have had* a reason or motivation to break it. However, in advocating this idea a libertarian would be backing away from a standard incompatibilist criticism of compatibilist accounts of ability.

Traditional compatibilists agree with libertarians that freely *A*-ing requires the ability at the time to do otherwise than *A* then. In their accounts of ability, they typically do not hold the past fixed. For example, the past is not held fixed in a compatibilist's claim that Ann was able at noon to do otherwise than toss the coin then because if she had decided just before noon to toss the coin no earlier than 12:01, she would have held on to the coin at noon.[34] A libertarian who allows that an agent, in a world *W*, who did not *A* at *t* was able at *t* to *A* at *t* even though the only worlds with the same laws as *W* in which she *A*-s at *t* have different pasts than *W* at *t* opens the door to compatibilist accounts of ability to do otherwise. This is a door that libertarians definitely want to be closed.

Libertarians who find themselves drifting away from an inclination to maintain that we can freely keep unopposed promises are heading toward a reaction I mentioned earlier to worries about *P*-ability. This is the *restrictivist* idea that agents freely *A*-ed only at times at which they had significant reasons (or motivation) for doing otherwise than *A*. Versions of this idea have been defended in the literature: for example, in van Inwagen's 'When Is the Will Free?'.[35] And they have drawn criticism.[36] An attempt to settle this issue would require a paper of its own. However, a brief commentary on restrictivism about free promise keeping is appropriate.

In 'When Is the Will Free?' van Inwagen argues that 'there are at most *two* sorts of occasion on which the incompatibilist can admit that we exercise free will: cases of an actual struggle between perceived moral duty or long-term self-interest ... and immediate

---

[34] See G. E. Moore, *Ethics* (Oxford: Oxford University Press, 1912), ch. 6 and A. J. Ayer, 'Freedom and Necessity', in Ayer's *Philosophical Essays* (London: Macmillan, 1954), ch. 12.

[35] Peter van Inwagen, 'When Is the Will Free?', *Philosophical Perspectives* 3 (1989), 399–422.

[36] See John Fischer and Mark Ravizza, 'When the Will is Free', *Philosophical Perspectives* 6 (1992), 423–51 and O'Connor, *Persons and Causes*, 101–7.

desire, ... and cases of a conflict of incommensurable values.'[37] Imagine a libertarian, Libby, who believes that agents can act freely only in scenarios of these two kinds. Accordingly, she believes that she keeps a promise *freely*, and freely performs an action of the promised kind, only if at the time of action she is involved in a struggle of the kind van Inwagen mentions or has relevant conflicting incommensurable values. Van Inwagen's position on the occasions on which exercising free will is possible is motivated by arguments that on occasions of other kinds the agent lacks genuine alternatives. Libby agrees. Her view is that whenever she has the latitude needed for free action, there are at least two relevant options, each of which is such that there is a significant chance that, owing to her own indeterministic psychology, she will pursue it: for example, she may act on an 'immediate desire' opposed by 'perceived moral duty' and may act instead on the latter consideration, and she may act in accordance with each (but not both) of two 'incommensurable values' that recommend competing courses of action. Consequently, she takes herself not to be in a position to promise any course of action that she expects to be opposed by any of the factors van Inwagen mentions; for she believes that she cannot trust herself to keep her promises in such cases. In short, she takes herself not to be in a position to promise to do anything she believes she will do freely (and anything she believes she would do freely, if she were to do it).

The idea that informed, consistent libertarians can make sincere promises only if they expect to keep them unfreely sounds weird. But when one realizes that someone propounding this idea narrows the occasions for free action in the way van Inwagen does for exercises of free will, one should not be at all surprised. In any case, a fan of *CFI* will reject Libby's restrictive position on occasions for free action.

Brief commentary on what I called the *close enough* view is also in order here. This, again, is the view that if the chance of an agent's deciding for no good reason not to do what she promised—namely, to *A*—is minuscule, her ability to *A* is sufficiently robust or reliable to be deemed a promise-level ability to *A*. In ordinary scenarios, this slight chance is a chance of deciding *irrationally*, if it is irrational to decide for no good reason not to do something that one recognizes one has a good reason to do. A nonlibertarian may ask how (on earth) a chance of going off the rails and deciding irrationally can contribute to freedom. And a libertarian may reply

---

[37] 'When Is the Will Free?', 417.

that although the chance itself makes no contribution to freedom, it entails something that does—the falsity of determinism.[38] Be this as it may, a fan of *CFI*, having no commitment to the thesis that agents act freely at *t* only if they are able at *t* to perform an alternative intentional action at *t*, will see no immediate need for the *close enough* thesis.

6. The Conferred Freedom Idea Explored: Freely Making and Keeping Promises

Keeping promises is one thing; making them is another. There are cases in which one is asked to make a sincere promise that one has no reason and no motivation not to make. Can one who makes such a promise make it freely?

Consider the following example. Because Anton thinks that Angela is ambivalent about going to the prom with him, his invitation takes the form of a request that she promise to go with him. Angela, who had been hoping that he would ask, is delighted by the invitation. She has no reason and no motivation not to make the promise, and she sincerely makes it, expressing an intention to accompany Anton to the prom. On prom night, she happily keeps her promise.

Suppose that because, at the time of the request, Angela had no reason and no motivation not to make that sincere promise, she was not *I*-able at the time to do otherwise than make it. Suppose also that because, on prom night, she had no reason and no motivation not to attend the prom with Anton and not to keep her promise, she was not *I*-able at the time to do otherwise than attend the prom with him and keep her promise. Would a libertarian be forced to conclude that Angela did not freely attend the prom with Anton and did not freely keep her promise? Not if Angela's making the promise and her subsequently keeping it are suitably related to earlier free actions of hers performed at times at which she was *I*-able to do otherwise than perform those actions. Perhaps those earlier free actions confer freedom on her promising act and on her keeping her promise.

I will say something about how this can be shortly. First, a little more motivation for *CFI* is in order. By far the most popular style of argument among libertarians for incompatibilism is 'the consequence argument'. Here is a short version from van Inwagen:

[38] See Mele, 'Soft Libertarianism and Frankfurt-Style Scenarios', 134.

'If determinism is true, then our acts are the consequences of the laws of nature and events in the remote past. But it is not up to us what went on before we were born, and neither is it up to us what the laws of nature are. Therefore, the consequences of these things (including our present acts) are not up to us.'[39] Libertarians abhor the thought that our actions are part of the unfolding of deterministic chains of events that were in progress even 'before we were born'. If libertarians can view themselves as making some causally undetermined decisions, then they can view themselves as initiating causal chains without what goes on in them at the time of initiation constituting an intermediate link in a long deterministic causal chain extending back before their birth. Successful exercises of such initiatory power are incompatible with the truth of the abhorred thought; they block the abhorred connection to the 'remote past'. Requiring that this power be exercised in the performance of each and every free action—if the power is claimed to encompass or entail the I-ability at the time to act otherwise then—may be overkill.

What past free actions of Angela's performed at times at which she was I-able to do otherwise—what 'basically free actions' of hers, one may say—might have contributed to the freedom of her promise-making act and to the freedom of her keeping her promise? Natural candidates include basically free actions performed in the course of interactions with Anton that contributed to Angela's having the attitude toward him that she does by the time he asks her to be his prom date. Given the basic freedom of these earlier actions, Angela's promise making and promise keeping are not causally determined consequences of 'events in the remote past'. In light of that, of the apparent connections between I-ability to A and reasons and motivation for A-ing, and of the etiology of Angela's attitude toward Anton at the time of his request and at the time of the prom, perhaps libertarians should not be put off by the fact that Angela was not I-able at the pertinent times to do otherwise than make the promise and keep the promise.

It is natural to worry that my move to past basically free actions simply postpones the sort of problem for libertarians that van Inwagen tried to motivate. That worry merits attention. As I have explained, if van Inwagen's argument raises a problem about agents' abilities for libertarians, it is not a problem about S-ability or I-ability. People who do not have high standards for intentional action will take van Inwagen, in his thought experiment, to be both

[39] *An Essay on Free Will*, 16.

S-able and *I*-able to keep silent, and people with higher standards for intentional action will find both abilities in my variant of van Inwagen's scenario with adjusted probabilities. If there is a genuine problem here, it is about promise-level ability, or something similar.

Here is a fact. Although I have heard people promise to decide by a certain time *whether* they will *A* (e.g. promise to decide by 9:00 p.m. Thursday whether they will accompany a friend to a party on Friday), I have never heard anyone promise to *decide to A*. The many things I have heard people promise do not include such things as deciding to go to the prom, deciding to toss a coin, and deciding to keep silent about a friend. A plausible diagnosis of that fact is ready to hand. With some possible exceptions (see n. 14), in sincerely promising to *A* one expresses an intention to *A*. For example, in promising to accompany Anton to the prom next month, Angela expresses an intention to accompany him. A promise now to decide next month to *A*, understood on this model, would express an intention now to decide next month to *A*, and it is only in very unusual cases that an agent would intend now to *decide* later to *A*— for example, intend now to decide later to accompany Anton.[40] Someone in a normal state of mind in the ballpark of this unusual intention would simply intend or decide to *A*.

This suggests that promise-level ability is not well-suited for exercise in deciding to *A* and is instead much more suitable for exercise in the doing of some of the things we sincerely promise to do, which things are executions of the decisions or intentions expressed in our sincere promises.[41] Now, it is natural to suppose that among Angela's basically free actions that contributed to her subsequent attitude toward Anton were various decisions—for example, decisions to join him for lunch, to invite him to a movie, and the like. These decisions issued in actions that helped shape Angela's attitude toward Anton. It is very unlikely that in making these decisions Angela exercised a promise-level ability to make them, and there is nothing problematic about that. Given that decisions are essentially intentional, Angela did exercise *I*-abilities in making her decisions, and if her decisions were 'basically free actions', she was *I*-able at the time to have done otherwise.[42]

[40] For an unusual science fiction case of this kind, see Mele, *Motivation and Agency*, 203–4.

[41] This claim is compatible, of course, with the idea that promise-level ability is sometimes exercised in performing actions that we have not promised to perform.

[42] The second conjunct is explained by the definition of 'basically free action' with which I am working.

236

It may be claimed that if Angela were to know that, owing to her indeterministic constitution as an agent, 'it is undetermined' whether, given that she decides to invite Anton to lunch, she will invite him, she would not be in a position to decide to invite him to lunch. This is an attempt to rescue van Inwagen's problem at another level. But the claim is implausible. Deciding to A is compatible with believing that there is some chance that one will not A even given that one decides to A. (Some months ago I decided to fly to Helsinki next Tuesday, knowing full well that any number of things might prevent me from doing so. I was confident, but not certain, that I would make the flight.) And deciding to A is compatible with believing that there is a chance that one will not execute that decision owing to one's indeterministic constitution. Belief constraints on deciding to A are weaker than those on sincerely promising to A. One can decide to do some things one takes oneself to be able to do intentionally even if one takes oneself not to be in a position sincerely to promise to do these things, owing to one's estimate of the chance of failure. Ann can decide now to call her dentist tomorrow to schedule a painful procedure even if she believes that there is a 0.05 chance that she would chicken out and fail to call even if she were sincerely to promise someone that she will make that call. But as long as she has that belief, she is not in a position sincerely to make that promise.

The abilities required for freely deciding to A, whatever exactly they are, do not include a promise-level ability to decide to A. Promise-level ability to A is, very roughly, the kind or level of ability to A that would ground promise-level confidence that if one promises to A, one will A. This itself suggests that we do not exercise P-abilities in deciding to A, since we never promise to decide to A. Furthermore, a libertarian view of free agents need not exclude their having P-abilities. Lacking a P-ability to decide to A is compatible with having P-abilities in other practical spheres. Depending on the details of her indeterministic make-up, even an agent who knows her indeterministic constitution can count on herself to keep her promises and have a kind or level of ability that grounds such confidence. Such an agent also can *freely* keep her promises while having a promise-level ability to keep them, given the conferred freedom idea.

7. A Distinct Worry for Libertarians

There is a genuine worry for libertarians in the neighborhood of the worry van Inwagen tried to develop. I have motivated it myself elsewhere, as have others.[43] To avoid repetition, I lead up to it with the following thought experiment. Suppose you are a libertarian demigod in an indeterministic world who wants to build rational free human beings capable of being very efficient agents. You believe that proximal decisions—decisions to A straightaway—are causes of actions that execute them, and you see no benefit in designing agents who have a chance of not even trying to A when they have decided to A straightaway and the intention to A formed in that act of deciding persists in the absence of any biological damage. Fortunately, the indeterministic fabric of your world allows you to build a deterministic connection between proximal decisions and attempts, and you do. Now, because you are a relatively typical libertarian, you believe that basically free decisions cannot be deterministically caused—even by something that centrally involves a considered judgment that it would be best to A straightaway. However, you think that agents can make basically free decisions on the basis of such judgments. So you design your agents in such a way that, even though they have just made such a judgment, and even though the judgment persists in the absence of biological damage, there is a chance that they decide contrary to it.

Given your brand of libertarianism, you believe that whenever agents perform a basically free action of deciding to A, they could have *freely* performed some alternative intentional action.[44] You worry that the indeterministic connection you built might not accommodate this. If the difference between the actual world, in which one of your agents judges it best to A straightaway and then decides accordingly, and any world with the same past and laws in which while the judgment persists he makes an alternative decision is just a matter of chance, you worry that he does not freely make that decision in that possible world, W. You suspect that his making that alternative decision rather than deciding in accordance with his best judgment—that is, that difference between W and the actual world—is just a matter of bad luck (or, more precisely, of worse luck in W for the agent than in the actual world). This leads you to suspect that, in W, the agent should not be blamed for making the decision he makes there.[45] And that he should not be blamed, you think, indicates that he did not freely make it.

---

[43] See 'Ultimate Responsibility and Dumb Luck'.

[44] See Kane, *The Significance of Free Will*, 109–14, 134–35, 143, 179–80, 191.

[45] You toy with the thought that the agent may be blamed for the decision if past free decisions of his had the result, by way of their effect on his character, that there was a significant chance that he would decide contrary to his best judgment. But it occurs to you that the same worry arises about past free decisions the agent made.

You can think of nothing that stops your worry from generalizing to all cases of deciding, whether the agent makes a judgment about what it is best to do or not. In the actual world, Ann decides at t to A. In another world with the same laws of nature and the same past, she decides at t not to A. If there is nothing about Ann's powers, capacities, states of mind, moral character, and the like in either world that accounts for this difference, then the difference seems to be just a matter of luck. And given that neither world diverges from the other in any respect until t, there is no difference at all in Ann in these two worlds that can account for the difference in her decisions. To be sure, something about Ann may explain why it is *possible* for her to decide to A in the actual world and decide not to A in another world with the same laws and past. That she is an indeterministic decision maker may explain this. That, of course, is consistent with the difference in her decisions being just a matter of luck. This is a relatively typical worry for libertarians. It is a worry about whether, on typical libertarian views, according to which one freely A-ed only if one could have freely done otherwise at the time, one was able to A freely.

The basic problem for libertarians is about what I called basically free actions. All libertarians who hold that A's being a basically free action depends on the agent's being able at the time to do otherwise freely then should tell us what it could possibly be about an agent who freely A-ed at t in virtue of which it is true that, in another world with the same past and laws, he freely does something else at t. Of course, they can *say* that the answer is free will. But what they need to explain is how free will, as they understand it, can be a feature of agents—or, more fully, how this can be so where 'free will', on their account of it, really does answer the question. Some libertarians have tried to explain this. I cannot honestly say that I have been persuaded by their proposals. But I certainly would not infer from this that the worry cannot be laid to rest.

My aim in this essay does not include offering a solution to this worry—call it the *Big Worry* for libertarians. I sketched it in order to make the point that it is not the same worry as the one I presented about promise-level ability. The Big Worry is not a worry about whether, on typical libertarian views, according to which one freely A-ed only if one could have freely done otherwise at the time, one was *P-able* to A (contrast van Inwagen's 'Free Will Remains a Mystery'). Nor is it a worry about whether one was able to act at all at the time (contrast van Inwagen's *An Essay on Free Will*,

239

Alfred Mele

129–35).[46] Instead, it is a worry about whether the agent was able to *A freely*. Being *P*-able to *A* is not required for being able to *A* freely. If it were, we could never freely do things that we rightly take ourselves to be insufficiently adept at doing to promise sincerely to do. Being able to act obviously is required for being able to act freely. But I have argued elsewhere that many libertarians need not worry that their view of free action precludes the ability to act.[47]

8. Conclusion

At the end of Section 1, I asked the following questions about my scenario in which Peter van Inwagen knows that there is a 0.05 objective probability that he will not keep silent about his friend even given that he promises to keep silent. (1) Is he in a position sincerely to promise to keep silent? (2) Is he *P*-able to keep silent? (3) If the correct answer to either 1 or 2 is *no*, is that a serious problem for libertarians? Given what van Inwagen knows in this scenario, the correct answer to 1 seems to be *no*. Seemingly, his self-knowledge cuts him off from the self-confidence required for being in a position sincerely to promise to keep silent. If my suggested account of *P*-ability is correct, or close to correct, the true answer to 2 also is *no*. Van Inwagen's ability to keep silent is not sufficiently reliable to meet standards for *P*-ability. Fortunately for libertarians, the correct answer to 3 is *no* as well. Libertarian proponents of the conferred freedom idea can consistently hold that free agents are *P*-able to keep promises and that free agents can believe, correctly, that they are in a position to make promises. Such libertarians do not share with van Inwagen views about free action that commit them to holding that the objective probability that a given free agent will break a promise is always such as to preclude *P*-ability to keep it.

As I pointed out, libertarians who shun the conferred freedom idea also have room to maneuver. Those who hold van Inwagen's restrictive view of opportunities for free action can consistently hold that they themselves are free agents and that their knowing the probability that they will *A* given that they promise to *A* is compatible with their being in a position to promise to *A*. Of course, if their subjective probability is sufficiently high that they regard themselves as being in a position sincerely to promise to *A*, they will believe that if they promise to *A* they will keep the promise

---

[46] For discussion of the cited material, see *Autonomous Agents*, 197–203.
[47] *Autonomous Agents*, 197–98.

unfreely. Libertarians who favor the *close enough* view can maintain that although van Inwagen lacks a P-ability to keep silent even in my version of his thought experiment with adjusted probabilities, there are versions of the case in which the chance of going off the rails is small enough to permit P-ability to keep silent and they can maintain as well that, as long as the small chance is not zero, the agent can keep her promise freely. Readers are free to judge which of the three ideas—the conferred freedom idea, restrictivism, or the close enough view—most merits further exploration and development.

The guiding question I posed for this essay is this: Can libertarians who know that they are right and know that they themselves are free agents make sincere promises in cases in which they assume that should they do what they promise to do, they would do it freely? The answer I have defended is *yes*. Libertarians who hold that every free action is what I called a 'basically free action' should worry about the problem that van Inwagen was trying to pose, if they believe that we can freely keep sincere promises. Libertarians who believe that their indeterministic constitution as agents is such that at any time they freely keep a promise there was a significant chance that they would break it—genuinely break it, as opposed to acting otherwise than as promised owing to their having a legitimate excuse—*should* wonder whether they are sufficiently reliable to be in the business of making sincere promises. However, this belief is optional for libertarians, as I have explained. The conferred freedom alternative is open to them.[48]

[48] Earlier versions of this article were presented at the Jean Nicod Institute (Paris; May 2002) and the University of Oxford (September 2002). I am grateful to my audiences for fruitful discussion.

Intention as Faith

RAE LANGTON

1. Introduction

What, if anything, has faith to do with intention?[1] By 'faith' I have in mind the attitude described by William James:

> Suppose ... that I am climbing in the Alps, and have had the ill-luck to work myself into a position from which the only escape is by a terrible leap. Being without similar experience, I have no evidence of my ability to perform it successfully; but hope and confidence in myself make me sure I shall not miss my aim, and nerve my feet to execute what without those subjective emotions would perhaps have been impossible. But suppose that, on the contrary, the emotions of fear and mistrust preponderate; or suppose that...I feel it would be sinful to act upon an assumption unverified by previous experience,—why, then I shall hesitate so long that at last, exhausted and trembling, and launching myself in a moment of despair, I miss my foothold and roll into the abyss....*There are then cases where faith creates its own verification.* Believe, and you shall be right, for you shall save yourself; doubt, and you shall again be right, for you shall perish.[2]

The climber has 'no evidence' about his ability to leap across the chasm: his faith goes beyond evidence.[3] The desire to leap across enables the climber to believe he will leap across: his faith is wishful. Belief that he will leap across enables him to leap across: his faith is self-fulfilling. When it comes to faith, the 'no evidence' issue is usually at the fore; but I shall mostly ignore it here, and focus on faith as a wishful and self-fulfilling attitude.

[1] I am grateful for comments from the audience at the RIP conference on *Action and Agency*, and from Richard Holton, Lloyd Humberstone, Matthew Nudds, Mike Ridge, David Velleman, Denis Walsh and Timothy Williamson. I'm aware I have not always profited by their generous responses as well as I should.

[2] William James, 'The Sentiment of Rationality', in *The Will to Believe and Other Essays in Popular Philosophy* (Norwood, Mass: Plimpton Press, 1896), 96–7.

[3] 'Faith means belief in something concerning which doubt is still theoretically possible; and as the test of belief is willingness to act, one may say that faith is the readiness to act in a cause the prosperous issue of which is not certified to us in advance' (*The Will to Believe*, 90.)

Rae Langton

Skirting alpine melodrama, and making a modest start: if faith is a kind of belief, we can begin with the wider question of what belief has to do with intention. Some philosophers give belief a modest role: perhaps intending to do something implies believing it at least *possible* you will do it; perhaps it implies believing you *will* do it; perhaps it implies *not* believing you *won't* do it; perhaps it implies believing you *intend* to do it. But among the propositional attitudes it is desire rather than belief that is usually thought closest to intention, and a popular view has it that intending just *is* a sort of *desiring*. After all, desire and intention apparently share a 'direction of fit', however one attempts to characterize this intuitive idea. When Elizabeth Anscombe famously contrasted the detective's list from the spied-upon shopper's list, she was` contrasting belief, which aims to fit the world, from an attitude that aims rather for the world to fit itself: intention, or desire? The shopper lists what he wants and intends to get. Why not put the two together and say that intending is a sort of desiring? The shopper intends to buy butter when he most strongly desires to buy butter, and desires not to deliberate further about buying it.[4]

An opposing hypothesis says intending just *is* a sort of *believing*. This is the doxastic account of intention, sometimes called 'cognitivism about practical reason'.[5] An elegant account along these lines is given by David Velleman, who says intentions are future-directed beliefs about what one will do—they are 'self-fulfilling expectations that are motivated by a desire for their fulfilment and that represent themselves as such'[6]. The shopper intends to buy butter when he has made up his mind that *he will buy butter:*

---

[4] See e.g. Michael Ridge, 'Humean Intentions', *American Philosophical Quarterly* 35 (1998), 157–78 (this description massively oversimplifies his proposed view). Anscombe's example is in *Intention* (Oxford: Blackwell, 1957), p. 56.

[5] See e.g. Michael Bratman, 'Cognitivism about Practical Reason', 250–1, in *Faces of Intention* (Cambridge: Cambridge University Press, 1999).

[6] David Velleman, *Practical Reflection* (Princeton: Princeton University Press, 1989), 109; also available on-line at Velleman's website. Intention is belief-like in its direction of fit (representing its content as true) and in its aim for truth (being regulated by mechanisms which revise it in the face of counter-evidence); these features justify the label 'belief', according to Velleman, but the label is not what matters. Extensive references to views ascribing a more modest role to belief in intention, such as those of Gilbert Harman, Paul Grice, and Robert Audi, are cited at p. 113 note 8.

'making up what we will do is, in fact, our way of making up our minds to do it.' Intention

> represents as true that we are going to do something;... it aims therein to represent something that really is true; and...it causes the truth of what it represents.[7]

The leaper's faith likewise represents as true that he is going to do something; it aims therein to represent something that really is true; and it causes the truth of what it represents. James' courageous leaper seems worlds away from Anscombe's shopper, but if the doxastic proposal is right there may be a connection between the leaper's faith and the shopper's intention; and I shall be interested in what the comparison can tell us about the proposal's merits. My conclusion will be a critical one—which is churlish, given that as a newcomer to this topic, I have nothing better to offer in its place; but there it is.

Both the leaper and shopper possess, on this account, a self-fulfilling expectation that is motivated by a desire for its fulfilment. Desire comes in as the spring of belief, rather than directly as the spring of action. The leaper and the shopper alike possess a belief that is both wishful, and self-fulfilling. This means that, on the face of it, intention and faith are alike in possessing certain 'misdirections' of fit, as we might provisionally dub them. On neat rules about direction of fit, belief is supposed to fit the world, and the world is supposed to fit desire; but in wishful thought, belief comes to fit desire, instead of the world; and in self-fulfilling thought, the world comes to fit belief, instead of desire.

These misdirections of fit are at once the source of the doxastic account's considerable virtues, and also of its ultimate failure, or so I shall suggest. They make intention a sort of faith; and, even if they did not, they would make intention as bad as faith—as difficult to achieve, and as dubious, epistemologically speaking. They deserve some brief preliminary comment.

2. Misdirections of fit: wishful and self-fulfilling belief

Taking wishful thinking first, it is worth distinguishing two forms. (i) I may believe that p because *I desire that p be true*. I desire to leap

[7] Velleman, *The Possibility of Practical Reason* (Oxford: Clarendon Press, 2000), 26. I do not attend here to the development of his view since the original presentation; in particular I shall skate over the distinction between a drive for self-knowledge as a desire, and as a regulative aim.

across the chasm, so I believe I will leap across the chasm. I desire that my cancer will be cured, and so I believe that my cancer will be cured. I desire that God exists, so I believe that God exists. (ii) I may believe that p because *I desire that I believe that p*. Wishing to avoid risk of damnation, and wagering as Pascal wagered, I desire to *believe* that God exists; so I believe that God exists. These two forms may also be combined, as when—(i + ii) I believe that p because *I desire that p be true, and I believe that believing p will make p true*. I desire to leap across the chasm, and believe that believing I shall leap across will enable me to leap across; so I believe I shall leap across. I desire that my cancer will be cured, and believe that believing my cancer will be cured will help cure it; so I believe my cancer will be cured. If (i) presents naive wishful thinking, (i + ii) presents sophisticated wishful thinking, assisted by faith in the efficacy of belief itself.[8]

Wishful thinking presents a puzzle, since it is widely thought by philosophers that you cannot, just like that, believe something because you want to believe it, or because it would be useful to believe it. *Acting* like a theist is something you might, all of a sudden, come to do, offered suitable incentives (the knife of the Inquisitor at your throat). *Believing* God exists is not something you might, all of a sudden, come to do, whatever the incentives. The reasons for this have been linked to belief's proper direction of fit. As Bernard Williams says,

it is not a contingent fact that I cannot bring it about, just like that, that I believe something ... Why is this? One reason is connected with the characteristic of beliefs that they aim at truth. If I could acquire a belief at will, I could acquire it whether it was true or not; moreover, I would know that I could acquire it whether it was true or not. If in full consciousness I could will to acquire a 'belief' irrespective of its truth, it is unclear that before

---

[8] Paralleling this phenomenon of *desire-driven belief*, one might identify *belief-driven desire* of these two corresponding varieties: (a) I desire that p because *I believe that p is true*. What would be envisaged here is a stoical matching of desire to what the world is believed to offer. I believe I am destined to be a housewife, so being a housewife is what I desire. (b) I desire that p because *I believe that I desire that p*. I am told, by credible authority, that all Australians love to watch cricket. Believing I am Australian, I believe I will love to watch cricket. As a result, I come to love to watch cricket. This contrast is discussed in joint work by Richard Holton and Langton, in progress.

the event I could seriously think of it as a belief, i.e. as something purporting to represent reality.[9]

Fear of hell provides Pascal, or his contemporary successor, with pragmatic reason for belief in God, but he cannot believe it, just like that. He may, of course, *do* something, just like that (go to church, say his prayers, announce his so-called 'decision for Christ' at the altar), actions which may lead to useful belief. Wishful thinking is thought to need assistance from a blindness or forgetfulness at odds with the 'full consciousness' Williams mentioned. The associated principle is sometimes cast as a point about the ethics of belief, a normative constraint—we *ought not* to indulge in wishful belief. This is the target James had in mind when he complained of those who 'feel it would be *sinful* to act upon an assumption unverified by previous experience'. Williams casts the principle as a constitutive constraint on belief: we *cannot* wishfully believe, or at least, we cannot wishfully believe 'in full consciousness'. If faith is wishful belief, and wishful belief impossible, little wonder faith is listed by St. Paul as a special gift, along with the power to work miracles.[10] It would be peculiar, though, if we had to place intention on the same list.

We turn from wishful to self-fulfilling beliefs, that 'class of truths of whose reality belief is a factor as well as a confessor', to borrow James' phrase. With this misdirection of fit, the world accommodates itself to fit belief, instead of belief accommodating itself to fit the world. Among self-fulfilling beliefs are some wishful beliefs, including the cases which occupied James. My desire-driven belief that I am able to leap across the chasm may enable me to leap across the chasm. My desire-driven belief that my cancer will be cured may cure my cancer. Belief may be self-fulfilling independently of the workings of desire: my belief in my chasm-leaping ability, my belief in a happy cancer prognosis, may stem from misleading evidence rather than desire, and, if I am lucky, be equally

---

[9] Bernard Williams, 'Deciding to Believe', in *Problems of the Self* (1973), 136–51; 148. Implications of this for feminist critique of reason are drawn in Langton, 'Beyond a Pragmatic Critique of Reason', *Australasian Journal of Philosophy* 71 (1993), 364–84, where I argue that pragmatic critique of 'male' cognitive strategies—for example, that they serve men's interests and hurt those of women—fails adequately to explain them, or damn them. (Reprinted in Langton, *Sexual Solipsism: Philosophical Essays on Pornography and Objectification* (Oxford: Oxford University Press, 2005), forthcoming.)

[10] 1 Corinthians 12: 9–10. Thanks to my mother, Valda Langton, for reminder of the reference.

self-fulfilling. For the leaper and the cancer patient, the world that accommodates itself to fit belief is the immediate psychological or physiological world of the believer; but belief's self-fulfilment may stretch futher afield. Here is James again:

> Do you like me or not?...Whether you do or not depends, in countless instances, on whether I meet you half-way, am willing to assume that you must like me, and show you trust and expectation. The previous faith on my part in your liking's existence is in such cases what makes your liking come.

> How many women's hearts are vanquished by the mere sanguine insistence of some man that they must love him! he will not consent to the hypothesis that they cannot. The desire for a certain kind of truth here brings about that special truth's existence; and so it is in innumerable cases of other sorts.

> Who gains promotions, boons, appointments, but the man in whose life they are seen to play the part of live hypotheses, who...takes risks for them in advance? His faith acts on the powers above him as a claim, and creates its own verification.[11]

> A whole train of passengers...will be looted by a few highwaymen, simply because the latter can count on one another, while each passenger fears that if he makes a movement of resistance, he will be shot before any one else backs him up. If we believed that the whole car-full would rise at once with us, we should each severally rise, and train-robbing would never even be attempted. There are then, cases where a fact cannot come at all unless a preliminary faith exists in its coming.

Less sanguine examples from the social domain might include a teacher's belief that a child will be stupid, which helps to make the child stupid; and a domineering man's belief that a woman will be submissive, which helps to make her submissive. These latter cases illustrate the way belief's self-fulfilment might have a moral and political dimension—might even be, as I have elsewhere argued, a central feature of objectification, though that is not my topic here.[12] Still further afield is the far-fetched hypothesis countenanced by James, that belief in God may be self-fulfilling:

[11] James, 'The Will to Believe', in *The Will to Believe*, 23–4.
[12] See e.g. Langton, 'Feminism in Epistemology: Exclusion and Objectification', in *Cambridge Companion to Feminism in Philosophy*, eds. Jennifer Hornsby and Miranda Fricker (Cambridge: Cambridge University Press, 2001).

[W]ill our faith in the unseen world...verify itself? Who knows? ...I confess that I do not see why the very existence of an invisible world may not in part depend on the personal response which any one of us may make to the religious appeal. God himself, in short, may draw vital strength and increase of very being from our fidelity. For my own part, I do not know what the sweat and blood and tragedy of this life mean, if they mean anything short of this.[13]

(This, if taken seriously, makes James' theism an instance of (i + ii), above.) These various examples are all, I take it, causally self-fulfilling. Non-causally self-fulfilling beliefs might include the classic Cartesian examples: 'I am thinking' and such; we shall, for present purposes, be ignoring those.

Now self-fulfilment is thought to have implications for the aforementioned puzzle about wishful thinking. While philosophers may wonder about the possibility, or rationality, of believing something 'just like that', given pragmatic incentives, their worries are groundless when it comes to wishful belief that is also self-fulfilling belief—so James argues. Wishful belief is no miracle, and it is no sin:

we may logically, legitimately, and inexpugnably believe what we desire [when] the belief creates its verification. The thought becomes literally father to the fact, as the wish was father to the thought.[14]

He castigates those who question the rationality of self-fulfilling faith:

[W]here faith in a fact can help create the fact, that would be an insane logic which should say that faith running ahead of scientific evidence is the 'lowest kind of immorality' into which a thinking being can fall.[15]

---

[13] James, *The Will to Believe*, 61.

[14] James, *The Will to Believe*, 103. Self-verifying belief is not quite the same as self-fulfilling belief—belief that produces evidence for itself might not be belief that fulfils itself—but the talk of 'fact' shows that what James has in mind here is belief that is self-verifying because it is self-fulfilling. Mind you, such a contrast will be relevant to his example of theism, given the contrast between theistic belief supplying subsequent evidence for itself, and making itself true (the latter being a considerably stranger doctrine than the former).

[15] James, 'The Will to Believe', in *The Will to Believe*, 25.

Rae Langton

In the context of intention rather than faith, Velleman argues likewise that wishful belief is not only possible but rational, when self-fulfilling. He says in response to Williams:

> If a person thinks of his beliefs as self-fulfilling, then he will see that aligning them with his wishes won't entail taking them out of alignment with the truth, for the simple reason that the truth will take care of aligning itself with them. He can therefore think of himself both as believing what he likes and as believing only what's true, because what's true depends on what he believes... Because self-fulfilling beliefs cause their own truth, instead of being caused by it, they remain reliably connected to the truth even if they are determined by what the subject wants to believe, and so they afford an opportunity for deliberate wishful thinking.[16]

Note that if it is supposed to be a matter of what the believer can 'think of himself', this argument should apply, not to beliefs that *are* self-fulfilling, but to beliefs that are *believed to be* self-fulfilling. Here we merely record the latter worry for later attention.

This talk of truth and the direction of causation brings us to a central feature of the doxastic account, which, if it works, achieves something far more ambitious than just an answer to the puzzle about how one can believe what one wants to believe. Intention, recall,

> (i) represents as true that we are going to do something;... (ii) it aims therein to represent something that really is true; and...(iii) it causes the truth of what it represents.[17]

Velleman here draws apart three features each of which have been taken by other philosophers to characterize the intuitive notion of direction of fit: whether a state represents something as true; whether it aims at truth; and whether it is caused by or causes the truth of what it represents.[18] Intention, as he describes it, involves no *misdirections* of fit; it does have an unusual combination of direction of fit-like features, which is what allows it to be both wishful, and truth-aiming. Our chief interest is in the second and third

[16] Velleman, *Practical Reflection,* 129
[17] Velleman, *Practical Reason,* 26; roman numerals added.
[18] For a survey of a range of attempts to identify what 'direction of fit' consists in, together with an original alternative proposal, see Lloyd Humberstone, 'Direction of Fit', *Mind* 101 (1992), 59–83; a paper to which I owe a great deal.

features.[19] The second he calls a 'constitutive aim', the aim to represent something as true only if it is true.[20] The third he calls 'direction of guidance', and it concerns the direction of causation: whether the state *causes*, or *is caused by* the truth of what it represents—or, to supply a Kantian label he does not use, whether the state in question is 'spontaneous' or 'receptive'.

Intention thus has two features which earn it the name of belief: it represents a proposition as true, and it aims at the truth. The third feature supplies a 'direction of guidance' which is not belief-like: it is practical, and more traditionally associated with desire rather than belief. Velleman concedes there is a temptation confine practicality to desire: to suppose that if a mental state is cognitive, representing how things are, it must be caused by how they are, or (borrowing the Kantian label) it must be receptive; to assume correspondingly that if the mental state causes what it represents, it must be representing how things *are to be*, and therefore it must be spontaneous, conative rather than cognitive; and to conclude belief cannot be practical. This temptation, he says, must be resisted:

> when I make a choice, a question is resolved in the world by being resolved in my mind. That I am going to do something is made true by my representing it as true. So choice has the same direction of fit as belief but the same direction of guidance as desire: it is a case of practical cognition.[21]

While Humeans allege that a state cannot have two directions of fit, Velleman's distinctions make space for a state which does, effectively, have two directions of fit; or better (putting the point in his terms), intention has a 'constitutive aim' that is cognitive—it aims at truth—and a 'direction of guidance' that is conative—it causes its truth. That is how intention can be 'practical cognition'.

We return now to the question of what faith might have to do with intention, given a doxastic account of intention.

---

[19] For Velleman only the first of the three listed features deserves the name 'direction of fit', which he uses in a narrow sense for the distinction between representing something *as* true and representing something as *to be made* true. This feature distinguishes beliefs *and* imaginings, together, from desires.

[20] This distinguishes beliefs from imaginings, as well as from desires. When you imagine something, you represent something as true without aiming to represent something that really is true; when you believe something you aim to represent it as true only if it really is true.

[21] *Practical Reason*, p. 25.

Rae Langton

3. Is intention a sort of faith?

Faith, as I am understanding it, is not merely predictive belief. Distinguishing intention and merely predictive belief is easy. The difference between merely predictive belief and intention lies in the direction of guidance. Merely predictive belief will be like an intention in representing as true that I am going to do something, and in aiming therein to represent something that really is true; but merely predictive belief, unlike an intention, does not cause the truth of what it represents. A merely predictive belief is receptive, not spontaneous. (Note that, contrary to what Velleman's dichotomy suggests, merely predictive belief is not receptive in virtue of being caused by the truth *of what it represents*, since what it represents is in the future; it is presumably receptive in virtue of being caused by the truth of propositions about the present or past that are evidence for the future.) Intention diverges from predictive belief about what one will do in being spontaneous—uncaused by what it represents—and by being self-fulfilling—causing the truth of what it represents. Intention is a wishful, spontaneous, self-fulfilling belief about what one will do.

When it comes to faith, distinguishing faith from intention is less easy. Faith so far matches intention, point for point: faith shares intention's belief-like features—the leaper represents as true that he is able to leap the chasm, and he aims to represent it as true only if it is true. Moreover, faith shares intention's direction of guidance, for it causes its truth: the leaper's faith enables him to leap the chasm. This might tempt us to think that what James has described simply *is* the climber's intention to leap across the chasm. If Velleman were right, that would seem an appropriate conclusion.

That would be a surprising outcome: for James is surely describing something quite different to the mere intention to leap across. He is describing a process of wishful confidence building, that is lucky in its outcome. To be sure, the leaper also *intends* to leap across, on anybody's story, and the presence of this intention—however understood—complicates the example. But the intention is not the same thing as this wishful, and fortunate, confidence building manoevre. To bring that out, consider the difference between this climber and the experienced climber who simply leaps across, without psychic drama, when he intends to do so. In both cases we have intention: each climber has, on Velleman's hypothesis, a motivated belief whose content is 'I shall leap across', and it is a belief that fulfils itself; but the James example supplies something extra, in addition to the intention. The experienced climber has intention;

252

the inexperienced climber has intention *and faith*. The faith is surely not the same thing as the intention. This gives us some preliminary reasons for doubting the doxastic account of intention, at least as so far described.

In the example just considered, there is intention without faith. There can equally be faith without intention. The faith which James describes that wins friends, wins love, and wins promotions, may work without thereby being an intention to win friends, win love, and win promotion. (Indeed, it will work better if it is no part of an intentional strategy.) My wishful, self-fulfilling belief that you will be friendly is not *ipso facto* my intention that you will be friendly, still less (to take James' far-fetched example) is my wishful, self-ful-filling belief that God exists is my intention that God exists.

Intuitively then, faith and intention are not the same. How are they to be distinguished, given the doxastic account of intention? Well, there are some more resources to draw upon.

In the first place, intention is supposed to be a wishful, self-ful-filling belief about *my own future action*: so your friendliness, my employer's rewarding actions, and God's existence do not obviously qualify. (But they might—perhaps the scope of one's own action reaches further than one thought, and in any case how else am I to identify what is my action if not via the notion of my intention?) Leaving aside this complex issue, it leaves untouched the basic hunch that the climber's faith in his future leap is indeed a belief about his future action; but it is not identical with his intention to act.

In the second place, intention is supposed to be a wishful, self-fulfilling belief that *consciously represents itself as self-fulfilling*. Intentions, recall, are 'self-fulfilling expectations that are motivated by a desire for their fulfilment and *that represent themselves as such*'. This constraint distinguishes intention from the faith of the naive wishful thinker—the leaper whose faith enables him to leap across, though he does not know it. But consider now a sophisticated leaper, who has read his William James and *knows* that faith will enable him to leap. The sophisticate has a wishful, self-fulfilling belief that does indeed consciously represent itself as self-fulfilling. But nonetheless that belief is, surely, not his intention.

In the third place, intention, unlike faith, is supposed to be a belief that fulfils itself via a mechanism involving an *aim for self-knowledge*. Here we come to the most daring part of Velleman's pro-posal, and a feature which promises at last to distinguish intention from faith. How does faith fulfil itself? We do not know, and it would presumably take a team of psychologists (or theologians) to

253

tell us. How does intention fulfil itself—why is it that when I intend something, I act on that intention, making true the belief that I will do it? My belief that I *will* do something comes true because *I want to know what I am doing*, or (better) because I *aim to know what I am doing*. On this view, self-knowledge is a constitutive aim of action, and this is what drives intention's direction of guidance. The shopper's belief that he will buy butter makes him put the butter in his basket because, roughly, he wants (or aims for) his belief to be true.

This want or aim is, Velleman concedes, not usually our end in view, consciously represented in our practical reasoning. The shopper may place butter in his basket without sparing a thought to the question of whether that is what he believed he would do, and without sparing a thought to the question of whether he wants to do what he believes he will do. The push towards self-knowledge is a sub-agential aim, comparable to the aim of avoiding pain in our movements about the world, likewise an aim which regulates behaviour without (usually) being an end. When the shopper places butter in his basket, what happens is this: he antecedently believes he is going to place butter in his basket, and his belief aims to be true; given his aim to know what he is doing, action makes his belief true. On Velleman's account, intention is not only a species of self-fulfilling belief, but a species of self-fulfilling belief that (when successful) counts as *knowledge*, and the achievement of this knowledge is—wittingly or otherwise—the aim of our intended actions.

What are we to make of this special mechanism? It does present a promising means of distinguishing faith from intention, on the doxastic account: for when my faith is self-fulfilling it is not mediated by an aim to know what I am doing. At least, I don't *think* it is mediated that way. But then it is news to me that my intention's self-fulfillment is mediated by an aim to know what I am doing. Perhaps a psychologist, or a philosopher, could convince me that the aim for self-knowledge is, in many cases, what drives faith as well. That would be an interesting surprise, but no more of an interesting surprise than the revelation that an aim for self-knowledge is what drives intention. Suppose a psychologist *were* to deliver us the news, after careful research, that the climber's faith was so mediated: he leapt across because he wanted his belief about himself to be self-knowledge. Would we then think of the climber's faith as his intention? Surely not—though I have no theory to back up this basic intuition. Supplying this extra ingredient does not yet add up to intention: faith mediated by a drive for self-knowledge is still just faith. But the doxastic account must call this faith intention. It must, effectively, concede that intention is a sort of faith.

4. Is intention as bad as faith?

The doxastic account effectively makes intention a sort of faith; it lacks resources adequately to distinguish intention from faith, or so I have argued. Suppose my argument is mistaken. It may nonetheless be that intention resembles faith closely enough that the pitfalls of faith are also the pitfalls of intention—that there are problems posed both by wishfulness, and by self-fulfilment.

What problems? After all, if wishfulness is supposed to be the problem, isn't self-fulfilment supposed to be the solution? That was certainly the idea. Faith is no miracle, and no sin, according to James: being self-fulfilling allows and entitles faith to be wishful, and still aim at truth. Intention, likewise, is no miracle, and no sin, for the same reason: being self-fulfilling allows and entitles intention to be wishful, and still aim at truth. Self-fulfilment is the key to the possibility, and epistemological laudability, of these attitudes—so James and Velleman argue, and we have been taking their word for it. But it is time to look at that idea more critically.

Let us consider whether faith can indeed be adopted directly, 'in full consciousness', when self-fulfilling. Pascal's wishful belief is *not* adopted directly, 'just like that', but cultivated gradually out of new habits and behaviour, assisted, presumably, by forgetfulness and inattention to earlier strategic thinking—but then Pascal did not suppose faith in God was self-fulfilling. Imagine instead a wishful theist who thought as James apparently thought, that God's very *existence* is a result of belief. Never mind that the point of Pascal's wager disappears (no threat of hell after all, if I don't believe in an avenging God!). Would the believer, in these circumstances, be able to believe in God, 'just like that'? The answer should be yes, if self-fulfilling beliefs 'cause their own truth, instead of being caused by it', as Velleman says, and therefore 'afford an opportunity for deliberate wishful thinking'. Ah, you say, but Velleman is here speaking of *truly* self-fulfilling belief: he is not speaking of belief that is merely *believed* self-fulfilling, on the basis of—not to put too fine a point on it—lunatic theology.

Well, let's see. Merely *being* self-fulfilling is never going to be enough to make wishful belief possible, 'in full consciousness'. To an agent ignorant of their potential self-fulfilment, such beliefs will come no more easily than any others. The argument against Williams implies, though this is not made explicit, that what matters is *believed* self-fulfilment, not self-fulfilment—and here we return to the worry recorded earlier. It is *believed* self-fulfilment, not self-fulfilment, that makes deliberate wishful thinking possible, if anything does:

> If a person *thinks of his beliefs as self-fulfilling*, then he will see that aligning them with his wishes won't entail taking them out of alignment with the truth, for the simple reason that the truth will take care of aligning itself with them. He can therefore *think of himself* both as believing what he likes and as believing only what's true, because what's true depends on what he believes. (emphasis added).

Being self-fulfilling won't achieve this; being *thought* self-fulfilling just might. So if Velleman is right, the lunatic theist should indeed be able to wishfully believe in God *just like that*, 'in full consciousness', without recourse to Pascal's method of religious habit and inattention. Since he thinks of his belief in God as self-fulfilling, he ought to see that aligning them with his wishes won't entail taking them out of alignment with the truth.

Can he believe in God, just like that? Surely not. The lunatic theist would be no better equipped than Pascal in the task of working up belief. I conclude that, contrary to the implicit views of James and Velleman, being *believed* self-fulfilling is not enough to make wishful belief possible, 'in full consciousness'. Faith would still, in these circumstances, be more or less a miracle. So too, I suggest, would intention, and for the same reason. The constitutive constraint on belief identified by Williams is not adequately met either by self-fulfilment, or by believed self-fulfilment.[22] Wishfulness creates a problem which self-fulfilment, believed or actual, does not adequately solve.

What of the normative constraint on belief? For James, it is no epistemological sin to wishfully believe, when belief is self-fulfilling: belief, though wishful, can still aim at truth, and can even count as knowledge.[23] The same goes for intention, on the doxastic account: belief can, though wishful, still aim at truth, and count as *knowledge*. How else could it be a drive for self-knowledge which makes one fulfil one's intention? When successful, intention is a true belief about one's future action, and non-accidentally true: it is

[22] So much for possibility: what of rationality? Here it may depend whether one has an internalist or externalist understanding of what makes belief rational. If his religious belief is not *in fact* 'reliably connected to the truth', it is, though possible, irrational, by externalist standards. But if instead what matters is internal to the mind, the belief may be not only possible but rational. To be sure, it rests on a false belief that belief in God is self-fulfilling (which in turn may have an irrational source): but the wishful belief-forming process is itself a rational one, since it can be regarded as aiming at the truth.

[23] James, 'The Will to Believe', 12. He thought that when we have faith, we know, but we do not know that we know.

reliably connected with the truth, because it is self-fulfilling. So it is knowledge.

Now faith has a number of features which may undermine its claim to be knowledge, including its wishful origins, but I wish to consider the possibility that *self-fulfillingness* may undermine faith's claim to knowledge. What applies to faith will then extend, I think, to intention, doxastically understood. Knowledge is thought to require appropriate direction of fit—not merely truth, justification, and non-accidentality. For those who think non-accidentality will do the job, Lloyd Humberstone supplies the following story as counterexample:

> Consider the case of a subject, S, whose beliefs about the future are monitored by a supernatural being who, taking (for whatever reason) a special interest in minimizing falsity amongst S's beliefs, intervenes in the course of history so as to make these future-oriented beliefs of S true. Note that we do not suppose that S has the slightest inkling that this is going on. It does not seem correct to say that S, who believes, for example, that Islam will be the state religion of a United Europe by the year 2100, knows this to be the case, even though it is not at all accidental that S's belief here is true. The trouble is that the non-accidentality pertains to a matching of the world to S's mental state rather than in the converse direction that befits a thetic attitude.[24]

The beliefs of this believer are not wishful, nor is he aware of his epistemological good fortune: yet, saliently, his beliefs are reliably self-fulfilling, reliably rendered true by his divine guardian. This agent presents a vivid example of faith in a fact helping to create a fact, in James' terms; his beliefs have, in Velleman's terms, a practical direction of guidance, since they cause the truth of what they represent, albeit by a rather unusual mechanism. He believes that Islam will be the religion of a United Europe by the year 2100, his belief is no accident—but it is not knowledge, or so Humberstone assumes, and I for present purposes agree. Why does it fail, as knowledge? Because of its anomalous direction of fit, its anomalous direction of guidance: his belief has not come to fit the world, but the world, rather, has come to fit his belief. Having a reliable connection to the truth is just not good enough.

Suppose we alter the example to make it, roughly, faith. The agent, out of religious devotion, *wishfully* believes that Islam will be the religion of a United Europe. That, I presume, would not improve its epistemological standing: so faith, even though self-fulfilling, would not be knowledge. Suppose we further alter the

[24] Humberstone, 'Direction of Fit', 62.

example to make it, roughly, intention, doxastically understood. We add Velleman's conditions: the agent is *aware* of his epistemic good fortune, and can *represent* his beliefs as self-fulfilling; we narrow down the scope of his beliefs to the domain of his own future action, so instead of thinking about Europe in a hundred years, he thinks, predictively, about his own doings, in a day's time. I presume these conditions do not, saliently, improve the beliefs' epistemological standing, though this may take more argument. So intention, even though self-fulfilling, would not be knowledge either.[25]

Summing up then, it seems that faith, even if self-fulfilling, or believed to be self-fulfilling, can probably not be achieved 'just like that'—so neither can intention, doxastically understood. Construed as 'deliberate wishful thinking', intention would be as impossible as faith. Moreover, faith, even if self-fulfilling, is not knowledge—so neither is intention, doxastically understood. We concluded before that the doxastic account makes intention a sort of faith. We conclude here that, in any case, it makes intention as bad as faith. James hoped for a faith achievable without miracle, and without epistemological sin. Velleman hopes the same, effectively, for intention. I fear such hopes are forlorn.

[25] This is not supposed to be a merely terminological point about how the label 'knowledge' is to be used. Observe too that even if one were to allow intention to count as knowledge of what one will do, it would be a knowledge so deeply entwined with error it is not obvious that it deserves the name (intellectualist rhetoric notwithstanding). When I intend to buy butter, I believe I will buy butter, and my belief makes me buy butter—given my background aim of *knowing what I am doing*. That is, in some sense, why I do it. But if asked, I will surely deny that is why I do it. If Velleman is right, my answer shows that I am profoundly in error. Velleman does not pretend that this is what we—consciously, explicitly—think we are up to when we act on our intentions. He allows that the background aim for self-knowledge is regulative, comparable to the background aim of avoiding pain when moving about, something that guides what we do without presenting itself as an explicit goal. He allows that we may be ignorant of our actions' constitutive aim. But ignorance understates the point. Ignorance is not mistake. If asked, 'in moving about like that, were you aiming to avoid hurting yourself?', a reflective response might well be 'yes, perhaps so—I hadn't realized'. If asked, 'in putting the butter in the basket, were you aiming to know what you are doing?' a reflective response is likely to be a simple no. The account implies that here we have mistake, and not just ignorance. The aim ascribed to us is not simply sub-agential, unconscious: it is actually at odds with what we believe we believe we are up to. So whenever I intend to do something, I am making a cognitive mistake. This, if nothing else, is a strange outcome for so vividly rationalistic an account of intention.

The Destruction of the World Trade Center and the Law on Event-identity

MICHAEL S. MOORE

1. Introduction

September 11, 2001 brought to legal awareness an issue that has long puzzled metaphysicians. The general issue is that of event-identity, drawing the boundaries of events so that we can tell when there is one event and when there are two. The September 11th version of that issue is: how many occurrences of insured events were there on September 11, 2001 in New York? Was the collapse of the two World Trade Center Towers one event, despite the two separate airliners crashing into each tower? Or were these two separate insured events?

Usually such puzzles are the stuff of academic debate amongst professional philosophers specializing in the metaphysics of event identity. Metaphysics is an arcane speciality carried on by 'those happy few who feel the intellectual fascination in ... grubbing around in the roots of being.'[1] The metaphysics of events is a specialty within metaphysics, capturing the attention of many professional philosophers in the 1970s, but otherwise remaining esoteric even within the confines of professional philosophy. Now such an issue has emerged from the academic shadows into the bright light of a 3-$\frac{1}{2}$ billion dollar legal controversy. For the owners of the World Trade Center lease, the Silverstein group, had obtained casualty ('first party') insurance for property damage with a limit of approximately 3-$\frac{1}{2}$ billion dollars 'per occurrence.' The question in the current lawsuits between those owners and the insurance companies, is whether there was one such occurrence or two when al Qaeda terrorists destroyed the World Trade Center. Such questions of individuation have often been scorned as pejoratively academic questions—like asking how many angels can dance on the head of a pin[2]—but now the financing of

[1] David Armstrong, *Universals* (Boulder, Colo.: Westview Press, 1989), at p. 139.
[2] Isaac D'Israeli, *Curiosities of Literature*, 1791.

Michael Moore

the rebuilding of a major American monument turns on the question.

The basic facts of what transpired on September 11 are known to everyone. Still, the details are important.[3] At 7:59 a.m. on September 11 American Airlines Flight number 11 departed Boston's Logan Airport. This Boeing 767 was hijacked shortly after takeoff by five members of al Qaeda, the terrorist organization headed by Osama Bin Laden. At 8:46 a.m. the plane crashed into the North Tower of the World Trade Center and at 10:29 a.m. that Tower collapsed because of the weakening of the steel columns due to the fire resulting from the crash. At 7:58 a.m. that same day United Flight number 175 departed Logan Airport. It too was hijacked shortly after takeoff by another five members of al Qaeda. In a co-ordinated attack, that plane, also a Boeing 767, struck the South Tower of the World Trade Center at 9:06 a.m. and at 10:00 a.m. that Tower also collapsed from the weakened steel columns due to another fire resulting from the second crash. The two Towers were completely destroyed, as were a number of the other buildings comprising the World Trade Center that were also leased to the Silverstein group. The reconstruction cost and lost rental income likely exceeds the $7,073,600,000 dollars sought by the Silverstein group from their insurance companies.[4]

Given the disparity between the foreseeably large loss if both Towers were completely destroyed and the roughly 3.5 billion dollar per occurrence limitation, the WTC leaseholders were obviously taking a risk in underinsuring. Much has been made of this fact in the controversy between the leaseholders and their insurance companies.[5] Yet that *a* risk was taken by the Silverstein group does not answer the question of whether *this* risk was taken. The bet being placed by insureds such as the Silverstein group is that no one thing is likely to destroy their property entirely; the most harm they can suffer from any one thing, they might think, is the loss of half of their property (such as one Tower). Whether the insureds win or lose in placing such bets is determined by the question of whether indeed 'one thing' caused the whole loss—and that is determined by

[3] The details on the attack on the Twin Towers were reconstructed and presented in *USA Today*, December 19, 2001, p. 1A, col. 2-3, pp. 3A-4A. The details on the exact nature of the collapse of the Towers are given in the Affidavit of Matthys P. Levy filed January 19, 2002, in support of Defendant's Motion for Summary Judgment.

[4] *Wall Street Journal*, Nov. 2, 2001, pp. A-1, A-11.

[5] See, e.g., the complaint of Swiss re filed October 22, 2001, paragraphs 28, 46.

what the parties meant by 'one thing,' which is the subject of this paper.

Because the WTC leaseholders had commenced ownership of the lease in July of 2001, only months before September 11, the wording of their casualty insurance policy had not been finalized. Instead, their insurance broker had obtained for them a 'binder' of insurance, which is legally effective in initiating insurance coverage. The binder provided for coverage against 'all risks of physical loss or damage' to a sum insured of 3,536,800,000 dollars *per occurrence*. The binder did not define the crucial 'per occurrence' language.

Earlier, however, on June 25, 2001, the WTC lease-holders' insurance broker had submitted a proposed policy form for the approval of the various insurance companies insuring or reinsuring the WTC lease. Those proposed terms of coverage did include the following definition of 'occurrence.'

> 'Occurrence' shall mean all losses or damages that are attributable directly or indirectly to one cause or to one series of similar causes. All such losses will be added together and the total amount of such losses will be treated as one occurrence irrespective of the period of time or area over which such losses occur.[6]

The lead reinsurance company, SR International Business Insurance Co. ('Swiss Re'), did not sign off on this form. Instead, in its binder Swiss Re referenced two of its own forms (neither of which defines 'occurrence') and then added to its binder, 'wording to be agreed by SRI.' Swiss Re executed its binder on July 9, 2001, adding that its agreement was 'subject to wording to be agreed.' No reference was made to the June 25 insurance form containing the definition of 'occurrence' quoted above.

Two other insurance companies, Ace Ltd. and XL Capital, covering 365 million of the $3.5368 billion dollars, did agree to the definition of 'occurrence' quoted earlier. Those two companies settled with the Silvestein group on a 'one occurrence' basis, namely, with a payout of only 365 million dollars.[7] In addition, on September 25, 2002, three more insurance companies (totaling $112 million in coverage) obtained the same result by the granting of summary judgment in their favour; the liability of these three insurance companies has also held to turn on the definition of 'occurrence' quoted earlier. Such settlements and judgments reflects a consensus between the parties and the judge that the definition quoted above is 'definitive' of the issue. I question in section

---

[6] Quoted in Swiss Re complaint, *supra* note 5, paragraph 31.
[7] *The Australian Financial Review*, 18 February 2002, p. 44.

5 whether the definition makes the large difference the judge and the attorneys apparently thought that it did.

On October 22, 2001, Swiss Re filed for a declaratory judgment in federal district court in New York for a declaration of its liabilities under the binder of insurance.[8] This suit has been joined with other lawsuits filed between the leaseholders and other insurance companies. In January, 2002 the Silverstein group filed a motion for summary judgment, which was denied in June, 2002. The matter is currently set for trial in November, 2002. Many predict that the amount of money involved, together with the murkiness of the issue, will require years worth of appeals to resolve the issue.[9]

2. The General Insurance Law Understanding of 'Occurrence'

Not surprisingly, the 'per occurrence' language of the WTC binder is not unique to that contract. It is common in America to write both casualty and liability insurance policies with a 'per occurrence' or 'per accident' upper and lower limit in exposure.[10] What is surprising are the complexities in the treatment of this issue by American insurance law. As I shall explore shortly, there are some detailed causal doctrines and some sophisticated views of event-identity presupposed by American decisions in this context.

---

[8] *SR International Business Insurance Co. v. World Trade Center Properties LLC, Silverstein Properties Inc. et al.* Civil. No.01CV12738(JSM), United States District Court for the Southern District of New York. The declaratory judgment action has been set for expedited trial on September 3, 2002. *Wall Street Journal*, Dec. 14, 2001, p. B-4; *Wall Street Journal*, Dec. 18, 2001, p. B-6.

[9] *Wall Street Journal*, Nov. 2, 2001, p. A16.

[10] Although nuanced differences in meaning between 'occurrence' and 'accident,' have been suggested, the tendency of the insurance cases is to equate the terms. See, e.g., *Hartford Accident and Indemnity Co. v. Wesolowski*, 33 N.Y.2d 169, 350 N.Y.2d 895, 305 N.E.2d 907 (1973), where the New York Court of Appeals held there to be no distinction in meaning between 'per occurrence' and 'per accident' limitations in insurance policies. Accord, *Truck Insurance Exchange v. Rohde*, 49 Wash.2d 465, 469, 303 P.2d 659, 661 (1957). For some suggestions regarding the differences between such terms when the issue is the kind of risks covered (not how many occurrences there were), see *Stauffer Chemical Co. v. Insurance Co. of North America*, 372 F.Supp. 1303, 1307 (S.D.N.Y. 1973) ('occurrence' a broader term than 'accident' in terms of the range of items covered).

a. *Simple, Intuitive Tests of 'One Occurrence'*

Before coming to the complexities, however, it may be well to put aside a tempting (because simpler) view. This is the view that takes at face value whatever bottom-line intuitions one might have about how many occurrences there were on the facts of particular cases. I have discovered, for example, that without knowing anything about insurance law many people have definite intuitions about how many occurrences took place when the Twin Towers were destroyed. The simple approach is to ask a judge or jury to resolve such cases by repairing to their own intuitions without further definition of, or instruction about, the meaning of 'occurrence.'

The simple view in this insurance context is reminiscent of Justice Potter Stewart's famous 'test' for hard core pornography: 'I cannot define it,' Steward opined, 'but I know it when I see it and this film is not that.'[11] The simple view is also reminiscent of Justice William Brennan's proposed test for when two criminal prosecutions are barred because they would prosecute 'the same offense: we should simply ask, Brennan urged, whether the 'same act, transaction, or episode' is being prosecuted in the two proceedings.[12] Arguably the New York Court of Appeals has also succumbed to the beguiling simplicity of intuitive tests in the present insurance context. For that court has said that all that needs asking in cases like that involving the World Trade Center is whether there is a 'single event' or not.[13]

The problem with these simple intuitive tests is not that we are bereft of intuitions about such matters, for often we are not. Rather, the problem is that such unguided intuitions may be answering the wrong question. This was certainly true of Brennan's proposed 'single act, transaction or episode' test of double jeopardy: such a test elides two distinct questions that require separate answers in the double jeopardy context. A proper understanding of double jeopardy's concern with disproportionate punishment requires that we ask *both*: (a) whether the accused performed one or more than one particular act on the occasion in question; and, if the accused did perform but one particular act, (b) whether the particular act the accused performed instantiated one or more than one type of action prohibited by the criminal code.[14] Only individuals who suffer

[11] *Jacobellis v. Ohio*, 378 U.S. 184, 197 (1961) (Stewart, J., concurring).

[12] *Ashe v. Swenson*, 397 U.S. 436 (1970) (concurring opinion).

[13] *Johnson v. Indemnity Insurance Company of North America*, 7 N.Y.2d 222, 196 N.Y.S.2d 678, 164 N.Ed.2d 704 (1959).

[14] Argued at length in Michael Moore, *Act and Crime: The Philosophy of Action and Its Implications for Criminal Law* (Oxford: Clarendon Press, 1993), Chapters 12–14.

Michael Moore

separate punishments for having done only one particular act instantiating only one prohibited act-type are multiply punished for 'the same offense,' and Brennan's simple intuitive test ignored this. The same is true of any simple, intuitive 'single event' test in the insurance law context. Such a test simply finesses the obvious question to ask about 'per occurrence' limitations in insurance policies. That question is, per occurrence *of what?* We can count instances of a kind only when we have some idea of the kind in question. Without specification of the kind, an untutored, intuitive approach may well count instances of very different (and very irrelevant) kinds.

b. *The Policies Guiding a Default Rule about 'One Occurrence'*

As in the double jeopardy context, the only way to get a handle on the relevant kind (whose instances we are to count) is by repairing to the policies that guide the law. Since in the insurance context we are dealing with a default rule of contract interpretation[15]—a rule that gives an interpretation of 'occurrence' in default of the parties' expressly supplying one—the dominant policy is that of freedom of contract.[16] Freedom of contract is the principle that recognizes the self-imposed nature of contractual obligations. Such principle dictates that parties be bound only to obligations that they have voluntarily undertaken (or at least that they could have been reasonably understood by their promisees to have undertaken).

Such a principle can be justified either on grounds of utility or on grounds of justice. That is, such a principle arguably furthers the maximization of utility by allowing them in the best position to judge the state of their own preferences to be legally obligated over

[15] The line between supplying an omitted term by a default rule, and finding the meaning of an express term by an interpretive process, is a vague one. For present purposes it does not matter how the issue is characterized, because the desiderata of a good supplied term match those of a good interpretation of an existing term. See generally E. Allan Farnsworth, *Contracts*, 3rd edit. (New York, Aspen Law and Business, 1999), pp. 461–6, 499–501.

[16] See Randy E. Barnett, *The Structure of Liberty: Justice and the Rule of Law*, (Oxford: Clarendon Press, 1998), pp. 29–83 (explaining the need for freedom of contract and what its limits should be); Randy E. Barnett, "The Sound of Silence: Default Rules and Contractual Consent," *Virginia Law Review*, Vol. 78 (1992), 821–911, at pp. 859–911 (explaining how default rules in contract law are consistent with contractual consent and should be chosen).

by their own judgments. Alternatively, such principle is fair and just in that it limits their legal obligations to their moral obligations (and the latter are limited to those created by promise).

This principle has several implications for default rules of contract interpretation. One, insofar as the parties to a particular contract had the same actual expectations about how a term in the contract is to be understood, then that understanding should govern the contract's interpretation (so long as such understanding can be proven consistently with the parol evidence rule).[17] This follows from the self-imposed nature of contractual obligation. Second, if the parties to a contract have actual expectations about how a term of the contract is to be interpreted, but these expectations differ and one of them is reasonable and the other unreasonable, then the reasonably expected interpretation governs.[18] Third, if neither party has any actual expectations with respect to the matter in issue, but the parties do share the same hypothetical expectations—counterfactually, if they knew ex ante what they come to know ex post, what they have thought about it?—then those hypothetical expectations should govern the contract's interpretation.[19] Fourthly, if there are no actual or hypothetical expectations on the interpretation at issue, but there still is a contract,[20] then the best default rule is one that forms the best 'seed-crystal' around which the actual expectations of future parties to future contracts can crystallize. In short, the best default rule of contract interpretation is one looking to the actual, reasonable, or hypothetical expectations of one or both contracting parties, or in the absence of these, looks to the expectations (for future contracting parties) foreseeably generated by the rule in this class of cases.

If we apply these general policies to interpret the undefined 'per occurrence' language specific to insurance policies, several desiderata of a good interpretation emerge. The first and by far the most important of these desiderata is to link the 'per occurrence' limitation to two items the parties to insurance contracts are certainly thinking about when they enter into such contracts. Insurance

---

[17] See Farnsworth, *supra* note 15, at pp. 461, 499.

[18] *Id.* at 462–3, 500-501.

[19] The hypothetical expectations of the parties tend to be the reasonable expectations parties generally to such transactions would have had. See *id.* at 465–6, 500.

[20] As in the case of different and equally reasonable expectations, the absence of any expectations may preclude there being an enforceable contract. See, e.g., *Ruckles v. Wicklehaus,* 2 H. and C. 906, 159 Eng. Rep. 375 (Exch. 1864).

Michael Moore

contracts are gambling contracts on future events about which the parties may have little or no control. The gamble in insurance contracts is two-fold: (1) what kind of loss or injury might the insured sustain during the policy period? And: (2) what kind of event that can cause the loss anticipated might occur during the policy period? In California, for example, homeowners typically purchase separate insurance policies insuring against: (1) property damage caused by (2) earthquake. Automobile liability policies, to take another example, insure against: (1) liability for personal injury damage and property damage to a non-insured, caused by (2) the tortious actions of the insured. Let us call the first of these the kind of *loss* insured against, and the second, the kind of *risk* insured against.

The parameters of loss and risk have to be the central focus of the actual expectations of parties to insurance contracts, for these two together define the gamble taken in such contracts. Hence, any reasonable party to an insurance contract containing a 'per occurrence' limitation in it has only one of two possible answers to the question, 'per occurrence of what?' It must be, per occurrence of the kind of loss insured against, or per occurrence of the kind of risk insured against. The 'per occurrence' limitation has to be read as part of these two larger limitations defining the gamble taken in insurance contracts.

It is of course logically possible to divorce 'per occurrence' limitations from the kinds of losses or kinds of risks insured against. One might limit the insurance company's exposure by the occurrence of eclipses during the policy period, for example. But this would be deranged. Reasonable contractors have to mean what real contractors surely do mean: they mean per occurrence of those kinds of losses or risks that define the gamble they are taking.

Subsidiary desiderata of a good default rule of contract interpretation here are something akin to corollaries of the prime desideratum above. They are four in number. First, whatever test is used to determine whether a given kind of loss has occurred, or whether a given kind of risk has materialized, should be consistent with the test used to individuate occurrences under 'per occurrence' language. By way of illustration, suppose a single earthquake causes two separate fires (from ruptured gas lines) that destroy a house; under a property damage/earthquake policy, if one tests whether there is coverage for this kind of risk (earthquake risk) looking to the original cause (the earthquake) rather than to the immediate cause (the fires), then one should test how many occurrences there are by counting earthquakes and not fires. Similarly, suppose two separate arsonists burn down two buildings of a company, the loss of both of which bankrupts the company; under a property damage/fire policy,

266

if one tests whether there is coverage by looking to the initial damage suffered (building destruction) rather than the ultimate damage suffered (economic injury), then one should test how many occurrences there are by counting building losses and not bankruptcies.

Second, whatever test is used to determine whether a loss occurs, or a risk materializes, *during the policy period,* should be consistent with the test used to individuate occurrences under 'per occurrence' limitations. By way of illustration, suppose an earthquake occurs at t_1 this causes two aftershocks to occur at t_2, and all three cause a building to collapse at t_3. Under a property damage/earthquake policy whose period ends prior to t_2, if coverage is found to exist then one should be counting earthquakes at t_1, and not at t_2. (And of course one would not be counting building collapses at t_3.)

Third, 'per occurrence' limitations are commonly used to fix the upper limits of exposure and also to fix the threshold of exposure (the 'deductible') of a policy.[21] Whatever t est is used to individuate occurrences for the upper limits of exposure should also be used to fix the thresholds of exposure.[22]

Fourth, 'per occurrence' limitations are used in both first and third party insurance policies (casualty and liability policies, respectively). Moreover, such limitations appear in both limited (or defined) risk, as well as in all-risk, casualty policies. Other things equal, whatever test is used for individuating occurrences for one kind of policy should also be used to individuate occurrences for the other kinds of policies.[23] This keeps the rule for interpreting insur-

[21] See, e.g., *Champion International Corporation v. Continental Casualty Co.,* 546 F.2d 502 (2d Cir. 1976), when the per occurrence limitation was involved for both the deductible and the upper limit on liability.

[22] This is particularly true in cases like *Champion, supra* note 21, where both upper and lower limits are in issue. In such cases, if there are too many occurrences, then each separate loss falls below the deductible; if there is only one occurrence, there is only one recovery. The roofing company in *Champion* successfully avoided both the upper and lower limits by obtaining a finding of 27 occurrences for 27 batches of defective roofing materials—despite the materials going into hundreds of separate roofs, and despite the defect being one kind of defect of manufacture. One needs a common meaning to 'occurrence' in both the upper and lower limits of liability for this threading of the needle to be anything but arbitrary.

[23] As one court has observed, a liability policy is just a kind of casualty policy, one where the event insured against is liability to another for her losses as opposed to the losses the insured suffer directly by fires, earthquakes, and the like. See *Hyer v. Inter-Insurance Exchange of the Automobile Club of Southern California,* 77 Cal.App. 343, 349, 246 Pac. 1055, 1057 (1926) ('Liability insurance is but a branch of accident and casualty insurance.')

Michael Moore

ance contracts simple enough that it can perform the 'seed-crystal' function mentioned earlier.

c. *Per Occurrence of What: Losses, Risks, or Both?*

If we apply these desiderata to the present issue, it should be apparent that there are two main candidates for what kinds of occurrences we should be counting under 'per occurrence' limitations in insurance contracts. We could count occurrences of the kinds of losses insured against, or we could count occurrences of the kinds of risks insured against. These are, respectively, the dominant approaches of English versus American insurance law.[24]

Under older English law, 'per occurrence' limits were interpreted to allow multiple recoveries by multiple parties who separately make claims for their injuries. By contrast, a 'per occurrence' limit in America is commonly held to focus on the event(s) that cause injuries, not on the number of injuries caused.[25] American insurance law thus focuses on the cause of injury, not on the effects of injurious behaviour, in ascertaining when there is one or more occurrence. This is commonly termed the causal test (as opposed to the 'effects test') of whether two or more putatively distinct events are in reality one and the same occurrence.[26]

It is important to see what questions the causal test both does, and does not, purport to answer. The test resolves the basic question of interpreting the contracting parties' intentions: as we have seen, when contracting on a per occurrence basis the 'per occurrence' language leaves open the question, 'per occurrence *of what?*' Per occurrence of the damage insured against, such as physical damage to a building? Or per occurrence of the kind of event that

[24] The English doctrine is set out in *Southern Staffordshire Tramways Co., Ltd. v. Sickness and Accident Assurance Association, Ltd.*, 1 Q.B. 402 (1891). It is discussed and rejected in one of the leading American cases, *Hyer, supra* note 23.

[25] One can, of course, write a 'per claim' version of per occurrence limitations in American insurance contracts; but the default rule is that unless otherwise specified, per occurrence limitations in American insurance contracts are per cause, not per claim. See, e.g., *Champion International Corporation v. Continental Casualty Co., supra* note 21, 546 F.2d at 505–6; *Lamberton v. Travelers Indemnity Co.*, 325 A.2d 104 (Del.Sup.Ct. 1974), *aff'd*, 346 A.2d 167 (Del. 1975).

[26] The 'effects test' is but another name for a 'per claim' or 'per injury' basis of coverage limitation. See, e.g., *American Indemnity Co. v. McQuaig*, 435 So.2d 414, 415 n. 1 (Fla. App. 1983).

268

produces such damage and the risk of which was also insured against, such as earthquake, fire, or terrorist acts? By the majority position in American insurance law,[27] parties to an insurance contract are taken to refer to the number of covered kinds of damage-causing-events that occur, not the number of injuries or injured persons such events may cause and not the number of claims such injuries may spawn. What the test does not answer is how we are to individuate events. The test, in other words, tells us what sort of events must be individuated for insurance purposes, *viz*, events that cause the relevant kinds of injuries. It does not even purport to tell us how to individuate such injuries-causing events.

One might be tempted to regard the causal test of American insurance law as being more ambitious than this. In the philosophy of events there is a well known view of event-identity which holds that any two putatively distinct events are in reality one and the same event if and only if such event(s) have the same causes and same effects.[28] On a modified version of this view one might think that the causal test of American insurance law *is* giving a test of event-identity for damage events, namely: Two putatively distinct instances of physical loss or damage events are in reality one and the same physical loss or damage event whenever they have the same causes.[29] On such a view the answer to the interpretive question, 'per occurrence of what?,' is the older, English answer: 'the kind of damages insured against' (and not the American answer, 'the kind of risks insured against'). The causal test would then be giving a theory of when two putatively distinct damage events are really one and the same event. Yet even if the causal test of American insurance law were this ambitious metaphysically, such test would still but regress the problem of event-identity: for to know when two

[27] There are occasional adoptions of the English per claim (or 'effects') view in America. See, e.g., *Anchor Casualty v. McCaleb*, 178 F.2d 322 (5th Cir. 1949).

[28] Donald Davidson, *Essays on Actions and Events* (Oxford: Oxford University Press, 1980), at p. 179. See also Laurence Lombard, *Events: A Metaphysical Study* (London: Routledge and Kegan Paul, 1986), pp. 74–5.

[29] In construing state statutory bans against multiply punishing 'the same act,' some courts have adopted a version of such a causal test of event-token individuation. See, e.g., *People v. Neal*, 55 Cal.2d 11, 357 P.2d 839 (1960), where the California Supreme Court held two acts to be the same when they are the products of a single intention. See also *Spinnell v. State*, 83 Tex. Crim. App. 418, 203 S.W. 357 (1918) ('A series of shots may constitute one act ... where they are fired with one volition.') The same intent test of act-token individuation is discussed briefly in Moore, *Act and Crime, supra* note 14, at pp. 381–3.

Michael Moore

damage events are the same, one would need to know whether they have the same cause-event, yet to know that, we must know when we have one cause-event versus two—and this the causal test cannot tell us, on pain of infinite regress.[30] In any case, the causal test of American law is not taken to be a metaphysical test of when two putatively distinct loss events are in reality one and the same event; rather, the causal test is regarded as the American answer to the basic question of contract interpretation in this class of cases, *viz*, 'per occurrence *of what?*'

It is difficult to pinpoint any very plausible rationale for the American choice of the causal over the effects interpretation of 'per occurrence' language. One explanation (not justification) for the American doctrine lies in the accidents of case selection. In some of the early cases, the specific policy language at issue suggested the causal test. For example, in a much-cited early California opinion the policy language was that the insurance company 'in no case shall ... be liable with respect to claims ... arising from one accident for more than one thousand dollars.'[31] As the California court pointed out,[32] such language plainly suggests that two or more injuries could nonetheless arise from but one accident. Moreover, the word 'accident' itself connotes something different than damage or loss; it is not as easily taken to refer to an instance of kinds of loss insured against as is the more general word, 'occurrence.' Once 'per occurrence' limitations are equated to 'per accident' limitations,[33] these connotations of the latter were read into the former.

If we put aside these matters of historical accident and approach the matter afresh, it is difficult to see why one should think contracting parties would focus on the number of times the kinds of risks insured against materialize (to the exclusion of the number of instances of the kind of losses insured against) when they use undefined 'per occurrence' limitations. After all, both the kinds of risks insured against, and the kinds of losses insured against, form the core of the gamble taken by parties to insurance contracts.

---

[30] In addition the Davidsonian test itself seems false as a test of event identity. See Michael Moore, *Act and Crime*, supra n. 14, at p. 383; Myles Brand, *Intending and Acting* (Cambridge, Mass.: M.I.T. Press, 1984), p. 69; Judith Jarvis Thomson, *Acts and Other Events* (Ithaca, N.Y.: Cornell University Press, 1977), p. 70.

[31] Hyer, supra note 23, 77 Cal.pp. at 345, 246 Pac. at 1055.

[32] *Id.*, 77 Cal.App. at 354, 246 Pac. at 1059.

[33] See cases cited, *supra* note 10

Presumably the parties focus on both matters equally when they decide how much protection to buy or sell.

If this is so, then the preferable interpretation of 'per occurrence' insurance language is one asking *both*: How many *risked* events, and how many *loss* events, were there? Only if there were both two separate cause-events of the kind risked, and two separate loss-events of the kind covered by the policy, should there be two recoveries under a 'per occurrence' limited policy.[34]

Arguably this is in fact the correct reading of the causal test of American insurance law. The kind of case that tests this is a case in which there are two separate cause-events of the kind risked yet there is but one loss-event (of the kind covered) that is the common effect of the two cause-events. Imagine that it required the crashing of two airliners to bring down a single Tower. Suppose two airliners crashed into a single Tower, ignited the same portion of the Tower, causing its collapse by the fire-related weakening of the structural steel. We might display such a single, indivisible loss-event caused by two separate cause-events as in schema (1):

(1)

By the best reading of the causal test of 'occurrence,' there is but one occurrence here for purposes of insurance recovery. There is but one injury-event, the collapse of the Tower, even though there were two distinct causes of that collapse.

Part of my confidence that this is the right result stems from the commonness of (1). Events are rarely, if ever, caused by single, other events. Even where one airliner alone crashes into a tower which collapses, the crash of the Boeing 767 does not by itself cause the collapse of a skyscraper. Such collapse requires, in addition: the fueling of such aircraft with sufficient gasoline to fire the building sufficiently as to weaken its structural steel, the decision to use only such-and-such amount of steel columns in the center and at the perimeter of the skyscraper; the presence of sufficient ventilation to allow the flames to build to the required intensity; the use of

---

[34] I put aside as too expansive the alternative, disjunctive combination of risk and loss.

Michael Moore

combustible items in constructing and furnishing the part of the skyscraper hit by the airline, etc.

It is true that ordinary thought often distinguishes between various states and events equally necessary for the happening of the event to be explained, honouring only one as 'the cause' of the latter event.[35] Such thought thus rules out many conditions necessary to the happening of some event as eligible to be called its cause. The arson investigator who reports that the cause of some suspicious fire was 'oxygen in the air' will surely lose his job, just as the doctor who tells his patients that the cause of their tennis elbow condition is the playing of tennis, will lose his patients. Each of these items may be necessary to the events in question, yet no one singles them out as causes.

The factors that allow such discriminations, however, are no part of the notion of causation itself. Rather, these are pragmatic factors wholly dependent on context for their sensible use. Doctors, for example, list as causes those things they can treat, arson investigators list as causes of fires more unusual factors like sparks or human intervenors, historians tend to isolate extraordinary or surprising events, etc. These are matters having to do with the interest of the enquirer, not with the nature of the causal relation. There is nothing general to be found here, thus, that can be used to narrow the number of causes for any insured injury.

It is also not the case that the law narrows sufficiently the range of items eligible to be considered 'the cause' such that one and only one item is *the* proximate cause of an event such as a skyscraper's collapse. None of the dominant proximate cause tests even purport to limit the causes of any event to just one preceding event. Both simultaneous and temporally successive sets of events may contain numerous proximate causes for any given loss.[36]

Thus, in neither ordinary thought nor in the law is there any way to debar numerous events and states as the plural causes of any

[35] On the criteria used in ordinary thought for honouring one item as "the cause" of some events see Joel Feinberg, *Doing and Deserving* (Princeton: Princeton University Press, 1970), pp. 142–8.

[36] For examples of simultaneous proximate causes, see Michael Moore, 'Causation and Responsibility,' *Social Philosophy and Policy*, Vol. 16 (1999), pp. 1–51, at pp. 9–13, reprinted in E. F. Paul, F. D. Miller, and J. Paul, eds., *Responsibility* (Cambridge: Cambridge University Press, 1999). For examples of successive proximate causes, see Michael Moore, 'The Metaphysics of Causal Intervention,' *California Law Review*, Vol. 88 (2000), pp. 827–77, *passim*. Both articles are rewritten as Chapters 2–6 of Michael Moore, *Causation and Responsibility* (Oxford: Oxford University Press, forthcoming).

given injury event. It cannot be the case, then, that for an indivisible injury there can be more than one occurrence within the meaning of some insurance policy just because there are multiple causes of that injury—on pain of all accidents being such multiple occurrences.

Surprisingly, some American court opinions appear to assert the contrary. Consider, for example, this language of the Arizona Supreme Court:

> The Fund also, argues that there was only one 'occurrence' because there was only one injury. The cases, however, show that the number of causative acts, and not the number of injuries produced, determines the number of 'occurrences.'... We conclude that the number of acts producing injury or damage, rather than the number of injuries caused, is the key on which the definition of 'occurrence' turns. *Multiple acts causing a single injury will constitute multiple occurrences*, while a single act will constitute a single occurrence even though it causes multiple injuries or multiple episodes of injury.[37]

What the Arizona Supreme Court seems to be asserting is a broad principle of symmetry: just as one cause producing multiple injuries is but one occurrence, so multiple causes of but one injury constitutes multiple occurrences. Yet this language cannot be taken so broadly, however, on pain of the *reductio* about showing that all injuries are multiple occurrences because multiply caused.

At the very least, to avoid the *reductio* making all incidents into multiple occurrences, courts such as that in Arizona have to restrict their multiple cause/multiple occurrence idea to liability policies where the multiple causes are each acts of someone for whom the insurance company is liable. Thus, in *Arizona Property and Casualty Co. v. Helme*,[38] quoted above, the multiple causes were acts of different doctors within the same professional corporation (the insured under the per occurrence liability policy); one doctor negligently diagnosed the victim and another doctor negligently operated on the victim, the victim dying as a joint result of an undiagnosed and untreated fracture dislocation of his cervical vertebra. Similarly, courts have held that other kinds of successive misdiagnoses by doctors insured under a liability policy,[39] as well as

---

[37] *Arizona Property and Casualty Insurance Guaranty Fund v. Helme*, 153 Ariz. 129, 735 P.2d 451, 457 (1987).

[38] *Id.*

[39] *Insurance Corporation of America v. Rubin*, 107 Nev. 610, 818 P.2d 389 (1991).

Michael Moore

successive shots fired by a single insured under a liability policy,[40] constitute multiple occurrences despite their joint production of but a single injury.

Such a liability insurance doctrine avoids my *reductio* by limiting the multiple causes (that can lead to a 'multiple occurrence' characterization) to those negligent acts insured against by a liability policy. The apparent rationale of such a restriction is that the focus of liability policies is on the acts of the insured that generate liability; 'occurrences' can thus be taken to refer to such acts in measuring how many occurrences there were, not the loss(es) such acts cause. The idea is that the contracting parties to a liability insurance contract would contemplate a per-act-giving-rise-to liability basis in their per occurrence limitations.

If this is true, of course, such a rationale has no application to first party casualty insurance. In first party insurance there is no focus on acts of some insured or its employees; rather, under all risk policies, the focus is on the kind of loss suffered, such as physical property damage, not on the causes of such loss. Storms, rains, natural coincidences, as well as negligent acts of individuals, may cause a loss compensable under a casualty policy. Therefore, if a court were to count occurrences here by the number of causes alone, it would be fully subject to my earlier *reductio*: all cases would involve multiple occurrences.

In fact, my own view is that the liability policy cases are mistaken even in the liability context. Negligent acts do not by themselves make for liability; only negligent acts that cause losses make for liability. The focus in the liability policy context should look to both separate losses and separate causes, on the more accurate assumption that contracting parties focus on both in setting limits of coverage. This is particularly clear in cases where t he multiple causes of a single injury are overdetermining causes.[41] In the classic joint fire cases,[42] for example, two fires of independent origin burn down some victim's house. Each fire independently was sufficient for the job, but the joint fire they created was too. Suppose $fire_1$ was started by one of insured's employees and $fire_2$ was started by another employee of the insured. When the employer is held liable for the destruction of the house by fire, and seeks coverage of

[40] *McQuaig, supra* note 26.

[41] The overdetermination cases are discussed in Moore, 'Causation and Responsibility,' *supra* note 36, at pp. 9–13.

[42] *Anderson v. Minneapolis St. Paul and S. St. Marie R.R. Co.*, 146 Minn. 430, 179 N.W. 45 (1920); *Kingston v. Chicago and N.W. Ry.*, 191 Wis. 610, 211 N.W. 913 (1927).

his liability from his liability carrier, surely this is only one occurrence for purposes of the per occurrence limitation in the employer's policy. The employer could not have expected to benefit by having more than one negligent employee causally contribute to some injury; for the employer has no more liability with the two negligent employees than he would have with only one.

What courts like those in Arizona may have mistakenly assumed is that where there is more than one negligent act causing injury for which an insured is liable, there must be more injury (even if not more separable injuries), thus, more liability, thus more need for a higher limit of insurance. Yet the overdetermination cases show that this is not true. Moreover, it is not even clearly true in the more ordinary kind of multiple cause cases, where each cause is necessary (and the causes together are jointly sufficient) for some indivisible injury. The only case where the assumption is clearly true are cases where each negligent act of employees cause separate injuries—but in such cases, there should be as many occurrences as there are such separately caused, separate injuries.

The correct interpretation of the American causal test is that fleetingly suggested by one federal district court: the question is whether multiple negligent acts or omissions of an insured doctor, or each act of treatment he prescribed, 'resulted in independent, compensable injuries.'[43] If they did, then each such act or omission should be a separate occurrence; but if, as in the actual case cited, each visit to the doctor and each treatment caused no separate damage but together jointly caused the blindness of the patient, then there is but one occurrence even for liability policy coverage purposes.[44]

In cases where there are two or more injuries *and* each injury has its own separate cause(s), then there should be two or more occurrences. Thus, if officers of a bank make a series of bad loans, each

[43] *Aetna Casualty and Surety Company of Illinois v. The Medical Protective Company of Fort Wayne, Indiana*, 575 F.Supp. 901 (N.D. Ill. 1983). This federal district court better characterized the causal test as:

'Whether the events in question are properly characterized as a single "occurrence" or multiple is a question of causation. A series of related injuries comprise a single "occurrence," for the purposes of an insurance contract, where they all flow from a single cause.... . *Where each injury results from an independent cause* (emphasis added), there are a series of occurrences.' 575 F.Supp. at 903.

[44] The insurance carrier lost in *Aetna Casualty, supra* note 43, because it could not prove the separate injuries to the eyes of the patient with each application of the prescribed medicine to the patient's eyes. *Id.*

Michael Moore

loan resulting in a loss equal to the amount of the loan, there are as many occurrences as there are acts of making a loan productive of loss of the money loaned [45]. Likewise, if a ship grounds its bow on a ledge, causing damage to its bow, and then it grounds its stern on the same ledge, causing damage to its stern, prima facie there are two acts causing two damages and thus there are two occurrences.[46]

This is not to say that the injury individuation question is always easy. If it could be proved that each administration of a chemical to the eyes of a patient caused some damage to the eye and optic nerve, and all administrations together caused total blindness, is there one injury (blindness) or as many injuries as there were administrations causing some loss of sight?[47] Or if a bank employee writes forty bad checks, are there forty small losses or one big one?[48] Or if officers and directors make a series of bad decisions, each resulting in the loss of a certain amount of money to the company, and all such losses together bankrupt the company, are there numerous smaller losses or one big loss?[49] These questions are no easier to answer than are the similar individuation question about the events which cause such losses (both such questions will be considered in § 4). The only point here is that both such questions of event-individuation need to be asked to properly apply the causal test for 'same occurrence.' I shall henceforth take the causal test of American insurance law to ask both of these questions of event-individuation.

d. *The Two Kinds of Metaphysical Questions Asked by the Causal Test*

I shall call both these last questions the pure questions of event-identity: when is there one (versus two or more) events that cause injuries and when is there one (versus two or more) events of an injurious kind? Because the causal test makes the notion of 'same

---

[45] *North River Insurance Co. v. Huff*, 638 F.Supp. 1129 (D. Kan. 1985).

[46] *Newark Insurance Company v. Continental Casualty Company*, 46 App. Div.2d 514, 363 N.Y.S.2d 327 (1975). The 'prima facie' qualifier in the text, to leave open the possibilities discussed later in this section, that the second grounding was not causally independent of the first, and that there might be some common cause of both groundings in some general decision or policy of the captain or the ship owner.

[47] The facts of *Aetna Casualty, supra* note 43.

[48] *Business Interiors v. Aetna Casualty and Surety Company*, 751 F.2d 361 (10th Cir. 1984).

[49] *Okada et al. v. MGIC Indemnity Corp.*, 608 F.Supp.383 (D. Hawaii 1985), *aff'd in part and rev'd in part*, 823 F.2d 276 (9th Cir. 1986).

276

occurrence' as dependent on the causal relations between such events as on the question of whether these are separate events, the test requires that we answer an additional kind of metaphysical question.[50] This second question is what I shall call the causal relation question: even when there are distinct cause-events and distinct injury-events, are the causal relations between them such that they should be classified as one occurrence under the causal test?

Although these two kinds of questions each form a leg of a single pair of trousers, the causal question is logically prior to the pure event-identity questions. This is because it is the answer to the causal question that tells us how far back in time we are to look when we seek to individuate events. One possibility would be to look for occurrences of the kinds of events most proximate to the loss events insured against. In the destruction of the Twin Towers, for example, this would be to focus on fire kinds of events, since it was the fires that most immediately caused the collapse of the Towers. Another possibility would be to look to the causes of those fires, in terms of the airplanes crashing into the Towers. A third possibility is to look for more remote causes, such as the making of the decision within al Qaeda to destroy the Towers with passenger aircraft. It is only after we have used causal doctrines to settle on the temporal slice(s) on which to focus that we can then ask the pure event-identity question of how many collapse-events, crash-events, decision-events, etc. there might have been at the relevant slice of time. For this reason I shall put on the causal leg of the trousers first.

3. The Causal Relation Question

The causal test of American insurance law demands a great deal from our notion of causation, as we shall see. Let us start with four

[50] Arguably, this point was obliquely recognized by the Appellate Division of New York when it stated that 'events of injury or loss are one "accident" within the meaning of the policy provided that they are (1) completely indistinguishable in time and space, or (2) that one event caused the other.' *Hartford Accident and Indemnity Company v. Wesolowski*, 39 App.Div.2d 833, 333 N.Y.S.2d 289, 292 (1972), *rev'd on other grounds, Wesolowski supra* note 6. Such a disjunctive test seemingly utilizes what I shall (in § 4 *infra*) call a spatio-temporal test of event identity, uses the clumping of two events together as one if they are causally related (what I call in § 3 the causal chain doctrine), and sees that the test is disjunctive so that both questions must be answered to determine occurrence identity. Whether New York follows the causal test of occurrence identity is a matter requiring some discussion, pursued later in this § 3.

Michael Moore

simple models where the implications of the causal test are thought to be plain. These are highly idealized models, freed of the complexities of most real world cases in order to keep the analysis simple. We can then seek to complicate the analysis in order to deal with the complexities of real world cases.

a. *The Four Simple Models*

i. The Common Cause Model

The first of the models is what I shall call the 'common cause,' or 'epiphenomenal,' cases. Suppose, for example, a single passenger airliner had crashed between the Towers, causing their collapse. Then a single cause-event caused two damage-events, which we might display as done below in schema (2):

(2)

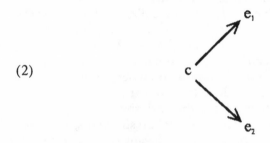

If anything is clear from the causal test, it is that in epiphenomenal cases of this kind there is but one occurrence despite the existence of two damage events.[51] This is the payoff of distinguishing the English from the American interpretation of 'per occurrence' insurance policies; under the latter scheme for interpretation, we focus on the number of causes of loss-events as much as on the number of such loss-events themselves.

ii. The Causal Chain Model

The second simple causal pattern is that of a chain of dependent causes. Imagine that the al Qaeda plan had been (as it apparently

[51] The multiple car collision cases are illustrative: if one piece of bad driving causes three collisions with three motorcycles, injuring five separate motorcycle riders or passengers, there is but one accident for insurance limitation purposes under the causal test. *Truck Insurance Exchange v. Rohde, supra* note 10. The New York Court of Appeals in another multiple collision case, *Wesolowski, supra* note 6, reaches a like result with its so-called 'event test.'

278

was in 1993) to topple the second WTC Tower by crashing the first such Tower into it. Suppose both planes hit the same Tower with the result intended. Then we may schematize the relation between the two 767's crashing into the first tower (c_1 c_2), causing the toppling of that tower (e_1), which causes the collapse of the second tower (e_2), thusly:

(3)

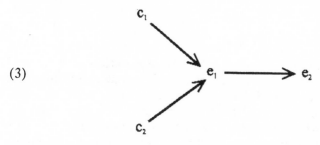

Notice that in such cases there are two cause-events of two injury-events, and yet the courts are uniform under the causal test in denying that there is more than one occurrence. The reason, it is said, is because e_1 and e_2 are not causally independent of one another; rather, e_1 causes e_2, and thus there is but one occurrence.

Illustrative of this causal independence aspect of the causal test are the multiple car collision cases.[52] When the insured's car hits multiple other cars, it matters whether he ricocheted off the first car into the second or whether, having regained control of his vehicle after the first collision, he then has a second collision. In the former case there is no causal independence between the successive collisions, so that there is a causal chain and thus but one occurrence; in the latter case the second collision is causally independent of the first and there are two occurrences.

The best way to think of this causal dependence notion is as a kind of clumping device: any cause-events that are causally linked are clumped together to count as one cause-event (even though as events they are in fact distinct), and any injury-events that are causally linked are clumped together to count as one injury-event (even though as events they are in fact distinct). The rationale for such clumping is of a piece with the rationale for the causal test of 'occurrence' in general: contracting parties using a 'per occurrence' (rather than a 'per claim') limitation of coverage are focusing on the events that cause injuries as much as they are focusing on the injuries themselves. In the former focus they are presumably using

[52] See, e.g., *Wesolowski, supra* note 10; *Rohde, supra* note 10; *Hyer, supra* note 23; *Olsen v. Moore,* 56 Wis.2d 340, 202 N.W.2d 236 (1972).

Michael Moore

a causal notion of separateness of events, so that only events that are causally separate can count as separate occurrences; they are betting on how much damage they are likely to sustain with any one visitation of the whims of nature. In counting 'whims,' any one event that causes numerous injuries via numerous intermediate events is but one visitation.

iii. The Common Injury Model

As was discussed in § 2 above, the best interpretation of American insurance law's causal test is that it counts instances of injury as well as instances of risked causes of injury. Under such an interpretation of American law, the third model precluding multiple recovery is one where were this is but one indivisible injury, the common effect of multiple causes. This was represented in schema (1) above.

iv. The Separate Causes of Separate Injuries Model

The common cause, common injury, and causal chain cases make up what I call the three idealized patterns to show but one occurrence under the causal test. These three contrast with the equally idealized pattern of two independent causes of two separate injuries, where there are two occurrences under the causal test:

$$c_1 \longrightarrow e_1$$

(4)

$$c_2 \longrightarrow e_2$$

b. *Some Real World Applications of the Four Models*

To apply the four simple models to the complex facts of real world cases requires two kinds of knowledge: (1) knowledge of event-individuation, i.e., when there is one and when there are two or more distinct cause-events and injury-events; and (2) knowledge of the nature of the causal relation. The first kind of knowledge I deal with in § 4; it is the second kind of knowledge on which I shall here focus.

The concept of causation that the courts adopt in 'per occurrence' insurance litigation is often said to be the same as is used throughout the law in assigning primary liability to actors. That is,

280

'cause' here is often taken to means both cause-in fact and proximate cause. It is this latter notion, of proximate causation, that is of particular importance to the classification of real world cases into one of the four basic patterns:

> 'Proximate cause is an integral part of any interpretation of the words 'accident' or 'occurrence' as used in a contract for liability insurance which indemnifies the insured for his tortious acts...'[53]

Consider by way of illustration one of the cases of considerable interest to the Twin Towers litigation, *Arthur Johnson Corp. v. Indemnity Insurance Co.*[54] In that case the basements of two adjacent buildings (at 300 and 304 Fourth Avenue) were flooded by the waters from an extraordinary rainstorm. This was not a first party insurance case, but a liability policy case; the party whose actions were at issue was a contractor who had contracted with the City of New York to construct subway platform extensions for the various stations of the Lexington Avenue Subway. In constructing one such platform extension under Fourth Avenue, the contractor: (1) dug a continuous trench in the street before the two buildings, 300 and 304 Fourth Avenue; (2) removed the front vault walls of each of the buildings, exposing their basements to the trench; and (3) constructed (in a manner stipulated not to be negligent)[55] a six-inch thick, cinder block retaining wall sealing off the basement of each building from the trench in the street.

A rainstorm, characterized by the New York Court of Appeals as one of 'unprecedented intensity,'[56] occurred, dropping 3.52 inches of rain in just two hours. The rain waters filled the trench, causing one retaining wall to collapse at 5:10 p.m. and causing the second to collapse at 6:00 p.m. The collapse of the retaining walls resulted in the flooding of each of the two basements, causing water damage to each of the buildings.

The loss insured against by the contractor was liability for the property damage of others, so long as the property damage arose out of this work. As the policy recognized, the liability might be a tortious liability of the contractor to various building owners, or the liability might be a contractual liability of the contractor to the City of New York. The latter liability arose out of an indemnity agreement entered into between the contractor and the City of New York

---

[53] *Rohde, supra* note 10, 49 Wash.2d at 471, 303 P.2d at 662.
[54] *Johnson, supra* note 13.
[55] 7 N.Y.2d at 226, 196 N.Y.S.2d at 681, 164 N.Ed.2d at 705.
[56] 7 N.Y.2d at 225–6, 196 N.Y.S.2d at 680, 164 N.Ed.2d at 705.

Michael Moore

whereby the contractor agreed to indemnify the City against 'claims by persons, including abutting owners and their tenants for damage which ... may be occasioned by the work of construction, even in cases where such owners have no legal claim against the City for such injuries or damage.'[57]

If the liability at issue in *Johnson* were a tort-based liability, then the kind of risk insured against would be easy to state: any acts or omissions of the contractor that under tort law would make him liable to the building owners are the kind of injury-producing events, the risk of which was insured against. In such a case, those acts or omissions of the contractor would have to be the in fact and proximate causes of the flood damage events suffered by the buildings, for only such acts or omissions could be the basis of the contractor's tort liability.

The kind of risk insured against is the same under a contract-based liability, which was the kind of liability actually at issue in *Johnson*. For that contract-based liability of the contractor was only for such liability the City might have to those building owners suffering property damage 'occasioned by the work of construction...'[58] 'Occasioned' is one of those numerous synonyms in the English language for 'caused.'[59] Only property damage caused by the work of construction of the platform extension is insured against, so that the risk is again of injury-producing acts of the contractor.

The policy thus limited coverage to one kind of loss, property damage, and one kind of risk, *viz* work of the contractor causing such loss. The policy further limited the risk coverage to accidentally caused injury, and then limited such coverage to '$50,000 per accident.' The issue in the case was whether there was one or two accidents within the meaning if the policy.

One thing highlighted by a case like *Johnson* is the limited determinacy of the American causal test. The indeterminacy here does not stem from indeterminacies in the pure questions of event-individuation. There may be these latter indeterminacies as well—see section 4 following—but the causal test introduces its own indeterminacy. To isolate this latter source of indeterminacy, let us assume for now that we are clear on the relevant questions of event-identity: the digging of the one continuous platform trench was one event; that the destruction of the basement vaults at numbers 300

[57] 7 N.Y.2d at 224, 196 N.Y.S.2d at 679, 164 N.E.2d at 704.
[58] *Id.*
[59] Action verbs of English are often 'causally complex' in this way. See Moore, *Act and Crime, supra* note 14, chapter 8.

282

and 304 Fourth Avenue were two events; the construction of two cinderblock retaining walls in front of the two buildings constituted two events; the two-hour rainstorm was one event; that the filling of the trench was one event; the collapse of each retaining wall was each a separate event; and the flooding of each basement was a separate event. Then the causal relation of what happened in *Johnson* looks like schema (5), with some simplifications such as making the paired events (vault wall destructions, retaining wall constructions, retaining wall collapses, floodings) simultaneous when in fact some were not:

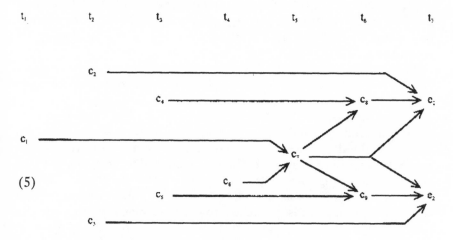

(5)

c_1 = digging of trench in street
c_2, c_3 = removals of vault walls of the two buildings
c_4, c_5 = constructions of retaining walls before the two buildings
c_6 = rainstorm
c_7 = filling of trench with rainwater
c_8, c_9 = collapses of two retaining walls
e_1, e_2 = floodings of the two basements

In English, what schema (5) depicts is that each of the two flooding-of-basement events was caused by: the removal of the basement vault walls (c_2, c_3), the collapse of the retaining walls (c_8, c_9), and the filling of the trench with water (c_7). The collapse of the retaining walls was caused in turn by the construction of them (c_4, c_5) with the strength they possessed, and the filling of the trench with water (c_7) to a depth where the pressure exceeded the strength of the walls. The filling of the trench with water was in turn caused by the digging of the trench (c_1) and the rainstorm (c_6).

The causal test tells us this much clearly: the fact that there were two injury-events (the two floodings) is not enough to make for two occurrences. For this could be a kind of common cause case where there is but one occurrence despite multiple separate injury-events. Still, while not sufficient the separation of the two injury events is necessary for there to be two occurrences, as we have seen. There is no causal relationship between them; no water entered one basement through the flooding of the other.[60] Indeed, as the Court of Appeals noted,[61] probably the flooding of the first basement lessened the pressure on the retaining wall protecting the second basement, so that the first flooding retarded, not accelerated, the second flooding.

Yet the harder question about a case like *Johnson* is how many cause-events there might be. For there to be two occurrences we need there to be two separate cause events of two separate injury events. If we ask this question globally, over the entire time-span t_1 –t_6 considered as a whole, there seems to be no answer. The two basement floodings were commonly caused by the one trench digging, the one rainstorm, and the one trench flooding; yet the two basement floodings were also separately caused by the removal of the separate vault walls, and the construction and collapse of the separate retaining walls. If we ask this question at any one time, we can get determinate answers (in terms of the two-wall collapses at t_6, for example), but how are we to pick the relevant slice of time on which to focus? Why not one rainstorm or one trench-digging as opposed to two wall collapses?

We might get some help here from the law's notion of proximate causation. If 'proximate cause' meant, 'cause nearest the injuries,' then we would get a lot of help, for that would focus us on the question of how many wall collapses there were. Yet 'proximate cause' doesn't mean, '*most* proximate cause.'[62] As one court noted in this context:

> 'Proximate cause' literally means the cause nearest to the effect produced; but in legal terminology it is not confined to its literal meaning. Though a negligent act or omission be removed from

[60] 7 N.Y.2d at 230, 196 N.Y.S.2d at 684, 164 N.E.2d at 708.
[61] *Id.*
[62] See generally, H. L. A. Hart and Tony Honore, *Causation in the Law*, 2d edit. (Oxford: Clarendon Press,1985); Moore, 'Metaphysics of Causal Intervention,' *supra* note 36.

the injury by intermediate causes or effects, yet if, in a natural and continuous sequence, unbroken by any new efficient cause, it produces that injury ... it is in law the proximate cause of such injury ...[63]

Still, even with a plurality of proximate causes possible for any given harm, the help potentially given by the notion of proximate cause lies in the *Hyers* court's idea of there being 'new efficient causes' that break causal chains. These are more usually called 'intervening,' 'superseding,' or 'extraneous' causes, items which constitute fresh causal starts and thereby end any causal relation between earlier events and the harm.

The extraordinary rainstorm in *Johnson* is a good candidate for being an intervening cause. The rainstorm was conceded by the *Johnson* court to be one of 'unprecedented intensity'—3.52 inches in two hours.[64] The Court further noted that the temporary retaining walls were not negligently constructed (or at least the parties so stipulated).[65] Although that leaves open the possibility that the walls were defective even if non-negligently made to be so, that seems unlikely given the failure of both walls and the great volume of water.

Such extraordinary natural events as an unprecedented rainstorm are good candidates for constituting an intervening or superseding cause. So long as they are events that are: (i) subsequent to some earlier event, (ii) causally independent of that earlier event while (iii) themselves causally contributing to the harm, and so long as such event is (iv) 'extraordinary' or 'abnormal,' while being (v) uncontrived by a defendant, then such states or events are intervening causes that break the causal chain between earlier events and the harm.[66] The rainstorm in *Johnson* is a good candidate for such an intervening cause, inasmuch as the only one of these five criteria for an intervening cause in doubt in *Johnson* is just how extraordinary a 3.52 inch downpour in two hours might be for New York City.

The Court of Appeals nonetheless found that 'The proximate cause cannot be said to be the heavy rainfall but separate negligent acts of preparing and constructing separate walls which, for all we know, may have been built at separate times by separate groups of workmen.'[67] Although the court does not tell us, perhaps the reason

[63] *Hyers, supra* note 23, 77 Cal.App. at 347, 246 Pac. at 1056.

[64] See note 56, *supra*.

[65] See note 55, *supra*.

[66] H.L.A. Hart and Tony Honore, *Causation in the Law*, 2d edit. (Oxford: Clarendon Press, 1985), pp. 79–80. See generally Moore, 'Metaphysics of Causal Intervention,' *supra* note 36, at pp. 832–9, 844–52.

[67] 7 N.Y.2d at 230, 196 N.Y.S.2d a t 684, 164 N.E.2d at 708.

was that a rainstorm of that intensity was not so unusual for New York City (despite the court calling it 'unprecedented'). In any case, had the rainstorm been held to have been an intervening cause, that would focus our attention on times subsequent to the rainstorm. We would not have to worry about how many trench-diggings (t_1), vault wall destructions (t_2), or retaining wall constructions (t_3) there were because none of these would have caused the flood damage complained of. We would still have to choose whether we are counting rainstorms, (t_4), trench fillings (t_5), or retaining wall collapses (t_6), but at least our choice is lessened in these alternate possibilities. Whereas if the rainstorm is not an intervening cause, all of these slices of time are eligible for selection as the time to ask, 'How many cause-events were there *then?*'

What helps to reduce the indeterminacy here more than anything else is to remember what I called the prime desideratum of an interpretation of 'per occurrence' limitations in insurance policies: make sure you are counting events that instantiate the kind of risks covered under the policy; if it's an earthquake policy, do not count the fires caused by an earthquake even if they go on to cause the harms; rather, count earthquakes.

In *Johnson* recall that the type of damage insured against was liability for property damage and the risk taken was that such liability would arise from the work of the contractor. When counting occurrences, we must thus count how many acts or omissions of the contractor—his 'work'—were the causes of the two basement floodings. This focuses the enquiry at t_1-t_3, for it was the digging of the trench, the destruction of the vaults, and the construction of the retaining walls, that was the work of the contractor leading to the floodings.

Now consider again the rainstorm as an intervening cause. If the rainstorm was an intervening cause, then the causal test is clear in its implication: there were *no* occurrences of work by the contractor causing the floodings. If the rainstorm was an intervening cause, then it and the events that followed it alone caused the floodings; and yet neither the rainstorm nor what followed it were the work of the contractor for which he could be liable in either torts or under his contract of indemnity. On the other hand, if the rainstorm is not an intervening cause, then the implications of the causal test are not so clear. To be sure, now we restrict our focus to t_1-t_3, but even so restricted the *Johnson* case could be construed as a common cause case (one trench digging) or as a separate causes of separate injuries case (two vault wall destructions and two retaining wall constructions).

The application of standard proximate cause notions, conjoined with the reminder that we only count cause-events of the kind risked in a policy, thus reduces but does not eliminate the indeterminacy of the causal test for liability policies like that in *Johnson*. A proper understanding of this highlights an important difference between liability and all-risk casualty policies. For notice in *Johnson* what makes possible a non-arbitrary selection of a time at which to ask, 'How many cause-events were there?', was the basis of the liability insured against: for an ordinary tort liability policy, that would mean negligent acts by the insured; for a contract-based strict liability, as in *Johnson*, that would mean any act of the insured—so long as such acts were among the proximate causes of the injuries.

For all risk policies such as that issued to the World Trade Center leaseholders, there is nothing analogous pinpointing *when* one should ask, 'How many causes were there?' For any kind of injury-causing event is the risk covered under an all-risk policy. Suppose in *Johnson* the two adjacent buildings were owned by one owner, who purchased a casualty policy, insuring against property damage from all risks, at $50,000 per occurrence. Suppose further we grant the New York Court of Appeals its conclusion that the rainstorm was not so extraordinary as to be an intervening cause. Whether there was one or two occurrences depends on whether we look at how many collapses there were (t_6), how many trench fillings there were (t_5), how many rainstorms there were (t_4), how many buildings of retaining walls there were (t_3), etc. Since all of these equally proximate causes of the physical damages suffered are covered risks, each seems equally eligible to be considered. And this has the embarrassing consequence that the causal test is much more indeterminate as a test of how many occurrences there might be for all-risk casualty policies than for liability policies.

c. *Three Approaches to Reduce the Indeterminacy of the Causal Test*

Given the indeteminacy of the causal test that remains even after one has both focused exclusively on events that instantiate covered risks and applied standard intervening cause doctrines, it is tempting to supplement the causal test with some more determinate subtest. Two obvious possibilities are temporal: pick the earliest of a series of covered, proximate causes, or pick the latest. The third possibility is more substantial: pick the 'most important' of a series of covered, proximate causes. I shall consider each such suggestion *seriatim*.

Michael Moore

i. The earliest proximate cause approach.

There is considerable case law support for the view that in cases where there are multiple proximate causes (of the kind that instantiates a covered risk) of damages (of the kind also covered by a policy) one should count occurrences by the earliest of the sequence of covered, proximate causes. Suppose an insured purchases an earthquake policy protecting against property damage. Suppose that insured's house is damaged by two aftershocks (c_2, c_3) of an earlier earthquake (c_1), each aftershock inflicting separate damage to a separate part of the house (e_1, e_2) but the initial earthquake causing no damage to these parts of the house. The picture is thus:

(6)

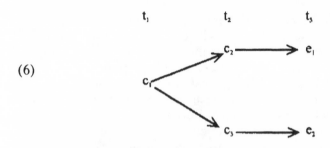

In such circumstances there is considerable authority for the view that there is one occurrence, not two. C_2 and c_3 are causally dependant on c_1, and therefore can be regarded as a mere means by which one earthquake caused multiple harms. Schema (6) thus reduces to schema (2), the common cause model for but one occurrence under the causal test.

The best case law support for the view that we are to look to the earliest proximate causes of harm when we are counting occurrences is to be found in the context of liability policies for automobile collisions.[68] The typical fact scenario involves the insured driving in a negligent manner at t_1 (typically a crossing of the center line); this results in a collision with victim number 1 at t_2; this collision ricochets the insured's vehicle into colliding with one or more other vehicles at t_3. The pattern is thus that of a causal chain (schema (3) above), and the courts uniformly hold there to be but one occurrence under the causal test.

The rationale for this 'first proximate cause' interpretation of the causal test is the same as the rationale for the 'one occurrence' construal of causal chains generally: so long as the subsequent

[68] See the cases cited *supra*, note 51.

288

causes of injury are dependant upon the earlier cause, that event is the one to count in deciding how many times the insured suffered one of the risks he insured against. All events produced by that earliest proximate cause are the mere means or mechanism by which that earlier event causes the multiple injuries that are its (covered by insurance) effects.

The limits of this rationale, and the limits of this 'first proximate cause' doctrine, are shown in cases where the later causes of injury are not causally dependant on the earliest proximate cause. We should thus contrast the causal chain multiple collision cases discussed above with a case where a negligent insured driver does not ricochet off the first car he hits nor does he make one mistake only. In *Liberty Mutual Insurance Co. v. Rawls,*[69] the insured was recklessly speeding because he was attempting to outrun two pursuing deputy sheriffs. He hit the left rear of one automobile in his own lane of travel, apparently in an attempt to pass it. Without losing control of his vehicle, he continued for several seconds across the center line, hitting a second vehicle head-on. Prima facie there were two acts of speeding, causing two separate injuries., thusly:

t_1 $\qquad\qquad$ t_2 $\qquad\qquad$ t_3 $\qquad\qquad$ t_4

c_1 (insured speeds $\longrightarrow$ e_1 (first collision)
and attempts to
pass)

(7) $\qquad$ c_2 (insured $\longrightarrow$ e_2 (second collision)
continues over center
line and continues
to speed)

As the Fifth Circuit emphasized in reaching its conclusion that there were two accidents, the insured 'had control of his vehicle after the initial collision.'[70] As subsequent courts have emphasized,[71] such control and continued reckless driving makes the second collision causally independent of the first. Therefore the model is that of schema (4), where there are two causes of two separate injuries, and thus, two occurrences under the causal test.

One way of construing cases like *Rawls* so as to make it fully consistent with always picking the earliest proximate cause when

---

[69] 404 F.2d 880 (5th Cir. 1968).

[70] *Id.* at 880.

[71] E.g., the Supreme Court of Wisconsin in *Olson v. Moore*, note 52 *supra*, 56 Wis.2d at 349, 202 N.W.2d at 240.

Michael Moore

counting occurrences, is to regard the second act of speeding by the insured as an intervening cause. Then the act of speeding and veering over the center line at t3 is the earliest proximate cause (of the kind instantiating the covered risk) of the second injury at t_4, just as the first act of speeding at t1 is the earliest proximate cause of the first injury at t_2. Yet suppose we were to think that the second act of speeding at t_3 was not an intervening cause. The control exercised by the injured in continuing to attempt to outrun the deputies at t_3 makes the second act of speeding causally independent of the first collision—this is not a ricochet case, in other words, where the first collision causes the second via an out-of-control automobile. But a later event that causally contributes to some harm can be causally independent of an earlier event without breaking the causal relationship between the earlier event and that harm. This is possible because causal independence is only a necessary condition for an event to be an intervening cause; it is not a sufficient condition.[72] Also necessary for a subsequent human action to be an intervening cause is that a human act intentionally takes advantage of the opportunity afforded by the earlier act so as to bring about the harm that resulted.[73]

Suppose that we were to think that the insured's decision to continue to evade the deputies in *Rawls* was not sufficiently intentional vis-a-vis the second collision as to be an intervening cause. The picture of the facts of *Rawls* then would be:

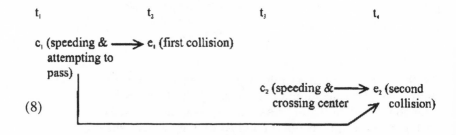

Because c_2 is not an intervening cause, the second collision can be a product of both the initial speeding at t_1 and the later swerving across the center line at t_3.

If one applied the 'pick the earliest proximate cause' idea to such a case, then this is but one occurrence—for there is one cause (c_2) of both collisions, and we have an instance of schema (2), the common

[72] See Moore, 'Metaphysics of Causal Intervention,' *supra* note 36.
[73] See Hart and Honore, *supra* note 62, at pp. 74–7.

290

cause model. Yet it seems quite doubtful that 'one' is the correct answer to such a case. Given the causal independence of c_2 from c_1, this is not a chain kind of case where one can say, 'The earliest proximate cause counts as one because it caused everything else.' Given the causal independence of c_2, there wasn't just one instance of the risk insured against materializing—there were two. And so long as each occurrence of the risk materializing caused its own separate injury (to put aside the common injury cases), there should be two occurrences here. Such a result is closer to the gamble the parties presumably took in affixing per occurrence limits to the kinds of events risked.

We can see the plausibility of the same point with the facts of *Johnson*. In *Johnson*, we should focus only on those events that constitute the work of the contractor that caused the flooding of the two basements. On the assumption that the rainstorm was not an intervening cause, there were three sorts of such causally relevant work: the digging of the one trench, the destruction of the two basement vault walls, and the construction of the two retaining walls. The earliest of these events was the digging of the trench, and on the 'earliest proximate cause counts' view, we should count events at t_1, in which case there was but one occurrence. Yet this to my mind is counterintuitive. Given the causal independence of the vault destruction and the retaining wall construction from the trench digging, one cannot say that everything leading to the flooding was caused by the trench digging. That event was first in time but equally important to the subsequent flooding was the replacement of strong vault walls with weaker cinder block retaining walls.

The upshot is that one cannot extend the 'first proximate cause' doctrine to cases where the other proximate causes are causally independent of the first proximate cause of some injuries. The causal test under this interpretation should be regarded as still indeterminate with regard to this class of cases.

ii. The last proximate cause approach

The other interpretation of the causal test having some explicit support in the case law is to pick the proximate cause(s) nearest in time to the harms and count how many of those there might be. This is the interpretation of the causal test accepted by the New York Court of Appeals as the main rationale for its decision in *Johnson*.[74]

There are two ways of taking this suggestion. One is to focus exclusively on the proximate cause(s) nearest the harm *no matter*

---

[74] *Johnson, supra* note 13.

Michael Moore

whether such events instantiate the risk insured against. This was apparently the view of the majority opinion in *Johnson*, for that opinion held there to be two occurrences because there were two wall collapse events. It was the collapse of the retaining walls that were the proximate causes most immediately preceding the flooding of the two basements, and because there were two such collapses, each causing a separate flooding-injury event, the court held there to be two occurrences under the policy. The court simply ignored how many trench-floodings, how many rainstorms, how many retaining wall constructions, how many vault wall destructions, and how many trench diggings there were, because these (admittedly proximate causes) were not the 'most proximate,' or immediate, causes of the flooding.

This 'last cause' interpretation is surely a very bad reading of per occurrence limitations in insurance contracts. As I argued earlier in section 2, both liability and casualty policies are issued against the risk of there being certain kinds of causes of certain kinds of injuries. 'per occurrence' limitations on coverage have to be read in light of this fact. The two kinds of occurrences of interest to parties to insurance contracts are occurrences of injuries and occurrences of causes of injuries, for these are the things (kinds of losses and kinds of risks) generally defining coverage.

There is thus only one sensible answer to the question, 'per occurrence of what?' That is the answer of the causal test (properly construed as above): 'per occurrence of injurious events of the kind covered in the policy, so long as each such injury is caused by a separate occurrence of the kind of event the risk of which was also covered in the policy.' One might argue for either a pure effects test, or a pure causal test, focusing respectively on covered kinds of damage or on covered kinds of risks. Although I argued earlier this would be erroneous, either of these arguments is at least intelligible. But focusing on events that are neither losses nor risks makes no sense. In particular, there is no sensible test focusing on events located temporally between the covered cause events and the covered damage events, such as the collapse of retaining walls in *Johnson*; for no contracting party is limiting coverage based on those events. Such events are neither covered types of injuries nor covered types of risks. One might as well construe per occurrence limits in insurance contracts based on the number of eclipses that occur during the policy period; such eclipses have as much to do with damages and risks insured against as do other non-covered events like retaining wall collapses.

Imagine buying a property damage policy covering the risk of earthquakes. Suppose an earthquake occurs, this causes two fires to break out in two separate parts of the building insured, and this results in separate injuries to the different parts of the building. Suppose further a court would construe the policy to cover this property damage, on the ground that it is still earthquake- caused damage even though the means by which the earthquake caused the damage was by two fires. If one were to apply the last proximate cause test in the manner of the court in *Johnson*, then one would conclude that there were two occurrences because there were two fires; this, despite the fact that fires are not risks covered by an earthquake policy. Such an approach divorces what one is counting under per occurrence limitations from what is covered by the policy, and that surely no party to an insurance contract either intends or expects.

The cases cited by the New York Court of Appeals do little to support its view in *Johnson* that there is some test of 'same occurrence' focusing exclusively on the last proximate cause of the injuries. The case that court considered 'most similar'[75] to *Johnson* was *Kuhn's of Brownsville*,[76] a case in which four buildings collapsed because of the excavation work done by the insured. Yet in the latter case the Supreme Court of Tennessee did not see itself as applying some last proximate cause kind of test. Rather, the court engaged in standard proximate cause analysis (called for by the causal test) to find that the insured's excavation(s) had caused the collapse of the four buildings. That court then mistakenly found there to be two excavation events to cause the two injury events,[77] but this mistake had nothing to do with any supposed invention of a last proximate cause test for 'per occurrence' limitations.

The subsequent application of the New York last proximate cause test also does little to support the idea that this is truly the test for 'same occurrence' being followed in New York. In the *Wesolowski* decision[78] issued 14 years after *Johnson*, the New York Court of Appeals purported to be applying the *Johnson* last event test. Yet in this ricochet-type multiple car collision case, the court in fact engaged in the standard proximate cause analysis. Because 'the continuum between the two impacts was unbroken, with no intervening agent or operative factor,'[79] the court held there to be but one occurrence despite the multiple car collisions. This is precisely the

[75] 7 N.Y.2d at 229, 190 N.Y.S.2d at 683, 164 N.E.2d at 707.

[76] *Kuhn's of Brownsville v. Bituminous Casualty Co.*, 197 Tenn. 60, 270 s.W.2d 358 (1954).

[77] See the discussion, text at nn.142–7, *infra*.

[78] *Wesolowski, supra* note 10.

[79] 33 N.Y.2d at 174, 350 N.Y.S.2d at , 305 N.E.2d at 910.

Michael Moore

result and the reasoning dictated by the standard version of the causal test.

I conclude that in reality New York cannot be following any last proximate cause test of 'same occurrence.' There is no such test that makes any sense in light of contracting parties presumed intentions, there is no such test to be found in the non-New York case law relied on by the New York courts, and the New York courts themselves have had the good sense to apply no such test in their multiple collision cases, despite what they may say. There is also a fourth reason to think that New York cannot be following any such last proximate test. This reason is supplied by a *reductio* suggested by the dissent in *Johnson*. Justice Van Voorhis noted in that dissent that 'something analogous to the collapse of these two walls can always be found, and would necessarily occur whenever damage is effected to more than one person.'[80] This would collapse the causal test supposedly distinctive of American insurance law, into the English effects test.

Justice Van Voorhis' point can be illustrated by one of the multiple collision cases, *Truck Insurance Exchange v. Rohde.*[81] In that case a truck negligently driven by the insured ran into three motorcycles successively. On two of the motorcycles there was a passenger in addition to a driver. All five persons on the motorcycle suffered serious injuries. Given the lack of causal connection between the collisions, this was not a ricochet case but rather, a common cause sort of case:

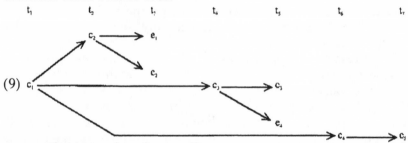

c_1 = negligent crossing of center line
c_2 = collision with first motorcycle
c_3 = collision with second motorcycle
c_4 = collision with third motorcycle
e_1 = injury of driver$_2$
e_2 = injury of passenger$_1$
e_3 = injury of driver$_2$
e_4 = injury of passenger$_2$
e_4 = injury of driver$_3$

[80] 7 N.Y.2d at 232, 196 N.Y.S.2d at 686, 164 N.E.2d at 709.
[81] *Rohde, supra* note 10.

294

If we look to the last proximate cause of the injuries (despite the fact that it is not a kind of risk covered in the policy), this was arguably the impact of the truck on each motorcycle—and there were three of those. Yet there should be but one occurrence here, as the Washington Supreme Court properly held.

But van Voorhis's *reductio* does not stop here. Once we free ourselves from looking only for proximate causes of injury that instantiate a covered risk, why not see *Rohde* this way:

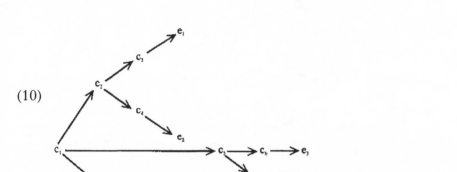

(10)

where c_1 = negligent driving
c_2, c_5, c_8 = the three collisions
e_1, e_2, e_3, e_4, e_5 = the five injuries, as before
c_3, c_4, c_6, c_7, c_9 = the impact of a passenger or a driver onto the pavement

Now there are five last proximate causes—the impact of each of the five motorcycle riders on the pavement—to match the number of persons injured. So long as the major injuries resulted from such impacts with the pavement, there will be as many of those as there are persons injured, and the causal test merges fully into the effects test avowedly rejected by American insurance law.

A second and much more sensible way of taking the suggestion about last proximate causes, would be to restrict the causes eligible to those that instantiate a covered risk. Then at least we would not be counting fires under earthquake policies, nor would we be counting non-acts like wall collapses or rainstorms under liability policies covering only actions of the insured.

Even this much more sensible version of the last proximate cause doctrine faces two problems. One is the problem that in cases where the last proximate cause is itself causally dependent on earlier proximate causes, the rationale for the *first* proximate cause test seems correct: all that is produced by this first proximate cause is the mere means by which it causes damages even though those means may be causes too of those damages. Suppose again a property damage/earthquake policy, and suppose one earthquake produces two aftershocks, each of which causes separate injury to the insured's building. The schema in such a case is:

$$t_1 \qquad\qquad t_2 \qquad\qquad t_3$$

(11)

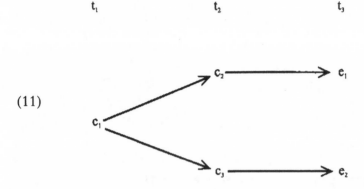

(Where c_1 = the initiating earthquakes, c_2 and c_3 = the two aftershocks, and e_1 and e_2 represent the two injury events.)

Intuitively the first proximate cause doctrine seems correct for this class of cases: there was one occurrence of an earthquake even though it caused two separate injuries via two separate aftershocks.

If this is right, it suggests restricting the last proximate cause test even further, namely, to those cases where there are two or more proximate causes (each of which instantiate a covered risk) *and* those causes are causally independent of one another. In a case like *Johnson*, for example, that would suggest a focus on the retaining wall constructions—and not the trench digging or the vault wall distinctions—when counting occurrences. This was in fact the alternative focus of the New York Court of Appeals in *Johnson*, who in the alternative held there to be two acts of retaining wall construction causing two separate instances of flood damage.

The problem with even this restricted an application of the *last* proximate cause doctrine is the same problem as beset the application of the *first* proximate cause doctrine to this class of case: it seems an arbitrary stipulation having no salience in the likely expectations of the contracting parties. It seems as arbitrary to focus on the retaining wall constructions alone as it is to focus on the trench digging alone when asking, 'How many instances of the work of the contractor were there that resulted in the two instances of flood damage?' Seemingly needed is some more holistic approach for this class of cases.

iii The most substantial proximate cause approach

It may seem that with the restrictions hitherto imposed we are dealing with a small and not very significant class of cases. To review, these are cases where: (1) standard intervening cause doctrines leave open the possibility that there is more than one proximate cause for a set of injuries; (2) when such proximate causes each instantiate the kind of risk insured against; and (3) when such proximate causes are each causally independent of one another. Yet these three restrictions in fact leave open a large number of cases, including both the *Johnson* case in New York and the current World Trade Center litigation.

Take the facts of *Johnson* again, and suppose we are dealing with an all risk casualty policy purchased by the common owner of both of the buildings flooded. Such an all-risk policy means that limit (2) above does very little work, for all risks are insured against, rainstorms as much as negligent contractors. Still, items (1) and (3) above do some work. Events prior to the digging of the trench on Fourth Avenue may be cut off by standard intervening cause (or other proximate cause) doctrines, and we should lump vault wall destructions with retaining wall constructions with retaining wall collapses under the causal dependance idea. Nonetheless, that leaves the digging of the trench, the wall replacements, and the rainstorm as equally proximate causes of the two floodings. That results in one or two occurrences, depending on which of these one counts as occurrences.

The way out of this indeterminacy is to leave temporal tests (of first or last proximate causes) for a more substantive test. Roughly: focus on the most important cause(s) of the floodings and count how many of those kinds of events there were. By the facts given in the *Johnson* opinion, that seems to be the 'unprecedented' rainstorm; there was one of those and so one occurrence under a single casualty policy purchased by the owner of the two buildings. True enough, there would have been no flooding if there were no trench dug or no vault walls replaced with weaker retaining walls, no less than if there had been no rainstorm. Each of these three factors, in other words, was equally necessary to the damage events, the floodings. Yet so long as the retaining walls were not defective in any way, the rainstorm was more of a cause of the floodings than was either the trench digging or the retaining wall substitution.

As should be apparent from the foregoing, there is a quite controversial notion of causation being presupposed by this suggestion. In particular, one has to reject (or highly qualify) the 'but for,' or necessary condition conception of causation, for necessity does not admit easily of degrees. One has to substitute an avowedly *scalar* notion of causation, a conception with which one can comfortably rank causes of a given effect by their size or importance. Elsewhere I have undertaken the two-fold showing needed to defend such a scalar view of causation.[82] In a forthcoming book[83] I seek to show, first, how many of the distinctions the law draws when it employs a concept of causation only make sense in light of the scalar conception; and second, how the most plausible metaphysics of causation endow that relation with scalarity as well. In this much shorter work I shall simply assume such showings have been made, and move on.

There is one objection to this scalar idea of causation that should be dealt with here. This is the objection that has been voiced in legal circles ever since a scalar notion of causation was defended by Jeremiah Smith in his introduction of a 'substantial factor' test for causation in tort law in 1911.[84] The objection is that there is a large area of indeterminacy introduced into causal questions if the causal relation can be one of degree. How much of the stuff must there be to be substantial? How do we individuate the units of the stuff so that we can compare degrees of causal contribution and pronounce one (of a set of causes) to be 'most substantial?'

The vagueness objection (as I shall call it) is a rather toothless objection here. As Aristotle once admonished us, it is folly to demand more precision than the subject matter at hand affords.[85] If causation is scalar then it is a matter of degree, and the matching of the continuous variation of the relation with the vagueness of the concept is a virtue for an analysis, not a vice. This is particularly true for the concept of causation used in the interpretation of contracts. Insofar as the parties limit their coverage by occurrences of certain sorts of risks that, when they materialize, cause injuries of certain sorts, the notion of cause employed should be no more precise than that understood by the parties. Big rainstorms, like terrorist acts, are big causes in ordinary understanding, in a way that

[82] Moore, 'Causation and Responsibility,' *supra* note 36.

[83] Moore, *Causation and Responsibility, supra*, note 36.

[84] Jeremiah Smith, 'Legal Cause in Actions of Tort,' *Harvard Law Review*, Vol. 25 (1911), pp. 103–28, 223–52, 303–27.

[85] Aristotle, *Nicomachean Ethics*, Bk. 1, ch. 3, in Richard McKeon, ed., *Introduction to Aristotle* (Chicago: University of Chicago Press, 2d edit., 1973), pp. 347–8.

non-defective retaining wall construction (and non-defective sky-scraper design) are not.

d. *Applying the Causal Test to the Destruction of the Twin Towers*

It is now time to apply this over-long analysis to the Twin Towers litigation. To begin with, that litigation involves an all risk policy on the Towers. All proximate causes of the Towers' destruction are thus eligible to be considered under the 'covered risk' criterion. That leaves the proximate cause, the causal dependence, and the most substantial cause criteria, to do all of the work in determining what kind of events we should be counting in this case.

Consider first the causal independence criterion. Many of the events included in the Twin Towers litigation are clear instances of causal dependance. The Twin Towers causal picture may be schematized as:

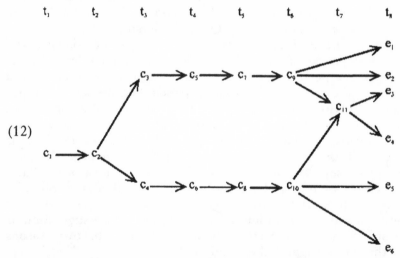

(12)

(Where c_1 = the decision at the top of al Qaeda to destroy both of the Twin Towers, c_2 = the agreement of the two pilots to destroy the Twin Towers, c_3, c_4 = the decisions of the two pilots after hijacking to crash the two 767's into the two Towers, c_5, c_6 = the crashing of the two 767's into the two Towers, c_7, c_8 = the intense fires that raged in each tower, c_9, c_{10} = the collapse of each tower, c_{11} = the collapse of other WTC buildings also leased by Silverstein, and e_1–e_6 = the reconstruction costs and non-payment of rent otherwise due on each Tower and on the other collapsed WTC buildings.)

299

Michael Moore

Despite the two different kinds of damage—property damage and lost income—these are t he effects of a common cause (the collapse of each Tower) and there are thus at most two occurrences of injury-events. Furthermore, despite the separate injuries flowing from the collapse of other WTC buildings also leased by the Silverstein group, the collapse of those buildings was caused by the collapse of the Towers and this (under the causal chain model) cannot constitute a separate occurrence. The fires at t_5 are causally dependant on the crashes at t_4 which are themselves the result of the decisions of the pilots on board each aircraft at t_3; there are thus at most but two occurrences of risked events to be found here as well. Further, if the decisions of the two teams was causally dependant on one earlier decision by the pilots themselves (t_2) or by the al Qaeda leadership (t_1), then all other causes in the chains (c_3–c_{11}) are the mere means or mechanisms by which one terrorist decision caused two injuries; this reduces to the common cause model for one occurrence. The trick, however, is to decide whether the decisions of the two pilots at t_3 causally depended on the general decision to destroy the Towers made by themselves or by the al Qaeda leadership.

When we are dealing with human actions and decisions to act, causal independence means motivational independence.[86] Put simply, if one person supplies the motivation for another to do a certain act, the latter act is causally dependant on the act of the first person supplying the motive; whereas if the second actor has his own reasons for wanting to do the act in question, then the later action is causally independent of the earlier suggestions. This is true even if the first actor's actions suggest or request the later action of another, and are in that sense a 'but for' cause of that later act. A clear case of supplying motivation to another is coercion by threats. Another is brainwashing. A clear case of the later actor bringing his own motivation to his action is where a suggestion or request is made to the second actor who decides for his own reasons to do the action suggested or requested.

From what we know thus far about the structure of al Qaeda it would appear most likely that the decisions of the two terrorist teams was causally independent of the decision of the leadership to destroy both Towers. There are three reasons for this. First, the pilots involved in crashing the planes were not indoctrinated 18 year olds typical of Palestinian suicide bombers. They were fathers, aged 23 and 33; then presumably had the maturity to reflect on what they were doing. They were thus far removed from the brain-washed

[86] Explored in Moore, 'Metaphysics of Causal Intervention,' *supra* note 36, at pp. 834–9.

300

automatons perhaps typical of some of the terrorist acts currently taking place in Israel. Second, al Qaeda is said to be an example of the new form of terrorist organization. It is said to consist of semi-autonomous cells, different from the more hierarchical structure of older terrorist organizations. If this is true then even the mild form of coercion supplied by military orders (not backed by threats) was not present in the suggestion by the leadership about destroying the Twin Towers. The pilots supplied their own motivations for their crashing of the planes (motivations consisting of their subscribing to a certain religious ideology); they were not moved to act by the coercive effect of threats, orders, or 'offers they could not refuse.' Third, the details of just how to bring down the Twin Towers seem to have been left to the 33-year-old leader of the terrorist teams. The speed of the aircraft differed (the second was at full throttle, while the first was operated at a more normal speed for that low altitude), as did the timing and the precise targeting of impact. The teams may also have picked which flights to hijack (so long as they were 767's loaded with fuel for a cross country flight). Such independent fixing of the content of the decisions by each team to hijack and crash the aircraft, lessens any causal dependence of those decisions on some general decision to destroy the Twin Towers with aircraft. Not only were the pilots bringing their own motivation to bear on their decisions to crash, but they also were exercising their independent cognitive abilities in deciding precisely how and when to crash.

The causal independence of the pilot's decisions to crash from the more general decision of the leadership to destroy the Twin Towers with aircraft, means that one cannot disregard the former decisions in counting occurrences. Such causal independence does not tell us to look to those decisions alone in counting occurrences, for perhaps both these decisions and the more general decisions are causes of the damage events. Whether this is so depends on whether the pilots' decisions meet the other conditions (in addition to causal independence) for being intervening causes.

In addition to c_2, c_3 being causally independent of c_1, for c_2 and c_3 to be intervening causes they must be intentional with respect to the harms suffered. This too seems to be satisfied here, from what we know or can surmise about al Qaeda's planning of these attacks. It is true that Osama bin Laden in one of the videos released during the recent war in Afghanistan laughed about the degree of ignorance of some of the hijackers of just what they were about to do. Insofar as those hijackers were ignorant dupes of al Qaeda's central leadership, their actions and choices would not be intentional with respect to the crash into, and damage to, the Twin

301

Michael Moore

Towers.[87] Yet the pilots surely knew what they were about and decided to go forward anyway. The pilots' decisions and actions, at least, were sufficiently intentional so as to constitute intervening causes.

A way to test this claim is to imagine that the pilots and bin Laden survived and were indicted for murder. Would the central leadership—bin Laden—be charged as a principal or as an accomplice? If the pilots' decisions were intervening causes, bin Laden could only be charged as an accomplice—one who intentionally *aids* another to cause some legally prohibited state of affairs but who does not himself *cause* such state of affairs. If the pilots were duped by bin Laden about what they were doing, then they would be like the innocent or partly innocent agents whose actions do not break causal chains; then bin Laden could be indicted as a principal.[88] From what we know thus far, it seems quite unlikely that the al Qaeda leadership would be charged as principals—this, because they procured others to act but did not themselves cause the harms the criminal law prohibits.

It should thus be relatively easy to reach the conclusion that the decision by the pilots to crash the planes constituted intervening causes robbing the earlier decision of the al Qaeda leadership (to destroy the World Trade Center) of the potential of being the common cause of both injuries. Yet this does not end the enquiry because of a second candidate for a common cause emerging from the facts behind September 11. One of the pilots, Mohamed Atta, was himself (apparently) the principal architect of the details of the plan as it evolved in the United States. If it was not his idea originally (which it appears it was not), it was his to plan in detail. Atta co-ordinated all of the other teams of terrorists in America, traveling constantly between the various groups.[89] Perhaps Atta's earlier, detailed intention constitutes the common cause of all injuries.

This event too, seems remote (in the law's sense) from the collapse of the Towers. Again, the decisions of the pilots (including Atta's) prima facie meets the standard criteria for an intervening cause: they were subsequent to Atta's planning activities, causally

---

[87] On the use of innocent agents and their status as non-intervening causes, see Sanford Kadish, 'Causation and Complicity: A Study in the Interpretation of Doctrine,' *California Law Review*, Vol. 73 (1985), pp. 323–410.

[88] *Id.*

[89] The evidence is summarized in the *New York Times'* anniversary retrospective, Sept. 11, 2002.

(motivationally) independent of those activities, causally significant themselves, intentional with respect to the damage, and voluntary in the sense of uncoerced by Atta as well as done by those in full possession of their faculties.[90] Hence, if we read the law's standard doctrines of intervening causation into this insurance contract's causal test for 'occurrence,' Atta's pre-flight intention was no more a common cause of the collapse than was bin Laden's much earlier intention.

In liability policies there is good reason to read tort law's detailed doctrines of intervening cause into the causal test of insurance law.[91] For liability policies, the liability of the insurance companies is for the liability of the insured to some third party, and the latter liability itself is based on the tort law's doctrines of proximate causation. When the loss insured against—liability in tort—itself is based on certain ideas of causation, it makes sense to read those ideas into the test for liability of the insurance company for that loss. The reasonable expectations of both parties to insurance contracts should be focused on these doctrines.

With casualty policies the issue is not so clear. In a first party casualty policy insuring against property damage caused by earthquakes, for example, the risk insured against is earthquakes. Unlike tort liability, earthquakes do not have the legal notion of intervening causation built into them. Of course, even in casualty policies earthquakes must *cause* damage of the requisite sort and it is open to read the law's notions of intervening causation into that requirement.

Whether such reading is a good idea depends in part on what one thinks is the status of the legal idea of intervening causation. If that legal idea is no more than a reflection of the ordinary person's conception of causation used throughout daily life, or if that legal idea captures the metaphysics of the causal relation, then there is good reason to read such ideas into the causal test for casualty policies as well as for liability policies. Yet despite the distinguished defense of one or both of these bases for the legal idea of intervening causation by Herbert Hart and Tony Honore,[92] there is reason to doubt the claims.[93] There is simply no plausible metaphysics that can make

[90] See generally Hart and Honore, *Causation in the Law*, *supra* note 62, at pp. 74–7, 136–62, 326–40; Moore, 'Metaphysics of Causal Intervention,' *supra* note 36, at pp. 839–44.

[91] As many courts do. See text *supra* at nn. 53–4.

[92] Hart and Honore, *Causation in the Law*, *supra* note 62, *passim*, but particularly the 'Preface to the Second Edition.'

[93] Moore, 'Metaphysics of Causal Intervention,' *supra* note 36.

sense of the law's idea that intervening (free, voluntary, informed) human choices always break causal chains, relegating what went before to mere background conditions (rather than causes) of the harm.[94]

It is true that there are many applications of the law's notion of intervening cause that common folk find intuitively compelling even outside legal contexts. Yet these, I have argued,[95] are accounted for by a metaphysically more plausible concept of causation, the 'substantial cause' idea adverted to before.[96] What makes both 'acts of God' and free human choices act like intervening causes in popular understanding is that such factors often swamp earlier causal factors in importance. Put crudely, such later factors are so much *more* of a cause than the earlier items that they dominate any causal account of the harms in question.[97]

If such 'substantial causation' idea captures both the true metaphysics and the popular understanding of the causal relation, then we might read this idea into the causal test for casualty policies, in preference to using the legal doctrines of intervening causation. If we frame the issue this way, then the question in the Twin Towers litigation is this one: when was (were) the decision(s) that had the largest role in causing the destruction of the Twin Towers, actually made? Was bin Laden's decision the major factor, or was it Atta's American planning, or was it the decisions of each pilot, that played the dominant role? This approach involves the subquestions, first, of content: how much of *what* was decided (the content) at the later time was identical to what was already decided at the earlier time? Were the details all worked out earlier, or was much planning done later? Second, there is the subquestion of resolve: how firm was the earlier intention? Except for some forms of mental disease, intentions are never fixed come hell or high water. Their firmness is rather a matter of degree, measured by their resistance to change even if it should turn out the action intended will conflict with other desires and intentions of the agent. Third, there is the subquestion of what could be called the counter-instinctual nature of the action intended. Some choices necessarily run counter to nearly universal human needs that are almost always deeply felt, or in that loose sense, 'instinctual.' Soldiers often say, for example, that one never

[94] *Id.*

[95] *Id.* at pp. 873-877.

[96] Text *supra* at nn. 81-85.

[97] Moore, 'Metaphysics of Causal Intervention,' *supra* note 36, at pp. 873–7, Richard Epstein, 'A Theory of Strict Liability,' *Journal of Legal Studies*, Vol. 2 (1973), pp. 151–204, at 183–4.

knows how one will perform in battle until one is there. In such cases even firm general intentions may call for fresh judgment when it comes time to execute them, for only then does the actor really face (emotionally) the costs of his action.

All three of these matters—of content, resolve and instinct—are matters of degree, but that hardly cuts against this approach, for the nature of the issue itself necessarily involves drawing lines on a matter of continuous variation. Without saying so, this is implicitly the approach adopted in some of the insurance cases dealing with the issue (of later, multiple decisions of an agent supplanting earlier, single decisions by that same agent). Consider again in this regard the *Rawls* case,[98] where the insured attempted to outrun two sheriff's deputies and successively collided with two cars. One might schematize the case as a kind of common cause case:

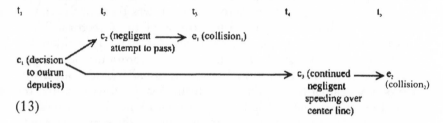

(13)

To decide the case as it did, the Fifth Circuit implicitly had to reject the earlier decision of the insured (to outrun the deputies) as the common cause of the two collisions; yet it could not do this on standard intervening cause notions. The insured's later decisions (to pass the first car, to continue to speed and to cross the center line) were not intentional or knowing with respect to the collisions that resulted; they were at most reckless and more likely only negligent. Usually negligent subsequent decisions do not constitute intervening causes.[99] To prevent the earlier, more general decision being considered the common cause of all injuries required the court to use some other approach.

Enter the most substantial cause question. *When* was the decision(s) really made that resulted in the collisions? In *Rawls*, the resolve of the earlier decision may have been quite firm, but the content was hardly identical to the content of the later decisions; they were responsive to situations unforeseen at the earlier time and about which no decision had therefore been taken. The later

[98] See note 69, *supra*.
[99] See Moore, 'Metaphysics of Causal Intervention,' *supra* note 33, at pp. 841–2.

decisions were *more of a cause* of their respective collisions than was the earlier, more general decision to outrun the deputies.

Consider these variations. Mentally disturbed insured fires his shotgun three times at arresting officers, the shots separated by about a minute apiece—is there a common cause in the initial decision to resist arrest, or several causes with each pull of the trigger?[100] Directors and officers of a savings and loan association (insured under a directors and officers liability policy) instituted a loan swap program under which four bad loans were made—is there a common cause in the initiation of the general loan swap policy, or several causes in the decision to make each individual loan?[101] Under another D and O liability policy, when officers of the insured separately authorize spot loans to unqualified home buyers, authorize five separate large condominium project loans that go bad, and authorize the move and renovation of corporate headquarters without having sufficient funds to pay for it, was there one common cause of all losses in the general ineptitude of the directors? Three causes of three unrelated series of losses? Or as many incidents of loss as there were bad spot loans, bad condominium loans, and unfundable moves and unfundable renovations?[102] Under an insurance policy against losses caused by dishonest employees, when the insured's employee embezzled a large sum of money by writing forty separate checks, was there one common cause in the employee's general decision to embezzle money via bogus checks, or forty causes of forty losses in the decision to write each bogus check?[103] Under a general liability policy for a business, when the insured company is held liable in a class action suit for sex discrimination in the hiring, promoting, and compensation of numerous of its female employees, was there one common cause in the initiation of a general company policy of discrimination or as many causes of separate injuries as there were acts of discrimination on particular occasions?[104]

In the first three of these five cases the courts held for multiple causes, in the last two, for a single common cause. The difference lies in the degree of firmness of the earlier decision and in the degree of content-independence to be found in the individual decisions, an independence increased by the lack of identity of content between the later decisions and some more general back-

[100] *McQuaig, supra* note 26.
[101] *Huff, supra* note 45.
[102] *Okada, supra* note 49.
[103] *Business Interiors, supra* note 48.
[104] *Appalachian Insurance Co. v. Liberty Mutual Insurance Co.*, 676 F.2d 56 (2rd Cir. 1982).

ground policy or decision. As the Tenth Circuit noted in *Business Interiors* (the 40 bogus checks case),[105] the question is whether the initial decision (e.g., to embezzle money) effectively decided that issue on each of 40 occasions where the opportunity arose to embezzle money, or whether each transaction required some kind of fresh decision. If the individual decisions (to make loans, write checks, offer less money to female employees) are each sufficiently unique as to call for fresh judgment, or if the original decisions were sufficiently shaky in their resolve as to call for fresh judgment, then the most substantial causes are the later decisions; whereas if such individual judgments are the routine application of one's own established policy, less judgment is called for and the less such individual decisions look like the most substantial causes of the injuries they admittedly do cause.

Suppose (as seems possible from the facts thus far revealed) that one decision was made by Mohamed Atta to destroy the World Trade Center by using two passenger aircraft, and that that decision was firmly fixed in his mind when he directed his own and the other teams. Whether that decision is a common cause of the two collapses of the Twin Towers then depends in part on whether the subsequent decisions of Atta and the other pilot while on their airplanes made significant additions or changes to what was originally decided. How much choice was left (by the general decision to destroy the World Trade Center) to the individual terrorist teams as to *how* such destruction was to be accomplished—was every detail decided in advance by the al Qaeda terrorist network or was much independent judgment required by the separate terrorist teams? Were the targets pre-assigned to each of the planes, or was choice required between alternative targets? Secondly, there is the question of a fresh judgment being made by each of the pilots because of the nature of the actions contemplated. It is one thing to form a firm intention to crash a plane into a building for the greater glory of god when that event is yet in the future; it must be something else to actually pilot a plane right at the face of that building. While in a general sense the pilots chose to do exactly what they earlier intended to do, it may well have required the kind of fresh decision just because of the counter-instinctual nature of the act chosen.

Some of these facts we will never know, but perhaps others will come to light, either at trial or later.[106] It is these kinds of facts that

---

[105] *Business Interiors, supra,* note 48, 751 F.2d at 363.

[106] We might learn, for example, whether the two pilots 'routinized' their crashing of an airliner into a building by using the publicly available software simulating flying an airplane between and into the Twin Towers. See *Time,* special issue of September 11, 2001, p. 28.

should determine how substantial a cause was the earlier (versus the later) decisions of the two pilots. This approach is thus somewhat less determinant than is the intervening cause approach, where the result seems pretty plain: the pilots' on board decisions were intervening causes cutting off any earlier, common cause, and there were two of such decisions.

4. The Pure Question of Event-Identity

In discussing and applying the causal test we assumed we knew how many events were involved in any given situation—one trench digging, two wall destructions, two wall constructions, one rainstorm, one trench filling, two wall collapses, two basement floodings, for example in *Johnson*.[107] We made such assumptions in order to focus on the causal relations between such events. Now we need to examine what I earlier called the pure question of event identity: when do we have one event, such as the flooding of the basements of New York City,[108] and when do we have two floodings, or many?

I shall proceed in the following way. Since it is easy to confuse qualitative identity with numerical identity in ordinary speech and in the law, I shall first examine these two notions, the relations that hold between them, and argue that only numerical identity is meant by the same occurrence limitation in insurance policies. Second, since the (numerical) identity conditions for a class of things like events depends on the essential nature of such things, I shall explore several different theories as to the nature of events, as well as their corresponding notions about the identity conditions of events. Third, I will then address what I shall call the sizing question: under the theory of the essential nature of events that I believe to be correct, there are three dimensions of indeterminacy in how big or small natural events might be. An answer to the sizing question should defend some point in each of these three areas of indeterminacy.

a. *Numerical and Qualitative Identity*

When we talk of identity, we are often ambiguous between two different ideas of identity. Consider statements about the identity of

---

[107] *Arthur Johnson Corp. v. Indemnity Insurance Co.*, *supra* note 13.

[108] Cf. Lombard, *supra* note 28, at pp. 123–4, where Lombard considers the singleness of very large events like the melting of the Antarctic ice cap, or even the melting of all the world's snows.

persons. We often say of a reformed criminal, for example, 'Smith is no longer the same person.' We sometimes say the same of a multiple-personalitied person when he shifts to his alter ego. In such statements we could mean that Smith is no longer numerically the same person, so that, for example, the person he now is: can't be punished for the crimes of someone else, can't benefit from contracts made by someone else, or wills leaving property to someone else, is not married to the Mrs. Smith the other guy was married to, cannot trespass on the other's person's real property, etc.[109] More likely such statements should be taken to refer to qualitative, not numerical, identity. We likely mean that 'Smith is not quite himself' in the sense that his personality traits are markedly different from those that are usually in character for him. We mean, that is, that Smith is not the same *kind* of person today, not that he isn't literally the same person as he was yesterday.[110]

True qualitative identity—where two numerically distinct particulars share all the same properties—is rare to the point of non-existence. The 17th Century German logician, Leibniz, noticed this with his famous two principles of identity.[111] The first is called the Indiscernability of Identicals, or sometimes called Leibniz's Law. This principle asserts that if two putatively distinct particulars are in reality one and the same thing, then necessarily they (it) share all the same properties at any given point of time. (Over an interval of time, they necessarily share only their (its) essential properties.) In a phrase, at any one time numerical identity implies true qualitative identity.

Leibniz also thought the converse was true, namely, that if two putatively distinct particulars shared all of their properties, then such particulars were in reality one and the same thing. Leibniz thought, in other words, that no two truly distinct items could share all of their properties. This is usually called the Identity of Indiscernibles principle.

The former of these principles, Leibniz's Law, is usually thought

---

[109] Rebecca Dresser examines the sense of taking statements of personal identity over time in this numerical sense of identity. See Dresser, 'Personal Identity and Punishment,' *Boston University Law Review*, Vol. 70 (1990), pp. 395-446.

[110] I so construe most of such statements in Michael Moore, *Law and Psychiatry: Rethinking the Relationship* (Cambridge: Cambridge University Press, 1984), pp. 398–407.

[111] A brief introduction to these principles of identity may be found in Baruch Brody, *Identity and Essence* (Princeton: Princeton University Press, 1980), pp. 6–10.

Michael Moore

to be partly constitutive of the idea of identity. If two descriptions literally describe the same thing, it is difficult to conceive how that thing could possess different properties depending on how it is described. As philosophers often put it, 'If identity does not mean universal interchangeability, then I do not really understand identity.'[112] Or again, 'tampering with the substitutivity of identity may easily make the notion of identity unintelligible.'[113] By contrast, the second principle, the Identity of Indiscernibles, seems less likely true and, even if true, less closely connected to the very meaning of identity.

In most ordinary and legal contexts, when we speak of two numerically distinct particulars being the same kind of things, we almost never mean, 'the same in all respects.' Rather, we mean, 'the same in certain respects relevant to this context.' One diamond may be 'the same' as another in terms of: its monetary value; its colour and cut; its clarity and degree of imperfections; its source of origin; etc. In assessing qualitative sameness, usually the context picks out the relevant qualities. A husband replacing his wife's lost engagement ring may focus on the value, the wife, on the appearance, the jeweler, on the rated quality, and the customs inspector, on the country of origin.

Judgments of qualitative identity thus focus on one or a few properties and ask whether two particulars do or do not share those properties. Of course, particulars 'share' a property only if the property each particular possesses is 'the same.' Qualitative identity judgments thus require judgments about the numerical identity of properties (or types). The elusiveness of the identity conditions for universals (properties and types) makes this question often a perplexing one.[114]

Nonetheless, this question of the numerical identity of properties lies at the root of judgments of the qualitative identity of particulars, which in turn impacts upon judgments about the numerical identity of particulars. To distinguish between the two uses of numerical identity, we should introduce a standard convention. When speaking of the numerical identity of particular events, we shall call them 'event-tokens'; when speaking of the identity of the properties that events may possess, we shall call them 'event-types.'[115]

[112] Neil Wilson, *The Concept of Language* (University of Toronto Press, 1959), at p. 39.

[113] D. Follesdal, 'Quantification into Causal Contexts,' in L. Linsky, eds., *Reference and Modality* (Oxford: Oxford University Press, 1971), at p. 56.

[114] See Armstrong, *supra* note 1.

[115] See Moore, *Act and Crime, supra* note 14, at p. 80.

310

Having distinguished numerical from qualitative identity, it remains to enquire which notion of identity is involved in insurance law's question of 'same occurrence.' It is of course possible that insurance law elliptically asks both sorts of identity questions when it asks after 'same occurrences.' In double jeopardy contexts, for example, the law rather plainly asks both sorts of questions when it asks whether an accused has been prosecuted or punished twice for 'the same offense.' In the latter context the law asks first, whether the same type of act is being twice prosecuted or punished,[116] and second, whether the same instance of each type is being twice prosecuted or punished.[117] Double jeopardy att aches only if the same act-token is being multiply prosecuted or punished for instantiating the same act-type.

In insurance law, by contrast, 'same occurrence' is univocal: it asks only after the numerical identity of event-tokens. There is a concern with types of events in insurance law: the injury event-token must be an instance of the type of injury ('physical damage to property,' for example) covered by a policy; in addition, the cause event-token must be an instance of the type of causes (earthquake, fire, liability for negligence, etc.) covered by a policy. Yet there is much less concern with the identity of types in insurance law analogous to the concern with types of acts in double jeopardy law. The usual concerns in insurance law are the concerns about the numerical identity of both injury event-tokens and cause event-tokens. So long as each such event-token is an instance of the types (of damage and risks, respectively) covered by the policy, the enquiry into types of events is usually satisfied.[118]

b. *The Essential Nature of Events*

We shall here examine several different views of when two putatively distinct event-tokens are in reality one and the same. Such theories each purport to give the 'identity conditions' of event-tokens. The first such theory utilizes the Leibnizian principles above discussed. More specifically, Baruch Brody has urged that the identity conditions of event-tokens are no different than the identity conditions for all particulars, namely: two putatively distinct event

---

[116] *Id.* at Chap. 13.

[117] *Id.* at Chap. 14. In double jeopardy adjudication, this is called the 'unit of offense' question.

[118] As we shall see, however, questions about the identity of particulars quickly involve one in questions about the identity of properties.

Michael Moore

tokens x and y are in reality one and the same event token if and only if x and y share all of their (its) properties.[119] If both of Leibnizian principles are true of identity generally, then of course they are true of the identity of event-tokens. I nonetheless shall put aside the Leibnizian criteria, not on the grounds of falsity, but rather on the grounds of generality.[120] More powerful identity conditions for event-tokens are wanted, conditions that are distinctive of events as a class of things. Such more specific and more powerful identity conditions for events will focus on some properties that, if shared, make for identity of event-tokens. Such more powerful identity conditions do not require us to examine all properties in order to reach conclusions of sameness when faced with questions of identity and individuation of act-tokens.

The properties on which to focus in building more powerful identity conditions for events are the essential properties of something being an event. If two putatively distinct items x and y are events, and if they share the properties essential to events, then they are one and the same event. This means they of course do share *all* of their properties (by Leibniz's Law), but one advantage of these more powerful identity conditions is that we don't have to look at all properties to reach conclusions on identity.

Another advantage of seeking more powerful identity conditions for events based on their essential properties lies in the capacity of such conditions to make identifications over time. For events exist over intervals of time[121] and it is possible for a single event to have some property P at the beginning of the interval but to lack it at the end. The Leibnizian criteria of identity hold only for identity at a time; for identity over time, we need the more powerful identity conditions of events that focuses exclusively on their essential properties—for these cannot change over time for the same thing.[122]

If we put aside the general Leibnizian criteria of identity as too broad for a useful theory of event-identity, then we need a theory about the essential nature of events in order to know how many of them may exist at any given time. Very generally, there are two sorts of theories about the nature of events. The first view likens events

[119] Baruch Brody, *Identity and Essence, supra* note 111.

[120] For variations of this critique, see Moore, *Act and Crime, supra* note 14, at pp. 366-367; Lombard, *supra* note 28, at pp. 23–30; Brand, *supra* note 30, at pp. 59-65.

[121] Moore, *supra* note 14, at p. 72.

[122] For Brody's attempt to deal with this, see Brody, *supra* note 108, at pp. 20–23.

to proposition-like things we call facts.[123] The second conceives of events as spatio-temporally located particulars. On the first view events are linguistic in the same way that facts are linguistic: both are constituted by descriptions in a language such as English. The event of some snow moving—the avalanche—for example, just is the fact that the snow moved. On this view there is no such thing as facts *about* events, for events just are such facts.[124]

Fortunately the propositional view of events is neither well received in the metaphysics of events nor is it reflective of popular understanding of events. For both ordinary folk and metaphysicians distinguish facts about events from the events themselves. This is fortunate because the identity conditions for events would become very murky if events were propositional in nature, given the murkiness of the idea of propositional identity. As one prominent logician once said, 'nobody really has the faintest idea what he means when he says, the proposition that p is the same as the proposition that q.'[125]

Ordinary thought and most metaphysicians conceive of events the other way, as spatio-temporally located particulars. There are three main variants of this view, the middle-sized view of events of Donald Davidson,[126] the fine-grained view of Jaegwon Kim,[127] and

---

[123] See Roderick Chisholm, 'Events and Propositions,' *Nous*, vol. 4 (1970), pp. 15–24; Chisholm, 'States of Affairs Again,' *Nous*, Vol. 5 (1971), pp. 179–89; Chisholm, 'The Structure of States of Affairs,' in B. Vermazan and M. Hintikka, eds., *Essays on Davidson Actions and Events* (Oxford: Clarendon Press, 1985); Chisholm, *A Realistic Theory of Categories*, (Cambridge: Cambridge University Press, (1996), pp. 71–8. See also Neil Wilson, 'Facts, Events, and Their Identity-Conditions,' *Philosophical Studies*, Vol. 25 (1974), pp. 303–21; Wilfred Sellars, 'Actions and Events,' *Nous*, Vol. 7 (1973), pp. 179–202.

[124] For an excellent discussion of the distinction (and of the importance of making the distinction) between events and facts about events, see Jonathan Bennett, *Events and Their Names* (Indianapolis: Hackett Pub., 1988); Anthony Quinton, 'Objects and Events,' *Mind*, Vol. 88 (1979), pp. 197–214, at p. 206.

[125] Peter Geach, *Logic Matters* (Berkeley: University of California Press, 1980), at p. 176.

[126] Davidson, *supra* note 28.

[127] Jaegwon Kim, 'On the Psycho-Physical Identity Theory,' *American Philosophical Quarterly*, Vol. 3 (1966), pp. 227–35; Kim, 'Causation, Nomic Subsumption, and the Concept of Event,' *Journal of Philosophy*, Vol. 70 (1973), pp. 217–36; Kim, 'Events as Property-Exemplifications,' in M. Brand and D. Walton, eds., *Action Theory* (Dordrecht, Holland: Reidel, 1976). Alvin Goldman also adopts this view in his *A Theory of*

the coarse-grained view of Willard Quine.[128] On the Davidsonian view, the first I shall examine, events are particulars having spatio-temporal location. Such particulars have many properties, and we often use the names of such properties to pick out the event in question. However, such non-essential properties are not parts of such events.

For example, suppose the snow in an avalanche begins moving down at t_1, it ceases moving at t_2, it dams a stream at t_3, it floods a village with the water backed up by the dam at t_4, and it is the most talked about event in the region in which it occurred until the end of the year (t_5). On a Davidsonian view, the avalanche has spatio-temporal location. Temporally, it existed during the interval t_1–t_2; spatially, it was located wherever the object avalanching (the snow) was located during t_1–t_2. This spatio-temporally located particular also has numerous non-essential properties: it caused the damming of the stream, it caused the flooding of the village, and it caused people to talk about it a lot. We can successfully refer to it by using these properties, as in: 'the stream-damming avalanche,' 'the cause of the flood of the village,' or 'the most talked-about event of the year.' Yet neither the damming of the stream, the flooding of the town, nor the discussions about the avalanche, are proper parts of the event itself. The event that was the avalanche ended when the snow stopped moving, even though its effects continued on.

The role of properties in this account of events is crucial. On what I shall call the standard version, an event is 'a having and then a lacking by an object of a static property at a time...'[129] Notice there are three aspects of events, on this account: a (spatially located) object that exists in its own right; a change (the having then the absence) in some property or properties of that object; and a

---

[128] Willard Quine, 'Events and Reification,' in E. Le Pore and B. McLaughlin, eds., *Actions and Events: Perspectives on the Philosophy of Donald Davidson* (Oxford: Oxford University Press, 1983); Quine, *Word and Object* (Cambridge, Mass.: MIT Press, 1960), p. 171; Quine, *Theories and Things* (New York: Columbia University Press, 1981), pp. 11–12. Davidson came to have some sympathy for Quine's view of events. See Davidson, 'Reply to Quine on Events,' in Le Pore and McLaughlin, eds., *supra*.

[129] Lombard, *supra* note 27, at p. 220.

Human Action (Englewood Cliffs, N.J.: Prentice-Hall, 1970). It is arguable that Kim's property exemplification view collapses into the facts/propositions view mentioned earlier, although that is not how Kim himself presents it. On this, see Helen Steward, *The Ontology of Mind* (Oxford: Oxford University Press, 1997), pp. 19–27.

temporal interval during which the change takes place. It is the properties essential to an avalanche-type event that are crucial here, properties such as the movement of snow down a mountain. The snow was at rest at t_0, began moving at t_1, ceased moving at t_2, was continuously moving during the interval t_1–t_2, and was at rest at t_4. Movement is one of those 'static properties' the absence of which, the having of which, and the absence of which again, fixes the temporal location of the avalanche event.

It is the presence/absence of properties essential to events like avalanches that is the sense in the common view that events are *changes* in some object in the world. As Aristotle characterized this view:

'There are three classes of things in connection with which we speak of change: the 'that which,' the 'that in respect of which,' and the 'that during which.' I mean that there must be something that changes, e.g., a man or gold, and it must change in respect of something, e.g., its place or some property, and during something, for all change takes place during a time.'[130]

It is the standard view of events as changes in the properties of objects during an interval of time—a view as old as Aristotle and as modern as the contemporary metaphysics of events—that I shall adopt.

The two main competitors for this standard, Davidsonian view of events can most easily be glimpsed via a problem for the standard view. The problem is this: since events on this standard view do not exclusively occupy the spatio-temporal region at which they occur, it is possible for two or more events to occur at the same place and during the same time. For example, the earth right now is both spinning on its axis, and cooling from core to crust.[131] The object involved is but one thing, the earth. The time interval, let us assume, is the same; that is, the earth began spinning when it began cooling, and both will cease at the same time. Despite the identity of spatio-temporal location, it seems intuitively that there are two events here, involving the same object. If there are two events here, that can only be because of the distinct properties (of motion and of temperature, respectively) exemplified during the interval of time. It is because we think the properties of motion involved in spinning are distinct from the properties of temperature involved in cooling that we individuate the (spatio-temporally identical) events of the earth spinning and the earth cooling.

[130] Aristotle, *Physics*. Book V, ch. 4 (227–621).
[131] A modification of Donald Davidson's example, *supra* note 28, at p. 178.

Michael Moore

The problem for the standard view is partly the problem of property individuation. As mentioned earlier, it is notoriously difficult to individuate properties. Yet matters are even thornier for the standard view of events, because event individuation on the standard view often involves a clumping of properties into groups. Consider a parachutist coming down in such a way that his path is a spiral one.[132] During the interval t_1 (when he jumps from the plane) to t_2 (when he lands) the parachutist is moving downward and he is moving in a spiral fashion. Is there one event here (a spiral descent) or two (a descent and a spiral motion)? If, as seems likely, the spiral motion is caused (in part) by the descent, we may be tempted to group the two properties and thus to find only one event to exist. The second aspect of the problem for the standard view of events stems from the fact that there are no obvious principles with which to group properties (even assuming that we can individuate the properties themselves). Jonathan Bennett concludes from examples such as these that on the standard view (as on Bennett's own view), 'our concept of particular event has a large dimension of vagueness...'[133]

The second view of events, the fine-grained view of Jaegwon Kim, finesses this grouping-of-properties problem by regarding every instance of each property a separate event-token—for then there can be no grouping-of-properties problem. On this view events just are property instances, or 'tropes.' There are thus as many events going on in a space/time region as there are properties instantiated. Thus, when John kisses Mary, it is their first kiss, the kiss is a tender, short, but passionate one, Mary is both surprised and pleased by the kiss, and Mary catches cold from John via the kiss, there were eight events going on then and there: a kissing event, a first kiss kissing event, a tender kiss kissing event, a short kiss kissing event, a passionate kiss kissing event, a pleasing kiss kissing event, a surprising kiss kissing event, and cold-transmitting kiss kissing event. In the Kimian world, a lot goes on when John kisses Mary (!), which is why this is called a fine-grained view of events.

The third major view of events, by contrast, is a very coarse-grained view. On the Quinean view of events, event-tokens are simply the whole of what exclusively occupies a space/time region. Whatever properties may be instanced during an interval of time at some place together constitute but one thing, what Quine would call

---

[132] Jonathan Bennett's example. Bennett, *supra* note 124, at pp. 127–8.
[133] *Id.* at p. 127.

the material content of that space/time zone. Such a view not only finesses the grouping of properties problem, but it also eliminates the individuation of properties problem. For this view makes no use of properties in determining what exists. As Bennett recognizes, 'a Quinean event is ... uniquely determined by the zone, with no need to mention properties at all.'[134]

Despite these benefits of Kimian and the Quinean views of events, we should hew to the standard, Davidsonian view of events. There are three reasons for this. One is my own metaphysical bet on where the truth of the matter lies about events. The standard view requires less revision of other things we rather deeply believe to be true than does its competitors. The Quinean view, for example, collapses events and objects together, regarding both as one thing, the material content of a space/time region.[135] The Kimian view, on the other hand, collapses events in the other direction, making them simply properties as instantiated at a particular time and place.[136] Both the Quinean and the Kimian demote events to subsidiary roles in our overall ontology, and do so by placing events in the shadow of items that seem to ordinary thought to be very different from events (objects and properties, respectively). Moreover, each of these views leads to very counterintuitive modes of individuating events: on the Quinean view there is only one thing going on at any time and place, whereas for a Kimian an impossibly large number of things is going on. The world as we know it does not seem either this boring or this busy.

The second reason to hew to the standard view of events is that the standard view is closest to the common sense view of events shared by non-metaphysically oriented citizens. Even if the correct metaphysics of events should turn out to be Quinean or Kimian, these are not the views presupposed by ordinary folk in their use of the event concept.[137] This is not said to elevate common sense generally over the correct metaphysics, as if common belief could not be shown to be mistaken by philosophical theory. Rather, the point is this: in contracts the contracting parties are free to limit their obligations as they see fit. If those parties have a dominant understanding of the limits of their obligations, courts have good reason

---

[134] *Id.* at p. 104.

[135] See Moore, *supra* note 14, at pp. 372–4.

[136] *Id.* at p. 66.

[137] It is doubtful that either Quine or Kim were even trying to capture any ordinary conception of event with their theories. On Kim's intention in this regard, see Steward, *supra* note 127, at p. 23.

Michael Moore

to follow that understanding in interpreting their contracts. The standard view of events, being the common sense view of events, is the most likely understanding parties to insurance contracts bring to their use of phrases like, 'per occurrence.'

Thirdly, courts too are not immune to the pull of common sense views of deep metaphysical puzzles like the nature of events. Insofar as there is any insurance law on what I have been calling the pure question of event-individuation, that law tends toward the standard view of events. Thus, for example, the New York Court of Appeals in *Johnson*[138] rather easily found there to be two retaining wall collapse events because: (1) there were two objects (the two separate buildings with the two separate walls in front of them); and (2) there were two separate time intervals involved; even though (3) there was (arguably) the same group of properties involved in the collapses. A Quinean about events would not rely on the separateness of objects in deciding how many events took place in *Johnson*, but would individuate the space/time zone differently (leading perhaps to a big enough zone in which there was but one event). A Kimian about events would presumably find there to be many events (not just two) in *Johnson*—as many as there were properties instantiated when the walls collapsed.

Consider also the court's conclusion in the *Okada* case mentioned earlier,[139] where the officers and directors under a D and O liability policy voted to authorize several bad spot loans to home buyers, five large condominium project loans, and the move and renovation of corporate headquarters. In holding these to be 'distinct acts,'[140] the court focused on the properties of the authorizing decision, not the place or time at which they were made. The decision on one of the condominium project loans, for example, was a decision to waive a participation requirement on the loan, immediately obliging the savings and loan to fund the entire loan commitment.[141] This was a property not shared by other acts of the officers and directors, even if (the facts are not given) those other acts of authorization took place where and when this one did, *viz.* in one Board resolution. A Quinean about events could not so finely individuate these authorization events, and a Kimian would even more finely individuate them.

Occasionally courts stray from the standard view of events. Consider, for example, the facts of *Kuhn's of Brownsville v.*

[138] *Johnson, supra* note 13.
[139] *Okada, supra* note 49.
[140] *Id.* at 388.
[141] *Id.*

318

Bituminous Casualty Co.[142] Kuhn's excavated beneath two adjoining buildings in an effort to remodel them. As part of the excavation Kuhn's removed the wall between the two buildings. The excavation and/or the removal caused the two buildings to collapse, which also caused the immediate collapse of the building to the east of the two buildings worked on by Kuhn's. Two days later a fourth building collapsed, the one to the west of the first two buildings. The court assumed there was liability of Kuhn's to property owners in all four buildings, because 'the excavation work ... was the proximate cause of the collapse of the [three] buildings on May 27th and the collapse of the [fourth] building on the west side on May 29th.'[143] The court held there to be two accidents within the meaning of Kuhn's policy with Bituminous Casualty Co. The reason given by the court was pure Kimian event theory. The court recognized the policy covered only liability of the insured for property damage caused by 'the collapse of or structural damage to any building or structure due to excavation ... or removal ... of any structural support ... while such operations are being performed by the named insured.'[144] Such coverage required the court to focus on the excavation/removal work of Kuhn's as it asked, how many covered accidents there were. The court apparently thought that there were two such excavation events:

> 'If the excavation was a single act, and constitutes a single accident, then the question comes as to when the accident occurred. The owners on the west suffered no loss and experienced no unforeseen event until the 29th.'[145]

Only a Kimian about events could think that the losses of the west side property owners was part of a separate excavation event.[146] For it is only Kimians who think that because an excavation event seemingly has two properties—a causing of the collapse of the east side building, and a causing of the collapse of the west side building—that there must in reality be two excavation events. This is a piece with the Kimian conclusion that when a defendant moves his finger

---

[142] *Kuhn's, supra* note 76.
[143] 197 Tenn. at 61, 270 S.W.2d at 359.
[144] 197 Tenn. at 64, 270 S.W.2d at 360.
[145] 197 Tenn. at 65-66, 270 S.W.2d at 360.
[146] The statement in the text is not quite true. One might construe the 'componential' theory of events of Judy Thomson and the late Irving Thalberg to hold there to be two distinct events here. See Thomson, *supra* note 30; Thalberg, Perception, Emotion, and Action (New Haven, Conn.: Yale University Press, 1977).

Michael Moore

on the trigger of a gun, and such finger movement causes the death of two people with a single bullet, there are at least three act-tokens by the defendant here—the act of finger movement, the act of killing the first victim, and the act of killing the second victim.[147]

Surely the reasoning in *Kuhn's* is as counterintuitive as is the Kimian theory of events generally. There was only one excavation in *Kuhn's* even though that event had numerous properties. What happened after Kuhn's ceased digging is no part of Kuhn's excavation event, even though we might use that later happening as a means of referring to Kuhn's excavation (as in, 'the four-building-destroying excavation').

Kuhn's is as aberrational as it is counterintuitive. Most of the time courts adopt the standard view of events that has captured common sense since Aristotle: an event is the change in some property (or group of properties) of some object during some interval of time. To individuate events on this dominant view is to individuate: (1) both properties and groups of properties; (2) objects; and (3) temporal intervals.

c. *The Sizing of Events*

If one adopts the standard view on the nature of events, then the individuation question at issue in the Twin Towers litigation has three parts to it, corresponding to the three attributes of events: (1) When is there one, or more than one, physical object? (2) When is there one property or one group of properties, and when are there two or more? (3) When is there one interval of time, and when are there two or more?

Here the happy coincidence of ordinary, legal, and true metaphysics (that I relied upon in defending Davidsonian versus other accounts of events) comes apart. For the true metaphysics on the size of events is unhelpful in this context. There are two plausible views of such true metaphysics of event sizes (assuming we restrict ourselves to the possibilities under a Davidsonian theory of the

---

[147] The explicit conclusion in double jeopardy contexts by a leading Kimian about events, Alvin Goldman. See his critique of my views in Goldman, 'Action and Crime: A Fine-Grained Approach,' *University of Pennsylvania Law Review*, Vol. 142 (1994), pp. 1563–86, and my response, 'More on Act and Crime,' *University of Pennsylvania Law Review*, Vol. 142 (1994), pp. 1749–1840, revised and reprinted as chapter 6 of Michael Moore, *Placing Blame: A General Theory of the Criminal Law* (Oxford: Oxford University Press, 1997), at pp. 318–29.

nature of events). One I shall call the *atomic* view.[148] On this view there are 'atomic events' defined as events out of which other larger events may be constructed but which themselves have no parts because they are the smallest events that exist. Such atomic events are thus basic, whereas all larger events are secondary constructions of the more basic events.

For atomic events to exist, three things must be true (corresponding to the three attributes of events). First, there must be atomic objects, that is, physical objects ('atoms' in the ancient Greek sense) that are composed of no parts. Second, there must be simple properties, that is, properties not themselves composed of combinations of other properties. Third, there must be atomic event-intervals, being the minimum amount of time it takes to cross an 'atomic quality space' (i.e., to constitute a *change* in some single properties).

The second view denies that there are any atomic events and also denies that there is any limit to the size of an event. The universe is one object, all of its parts are objects, and every change to every object (no matter what its size) is equally an event. We can fuse smaller events into bigger ones, and divide bigger ones into smaller ones, without limit, on this view.[149]

Neither of these possibilities as to the true metaphysics of event size can be of much use to the law of insurance. The second view yields no answer to the question of how many events took place in the collapse of the Twin Towers, for example, because the 'how many' question fully depends on the size of objects, properties, and time intervals selected for individuating *an* event. The first view, by contrast, yields *an* answer (in terms of atomic event sizes) to the 'how many' question, but it is surely the wrong answer. Surely no party to a 'per occurrence' insurance contract means to be counting atomic-sized events when payoffs per occurrence are being calculated. Presumably there were millions of such atomic events involved in the collapse of just one Tower, but that answer would make a 'per occurrence' limit on liability no limit at all.

The answer needed is one plausibly attributable to the actual or

[148] Lawrence Lombard adopts this view in his *Events*, *supra* note 28, at p. 168. Lombard's attempt to find metaphysically correct sizes for events is taken to task in Jonathan Bennett's *Events and Their Names*, *supra* note 124, at pp. 149–51, 155–56.

[149] Arguably the view of Judy Thomson in her *Acts and Other Events*, *supra* note 30. See particularly *id.* at 78, where she accepts a 'fusion principle' according to which there always exist larger events that are the fusion of smaller events sharing any given property.

Michael Moore

hypothetical expectations of the parties to insurance contracts. Such expectations are framed with neither very small nor very large sized events in mind; rather, they are framed with the middle-sized events of daily life in mind—events like a conversation, a speech, a wedding, a death, etc. There being no true metaphysics of events that can yield a determinate, intuitive mode of individuating such middle-sized events,[150] we do better to repair to the common sense metaphysics of event-individuation, if there is one.

Consider each of the attributes of an event (on the Davidsonian metaphysics of events) with an eye to sizing that event along the lines accepted by common sense (or 'the plain man's view'). Take the object question first. The ordinary notion of physical objects give some hope of offering up some determinate, non-arbitrary answers. The hope remains despite the fact that the identity conditions for physical objects are standardly given in term of such objects exclusively occupying spatio-temporal zones.[151] The hope is that physical objects like ships, tables, buildings, human bodies, etc., have natural sizings in a way that spatial zones do not.

Such hope is not dashed by recognition of the vagueness of the concept by which we clarify objects. Quine used the example of mountains: when two higher pieces of rock are joined by a high saddle, do we have one mountain or two?[152] Such vagueness diminishes but does not eliminate the determinateness in the boundaries of physical objects. If there are cases like Marian Peak and Jean's Peak in the San Jacinto Mountains of California—two barely discernible high spots on a 10,000 foot ridge[153]—where we are unclear, there are also easy cases like Chomolunga and Sagamantha (the Tibetan and

[150] Lombard appears to believe the contrary, urging that there is a metaphysics of objects such that we can resist fusions such as the fusion of Jones saying 'hello' and Smith saying 'hello' into one larger event, Smith's and Jones' greeting each other. For Lombard, Smith and Jones are separate objects, and the pair of them is in no sense an object, so there is no such event as a greeting between them. Similarly, although there can be a horse in the field, 'the horse in the field' does not name an object that can undergo change over an interval of time (and thus be a larger event). *Events*, *supra* note 28, at pp. 238–9. I shortly defend similar conclusions, but not based on any supposed true metaphysics of events and their objects.

[151] See Moore, *supra* note 14, at p. 368.

[152] Willard Quine, *Word and Object* (Cambridge, Mass.: M.I.T. Press, 1960), at p. 126.

[153] Named separately, incidentally, because the surveyor of the area in the 1890's had two lady friends at the time of his survey and did not wish to insult either one by naming *the* peak with just one of their names.

322

Nepalese names for Mt. Everest, one peak), and like Annapurna and Daligari (two 8,000 meter peaks separated by the deepest valley on earth).

More pernicious than vagueness for the hoped-for determinacy in the boundaries of common sense objects is the mereological problem I adverted to before in discussing true metaphysics: in ordinary thought, are not parts of objects, and aggregations of objects, often objects in their own right? A glacier is a physical object. But are not parts of glaciers, such as the Bergshrund at the top, the ice-fall in its middle, and the calving tip of it at its base in the ocean, also physical objects? Indeed, are not all the worlds glaciers in some sense one object, *viz*, the earth's glacial ice?[154] If so, then there is no more determinacy in the ordinary usage of an event than there is on the true metaphysics of the matter.

Yet in ordinary thought—the touchstone in contract interpretation—there is a primacy to ordinary-sized objects. In most contexts a table is an object in a way that the table's legs, or the furniture in the dining room, are not. Hilary Putnam imagines taking 'someone into a room with a chair, a table on which are a lamp and a notebook and a ballpoint pen, and nothing else, and I ask, "How many objects are there in this room?" My companion answers, let us suppose, "Five."'[155] Although Putnam himself views 'Five' as just one answer metaphysically no better than others (such as 'one,' for the mereological sum of these five objects, or 'twenty,' viewing each of the five objects as itself being the mereological sums of four other objects),[156] surely Putnam's companion is closer to ordinary thought than Putnam himself. If someone had contracted to pay one dollar for every object found in the room, the best interpretation of that contract would be that there is an obligation to pay five dollars.[157]

In a case such as the *Johnson* case mentioned earlier,[158] the New York Court of Appeal's characterization of a building as one object, and a retaining wall as one object, seems in accordance with the

[154] Lombard's kind of puzzle. Lombard, *supra* note 28, at pp. 123–4.

[155] Hilary Putnam, *Representation and Reality* (Cambridge, Mass.: M.I.T. Press, 1989), at p. 100.

[156] *Id.* See also Putnam, *The Many Faces of Realism* (La Salle, Ill.: Open Court, 1987), at pp. 18-19; Putnam, *Renewing Philosophy* (Cambridge, Mass.: Harvard University Press, 1992), at p. 120.

[157] Perhaps Putnam does not disagree with this, as a matter of common sense (not true metaphysics): 'Certain things are paradigmatically objects, for example tables and chairs but ... there is no fact of the matter as to whether ... mereological sums are objects or not.' Putnam, *Renewing Philosophy*, *supra* at p. 267.

[158] Johnson, *supra* note 13.

primacy given ordinary size objects in ordinary thought. The basement of a building, the front of a building, the front half of the basement of a building, are in some sense objects in their own right; two adjoining buildings, or a cluster of buildings such as the Rockefeller Center, are also objects in some sense; yet separate buildings seem primary in most contexts of ordinary thought, in a way that the parts of such buildings, or the aggregation of such buildings, do not.

More troublesome was how one should consider the subway station platform extension trench dug by the contractor-insured in the *Johnson* case. Was there one trench running the entire length of the block? Or as may trenches as there were buildings fronting the street in which the trench was dug? Common sense would probably consider the trench one object, at least until it intersected another trench. This is particularly true given the free flow of rainwater up and down the full length of the trench. If the relevant work of the contractor covered by the insurance were solely the digging of the trench, prima facie there was only one such event of trench digging because only one trench was dug. Such individuation of work-events is prima facie only, however, because perhaps one could show either temporally discontinuous bits of trench digging, and/or different properties of the trench-diggings when done in front of the two different buildings. As the Court of Appeals mentioned with respect to the cinder block retaining walls, even if they were spatially continuous (which they were not), perhaps they had been 'built at separate times by separate groups of workmen.'[159] As the court here implicitly reminds us, the singleness of an object is only one of the three things we need to look at in individuating events (on the standard account of the nature of events); in addition, we must look at both properties and temporal locations.

About the temporal location of events, we seem to have a greater sizing problem than we did for spatial location. For the latter sizing problem, we can rely on the primacy given by ordinary thought to the familiar objects of everyday life. For temporal sizings, we have no such natural sizings.

If the temporal locations of events were points in time, there would be no temporal sizing problem for events. Then *any* difference in temporal location would make for a difference in events. Yet the temporal locations of events are not points in time; they are intervals of time, intervals having a duration.[160] The 'how much'

[159] 7 N.Y.2d at 230, 196 N.Y.S.2d at 684, 164 N.E.2d at 708.
[160] Moore, *supra* note 14, at p. 72.

question is inevitable once one sees this fact about the temporal location of events. Squeezing five quick shots off only seconds apart has been held to be but one event in certain contexts,[161] but firing a shotgun three times, a minute between each blast, counts as three events in other contexts.[162] What is the natural sizing of temporal duration that makes these results justifiable?

Fortunately we get considerable help in the temporal sizing of events by repairing to the third aspect of events, the property or properties making each event-token the kind of event it is. Consider again the excavation events at issue in *Kuhn's of Brownsville*.[163] What makes an excavation event the kind of event it is—an excavation kind of event—is a change in the earth beneath a building: at t_1, it was there, at t_2 the first earth was removed, at t_3 it all was removed, and at t_4 buildings collapsed. On the standard account of events, we focus on the essential properties of the excavation event, here, earth-removal. (Causing the collapse of buildings is a property of the excavation, but it is not an essential property of it.) The essential property, earth removal, began at t_2, and ceased at t_3. Therefore, the relevant temporal interval is t_2–t_3.

Such examples might suggest that the temporal dimension of events is simply the tail wagged by the dog of the property dimension of events. In cases where there is no difference in essential properties between two putatively distinct events, however, the temporal dimension can do all of the individuating work. Consider the facts of *Newark Insurance Co.*[164] again, the case in which a tanker grounded itself twice on the same underwater ledge. In that case it is plausible to suppose that there were the same objects (ship, ledge) and the same essential properties involved (contact between ship and ledge). Nonetheless, the court was on solid ground (so to speak) in holding there to be two grounding events 'differentiated by the passage of time.'[165] Even if there had been no difference in properties between the two groundings,[166] the temporal separation made these two grounding events, not one.

Where the temporal dimension of events does depend on the duration of the change in essential properties making an event the kind of event that it is, the temporal dimension will be as vague as

[161] *Davis v. Herring*, 800 F.2d 513 (5th Cir. 1986).
[162] *American Indemnity Co. v. McQuaig, supra* note 26.
[163] *Kuhn's, supra* note 76.
[164] *Newark Insurance, supra* note 46.
[165] 46 App.Div.2d at 517, 303 N.Y.S.2d at 330.
[166] In fact, one was a bow grounding and the other was a stern grounding.

is the property dimension. As noted before, such vagueness in property individuation and property aggregation prevents determinate answers being given in all cases to the how many events question. As with the spatial sizing problem, however, there will also be clear cases, even though there are also unclear cases, of property (and thus temporal) individuation.

It might be thought that these three indeterminacies in event-individuation can be reduced considerably in the context of insurance law. Sometimes such contextualization of the event-individuations question surely does reduce these indeterminacies. When individuating events for purposes of answering the 'unit of offense' question in double jeopardy, for example, we use the type of act that is the offense in question and ask, 'how many instances of that type of act were there?'[167] This is a lot easier than asking how many events took place there and then, without regard to type. The difference is illustrated by comparing the question, how many kissings of Mary by John there were in a given space/time region, with the question asking how many events took place in that region.[168] The event-type, kissing, has its own essential nature to help in guiding the individuation of kisses, in addition to the identity conditions for events generally. As Helen Steward also notes, 'it seems clear that each event sortal [like "kiss"] brings with it its own bundle of relevance considerations.'[169]

Sometimes this aid is available in the insurance context, particularly when first party, defined risk policies are in issue. In a war-risk policy limiting coverage by occurrences of acts of wars, for example, many events that played a causal role in the production of the damage insured against would be irrelevant in counting acts of war. As Steward notes, 'The concept "war" ... suggests that we need to exclude most civilian activity events in the plant and animal kingdoms, and geological and meteorological events, and demands that we include all offensive and defensive operations.'[170] Similarly, for defined risk policies about earthquakes, floods, fires, and the like, we only need count causally relevant earthquakes, floods, fires, etc.; we need not count causally relevant events in general.

Similarly, for some liability policies like that in *Kuhn's*,[171] the liability insured against is limited to liability for harms caused by specific types of acts of the insured only, such as 'excavation or

---

[167] Moore, *Act and Crime*, *supra* note 14, at p. 371.
[168] *Id.*
[169] Seward, *supra* note 127, at p. 68.
[170] *Id.*
[171] *Kuhn's*, *supra* note 76.

removal work.' As I noted earlier,[172] we can count excavations more easily than events in general. For other liability policies like that in issue in *Johnson*,[173] however, notice that such help is only minimally available. For the defined risk of a liability policy is any act by the insured that causes damage of the kind insured against. This restricts the kinds of events we must count to actions by one human agent (and its agents), but this is not much of a restriction. It is not like counting occurrences of excavations, kisses, burglaries, or weddings, for example.

The situation is even worse with all risk casualty policies, for such policies make all types of events part of the risk insured against (so long of course as such events cause damage of the kind insured against). 'All risk' robs us of the greater determinacy promised by types like, 'earthquake', 'fire', etc. All risk policies throw us back to individuating events simplicatur, without regard to any particular types of events that must be instantiated. In the Twin Towers litigation, for example, we do not get to ask, 'how many acts of war caused the destruction of the World Trade Center' (as would be asked under a war risk policy). Rather, we must ask, 'how many events caused the destruction of the World Trade Center,' a much more open-ended question.

d. *Applying the Criteria of Event-Identity to the Destruction(s) of the Twin Towers*

If we apply these general observation to the facts of the Twin Towers litigation, we must do so separately with respect to the several different possibilities as to where in the causal sequence we are seeking to individuate events. If we focus on the last cause events and ask, how many building collapses were there, the answer rather patently seems to be, two. As to the object dimension of this conclusion, two 110 story towers, connected only by a subterranean shopping mall, undoubtedly constitute two buildings, on any ordinary concept of a building. Their common plan of construction, their common ownership, their common designation ('The World Trade Center'), and the single insurance policy issued on them, is not enough to overcome this conclusion. Even their popular name, 'The Twin Towers,' betokens the only qualitative but not numerical identity of the two buildings. Thus, even if these collapses were both qualitatively identical (which in fact they

---

[172] See text at n. 163 *supra*.
[173] *Johnson*, *supra* note 13.

nearly were) and temporally coincident (which they were not), there would have been two collapse events.

As it happened the collapses were separated by $29\text{-}1/_2$ minutes. Even if the two towers were each considered part of the same building, this temporal separation would make for two collapses. If part of a building collapses from one cause, and $29\text{-}1/_2$ minutes later another part of a building collapses from a distinct cause, with no causal connection between the collapses, there would be two collapses.

Moving back in time, if we focus on the dominant immediate causes of the two collapses, we get the same result. The immediate cause of each collapse was an intense fire that degraded the structural integrity of the columns of steel holding up the towers. Assuming there were two buildings (see above), there were then two fire events. This conclusion is reinforced by the slight lack of qualitative identity between the fires: the fire in the South Tower did not completely cover the floors involved in the impact, whereas the fire in the North Tower did completely seal off its impact floors.[174] The two fire-events conclusion is more strongly reinforced by the temporal distinctness of the fires: the South Tower fire existed for approximately 56 minutes, from 9 :03 a.m. to 9:59 a.m., whereas the North Tower fire existed for approximately 1 hour 42 minutes from 8:46 a.m. to 10:28 a.m.

Moving further back in time, to the dominant, immediate causes of the two fires, we also get the same result. There were two crash-events, first, because there were two sets of objects involved (two planes, two buildings), second, because there were some qualitative differences between the crashes (e.g., the floors hit, the speed of the airplanes and the resulting force of the impacts, the squareness of the hits[175]), and third, because the temporal locations of the crashes was distinct (8:46:26 a.m. on the North Tower, 9:02:54 on the South Tower).

My analysis in section 3 earlier would focus on none of these kinds of events when individuating occurrences under the WTC insurance policy. For each of these events causally depends on earlier events, and the real question is whether those earlier events were singular (and thus a common cause) or plural. The events on which we should focus are probably (see section 3) the decision(s) to crash made by the terrorist pilots aboard each aircraft. There is an easy sense, of course, in which those decisions were 'the same.' This is the sense we use in contract law, for example, when we ask whether

[174] See *USA Today, supra* note 3, at p. 4A.
[175] *Id.*

there was a 'meeting of the minds,' meaning by that phase that the intentions of the contracting parties were 'the same.'[176] What contract law means by 'the same,' however, is qualitative, not numerical, identity. Two numerically distinct people do not have numerically the same intention; they can only have qualitatively identical intentions.[177] Thus, the decisions of the two terrorist pilots when aboard their separate aircraft are two, no matter how similar such decisions might have been in terms of their properties and no matter how identical such decisions might have been in terms of their temporal location (e.g., 7:58–7:59 a.m. at Boston's Logan Airport, the place and times of departure of both flights) .

The only seriously contestable event-individuation issues are to be found if one moves even further back in time, as one might do if that is where the most substantial cause(s) of the crashes is to be found (see section 3). Suppose our causal analysis in section 3 lead us to focus on either the pre-highjacking decision of Mohamed Atta or on the even earlier decision(s) of the al Qaeda leadership in Afghanistan, presumably Osama bin Laden or Ayman al-Zawahiri.[178] Considered as individual decisions (or intentions) in either case there was but one intention-token as there was but one person making the decisions. Yet as the law of conspiracy shows us, we might not conceptualize this as a matter of individual decision; rather, we might do so as a matter of agreements, between bin Laden, al-Zawahiri, and their associates, or between Atta and his associates, or between all of them. We might well do that here (in the context of insurance law) for the same reason criminal law conceives of conspiracies as a crime separate from those crimes that are the objects of conspiratorial agreements: there is a special danger presented by group criminality. That special danger is often cashed out in causal terms: each individual's intention to do some criminal act in furtherance of a conspiracy is reinforced by the

---

[176] As in the classic contract formation case involving the good ships *Peerless, Raffles v. Wichelhaus*, 2 H. and C. 906, 159 Eng. Rep. 375 (Exch. 1864).

[177] Some aspects of the individuation of intentions can be quite tricky, namely, those aspects having to do with the content of such intentions. But on the objects involved with intentions—persons—the issues are easy: absent a group mind, different person makes for different intention. See Michael Moore, 'Intentions and *Mens Rea*,' in R. Gavison, ed., *Issues in Contemporary Legal Philosophy* (Oxford: Oxford University Press, 1987), reprinted as chap. 11 of Moore, *Placing Blame, supra* note 147.

[178] On al-Zawahiri's leadership role within al Qaeda, see 'The Man Behind Bin Laden', *The New Yorker* (Sept. 16, 2002), pp. 56–85.

group-reinforcements created by a common design involving others. Even if a sole pilot might have turned back if on his own, the reliance by others involved in a group action may have made the difference.

In any case, if we are counting agreements, there seemingly is only one. In double jeopardy contexts, as in ordinary thought, agreement events are individuated by the three attributes of events in metaphysics: the objects involved, *viz* the parties to the agreements; the time(s) of the agreeing acts; and the properties of the agreeing acts, and particularly those properties having to do with the content of the agreement(s), *viz*, *what* was agreed upon. By these criteria there would appear to be but one agreement between the relevant parties.

This conclusion about individuation makes even more crucial the resolution of the causal issues at the end of section 3. If the tentative conclusion favoured there is followed—that we should look at the in flight decisions of the pilots but no earlier—then there were two occurrences, not one. If, however, we look past the decisions of the pilots, there was but one decision or but one agreement operating as the common cause of all else that followed on September 11; this then would be but one occurrence.

5. Does a Definition of 'occurrence' as 'One Series of Similar Causes' Alter the Causal Test?

One of the issues that is being litigated in the World Trade Center litigation is whether the definition of 'occurrence' (quoted in § 1 above) is or is not part of the contract of insurance between the parties. Although there is a strong argument vis-à-vis most of the insurers that the definition is not part of the contract of insurance I shall assume the contrary. This allows us to reach the question of whether or not such a definition alters the meaning of 'occurrence' from the kind of meaning analyzed in §§ 3 and 4 of this article. For two reasons I conclude that such a definition, even if it were part of the contract of insurance, likely works no change in the meaning of per occurrence limitations in insurance contracts.

a. *The Language of the Definition is Consistent with the Causal Test*

The first reason lies in the language of the definition itself. It provides that '"occurrence" shall mean all losses or damages that are attributable ... to one cause ... All such losses will be added together and the total amount of such losses will be treated as one occurrence irrespective of the period of time or area over which such losses occur.' This part of the definition does no more than state the causal test for 'occurrence.' That is, such language affirms that the occurrences limiting coverage are cause-events, not injury-events. Moreover, the language simply states the common cause doctrine, the essence of the causal test of 'occurrence': if there is one cause of numerous injuries, there is but one occurrence, no matter how distinct the injuries may be *inter se*.

The language of 'damages ... attributable *directly or indirectly* to one cause ...' does not take the definition any distance from the causal test's standard formulation. Damages that are attributable indirectly to one cause are damages caused by some one cause-event through some intermediate cause-events. This is just the causal chain doctrine we examined earlier in § 3.

The only language in the definition raising a serious issue of divergence from the causal test is the language, 'damages ... attributable ... *to one series of similar causes*.' A possible reading of this language is that multiple causes of multiple injuries could count as one occurrence even if there are no causal relationships between such cause-events and even if they share no common cause. This is an interpretation diverging from the standard formulation of the causal test.

Any such interpretation of this language, interpreting it to diverge from the causal test, should be rejected. To begin with, the definition states that the causes must be similar. That leaves open the question, in what respect must two distinct cause-events be like one another to be relevantly 'similar.' Everything is similar in some respect to everything else, and everything is dissimilar to everything else in some respect.[179] So an interpreter must choose the respect or respects in which one thing must be like another to be adjudged 'similar.'

The best reading of the definition is that two distinct cause events are 'similar' if they possess similar causal properties. For example, if the employee of the insured writes forty bogus checks in his general scheme to embezzle money from his employer, the forty cause-events (the writing of each check) are similar in that they are the effects of a common cause, which was the general decision of the employee to embezzle the money.[180] As another example, in the

[179] Nelson Goodman, 'Seven Strictures on Similarity,' in his *Problems and Projects* (Indianapolis: Bobbs-Merrill, 1976).
[180] The facts of *Business Interiors, supra* note 48.

Michael Moore

ricocheting car collision cases,[181] two collisions are similar if one causes the other; they are then alike in sharing a causal relationship, one being the cause and the other being the effect of the same causal relationship.

This causal reading of 'similar,' of course, diverges not at all from the result reached under the causal test for 'occurrence' of standard American insurance law. The above examples of similarity are no more than applications of the common cause and causal chain doctrines discussed in § 3. Such a reading of 'similar' in the definition thus would change the causal test not at all.

This causal reading of the definition was adopted by the Arizona Supreme Court in *Arizona Property and Casualty Insurance Guaranty Fund v. Helme*, discussed earlier.[182] In that case the definition of 'occurrence' was "any incident, act or omission, or series of related incidents, acts or omissions resulting in injury ...'[183] As the court recognized, 'neither the Imperial policy, the parties, nor the court of appeals have defined the word "related" and our research does not reveal any generally accepted legal meaning ...'[184] The court proceeded to give the word 'related' a causal reading:

> 'We think it clear that Imperial limited "occurrence" by using the term, "series of related incidents ...," to protect itself from the contention that multiple, causally-connected negligent acts constituted more than one occurrence.'[185]

The court thus held that two doctor's qualitatively similar negligent acts constituted two occurrences because those acts were causally independent of one another.

This causal reading of the definitions in both the World Trade Center litigation and the *Helme* case, is reinforced by the use of the word, 'series.' Cause-events linked as a sequence in a causal chain is a natural reading of "series'; cause-events related as epiphenomena of a common cause is another natural reading of 'series.' Both of such readings are again, no more than standard applications of the causal test of general insurance law.

A second interpretation of the definition's language, 'one series of similar causes,' is alternative to the causal reading. This is an interpretation addressed to the indeterminacy in event-individuation we explored in § 4. More specifically, as I there mentioned, activities of

[181] See note 51 *supra*.
[182] See note 37, *supra*.
[183] 153 Ariz. at 134, 735 P.2d at 456.
[184] *Id.*
[185] 153 Ariz. at 135, 735 P.2d at 457.

a more or less continuous nature carried on over a long period of time are notoriously difficult to individuate. For double jeopardy purposes, for example, how many units of the offense of joy-riding take place when the defendant drives another's car without permission continuously over a twenty-four hour period?[186] For insurance purposes, how many insured events take place when a continuous trench the length of a street is dug by the same crew of workmen over the course of several weeks,[187] or when a continuously dug hole is excavated under two buildings over several days.[188] Definitions like that used in the World Trade Center situation can reduce the vagueness of event individuation in dealing with such continuing events.[189] What such definitions then do is not supplant the causal test but supplement it. They reduce the indeterminacy otherwise latent in the causal test with respect to continuous events of long duration.

The Texas Supreme Court has given such reading to a definition of 'occurrence' similar to that involved in the World Trade Center litigation. In *American Physicians Insurance Exchange et al. v. Garcia*[190] a medical malpractice policy defined 'occurrence' as including "a series of acts or occurrences arising out of one event."[191] The court's construal of this definition was:

"'[a] series of acts or occurrences," is apparently intended to have a coverage effect similar to the 'continuous or repeated exposure' unifying directive in commercial liability policies—but in a manner that is meaningful in the medical context. For example, medical malpractice frequently involves an operation or an extended course of treatment. A malpractice event may involve numerous independent grounds of negligence that cannot be unified as "repeated exposure to substantially the same conditions," but that nevertheless constitute "a series of acts or occurrences" that are related and form a single malpractice claim.'[192]

Both of the above two readings of a definition of 'occurrence' (as a series of similar causes) are acceptable readings; indeed, one could

---

[186] One of the issues in *Brown v. Ohio*, 432 U.S. 161 (1977), discussed in Moore, *supra* note 14, at pp. 320-323.

[187] One of the relevant events in *Johnson, supra* note 13.

[188] The relevant event in *Kuhn's of Brownsville, supra* note 76.

[189] On the ability of definitions to reduce or at least reallocate vagueness, see Michael Moore, 'The Semantics of Judging,' *Southern California Law Review*, Vol. 54 (1981), pp. 151–295, at pp. 196–7.

[190] 37 Tex. Sup. J. 561, 876 S.W.2d 842 (1994).

[191] 37 Tex. Sup.J. at ___, 876 S.W.2d at 854.

[192] *Id.*

give the definition both readings. Unacceptable would be a third reading, the one that would change the causal test in significant ways. On this reading one interprets 'similar' to mean any qualitative similarity between numerically distinct cause-events, and one would read 'one series' to mean any temporally ordered sequence of qualitatively similar events. What makes such a reading unacceptable are three factors.

One is the great indeterminacy opened up by such a reading. If any qualitative similarity counts—not just causal similarities or the similarity of being spatio-temporally contiguous and involved in continuous events—then no principled line-drawing is possible. For every event is similar to every other event in some respects. Moreover, a similar indeterminacy would affect the 'one series' language. How large a temporal slice should one use to find one series? The question has no obvious answer, once one abandons proximate cause doctrines or the limits of those spatio-temporally contiguous events making up one continuous event.

The second reason to reject this third reading of the definition lies in the reasonable expectations of insureds under a per occurrence limitation in a policy. Suppose a building were hit on the same day by two aircraft. The crashes are qualitatively as similar as you please, involving the same kind of aircraft, the same kind of negligent inadvertence by the pilots, the same kind of damage and injury, etc. Yet if each crash is causally independent of the other—it is a freak accident that they happened the same day to the same building—and if each crash causes its own separate damage, could anyone doubt that there would be two occurrences under the building owner's casualty policy? Yet the third reading of the definition at issue here—focusing as it does only on qualitative similarity and temporal sequencing—would hold this to be but one occurrence. That is so contrary to the reasonable expectations of the parties to insurance contracts that it is a sufficient reason to reject that reading.

The third reason to reject this reading lies in the language of the insurance form which contains the definition, for this language gives a partial definition of the phrase, 'one series of similar cases,' that is itself used to define 'occurrence.' With regard to perils of nature including floods or earthquakes, the insurance form in question defines 'one cause or a series of similar causes' explicitly to mean 'one single atmospheric disturbance as designated by the National Weather Service...'[193] Notice that a close temporal

---

[193] Willis North America, WILPROP 2000 sm, p. 3.

sequence of qualitatively identical storms would not qualify as a 'series of similar causes' under this definition, thus rejecting the third, most expansive reading of 'series of similar causes' for storms and other natural perils.

The stipulations for floods caused by tidal movements also rejects the expansive reading. If property is inundated with ocean water by a series of waves, tides, or tidal waves, there 'shall be deemed to be a single occurrence,' but only so long as each wave or tidal movement was 'caused by any one disturbance.'[194] Again, if one tidal wave hits, and then sixteen minutes later another tidal wave hits, and the waves are qualitatively as similar as you please, there are two occurrences because there is neither a causal connection between the waves nor a causal relationship between each wave and some one storm as a common cause.

Inland or stream flooding is handled differently. Here the problem is that adverted to before: how does one draw boundaries on matters of continuous variation (such as the gradual rise and fall of flood waters over an extended period of time)? As one philosopher of events noted recently, 'continuous, gradual change gives anyone trying to count [events] a headache...'[195] It is precisely to alleviate such headaches that stipulations such as 'series of similar causes' are introduced. For stream floods, the insurance form stipulates that any flood(s) occurring 'within a period of the continued rising or overflow of any natural or man-made bodies of water and the subsidence of same within their banks' shall be deemed to be a single occurrence.[196] Note this is the second use of the definition (the one adopted by the Texas Supreme Court),[197] not the third.

Earthquakes are treated differently: 'if more than one earthquake occurs within any period of 168 hours during the term of this policy, such earthquakes shall be deemed to be a single occurrence...'[198] This might seem to lump qualitatively similar but causally unconnected events together as a 'series of similar causes' and thus to support the third reading of that last phrase. This would be a mistake, however. What the 168 hour stipulation is doing is drawing a circle within with the following evidentiary presumption applies: any earthquakes in the same area following within one week (168 hours) of another earthquake are presumed to be aftershocks

[194] *Id.* at p. 4.
[195] Keith Campbell, *Abstract Particulars* (Oxford: Basil Blackwell, 1990), p. 140.
[196] WILPROP 2000 sm, p. 4.
[197] See text at nn. 190–1, *supra*.
[198] WILPROP 2000 sm, at p. 3.

Michael Moore

of the first quake. Seismology being the inexact science that it is, it is hard to prove that a later quake is an aftershock of an earlier one, but if they are in the same area, and occur within days of each other, almost always (and perhaps always) the later quake s are mere aftershocks of the earlier one. The causal test is thus once again intended by the 'series of similar causes' language, only aided by a conclusive presumption about relations of causal dependence between spatio-temporally close earthquakes.

To summarize, none of the language contained elsewhere in the insurance form at issue in the World Trade Center litigation goes any distance to support the third, expansive reading of the 'series of similar cause' definition of 'occurrence.' On the contrary, most of that language supports the first reading where 'similar' means, causally related. (What doesn't support the first reading does support the second reading, where the 'series of similar causes' language is taken to draw lines on matters of continuous variation.) Since the third reading also seems contrary to any reasonable expectations parties to such contracts could have, and because that reading results in greater vagueness than that it was designed to reduce, the third reading of the definition of 'occurrence' should be rejected.

b. *The Intention Could Be to Refer to the Causal Test Even if the Language of the Definition Were Inconsistent with the Causal Test*

Suppose (contrary to the argument of the immediately preceding subsection) that the most natural reading of the language, 'one series of similar causes,' is the third, most expansive reading. Even so the language should not be given that reading.

There are two ways that we use descriptive words and phrases, both in ordinary speech and in the law. One use is to fix the class of things being referred to by the description. In this use, a description gives a set of properties and those properties fix the reference entirely in the sense that anything possessing the properties mentioned in the description is meant as the subject being discussed. An example of such usage is to be found in the 'unborn widow' cases under the rule against perpetuities.[199] In such cases gifts over are made to a named person's 'widow.' The issue is whether the description, 'so-and-so's widow' should be taken to refer to the present wife of that person (who is a life in being), or whether the property of widowhood fixes the reference so that whoever is married to the husband when the latter dies is the one meant to take

---

[199] E.g., *Dickerson v. Union National Bank of Little Rock*, 595 S.W.2d 677 (Ark. 1980).

336

(who may not be a life in being). The right answer depends on the intention of the user of the word 'widow,' in this case, the testator: did he intend to make a gift to the present wife, using the phrase, 'John's widow,' to refer to her, or did he intend anyone to take the property so long as she turned out to be the widow of John? Courts reasonably enough interpret the description so that the property of widowhood fixes the reference, meaning whoever meets that description takes the property.

The second way to use a description is as a heuristic, a learning device that helps audiences pick out the thing(s) being described. In such use, the description does not fix the reference, however; what is referred to is fixed by the intention of the speaker, and the description is given to help the audience grasp the speaker's referential intention.[200] An example of this latter usage is given by Leo Katz:[201] your spouse directs you to go meet that man over there, described as, 'the one in the Brooks Brothers suit, Yves St. Laurent tie, and Gucci shoes.'[202] As Katz points out, typically this list of properties is not to be taken to fix the reference of the phrase, 'that man over there.' That is, your spouse probably intends you to meet a certain person irrespective of whether that person is wearing what your spouse thinks he is wearing. In such cases the description is not to be taken as fixing the reference of who it is you are to meet, but is used as a heuristic to get you to see to whom your spouse intends to refer.[203]

[200] Of the considerable literature on this topic, the classic article is Keith Donnellan, 'Reference and Definite Descriptions,' *The Philosophical Review*, Vol. (1966), pp. 281–304. One of Donnellan's examples: 'Smith's murderer is insane.' Are we using the phrase, 'Smith's murderer,' to pick out some one person, Jones say, who may or may not actually be Smith's murderer? Or are we using the phrase to pick out whoever turns out to be the murderer of Smith?

[201] Leo Katz, *Bad Acts and Guilty Minds* (Chicago: University of Chicago Press, 1987), pp. 85–7.

[202] *Id.* at p. 85.

[203] Alternatively, a spouse who is concerned to point out an example of a well-dressed man may well take the properties to fix the reference; she wants her husband to see someone dressed in just the outfit described.

[204] On these two usages of definition, and on the law's frequent use of the second sort, see Michael Moore, 'Justifying the Natural Law Theory of Constitutional Interpretation,' *Fordham Law Review*, Vol. 69 (2001), pp. 2087–2117, at pp. 2090–8; Moore, 'Do We Have an Unwritten Constitution?', *Southern California Law Review*, Vol. 63 (1989), pp. 107–39, at pp. 127–30, 134–5; Moore, 'A Natural Law Theory of Interpretation,' *Southern California Law Review*, Vol. 58 (1985), pp. 277–398, at pp. 291–301, 322–38, 340–1.

Michael Moore

Definitions do not differ from descriptive phrases in having these two distinct usages,[204] which is not surprising since definitions are simply descriptions framed in terms of properties the thing defined is supposed to possess. Consider the explicit definition of 'death' prevalent in American law pre-1970, which law defined death in terms of loss of consciousness and cessation of spontaneous heart and lung functioning.[205] Such definition could be taken to fix the reference of 'death' in the sense that any event that has the properties described necessarily is a death and anything lacking them is not. Alternatively, such definition could be taken as a heuristic to picking out the cases when someone is actually dead, but whether someone is or is not dead is not determined by the possession of these properties.

It is remarkable that despite the long-known marking of this distinction in linguistics, judges and lawyers regularly assume that definitions are used in legal documents only in the first way. Yet the reverse is actually true: usually definitions are used as heuristics, not determiners of reference. Take 'death' again. If we were to take the pre-1970 definition of 'death' to fix the reference of the word, a judge should find that a person submerged in very cold water for 40 minutes, who had lost consciousness and whose heart and lungs had ceased functioning, was legally dead—after all, the state of such a 'corpse' meets the legal definition of 'death.' Therefore a judge (in any organ transplant case, for example) should exclude medical testimony purporting to show that such a person is not really dead (as we know some such persons are not)—for if the proposed organ donor meets the legal definition of 'death,' he must be dead. Yet so to rule would be absurd.[206] The absurdity of the conclusion stems from the absurdity of thinking that the legal definition of 'death' fixes the class of things referred to by 'death.' The absurdity lies in the fact that the legal definition of 'death' was intended to help judges pick out the natural class of events that really are deaths, irrespective of whether or not all of the members of that class possess the properties contained in the legal definition.

It was this insight into the judicial tendency to take definitions the wrong way that lead the Presidential Commission on the Definition of Death in the 1980's to recommend that *no* statutory definition of death be given; for the Commission foresaw that judges might mistakenly think that a new definition of death (in

[205] See Moore, 'A Natural Law Theory of Interpretation,' *supra* note 204, at pp. 293–300, 322–8, for an extended discussion of the definition of 'death.'

[206] *Id.*

terms of brain function) fully determined what legal death was, rather than being simply another heuristic for judges (to be added to the heart/lung heuristic) often helpful to finding out when someone was really dead.[207]

Two law students at the Toronto Law School nicely captured the absurdity of taking definitions the wrong way, as judges often do, in creating the imaginary case of an Ojibway Indian who shot his pony because it was lame.[208] The defendant was prosecuted under the Ontario Small Birds Act, section two of which prohibited the killing of small birds. To the accused's objection that he had killed a horse and not a bird, the judge's reasoning was impeccable: section 1 of the Act defined a bird as a 'two-legged animal covered with feathers;' the pony met the definition, for it was: a) an animal; b) two-legged (indeed any four-legged creatures necessarily has two legs); and c) was covered with feathers (because the accused had placed a feather pillow on the pony's back in lieu of a saddle and anything artificially covered with feathers is *a fortiori* covered with feathers).

The absurdity of the judge's conclusion is fully generated by taking the legal definition to fix the class of things referred to by the word, 'bird.' Had he taken the definition to be used only as a heuristic, then he could have recognized that some things that met the definition (e.g., ponies with pillows) were not birds and that some things that failed to meet the definition (e.g., featherless birds) were still birds. In short, the use of the definition to fix the class referred to by the legislature ignores the legislature's own intention, which is to pick out *birds*—even if that very same legislature partly misdescribes that class with its definition.

Judge John Martin has unfortunately joined the long list of judges who assume that legal definitions must be taken to fix the class of things referred to. In granting summary judgment in favour of three insurance companies whose contract of insurance was held to contain the definition of 'occurrence' earlier quoted,[209] Judge Martin assumed there could be no triable issue of fact about how the definition of 'occurrence' was used.[210] But of course there was

[207] Report of the President's Commission, 'Defining Death: The Medical, Legal, and Ethical Issues in the Determination of Death,' excerpted in T. Beauchamp and L. Walters, ed., *Contemporary Issues in Bioethics* 2d edit., 1982), pp. 301–5.

[208] 'Judicial Humour—Construction of a Statute,' *Criminal Law Quarterly*, Vol. 8 (1966), pp. 137-139.

[209] Text at note 6, *supra*.

[210] Reported in *The Wall Street Journal*, September 26, 2002, p. B4, col. 3–4; *The New York Times*, September 26, 2002.

such an issue of fact: were those who used the definition—the contracting parties—using it to fix the class of things referred to by 'occurrence'? Or were they using the definition only as a heuristic, a way of directing attention to the fact that the intention was to refer to the causal test—a test whose nature is (perhaps) partly misdescribed by the very definition referring to it?

Not only was this factual issue open, but linguistics teaches us that the answer is probably the opposite of the one assumed by the judge in the case. That is, usually definitions are used as mere heuristics, aids to referring to something whose nature only approximates the properties described in the definition.[211] This usage fact is true even of phrases used to refer to legal tests, such as the causal test in insurance law. Consider in this regard the initiative in California that sought to return the state to the McNaughten test for legal insanity, yet defined that test badly: in lieu of McNaughten's 'or,' the initiative used, 'and.'[212] Nonetheless, the California Supreme Court properly held the definition to be a heuristic, aiding judges to pick out the thing referred to—the McNaughten test—even though that thing was very badly described by the definition.[213]

Another example is afforded by the British prohibition of *witchcraft* in their African colonies in the Nineteenth Century.[214] With their customary penchant for precision, the British not only prohibited witchcraft, they also defined it. Among other things, witchcraft was defined as the throwing of bones. Yet the social practice of witchcraft did not actually include the throwing of bones—such actions were part of the supposed antidote to witchcraft, not the practice of it. If the British courts had taken the definition to fix the class of things referred to by 'witchcraft,' then they should have acquitted witchcraft's practitioners and convicted its victims. They of course had the good sense to do no such thing, taking the definition to be a heuristic (a poor one, to be sure) to aid them in picking

---

[211] Hilary Putnam argues that most words are used referentially ('indexically') so that definitions of them give only stereotypes, but not the meanings of such words. 'The Meaning of "Meaning",' in Putnam, *Mind, Language, and Reality* (Cambridge: Cambridge University Press, 1975), pp. 215–71.

[212] The initiative is quoted in *People v. Skinner*, 704 P.2d 752 (Cal. Sup. Ct. 1985).

[213] *Id.*

[214] The tale of witchcraft is nicely told by Leo Katz in his *Bad Acts and Guilty Minds*, *supra* note 201, at pp. 82–96.

out 'true' witches (i.e. those regarded as witches by the test embedded in the social parties of the tribes in question).

The important lesson to be drawn in the present context from these two uses of definitions is this: a definition used in the first way cannot misdescribe the phenomenon to which it refers—because the phenomenon to which it refers is wholly fixed by the descriptions making up the definition. That is how Judge Martin used the definition of 'occurrence' in the World Trade Center litigation. Whereas a definition used in the second way can misdescribe the item meant by the word being defined, and yet the reference remains the same despite the misdescription in the definition— because again, the definition used in this second way does not fix the reference of the term being defined.

It thus should have remained an open issue in the World Trade Center litigation whether the contracting parties or their agents intended to refer to the causal test in their definition of 'occurrence,' even supposing that the definition partly misdescribes that test. If they did, then their intentions are honoured by using the thing referred to—the causal test—and not some misdescription of that test. The issue of which intentions they had required testimony to resolve, and was thus not a proper matter to be resolved on summary judgment.

6. Conclusion

So: was there one occurrence, or were there two occurrences, within the meaning of the insurance policy covering the destruction of the World Trade Center on September 11, 2001? On the facts presently available to us, my own conclusion is that there were two occurrences. This is a relatively clear conclusion if one applies New York's supposed 'last proximate cause' version of the causal test, almost as clear if one applies an 'intervening cause' version of the test, but also true (although less clearly so) under my own favoured version of the causal test, the 'most substantial cause' version.

This conclusion is less important, at least in academic settings, than is the route used to reach it. My hope for this paper, as for some of my earlier efforts, is to illustrate the potential help that philosophy can give to law. Everyone understands that at high levels of abstract legal theory—such as the general theory of punishment, the nature of corrective or distributive justice as the point of tort law, the nature of liberty as a restraint on legislation, the nature of law itself, and the like—philosophical analysis is an

Michael Moore

integral part of any legal analysis. Less generally accepted is the view sought here to be illustrated: even at the level of particular cases there is no escaping from doing some philosophy.[215] To resolve this case, strictly legal analyses (of the causal test, the policies behind it, the intervening cause doctrine) must be blended with: a philosophy of causation that is itself a blend of a metaphysical theory about the nature of the causal relation and a sociology of the popular conception of that relation; a philosophy of events that is similarly a blend of a metaphysical theory about the nature of events and a sociology of the popular conception of those entities; and a philosophy of language that distinguishes between referential and attributive uses of definitions. Legal decision-makers cannot afford the luxury of ignoring these kinds of philosophical analyses. Their only choices are whether to engage in such analyses consciously or unconsciously, with the help of another discipline (such a philosophy or linguistics), or without such help—ultimately, whether to do such analyses well, or to do them badly.

[215] Another example of attempting to use philosophy in the resolution of particular legal disputes is my attempt to bring the considerable literature on deontology to bear on Israel's practice of torturing terrorists possessing potentially life-saving information. Moore, 'Torture and the Balance of Evils,' *Israel law Review*, Vol. 23 (1989), pp. 280–344, reprinted in Moore, *Placing Blame: A General Theory of Criminal Law* (Oxford: Oxford University Press, 1997), chap. 17.

CPSIA information can be obtained
at www.ICGtesting.com
Printed in the USA
LVHW111924270722
724555LV00002B/128